ENDLESS STREET

Salisbury Market Place in 1782, by Thomas Rowlandson.

ENDLESS STREET
a history of Salisbury and its people

John Chandler

illustrated by

Alison Borthwick

DEDICATED TO MY FRIENDS
PICTURED WITHIN

First published in the United Kingdom in 1983
Reprinted with corrections in 1987 and 2001
First paperback edition 2010

Hobnob Press, PO Box 1838, East Knoyle, Salisbury, SP3 6FA
www.hobnobpress.co.uk

British Library Cataloguing in Publication Data
A catalogue record for this book is available from the British Library

ISBN 978-1-906978-23-5
Printed by Lightning Source

Contents

List of Plates

The plates will be found at the end of this volume.

Sources of plates: A. M. Borthwick, 7, 10, 11, 33, 36, 40, 44; M. J. Marshman, 3, 8, 9, 13, 15, 24, 41, 42, 43, 46; Salisbury District Council (copied by M. J. Marshman), 4, 12, 14, 22, 23, 31, 37, 47, 48; Salisbury and South Wilts Museum (copied by M. J. Marshman), frontispiece, 6, 16, 17, 18, 19, 20, 21, 25, 26, 27, 28, 29, 32, 34, 35, 38, 39, 45; Wiltshire Record Office (copied by author), 1; author, 2, 5, 30.

Figures 3, 13, 14, 15, 16, 19, 24, 27 are based upon Ordnance Survey maps with the permission of the Controller of Her Majesty's Stationery Office.

Introduction

Let us make a few things clear at the outset and so avoid misunderstandings later on. This is not a comprehensive history of Salisbury; nor is it an authoritative history of Salisbury. The world has become so wise, so laden with facts, so burdened with disagreements and uncertainties, that anyone who thinks that he has written a comprehensive or authoritative history of anything is deluding himself. Someone will always come along to tell him where he is wrong and what he has left out. So I make no such claim for the present work. Rather it is a personal exploration of some of the themes which I have found interesting and important whilst studying the history of Salisbury, and which I am bold enough to hope will likewise interest my readers. It may help if I explain how and why this book came to be written.

In the spring of 1980 Tony Martin, a Salisbury bookseller to whose qualities as a publisher and friend I shall return in due course, asked me to write a history of the city. He was dismayed by the lack of any full-length study to bridge the gap between the works designed for the professional historian, and those designed for the casual tourist. I was flattered by his request, and delighted, too, that he was giving me an opportunity to test a hypothesis which I have held for some years, that the divorce between academic and popular history is unnecessary, harmful to both traditions and insulting to the non-specialist reader, whom I hold in the highest regard. I therefore set about selecting those aspects of the city's history which I felt to be particularly relevant (to use a vogue word) to my generation, or which, in the light of recent advances in historical scholarship, could now be presented in a fresh and interesting new light. Relishing the freedom from editorial control which has inhibited some previous writers on Salisbury I have neglected many hallowed areas – including the Cathedral and its architecture – and have preferred less well-trodden paths – bedroom furniture in 1700, for instance, and the development of council housing – because I thought they were important.

Some of the topics which I have chosen to consider have required considerable original research in manuscript sources; others have been written largely from secondary material. I have tried to keep the apparatus of scholarship out of my narrative, but, in deference to those who may use this book for reference, I hope that I have footnoted, paragraph by paragraph, all the assertions made in the text, and I have tried to provide an adequate bibliography. I have no doubt that my critics will disagree with my choice of topic and my method of presentation. A work such as this is designed to stimulate discussion, and if I can infuriate others into setting down their own alternative views in print, that is all to the good.

I envisage this book as dividing into three parts. Chapters one and two view the city as a whole, as a living being, and trace its development from its conception to the present day. In the course of this account it becomes apparent that Salisbury's career has been unlike other places, and thus at the end of chapter two a number of questions are left unanswered. In chapters three, four and five, which are concerned with various aspects of economic history - trade, industry, communications and government - I try to answer these questions, and at the same time I introduce ordinary and extraordinary characters from Salisbury's past as examples of various facets of the city's history. The final part, chapter six, is an attempt to penetrate more deeply into the lives of former citizens by examining some of the most important areas of their lives - their schooling, religion, health, law and order - and concluding with a look inside their homes.

I make no excuse for adding yet another volume to the already extensive literature of Salisbury. The last serious attempt to write a full-scale history of the city for the general reader was made in 1957, a quarter of a century ago, and even that admirable work was rather less than half the length of the present volume. It is a truism that each generation must rewrite history to suit its own needs; if my book goes a little way to providing Salisbury with a history for the 1980s then I shall have achieved my aim.

Since coming to Wiltshire to work eight years ago it has been my privilege to make many friends in the field of local studies, and it is my great pleasure to acknowledge the help that they have given me in various ways whilst I have been writing this book. They have read and commented on parts of the typescript, produced documents, books and illustrations, willingly discussed points with me and gently corrected some of my wilder flights of fancy. They are not to blame for the mistakes that remain, of course, but, often without realising it, they have done a great deal to improve my work. In no particular order I should like to mention Peter Saunders, David Algar, Tiffany Hunt, Simon Olding and John Hadley of Salisbury and South Wiltshire Museum; Edward Boyle and Gillian Roberts of Salisbury Reference Library; Kenneth Rogers, Penelope Rundle, John d'Arcy, Andrew Crookston, Margaret Allen and Janet Lamble of the Wiltshire Record Office; Roy Canham, Alison Borthwick, Lesley Marshman and Robert Smith, my colleagues in the Archaeology and Museums Section of Wiltshire Library and Museum Service; Pamela Colman of Wiltshire

City of the Dead

If there is one thing that everyone knows – resident and visitor alike – it is that Salisbury has moved. The ramparts of Old Sarum dominate the northern skyline of the modern city, and we have all in our time gazed at that bleak outline and tried to visualise the streets of medieval houses dominated by the towers of a cathedral. Can it really be that there was once a city on this windswept hill? (Plate 2)

The so-called move from Old Sarum on the hill to New Sarum in the valley, which apparently took place around the year 1220, marks the birth of Salisbury as it exists today. Old Sarum, therefore, may be described as Salisbury's parent, and it is fitting that this study should begin with a discussion of that parent and the circumstances of the birth. But Old Sarum is an enigma, and very little, despite repeated archaeological exploration and concerted historical study, may be asserted about it with confidence. A series of questions waits to be answered, of which, 'Why did they move away?' is perhaps the simplest to answer. It is much harder to describe precisely what kind of place Old Sarum was, where it was situated, when and why it was established, and why it became a cathedral city. And what is meant by 'move'? When and how was the move effected, if indeed it happened at all?

It used to be thought that the city of Old Sarum lay within the massive oval bank and ditch which encompass the plateau of Old Sarum. Maps refer to this fortification as the 'city wall,' suggesting that the city lay inside, and indeed there is slight medieval evidence that this was so: 'The city stood in the castle and the castle in the city,' wrote a thirteenth-century poet. It was on this assumption that extensive excavations were undertaken within the ramparts in the early years of this century and a detailed model of the supposed city was made and exhibited in the former Salisbury Museum. As recently as 1978 a writer on Salisbury has claimed that, 'the city's commercial heart was contained within the Iron Age ramparts.' But no archaeological evidence has ever been found to support this claim. It is an assumption made in the absence of evidence and it typifies the problem of describing Old Sarum. The reconstruction which follows is likewise based on assumptions derived from inadequate evidence, and so is equally vulnerable to new evidence and new ideas.[1]

Old Sarum began life as an Iron Age hillfort, that is to say a fortified village or small town belonging to one of the Celtic tribes who were living in Britain at the time of the Roman invasion. It would have made a safe but unpleasant place to live, and it was probably used more as a refuge in times of emergency than as a permanent settlement. That it was built at all suggests both that there was felt to be a need for it and that the population of the surrounding countryside, whom it was designed to protect, was sufficiently large, strong and well-organised to undertake such a massive piece of civil engineering. In the first century after the Roman invasion towns were established near many of the most important hillforts, but this does not seem to have happened at Old Sarum. A town was perhaps intended, and certainly the hillfort was planned to be a key road junction, and an important staging-post and river-crossing on the Roman great west road (Figure 1), but there is no sign that Roman Salisbury (which was known as *Sorviodunum*) achieved the status of more than a small town. It probably consisted of little more than a *mansio* – a kind of government establishment which served as a hostelry for travellers using the road network on official business and as a depot for policing and regulating traffic along the roads. Where this *mansio* lay, together with any commercial or domestic buildings which may have been attracted to it, is not clear; there are three candidates: somewhere within the ramparts of Old Sarum itself, near the river-crossing at Stratford-sub-Castle, or on the high ground towards Bishop-down east of Old Sarum. Nor is it possible to say whether occupation of any or all of these sites continued to the end of the Roman period and beyond.

Sarum next occurs in history as *Searoburh*, the site of a battle between Saxon colonists and the indigenous population in 552 AD. But whether the battle, or perhaps a series of skirmishes, took place on the hillfort or somewhere in the surrounding countryside can only be guessed. There is no indication that Old Sarum was inhabited again until near the end of the Saxon period, in the tenth and eleventh centuries; indeed there is a little evidence that it was not, and that by this time *Sarisberie*, as the name had become, was being used to describe a much larger territory, of which Old Sarum was only the most prominent landmark.[2]

Three miles west of modern Salisbury, near the point where the Rivers Wylye and Nadder flow into one another, lies the small, but delightfully urban, town of Wilton. During the Saxon centuries, when nothing very much was happening at Old Sarum, Wilton was developing into one of the most important towns of Wessex. Besides its enviable position at the head of two important valleys, and the consequent trade that its market would attract, late Saxon Wilton was a place of great prestige, containing within its walls a royal palace and an important nunnery. It was moreover the chief town of Wiltshire, with which its name was synonymous, and it was at times second only to Winchester as the administrative centre of Wessex (Figure 2). Wilton's proximity to Old Sarum was probably not accidental. Another important town in Saxon Wiltshire, Ramsbury, the seat of a Bishop, stands in a somewhat similar relationship to the hillfort of Chisbury, four miles to its south, and Chisbury lies even closer to another Saxon town, Bedwyn. In

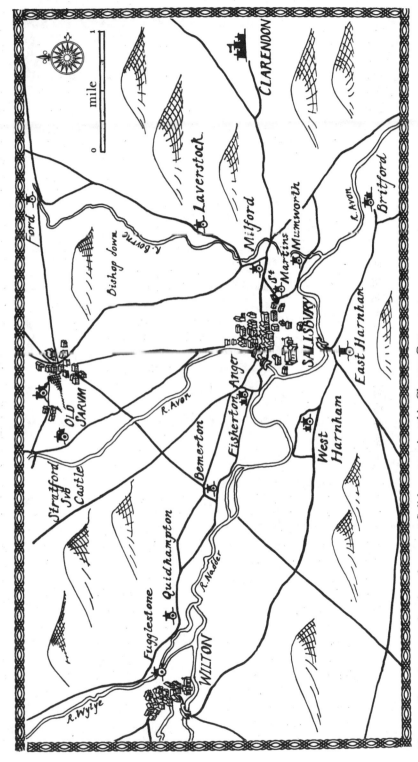

Figure 1. Location map, showing places near Salisbury mentioned in Chapter One.

5

Figure 2. Towns of Saxon and medieval Wessex.

Somerset the small Saxon town of Ilchester appears to have been linked to the important hillfort of South Cadbury, which, archaeological and documentary sources agree, was occupied in the Saxon period. The suggestion, therefore, is that Wilton felt able to develop in a commercially advantageous but strategically vulnerable position because of the reassuring profile of Old Sarum three miles along the road.[3]

The need to defend the towns of Wessex from Viking invasions was one of the main concerns of Alfred towards the end of the ninth century. A chain of strongholds, placed at regular intervals and with distinct territories, was thrown around the kingdom to offer co-ordinated protection on a scale not envisaged since the Romans. Chisbury was one such citadel, designated as a refuge for the inhabitants of Bedwyn, Ramsbury and the surrounding villages; other hillfort sites in Dorset and Devon were re-fortified in the same way. But surprisingly it was Wilton rather than Old Sarum that was chosen as the citadel for south Wiltshire, and this can only be explained by the importance of Wilton at this time and the economic loss that would have resulted if its inhabitants were encouraged to desert it for the safety of Old Sarum. Nevertheless, when put to the test a century later, this was precisely what they did. In 1003 Wilton was burnt to the ground by Danish invaders, but Old Sarum seems to have been left in peace. It is not clear whether inhabitants of Wilton took refuge in Old Sarum in anticipation of the events of 1003, or, as seems more likely, families who had lost their homes and possessions in 1003 decided, on the 'once bitten, twice shy' principle, to move up the hill rather than reconstruct their lives in Wilton. But we do know the names of three men – Godwine, Goldus and Saewine – who were living in Wilton before 1003 and Old Sarum after 1003. They were moneyers, the minters of coin, who were at the heart of any town's commercial success, and it may be assumed that they were part of a more general shift of tradesmen from Wilton to Old Sarum. No coin has ever been discovered which can be shown to have been minted at Old Sarum before 1003 and so it seems likely that Wilton's disaster was the prelude to Old Sarum's urban career.[4]

There is at present no archaeological evidence to suggest the position of the Saxon town of Old Sarum. It would be natural to assume that in 1003, with the Danes on their doorstep, the refugees would have made their camp inside the Iron Age hillfort, devoid at this period of any internal earthworks. It may be that for a few years, while the emergency continued, the ramparts of Old Sarum housed a quite considerable population, drawn not only from Wilton, but also from the villages and farmsteads of the larger tract known as the *Sarisberies* and from further afield. Such accommodation would have been temporary, as many, if not most, of the refugees would have had every intention of leaving the God-forsaken place as soon as it was safe for them to do so. It is unlikely that even those who decided to make Old Sarum their permanent home would have chosen to remain within the ramparts. Clearly the new settlement, if it were to survive, had to derive its livelihood from trade or agriculture, or both, and since the best agricultural land was undoubtedly already being farmed from settlements such as Avon and Stratford in the valley floor, Old Sarum had to stand by trade. Now Old Sarum had one great commercial advantage bequeathed to it by the Romans. It lay on the main highway from London to the West Country at a point where a number of other more or less important roads converged. None of these roads actually passed through the hillfort, but they seem to have met just outside the east gate, at a point now marked by a piece of waste land about one hundred metres north of the present Old Castle Inn (Figure 3). It would perhaps have been possible for the traders encamped inside Old Sarum to have diverted the main road to pass through the hillfort – such diversions were by no means uncommon in later new towns – but this would have required a very steep descent to the river west of the hillfort. Instead it seems that the town began to grow up outside the east gate around the road junction, where there is a small but relatively flat area now traversed by the main Salisbury to Amesbury (A345) road. Here the first of several churches, dedicated to St. Ethelreda, may have been built, and here, presumably along and around the main road junction, the first market would have been held.[5]

The Norman conquest in 1066 ushered in a period of reorganisation and reassessment throughout England. Decisions taken in such a climate are sometimes based on administrative tidiness and political expediency rather than common sense. It was an extraordinary notion to build a cathedral within the ramparts of Old Sarum, and the folly of that decision taken in 1075 very soon became apparent to the clergy and administrators who were forced to live and work there. But to the council of bishops who made that decision it was not unreasonable, and in the circumstances it was perhaps the best course open to them. Under the Norman administration pressure was placed on the church to abandon rural bishoprics based on villages and to transfer them to towns. The combined see of Sherborne and Ramsbury, which included Berkshire and Dorset as well as Wiltshire, was one such bishopric to come under scrutiny. The obvious choice for a diocesan centre, it could be argued, was Wilton, and indeed it is not altogether clear why Wilton did not become the cathedral city of Wessex, as it had been intermittently some two centuries earlier. Perhaps it was felt that Old Sarum was close enough to be identified as almost a suburb of Wilton, and that a cathedral at Old Sarum would carry all the prestige of a cathedral at Wilton, with the added advantage that it was surrounded by one of the Bishop's largest and most important endowments, the extensive manor of the *Sarisberies*. There may too have been an element of rivalry between the Bishop and the powerful Abbess of Wilton, whose nunnery dominated that town. The settlement at Old Sarum, it was true, was far smaller and less important than Wilton, but as a new town its future was not unpromising. In what was probably the first century of its existence it appears to have risen from nothing to become a rival to older Wiltshire boroughs such as Cricklade, Malmesbury and Marlborough. It was, as we have seen, a natural centre of communications – perhaps an important consideration in a diocese extending over three counties – and it had, after 1066, undergone some stimulus to development through the construction of an important wooden castle within the ramparts. There was, moreover, the opportunity to build from scratch on a virgin site in a commanding position, and the view from the solid Norman towers would be magnificent.[6]

8

settlements, to Wilton, or out of the area completely. And so the real decision taken by the Canons and their Bishop was whether to invest their ecclesiastical wealth in propping up the *status quo*, or whether to reverse the decision of 1075 and begin again. It is clear from the decisions of the Canons, preserved by William de Wanda, that financial considerations were uppermost, and the intricacy of the detail in which they are recorded is a sure sign of their authenticity.

And so the decision was taken to move. According to William de Wanda this decision had been taken, the site chosen, and even the individual tenements planned before 1199, but whether or not this was the same as the eventual site of New Sarum cannot now be known. Even as late as 1218, when the papal bull was issued, the Bishop was not committing himself to a named site. The alternatives seem to be as follows. He could resite the Cathedral outside the castle, in the existing town of Old Sarum, but this would not solve the physical discomforts, and Old Sarum was already in decline. He could resite the Cathedral at Wilton, and this was perhaps the obvious choice if, as seems likely, Old Sarum was still regarded as a satellite of Wilton. This, according to the legend, was the expected choice, and it is at pains to explain an acceptable reason why Wilton was not eventually chosen. A more plausible reason is that, since (as the legend admits) the Bishop would have had to build on land belonging to the Abbess, any profits accruing from settlement springing up around the Cathedral would pass to her rather than to him. A third option would have been to transfer the Cathedral and city from Old Sarum onto a new site owned by the Bishop, and this is what is popularly believed to have happened. But that is not what any of the sources we have discussed say, and there is no evidence that the Bishop interfered at all with the city of Old Sarum. The fourth option, and the course which was actually taken, was to transfer only the ecclesiastical buildings from Old Sarum – the Cathedral, Bishop's Palace and Canons' houses – and to resite them sufficiently close to an existing settlement – St. Martin's or Old Salisbury – to supply the needs of the builders, whilst allowing plenty of room for a new town to be laid out in a favourable commercial position. Whether Myrifield was chosen by divine inspiration, as the legend (but not the earlier sources) maintains, is a matter for conjecture. There is no need for such an explanation (except for the Bishop to cloak his commercial acumen under the guise of divine guidance) as the site chosen was probably the best available; it is perhaps more likely that the appearance of the Blessed Virgin Mary into the legend is the result of popular etymology of the name Myrifield as deriving from 'Mary-field.'

Most of the sources record, no doubt accurately, that before beginning the move the Bishop secured the approval of the Pope. The wording of the papal bull, and William de Wanda's remarks, seem to rule out the legend's assertion that Richard Poore actually visited the Pope in person, and the legend is certainly confused over the involvement of

King John and his successor, Henry III. William de Wanda records the interest shown in Herbert Poore's original scheme by Richard I, but does not mention any consultation with Henry III, other than an invitation to take part in the stone-laying ceremony in 1220. Richard Poore's charter of 1218 begins by announcing the Pope's agreement but does not mention the King, and the royal charter of 1227 says only that the King has taken note of the move. We should assume, therefore, that no official permission was sought from the King, and none given. But the legend may be correct in assuming that the Bishop had at least sounded out the royal attitude, since the success of the new city would depend very largely on securing the privileges conferred in the charter of 1227. Once the papal bull was received at Salisbury, probably in April 1218, the final decision to move was swiftly taken, and announced to the world at the beginning of July. A temporary church on the new site was started and completed in the course of the summer of 1219. At a Chapter meeting in August 1219 the moving date was fixed for November 1st, and invitations were sent all over England to attend a stone-laying ceremony to mark the commencement of building work on the new Cathedral, which was to take place on the feast of St Vitalis (April 28th) in 1220. And so, more than twenty years after it was planned and a little over two years after it was approved, New Salisbury was born.

Somewhere in this reconstruction of events we have lost the arrow that was lost in Myrifield, the brindle-cow grazing under the thorn, the Rogation-tide procession and the romance of the Bishop and the Abbess. Sometimes, regrettably, history and folklore must go their separate ways. We wish them well.

The Hen gathers her Chickens

The news that the Bishop of Salisbury was building a new town would have come as no surprise to anyone in thirteenth-century England. There had been new towns planned on a regular basis in Roman and Saxon times, and during the three centuries after the Norman conquest no fewer than 170 towns (and probably many more) were planted in the English countryside. Nearly 50 of them date from the period 1190–1230, when New Sarum was conceived and born, making these the busiest decades of all for the medieval town planner. These years too were to see the final flowering of the medieval new town, which after 1230 appeared only sporadically and for the most part without great success. Like so many other great achievements, therefore, the city of Salisbury stands near the end of the cultural epoch which created it, and could benefit from the experience gained in planning other, lesser, new towns.[21]

The most obvious feature of Salisbury's medieval plan is the grid or chequer pattern formed by many of the city streets, and it is often thought either that such a pattern is the hallmark by which all medieval planned towns may be recognised, or conversely that Salisbury is in some sense unique or unusual in possessing such a grid. Neither supposition is in fact true. Gridded plans are only one of several identifiable types found in new medieval towns; more commonly streets were planned around a central market place, often a triangular wedge or cigar shape; sometimes a semi-circular plan was used, as at Devizes, or the street pattern was dictated by natural features such as estuaries and important rivers. Nevertheless many of the most ambitious town plantations, such as New Winchelsea and Ludlow, do have grids, and many Roman and Saxon foundations were laid out along largely rectangular lines. Had its enormous medieval abbey survived Bury St. Edmunds in Suffolk, which was developed as a town soon after the Norman conquest, would perhaps present the closest English parallel to Salisbury.[22]

The difference between Salisbury and Bury – indeed the difference between Salisbury and all the other planned medieval towns – was that Salisbury was designed to be a cathedral city. Even without the medieval accounts of the foundation, which as we have seen might not tell the whole truth, it is clear from the city itself as it survives today that the Cathedral was planned first, surrounded by its Close, and that everything else – Market Place, streets and houses – took its cue from the work in Mary's field. The medieval church was at the heart of the new city – but to say that the city was church-centred or church-orientated would be to give a misleading impression of its piety. As we shall see in chapter five the medieval church was very big business, and the Bishop, as its chief executive, knew that the hubbub of workshops and the bustle of the Market Place were essential parts of his new foundation, bringing revenue to support the Cathedral and providing for the material needs of his staff. But Salisbury, uniquely among the medieval new towns, was not planned simply as a speculative venture to swell the coffers of a king, bishop or baron; it was designed to be the administrative and spiritual centre of a diocese which comprised a large tract of southern England. That it also proved to be the most spectacularly successful of all planned towns may not be unconnected with this original aim, but it should not be confused with the founder's intention. For much of its history the city has been trying to shake itself free from the Cathedral's dominance, but it cannot deny that it was the Cathedral that was the city's *raison d'être* and not the other way round.

We left Bishop Poore having decided to build his new Cathedral in the area known as Mary's field or Myrifield in the meadows near Milford, and now it is time to see how his decision was put into effect. The area he had chosen, and which he owned, was no more a blank on the map than any comparable piece of Wiltshire is today, and he had to contend with many of the problems – physical obstacles, boundaries and rights of way – that any modern developer has to face. He also had to weigh up the value of the rents he could expect to receive from the intended building plots against their existing value as agricultural land. Thirdly he had to devise a street plan which would allow for the best and most convenient division of land, and which would take into account the needs of special areas, such as a flat piece of ground for the Market Place, and adequate drainage for dwelling-houses and industrial premises (Plate 4).

The site chosen for the new Cathedral Close – Myrifield – seems to have been one of the common fields of the Bishop's manor of Milford. Low-lying and easily waterlogged, it was not ideal agricultural land, and the loss of rents and dues from the farmers who cultivated it would have been less than from some other potential sites. But as a common field it would have had divisions and boundaries, and some of these may have affected the plan of the development. The northern boundary of Myrifield is perhaps marked by the present-day Milford Street and New Canal, running along to a river crossing in the vicinity of Fisherton Bridge. It is probable that a medieval road from Winchester through Clarendon Forest to Wilton followed this course, which also marks the dividing line between the relatively firm river gravels and the muddier, boggier ground lying in the sweep of the river. The later town plan also suggests that this was a pre-existing landmark which the planners chose to – or had to – incorporate into their design (Figure 4). Close scrutiny of the alignment of streets shows that they all fall nearly parallel with or at right-angles to either New Canal or Milford Street, and this is a feature which we shall discuss in due course. A second road also seems to have crossed the Bishop's building site, running south from Old Sarum to a river crossing known as Aegel's ford, which gave its name to Ayleswade (or Harnham) Bridge. The modern Castle Street, Minster Street and High Street mark its course, and the Cathedral was built so that its west front abuts the line which it must have taken through the common field. Apart from these two roads and the headlands which must once have provided access to individual strips in the field the only topographical feature in Myrifield which may have affected the plan was the small village settlement clustered around the Church of St. Martin at the eastern edge of the field. The angle of St. Martin's Church Street, which is at odds with every other street in medieval Salisbury, suggests perhaps that it represents the line of a village street left undisturbed by the new town (for street names see Figure 11, page 49).[23]

These three features – the northern boundary, the north–south road and the village – seem to have provided the benchmarks on the surveyor's drawing board. The order in which the first artificial lines were planned and pegged out must remain a matter for conjecture, but it seems likely, from documentary as well as topographical evidence, that, after the Cathedral, the Bishop's Palace and the North and West Walks of the Close were decided first. The West Walk seems to have used the north–south road, with which it is parallel, as its yardstick, and

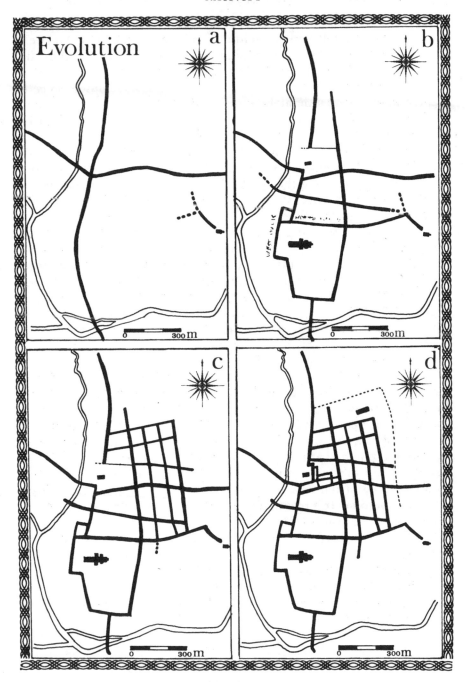

Figure 4. The evolution of Salisbury's plan in the thirteenth century – a hypothetical sequence. Precise dating is impossible, but it is suggested that a. depicts features existing pre-1220; b. represents the first artificial lines, laid *ca.* 1220–1230; c. shows additions made *ca.* 1230–1260; and d. marks subsequent modifications to the plan after *ca.* 1260. The defences are marked by a dashed line on map d.

the North Walk is aligned on an east–west axis which runs directly from the point where the Rivers Avon and Nadder converge to St. Martin's Church. On the north and west sides of the Close, fronting onto the walks and onto a small green in the north-west quadrant, were the first tenements of New Salisbury, the plots for the Canons' houses. Since it seems that they were ultimately responsible for the move, and since they carried a large part of the financial burden of the projected new Cathedral, it was natural that the Canons would award themselves the best ringside seats to watch it being built. Their tenements, by contrast with the cramped accommodation at Old Sarum, were of generous proportions, and those fronting the West Walk had the extra attraction of a garden stretching down to the river. The Close quickly gave the appearance of an enclave of affluence, as expensive houses were built to the pattern set by the Bishop at Leadenhall, a building so extravagant by the standards of its time that its mortgage continued for generations.[24]

This stage in the town plan may be dated with some confidence to the years 1219 and 1220, coinciding with the ceremonial stone-laying of the Cathedral on St. Vitalis's day, 1220. The Canons' houses were begun immediately and penalties were imposed on those who delayed. The city, by contrast, is portrayed in the earliest sources as something of an afterthought, springing up of its own accord as a result of the religious migration. This of couse cannot be true; it is simply the Bishop's propaganda, dissociating himself from any commercial or financial incentive, and emphasising the priority of the Cathedral over the city. In fact there was nothing haphazard about the new city, as its chequer-board pattern signifies, and some urban development, even if only to cater for the army of cathedral-builders, must have been anticipated and planned at the outset, and was indeed inevitable. But it is just as certain that no-one in 1220 would have predicted how enormously successful the new city was to be, and how populous it was quickly to become. It is reasonable to ask, therefore, how, where and to what extent the original planners intended the new city to develop, although any conclusion to this kind of question must rest largely on conjecture.[25]

We should perhaps begin by trying to decide which streets were next to be laid out (Figure 4). New Street, which certainly went under that name in the thirteenth century, and which seems to have included at first the whole sequence of modern streets from Crane Bridge to the junction with St. Martin's Church Street, would be a good candidate. Its name, if original, hints that it may have been the first street of the city to have been laid out along entirely new lines, and the straightness of its course suggests that there was no other development to stand in its way. Alone among the streets it gave its name to one of the four wards into which the city was from a very early date divided, and there is a tradition that Mitre House, which stands at the intersection of New Street and High Street, was the first house to be built in the city. A second candidate would be the street known today by various names, from Endless Street in the north, through Queen Street and Catherine Street to Exeter Street (formerly Draghall Street). The whole line, which was originally known as High Street, looks as if it was designed as a diversion, branching from the Old Sarum to Aegel's ford road at a point near the modern Castle Street railway bridge and leading the traveller to the east of the Cathedral instead of past the west door. Such a road was perhaps constructed before the town defences enclosing the city's northern and eastern sides were envisaged, and the name given its northern section – Endless Street – is evidence that it was not constrained by these defences. In its southern portion – the modern Exeter Street – it also serves to define the eastern boundary of the Close, which is perhaps an indication that it was conceived at the same time as the North and West Walks discussed earlier. A third street which may date from this earliest phase of the town planning is St. Ann Street. This leads slightly south of west from the point at which New Street joins St. Martin's Church Street, until it meets an extension of the line of the North Walk of the Close. Perhaps it was developed on the site of an earlier track leading into the common field from the settlement along St. Martin's Church Street. The alignment of its western end suggests that it was planned as a continuation of the North Walk.[26]

If these three roads were indeed the first to be laid out in the new city we may infer that the original intention was to develop the remainder of Myrifield, that is to say the area north of the Close as far as New Canal and east as far as St. Martin's Church. This view is supported by the earliest division of the city into administrative areas, the wards of aldermanries. There were four wards, and although the first mention in documents of the existence of wards does not occur until 1249, it has been suggested that they date from before the establishment of St. Thomas's Church in the 1230s. They belong, therefore, to a very early phase of the city's development, and it is interesting to see how they divide the city. Three of the four seem originally to have fallen south of the New Canal–Milford Street line, dividing Myrifield into New Street Ward (everything west of the former High Street line), Martins Ward (everything east of the former High Street line as far south as the New Street line), and Meads Ward (everything south and east of the High Street and New Street lines). The fourth, Market Ward, occupied the area north of the New Canal–Milford Street line around the market and site of St. Thomas's Church. If we may assume that these boundaries represent a division of the city into four equal parts at some time in the 1220s or 1230s then it is clear that the first urban development was taking place along either side of the New Street line.[27]

Both the original street plan and the ward boundaries as described above reinforce the view that the original city was planned on a rather more modest scale than it was eventually to become, sacrificing only the one common field to building development, and extending the existing settlement around St. Martin's Church. Three factors were perhaps responsible for a change of plan at the end of the 1220s. Firstly it seems that the south-eastern part of Myrifield, known as Bugmore, was found to be unsuitable for building; secondly the new city was showing itself to be popular and capable of further expansion; and thirdly the Bishop in 1227 succeeded in obtaining a royal charter conferring borough status on the new city, with the right to hold weekly markets, and with various privileges for the inhabitants which made New Sarum a very desirable place to live. And so the decision was taken to begin building on what was probably St. Martin's better common field, the valley floor north of the New Canal–Milford Street line. If our hypothesis about roads is correct this area was already traversed by two north–south routes, the original line following the modern Castle Street–High Street alignment, and a new 'by-pass' represented by Endless Street, Queen Street, Catherine Street and Exeter Street. Its southern boundary was also marked by an ancient road, the Winchester–Clarendon–Fisherton–Wilton road, now followed by New Canal and Milford Street. Defined on three sides by these roads a large area was now set aside for the city's Market Place, extending as far north as the present Blue Boar Row. This spacious, if slightly lop-sided, square quickly established itself as the heart of the city, outstripping even the Cathedral in importance, and becoming indeed one of the busiest, richest and most important pieces of land in medieval England.[28]

It is now, in about the year 1227, with the Bishop's city placed on a firm footing by the royal charter and development spreading from the Myrifield area to the Market Place, that we should consider the grid or chequer pattern of streets for which the city is famous. There is nothing particularly clever or original about a grid; indeed it would be absurd to suggest that men capable of designing and building Salisbury Cathedral could not have pegged out a far more sophisticated street plan had it suited their intentions. But in fact a square or rectangular grid is the most economical method of dividing land into tenements of regular and equal size, so that each has direct access from the street. If a city, such as New Winchelsea, was planned about a perfectly rectangular grid, it is a sign not of the designer's ingenuity but of a lack of constraints which might force him to deviate from the regular. And so at Salisbury we should be asking not, why is a grid pattern employed, but why is the grid not completely regular and what has caused the irregularities.[29]

Some of the irregularities may be explained by existing buildings which obstructed the plan. St. Martin's Church Street, we have suggested, is the way it is because it already existed as a village street before Salisbury was planned. It may be that the slightly awkward street plan in the area of St. Thomas's Church and Fisherton Bridge was caused by buildings near the river-crossing and the Bishop's mill. But the biggest spanner in the works was, as we have suggested, the irregularity of the

CHAPTER TWO

Maturity

Salisbury does not really belong to us. It has been given to us to look after for a few years, and we must make of it what we can until it is time to hand it on again. We are only the latest in a long line of occupants, and we, like each of them, will leave our mark on the place, for better or for worse. In this chapter an attempt is made to discover those who have gone before us, and how, by their weight of numbers as well as their power to create and destroy, they have contributed to the Salisbury we know. They have left us written records and they have left us buildings, and from these clues we can begin to see how the city has fared during its long, eventful life.

The Population of Salisbury

There is no better index to the development of a town than the number of people which it has accommodated throughout its history. Population has a bearing on every other topic covered in this book and may, in addition, be used as a basis for comparing Salisbury with other places. If it were possible to obtain accurate total population figures for every year or every decade since the city's foundation, we could pinpoint with confidence times of stability, of rapid influx and of sudden decline, and relate them to known events, such as epidemics and periods of economic growth. We could look for signs of new building in response to a rising population and dilapidation in times of decline, and we could discover critical periods when Salisbury has stepped out of line compared with its neighbours and rivals. But such precision is impossible. For most of Salisbury's history its citizens have had no sure indication of how many of them there were, and those estimates of population that have been made have usually only told part of the story – adults, men or households – or have omitted to define the area of the city which they cover. Even less reliable are those totals which have been collected for taxation purposes, since it is impossible to know how widespread was evasion, or how many individuals were legitimately excused payment. The best that we can do is to collect as many figures as possible from all periods and take each on its merits (Figure 5).

We should begin by examining statistics which claim to represent the total population of the city. (By city we shall for the time being include the three city parishes or four city wards, excluding the Close and the suburbs of Fisherton, Milford and the Harnhams.) The most reliable figures are those derived from the national censuses, held every ten years (except 1941) since 1801. Although slight inaccuracies may have crept into the early censuses, especially the first, there is no need to distrust the general picture that they present, nor to look for other sources since 1801 to supplement them. The 1801 figure is 7,126, and this rose each decade until 1841, when it reached 9,531. Thereafter the city parishes declined, but the city continued to grow at the outskirts, so that in 1871 the three city parishes stood at 9,212 whilst the total within the city boundary was 12,903. This trend of growth at the edges and decline at the centre continued, until by 1901 more than half the city's 17,117 people were living outside the historic city. In the present century the city's population has doubled again, and the latest estimate suggests that over 36,000 people now live in the city area of Salisbury, and nearly 44,000 if Laverstock, Wilton and other outliers are included.[1]

33

Figure 5. The population of Salisbury from the fourteenth to the nineteenth centuries. The vertical pilasters represent dates for which population estimates are made in the text. Because of the impossibility of precision before 1700 the tops of two walls are depicted, representing probable maximum and minimum totals; thereafter a single wall suffices.

Contrary to popular belief the 1801 census was not the first official total population census in this country. That took place in 1695 and, although it was never published and most of the returns and totals are believed no longer to exist, Salisbury is one of the relatively few places whose total was noted and has survived. Hatcher recorded a figure, 6,976, as an appendix to his history published in 1843, but he seems not to have known the source. In fact it is taken from a note made in St. Edmund's parish register in 1695, presumably by a churchwarden involved in compiling the figure. Unfortunately he seems to have made a mistake in one of his parish totals and there are strong reasons for believing that the true figure should read 6,676. Two other figures help to bridge the gap between 1695 and 1801: a writer in the *Gentleman's Magazine* in 1753 claimed that in the previous year (1752) the population of Salisbury was 6,586, although he offered no clue to his source; and a survey conducted by the city council in 1775 to discover what proportion of the population was native to the city revealed a total population of 6,856. There also exist two estimates of the total population at earlier periods. One, made by an Italian visitor to Salisbury in 1669, that the city contained over 16,000 inhabitants, seems improbable and may be discounted in the light of other evidence which we shall present. But the other is probably nearer the truth. This is an official figure of 1597, preserved among the city muniments, which gives an estimate of the total population as 7,000.[2]

So far, therefore, the evidence suggests a fairly stable population of 6,500–7,000 in the seventeenth and eighteenth centuries, which doubled through outward expansion in the nineteenth century and has doubled again since 1900. To take the story further back into the medieval period we must rely on the evidence of partial censuses and calculations made by modern writers. In 1377 a fourpenny poll-tax was imposed on everyone over the age of fourteen, except clergy and beggars. Various multipliers have been suggested to convert this tax into a total population figure, and if these are applied to the number of Salisbury poll-tax payers – 3,326 – the population of Salisbury would lie somewhere between 4,900 and 5,800. The fifteenth century, unfortunately, is a demographic desert, but in the 1520s another form of taxation, the lay subsidy, was imposed, and this gives an opportunity to make a very tentative population estimate, by comparing Salisbury's contribution with other towns of similar status, in particular Coventry, where a population census survives from the same period. It has been suggested that on this basis Salisbury's population may in the 1520s have been around 8,000, although both this and the 1377 assessment presumably include the Close, and so the total for the three city parishes should be reckoned betweeen 500 and 1,000 lower. Also in the sixteenth century an estimate survives of the number of communicants in St. Edmund's parish in 1548, and this conforms fairly well with the 1520s figure. In 1548 there were said to be 1,700 communicants, and if this is multiplied to include children, and the total considered to be 40–50% of the city's total population, as St. Edmund's parish was a century later, we arrive at a span of about 6,300–7,100 within which Salisbury's population should lie. We may, therefore, cautiously add some figures to our graph: 4,850±450 in 1377, 7,000–7,500 in the 1520s and 6,700±400 in 1548.[3]

The next minefield for the historical demographer is that body of statistics which lists households. Here we become embroiled in the world of tax returns, so that not only must a multiplier be applied to convert from families to individuals, but allowance must also be made for tax evaders. Some taxes, such as the window taxes, were so half-heartedly applied or so widely ignored that the figures they yield are meaningless as an index of total population. Many, like the hearth taxes, have perished or survive only as fragments and others became stereotyped over many years and continued to be applied at the old rates decades, even centuries, after the original assessment was made. But there are a few worthwhile lists which may be used to give at least an approximate population figure. The earliest, written on a small, insignificant-looking roll among the city muniments, has been shown to date from the years 1399 or 1400, and seems to list every tenant by the ward in which he lived (see Appendix one). The list contains 999 names, so that if (and it is a very big 'if') this represents 999 families, and we apply a multiplier of between four and five, a total population figure emerges of about 4,000–5,000, which is encouragingly close to the figure for the year 1377, which we have just calculated. Another list, dating from 1455, contains many fewer entries, only 742 in fact, and this is surprising because it is unlikely, in the light of other evidence, that the city was in decline at this period; and yet the list, which is a rental of the Bishop's tenants, seems to have been prepared with some care, and the rent could not easily have been avoided. The solution is probably that this rental omits sub-tenants, so that in certain cases a tenement appears only once even though it may have been shared between three or four families. Some idea of the extent to which tenements were divided is gained from a later list, of 1667, which records about 670 tenements but includes nearly 1,400 names, each presumably a householder. There is no way of knowing whether this ratio, of rather more than two families per tenement, can be carried back into the medieval period, but if it can, our 742 tenements of 1455 might have housed between 6,500 and 8,000 people. On the same basis the 1667 list would represent a total population of 6,200–6,800, which accords very well with the 1597 figure of 7,000 and the 1695 figure of 6,676. Two other figures should also be mentioned, which come not from lists of householders, but from estimates of the total number of houses themselves. An official figure of 1,290 houses in 1626 would suggest a population of 5,800–6,500 and a private survey of 1782 discovered 1,474 houses, or 6,600–7,400 people.[4]

Adding all these figures to our population graph we discover a certain degree of consistency, although it must be admitted that the medieval figures represent a foundation so shaky that no very elaborate structure may be built upon them. After 1600 the picture becomes much clearer and the graph may be presented with some confidence. We have now discussed all the principal sources available for calculating total populations at fixed points in the city's history, but there remains another area for exploration which may enable us to refine our graph and identify some of the fluctuations which must have occurred. The registers of the Salisbury parishes survive, in various states of preservation, from the 1560s onwards, and it is possible, by totalling and averaging the number of baptisms and burials each year, to reveal periods of increase and decline (Figure 6). Decline seems to have occurred in the 1590s and in the periods 1680–1710, 1725–1745 and 1790–1800, whilst the figures suggest increases between 1650 and 1680, in the years after 1710 and from 1745–1790. Particularly noticeable is the way in which the number of baptisms and burials seem to run in tandem, apart from occasional leaps and bounds in the burial figures.[5]

There are only two direct reasons for a decline in population – either the number of deaths exceeds the number of births, or the number of emigrants exceeds the number of immigrants. Obviously the reverse is also true, and if there are more births than deaths, or more immigrants than emigrants, the population rises. Of course questions about why people come and go or die before their time are very complicated and can only be answered in the light of the economic and social evidence which we shall present in later chapters. But whilst the statistics are in front of us it will be worth considering the direct causes of growth and decline – mortality, fecundity and migration. The most striking features revealed by parish register analysis is that whereas for about a century from 1620–1720 Salisbury was able to hold its own by producing sufficient children to make up for casualties and perhaps even achieving a modest natural increase, from 1720 until 1800 death was outstripping birth, so that, left to its own devices, the city would have declined by about 1,000 every twenty years, and found itself in 1800 with less than half its 1720 population. The ratio in the earlier period of the registers, 1560–1620, is less easy to judge, because of obvious discrepancies and omissions in their compilation. But the impression given is of births and deaths keeping pace with another, except in a few calamitious years of epidemic disease.

The cause of death is seldom recorded in the registers and so, apart from the occasional plaintive note of explanation, it is left to us to surmise what dreadful catastrophe overtook the city in years of high mortality (Figure 7). We can but shudder at the thought of 172 burials taking place at St. Edmund's Church in the space of a single month, September 1563. What is clear from the registers is that the years which decimated the city nearly always followed the same pattern, with no hint of danger until May or June, and then a devastating rate of casualties until August or September, tailing away to normal in the

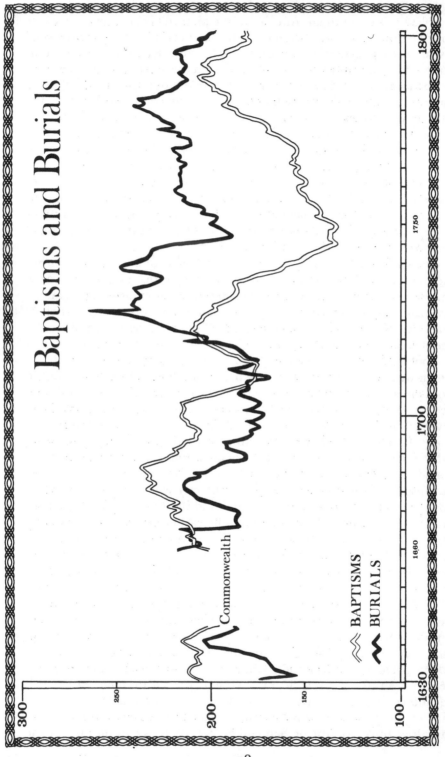

Figure 6. Baptisms and burials in Salisbury parish registers, 1631–1801. The vertical scale represents the annual totals for the three city parishes, which have been combined, and fluctuations have been reduced by employing a nine-year moving average (a technique whereby each year is represented as the average of its own total and the totals of the four preceding and four succeeding years).

autumn. Salisbury in high summer must have been a breeding ground for all kinds of disease, the open watercourses distributing every strain of unpleasantness along the refuse-laden streets. This ritual poisoning of the city by the city seems to have taken place every few years from the sixteenth to the nineteenth centuries, and probably through much of the medieval period as well. But paradoxically these self-inflicted wounds are not reflected in the total population figures which we have tried to reconstruct. There was no dramatic fall in the population after a bad summer had filled the graveyard; a never-ending supply of immigrants seems to have been ready and only too willing to subject themselves to the same dangers. In 1579 nearly 500 citizens succumbed, all but 80 of them between July and October, and yet in the following year the city council had to take action to try to prevent overcrowding. The position was no different after the devastating plagues of 1604 and 1627; there were always more mouths to feed.[6]

This raises the question of who were these immigrants and where had they come from? Did they move in from neighbouring villages, or from Salisbury's wider hinterland, or were they natives of remote cities seeking their fortunes away from home? Comparison of three groups of immigrants, of different social classes and from different periods in the city's history, suggests that a large proportion in each case had travelled quite a distance to Salisbury and originated outside the city's immediate sphere of influence. In the fourteenth century many men's names had not crystallised into surnames in the modern sense, but still contained a statement of their place of origin. Analysis of two lists of prominent citizens, of 1306 and 1334, suggests that a little over a quarter of them came from places within ten miles of Salisbury, and that about half were of towns and villages more than twenty miles away, mostly in Wiltshire and neighbouring counties, but including representatives of Exeter, Harpenden, Hereford, London and Wales. At the end of the sixteenth century, among the poorest classes of immigrants the distances travelled were much greater, and two-thirds of the vagrants sent on their way by the magistrates had strayed from places more than twenty miles from the city, many of them wandering from such exotic parts as Yorkshire, Cork, Northumberland and Kent. About one-quarter were natives of villages within ten miles of the city and a further 10% had come from other places up to twenty miles away. In the eighteenth century, by contrast, among young men arriving in the city to be apprenticed to Salisbury masters a much higher proportion came from nearby villages, nearly a quarter from places fewer than five miles from the city and over half from fewer than twenty miles away. There were still, nevertheless, considerable numbers from the manufacturing towns of the Wiltshire–Somerset border and from remote parts of Hampshire and Dorset.[7]

It would perhaps be reasonable to conclude from these various statistics that by 1400 Salisbury's population had reached 4,000–5,000. It

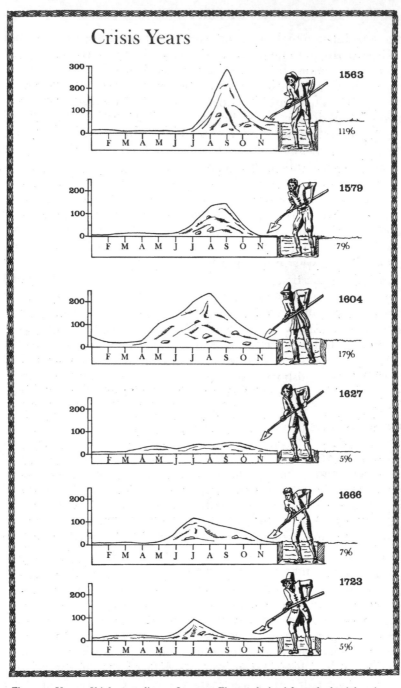

Figure 7. Years of high mortality, 1563–1723. Figures derived from the burial registers of the city parishes have been used to plot month-by-month totals for certain crisis years, and these are represented as gravediggers' spoil heaps. In 1604 all three parishes' registers are available, but for the other years only two of the three survive in a complete form, as follows: 1563, 1579, 1666, 1723 – St. Edmund's and St. Martin's; 1627 – St. Edmund's and St. Thomas's. The absence of St. Thomas's burials from four of the six totals is not so serious a drawback as it might appear; we suggest that the very limited churchyard accommodation at St. Thomas's led to casualties from St. Thomas's parish being buried elsewhere. Percentages of the total population are given.

continued to grow to a maximum of 7,000–8,000 a century later and then declined slightly. Thereafter, apart from minor fluctuations, there seems to have been little change for about two centuries, with the total hovering on either side of 6,500, until about 1780, when an inexorable rise began. Suburban expansion, which began in the early decades of the last century, has continued apace, so that now the city, although not large as cities go, has come to cater for a population approaching 40,000, more than five times its historic size. Its survival over the centuries has been ensured for the most part not by natural regeneration – its record for salubrity has not been good – but by attracting immigrants of all classes from near and far. This, in a nutshell, has been the story of Salisbury's maturity. How does its record compare with similar towns elsewhere?

Comparisons

In a world teeming with people, where towns extend mile after mile until they run into one another, and where the constant pressure to develop and redevelop is everywhere apparent, it is hard to imagine a medieval landscape in which villages predominated, subsistence agriculture was the order of the day, and the towns were modest, intimate communities distinguished less by their size than by their function and status. A town of 5,000 people nowadays is accounted little more than a village; but very few medieval towns supported such a population, and – London excepted – it is doubtful whether any ever grew beyond the size of today's Devizes or Warminster or Romsey. The great cities of medieval England, although their importance in the national and local economy may have been no less than their modern counterparts, were by today's standards tiny – urban arrangements in miniature. Our estimates of Salisbury's population at various periods, therefore, in the range 4,000–8,000, are by medieval standards those of a major town.

If Salisbury's population is placed alongside estimates of the total national population it is immediately apparent that the fluctuations do not correspond (Figure 8). Before the nineteenth century Salisbury seems to have achieved its maximum size in the late medieval period, when the population as a whole was in decline or stagnating. Conversely as the increase in the national total gathered momentum after 1500 Salisbury went into decline, and only recovered at the end of the eighteenth century. In fact the only 'normal' feature of Salisbury's fluctuating population seems to be the doubling and quadrupling which has taken place since 1800.

Salisbury's progress before that date seems just as erratic if it is compared with other towns of similar size and origin (Figure 9). Among the planted towns of England it ranked third in size in 1334 and most populous of all in 1377. The lateness of its foundation made such success

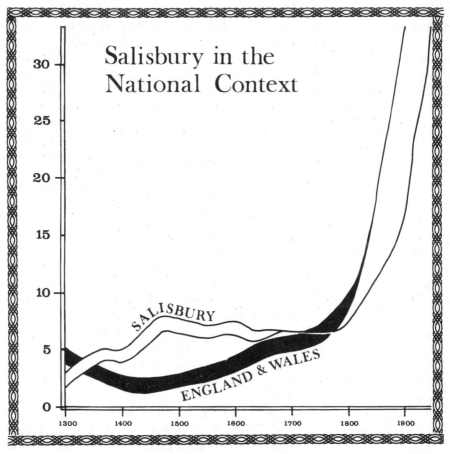

Salisbury in the National Context

Figure 8. Salisbury's development in the national context. Estimates of the population of Salisbury, since 1300 (see Figures 5 and 10) are compared with estimates of the total population of England and Wales during the same period (from Rogers, 1977, 12). Salisbury's population is expressed on the vertical scale in thousands, the national population (using the same calibration) in millions.

the more remarkable – only one town founded after Salisbury on a completely new site occurs among the twenty-five largest new towns in 1334. Already by this date, little more than a century after its creation, Salisbury was the tenth most important city in England, and by 1377 it had risen to seventh place. After 1377 there is no basis for comparison with other towns for nearly 150 years, but the next assessment, of *ca.* 1523, found Salisbury still seventh in importance, apparently having gained ground on all but four of its rivals – Norwich, Newcastle, Exeter and York. Whether Salisbury had in fact maintained this position throughout the fifteenth century or even ventured higher in the league table cannot now be known, but certainly in the Bishop's rental of 1455 there is no hint of the urban decay which many of its contemporaries

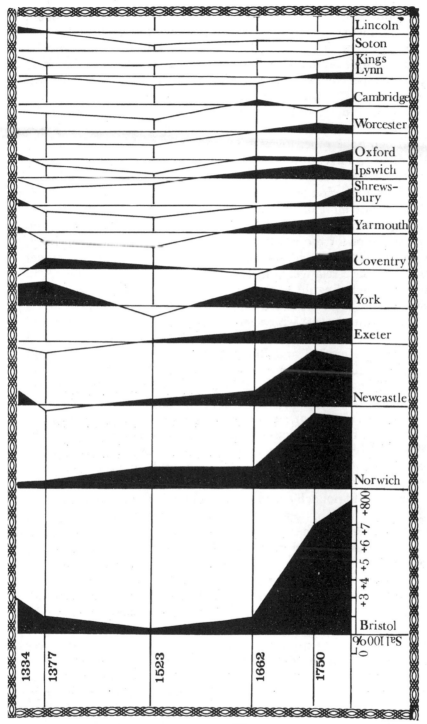

Figure 9. Salisbury compared with other major towns, 1334–1801. With the exception of London all English towns which exceeded Salisbury's population at any time in the medieval period are included. Salisbury is depicted as a constant (a vertical line) against which each town is compared. A profile to the right of this line (shown as a solid black mass) denotes that the town in question is larger than Salisbury, expressed as a percentage; a profile to the left of this line (shown as an outline) denotes that the town is smaller than Salisbury, expressed as a percentage.

were claiming to have suffered. Medieval Salisbury was clearly a boom town, one of the most notably successful places in England.[8]

But by 1523 the tide seems to have turned against the city, and for the next century Salisbury shared with Coventry the humiliation of being outstripped by each of its rivals. It was not that Salisbury was becoming a ghost town – the actual population, as we have seen, declined by no more than 10%, if at all, and there were times when the city was awash with immigrants – it was simply that Salisbury was being left behind as other towns grew and prospered. By 1662 the city had dropped to fifteenth in importance, and the comparative decline continued through the eighteenth century. Not only was Salisbury overtaken at this period by the upstart industrial towns of the Midlands and North, but most of the old sparring partners from the days of medieval prosperity had also left the city far behind. By 1801, when reliable statistics for the whole country become available, Salisbury, through its inactivity and stagnation, had dropped in the national stakes to become a relatively small and insignificant country town.[9]

Salisbury, including the Close and the three city parishes, was home to 7,668 souls in 1801. It ranked alongside a number of other cathedral cities and county towns, whose relative decline in the post-medieval period had not been unlike Salisbury's (Figure 10). Gloucester and Northampton, Hereford and Bury St. Edmunds, Southampton and Lincoln, were all included among the top 40 English towns at the end of the middle ages, but in 1801 all found themselves, like Salisbury, with a population around 7,000–8,000. Alongside them were other ancient, but less important, country towns – Durham, Kendal, Newark, Maidstone and Berwick-upon-Tweed – and one recent prodigy, Brighton. Without exception Salisbury and all these towns of comparable size increased their populations during the nineteenth century – indeed it would have been a symptom of some fatal cancer eating away at any town which could not achieve some growth while the national population quadrupled. Six of these thirteen towns succeeded in bettering the national increase, and these ranged from Brighton, where the population increased sixteen-fold during the century, to Maidstone, which mirrored the national growth fairly closely. The remaining seven, including Salisbury, barely managed to double their total populations, although Salisbury and Hereford fared slightly better than the other five. The criteria for success in an industrialised society were not, of course, the same as those which had favoured the medieval market town, and it might be expected that those towns with good rail connections or close to iron and coal fields might show the greatest increase. But that is not the conclusion to be drawn from towns in this size category. Newark and Durham, the only towns near mineral workings, were amongst the least successful of the thirteen; and already by 1841, before the railways had made their impact, the die seems to have been cast, in that the thirteen towns had already assumed the approximate

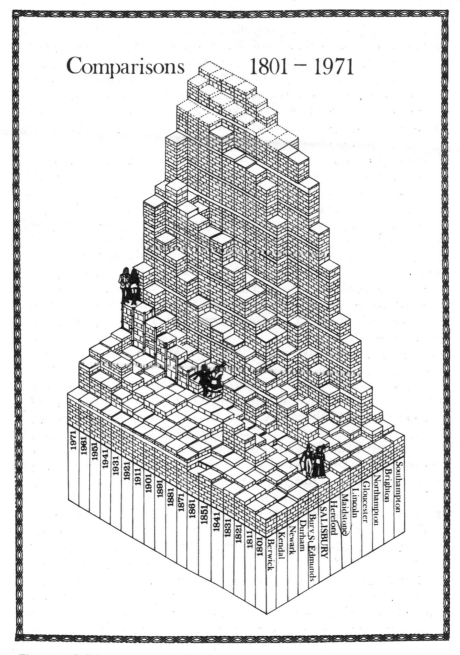

Comparisons   1801 – 1971

Figure 10. Salisbury compared with similar towns, 1801-1971. Salisbury's population totals at ten-year intervals are compared with those of twelve other towns, all of which were approximately the same size as Salisbury in 1801. The period figures mark the line of Salisbury's development. Dashed lines imply that the totals for certain towns exceed the graph's ceiling of 100,000. A plain string-course through the brickwork appears at 10,000 intervals.

positions relative to each other that they were to hold in 1901 and, moreover, in 1971. It seems, therefore, that for this kind of town its rate of growth in the early decades of the nineteenth century has set the seal on its later development. Only in the present century has Salisbury once again grown at a faster rate than the national population. Between 1901 and 1961 the number of Salisbury's inhabitants doubled, and although Hereford and Southampton approached this rate of increase, none of the original thirteen towns equalled the rate of Salisbury's growth during this period.[10]

Statistics such as these may be used to place Salisbury in its national context and draw comparisons with similar towns elsewhere. But to most of Salisbury's inhabitants such considerations have probably never seemed very important. And to the people of the Wiltshire villages such comparisons have always been meaningless – Salisbury, in W. H. Hudson's words, is 'the great market and emporium and place of all delights for all the great Plain.' Just as London has always dominated the towns of England, so Salisbury has until the last century dominated the towns of Wiltshire, the historic, though not the actual, capital of its dominion. And if Salisbury's performance is judged against these more local rivals, the towns of Wiltshire, a picture emerges rather similar to that which we have already described.[11]

Medieval Wiltshire occupied a far loftier position among the counties of England in terms of wealth and population than it does today. Salisbury's prosperity in the fifteenth century was not, therefore, achieved at the expense of neighbouring Wiltshire towns; it accompanied theirs and only slightly outmatched most of them. Nevertheless three towns – Trowbridge, Devizes and Marlborough – seem to have kept pace with, and bettered, Salisbury's growth, though on a much smaller scale, even at the height of its power. At the close of the middle ages, when Salisbury entered its period of stagnation, all the other towns in Wiltshire made rapid progress by comparison, a relative improvement against Salisbury's position which seems to have continued unabated in most cases until the nineteenth century. The exceptions to this pattern are Malmesbury, Bradford-on-Avon and Marlborough, which all declined, relatively speaking, after peaks in the seventeenth century. Salisbury continued to lose ground until the mid nineteenth century, when the positions began to change, so that between 1841 and 1921 everywhere except Swindon was growing less quickly than Salisbury. The present century has seen the trend reversed again, so that while Salisbury's population has doubled, most other Wiltshire towns have been growing even faster. Such growth has not been reflected in the total population of Wiltshire as a whole, with the result that the towns have grown at the expense of the villages and the countryside.[12]

Until the seventeenth century all the Wiltshire towns apart from Salisbury were very small. Probably none achieved a population much higher than 1,500, a figure exceeded by many self-respecting villages today. None, therefore, offered any serious threat to Salisbury's supremacy in the county. But by 1700 a number of places were creeping up on Salisbury; Bradford and Marlborough, if the figures are to be believed, each achieved 70% of Salisbury's population in 1676, and Devizes, Warminster and Trowbridge were all hovering around 50% in the eighteenth century. To Trowbridge fell the honour of overtaking Salisbury in the Wiltshire population stakes, at the end of the Napoleonic wars. By 1821 Salisbury's 8,763 was matched by Trowbridge's 9,545, and the two ran side-by-side until a third contender, Swindon, steamed past them both during the 1870s. The positions recorded by the 1881 census, with Salisbury a poor second to Swindon, but a long way in front of Trowbridge, remain to this day, although now Chippenham is battling with Trowbridge for third place. Modern Salisbury has claimed a territory of about twenty miles in every direction, in which the city has no serious rivals. There are small towns within this ambit – Romsey, Ringwood and Wilton – and the three populous parishes of Salisbury Plain – Amesbury, Bulford and Durrington – and in a roughly twenty-mile ring all around Salisbury, held at a safe distance, are towns of all shapes and sizes – Andover, Winchester, Eastleigh, Southampton, Bournemouth, Blandford, Shaftesbury, Warminster and Devizes – which sometimes seem to threaten its supremacy. But Salisbury remains the capital of the Plain, as it was in Hudson's day, and still, for those who live in it and around it, 'an exceedingly important place – the most important in the world.'[13]

The Fabric of Salisbury

If at some date in the future Salisbury were to disappear without leaving any archaeological evidence of its existence; and if some historian in the 21st century were set the task of reconstructing the city as it might have looked in the 1980s using only the kinds of documentary evidence which we have presented in this and the previous chapter, what deductions would he make? Is it possible, in fact, to offer a satisfactory explanation of our present townscape in terms of thirteenth-century planning, medieval prosperity, post-medieval decline and Victorian suburban development? And if it is, what are the features of modern Salisbury which point to the fluctuating fortunes of its past?

The first deduction which our historian might draw from our evidence is that during the nineteenth and twentieth centuries, as the city doubled and quadrupled its population without suffering a crisis of overcrowding, there must have been a considerable expansion of the urban area, achieved by pushing out beyond the original limits, along the main roads and in the wedge-shaped tracts of land between the main roads, engulfing – like lava from a volcano – any hamlets and villages which lay in the path. Such development occurred around towns everywhere, and how it was achieved in Salisbury will be the subject of the last section of this chapter. The second deduction that could be drawn is that for three centuries before 1800, when the population was static or in decline, there would have been little need to expand beyond the medieval limits of the city, and so we should not expect to find extensive suburban development occurring during this period. A third deduction might be that, since Salisbury seems to have achieved its greatest prosperity and national prestige around the fifteenth century, buildings which survive from this period should in general exhibit better craftsmanship and breathe more of an air of affluence than those which came later. By the same token, as the fifteenth century was followed by a serious reversal in the city's fortunes, medieval buildings would stand a better chance of survival in Salisbury than in other towns which grew prosperous – and so could afford to build anew – in later centuries. There would be other deductions, based perhaps on the original town plan, the influence of the Cathedral and Close, the form of tenure under which the citizens held their dwellings, the distinct functions of areas of the city, and the names given to the city's streets, all of which can be shown to be ingredients of Salisbury as seen today.

The building blocks of the city, as originally planned, were, as we have seen, the rectangular tenements of seven perches by three, or about 35 × 15 metres. These, we have suggested, were instrumental in deciding the layout of streets and the dimensions of the city as originally built, and their influence continued to be felt long after the pattern of regular tenements had disintegrated (Figure 11). Their relatively spacious proportions – in common with those of many other planted towns – meant that Salisbury embarked on its era of medieval wealth with plenty of spare capacity, and could accommodate a growing population without extending its boundaries beyond the limits set by the thirteenth-century planners. There was perhaps room for about 500 regular tenements (including some slightly larger or smaller plots on account of irregularities in the plan) within the thirteenth-century city. If Salisbury was settled at the density of one family per tenement the resulting population would be about 2,500, but if this was too optimistic and some tenements found no takers – as at New Winchelsea – the outlying chequers need not be developed or could be rented at a lower rate for agricultural or horticultural use. Or if, on the other hand, the population rose above 2,500 it was easily possible to build three or four dwellings on each tenement and so accommodate a population of 7,000–10,000 without undue overcrowding.[14]

The arrangement of the tenements, as well as their size, has had its consequences for the city's later development. The basic plan, as we have seen, involved chequers consisting of twelve or more tenements arranged in two rows, each tenement running east-west and fronting on either its eastern or western boundary a street running north–south.

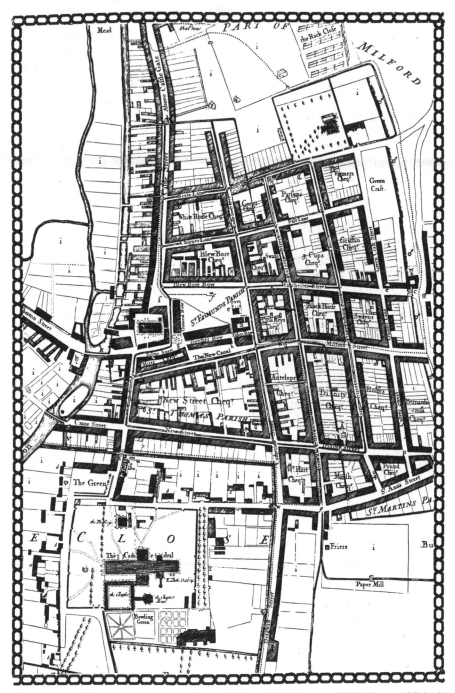

Figure 11. Salisbury in 1751. A portion of William Naish's map of Salisbury published in 1751. Few changes were made to the map between this and an earlier edition of 1716, and so it depicts a pattern of boundaries largely unaffected by eighteenth-century alterations. The remains of medieval tenement divisions are particularly noticeable in the eastern chequers, especially Griffin, Swayns and Rolfes.

Between the two rows, therefore, was a common boundary running north–south which bisected the chequer. Thus each tenement had a street frontage and, in most cases, this also served as its water supply, since most north–south streets carried canals. (It was perhaps because of the basically north–south orientation of the water supply, demanded by the contours, that the tenements were planned to run east–west.) But this arrangement of tenements also meant that they had no rear access by means of north–south alleys. Anyone planning to divide up his tenement, therefore, had either to make the division along its long axis, resulting in narrow strips of land and a narrow street frontage, or to forfeit part of the street frontage to an archway or entrance providing access to buildings ranged along the tenement with no street frontage of their own. In some parts of the city other solutions were possible, such as where rows of east–west and north–south tenements abutted one another, so that by obtaining parts of each an L-shaped plot could be made. Other possibilities presented themselves with corner tenements or where adjacent tenements on either side of a chequer could be acquired.[15]

The basic tenement structure, therefore, offered scope for modification and rearrangement in later periods whilst retaining vestiges of its original layout. By 1455 it is clear that throughout the city the original tenements had undergone very drastic modifications. Of the 750 or so parcels of land then described as tenements only nine were charged at the shilling rate which denoted the standard size of tenement. About one hundred were assessed at more than one shilling and so probably represented plots comprising parts of more than one original tenement. The remaining 640 were all charged at less than one shilling, signifying in most cases that an original tenement had been divided. Of these nearly one-third were assessed at either sixpence, fourpence or threepence, suggesting an original tenement divided into two, three or four respectively. Some insight into the complicated way in which tenements are known to have been divided is given by one detailed study of a building complex in the city. 'Balle's Place,' which lay in the south-west corner of Three Cups chequer, contained in 1386 a dwelling-house, some shops, a cottage, a gateway, a courtyard, a garden, a dovecot and other appurtenances. It occupied the whole of the original corner tenement, running east–west along Winchester Street, and the innermost two-thirds of the next tenement to the north, which, because the corner was not a right angle, was an irregular shape. Access to this portion was obtained from Winchester Street through a courtyard in the more southerly tenement, and the principal dwelling-house was built in the centre of the plot away from the road. But because the northern part of this plot was completely landlocked by other tenements a subsequent owner bought part of the next tenement to the north, which, although it had no street frontage of its own, had access to Rollestone Street through a passage made when it was divided. In due course the property passed to the city authorities who purchased the remaining parts of the original tenements which fronted onto Rollestone Street, and thus acquired the whole of three adjacent thirteenth-century tenements which in the course of about 150 years had been divided into no fewer than ten more or less unequal parts.[16]

A glance at Naish's map of 1751 shows that the city at that period still retained many examples of boundaries which corresponded to the original layout of tenements (Figure 11). A number of chequers retained, in whole or in part, the north-south boundary line bisecting them and marking the division of the two rows of tenements. Many of these have now vanished, but a good example can be seen by walking along the alley next to the Methodist Church in St. Edmund's Church Street. The alley, which runs to Greencroft Street, is approximately 70 metres long (fourteen perches) and exactly halfway along there is a very slight deflection. This marks the point where a standard tenement of seven perches in length fronting onto St Edmund's Church Street abutted a similar tenement on a slightly different alignment fronting onto Greencroft Street. Property boundaries are fairly resilient, and doubtless the observant explorer could find many another example, especially in the eastern chequers, of a surviving thirteenth-century boundary incorporated into a nineteenth- or twentieth-century development.

In the 1455 survey of the city, which we may regard as a description of Salisbury at the height of its medieval vigour, the various uses to which tenements might be put are enumerated. A large number are described simply as tenements, principal tenements or corner tenements, sometimes with the name and occupation of the tenant and the note, 'in which he is living.' Such entries presumably cover a wide range of dwelling-houses, often combined with the tenant's workshop, adapted to his own particular trade. Many other tenements, especially near the Market Place, are described as shops, whilst others contain cottages or gardens, which sometimes include racks used in making cloth. There is a sprinkling of 'hospitia' (inns) and a few 'tabernae' (taverns), as well as the occasional mention of a stall, a workshop, a storehouse, a dovecot and a latrine. Most of these buildings, we may assume from surviving examples, were built principally of wood, with little use made of stone. And although no domestic building remains (outside the Close) from the time when the city was new, a recent survey has identified remains of eighteen buildings of the fourteenth century and about 60 of the fifteenth century which may still be seen or which have only recently fallen victim to redevelopment. With the help of these ambassadors from the middle ages, therefore, it is possible to gain some impression of the city's appearance at the time of the 1455 survey, although we should bear in mind that only the fittest and most stoutly-constructed are likely to have survived, and that, then as now, many of the buildings lining the city streets would have stood little chance of lasting for one century, let alone five.[17]

The grandest houses in the medieval city, and often those which occupied the largest tenements, belonged to wealthy merchants and men of affairs, such as John Halle, whose house in New Canal dates from shortly after the 1455 survey. The surviving hall of his dwelling, which now serves as the entrance to a cinema, displays a finely-carved roof and painted window-glass. The hall is set at right-angles to the street, thus permitting access to the rear of the tenement by a passage which would have run alongside it. Perhaps more typical of Salisbury's merchant houses, and certainly more complete, is the complex of buildings in Crane Street now known as Church House. Here the fifteenth-century north range – roughly contemporary with the survey – runs parallel to the street and occupies the whole street frontage of the tenement. To gain access to the courtyard and suite of buildings beyond it, therefore, an arched gateway was built through the range of sufficient size to permit waggons to pass through to the courtyard beyond. Some smaller houses also followed this arrangement, although a hall at right-angles to the street was probably more usual. Beach's bookshop, on the corner of High Street and Crane Street, is an example of three small gabled houses crammed into the High Street frontage of a single tenement. And what is probably the oldest surviving building in the city, William Russel's house in Queen Street, dating from about 1306, is of this type, and its fine medieval features are clearly seen inside, even though it sports a much later facade.[18]

Another particularly interesting, though more specialised, medieval building is tucked away behind Debenham's store in Blue Boar Row, of which it now forms a part. It was built as accommodation for the Boar Inn and originally stood in the inn's courtyard. It is unusual in that not only has most of the structure survived but so has the contract for its building, and this stipulates precisely how long the work should take, who should be responsible for providing the materials, and at what points payments should be made to the carpenter. It also lays down the dimensions of the building and the thickness of the timbers to be used: 'And the groundsilles yn brede of xv ynche And yn thiknesse x ynche And xiii principal postis every post xvi fote of lengthe And yn brede xiii ynche and yn thiknesse xii ynche ...' That the building still stands is a tribute to the care with which the carpenter fulfilled his contract, although it appears that he was unable to provide timbers to the full twenty feet (six metres) stipulated as the width of the building. He therefore made the building slightly narrower but increased the overall length as compensation.[19]

As well as this purpose-built commercial building, shops lined many of the city's streets in 1455, especially in areas close to the Market Place. The distinction between dwelling-house and shop is not an important one, as many buildings served both functions, and many others must have alternated between one and the other in the hands of successive owners. Medieval buildings which survive along the rows adjacent to the Market

Place were originally shops, of course, and were, as we have seen, the permanent successors of portable stalls or shambles. They had no land beyond their own four walls, and the streets ran along either side, so there was no need for passages and alleyways. The Wheatsheaf Inn, which extends from Fish Row to New Canal, consists of two such medieval shops; the Haunch of Venison Inn and neighbouring buildings on either side of Minster Street probably began life in the same way. At the bottom end of the architectural scale, among the cottages and outbuildings, there are naturally fewer survivors from the medieval period, and most of the residential chequers away from the Market Place, where they would have been found, are now lined with terraced housing of the eighteenth or nineteenth centuries. In Guilder Lane, however, a row of seven cottages survives which is roughly contemporary with the 1455 survey, and so offers the best remaining example in the city of the kind of housing in which its poorer medieval citizens were accommodated (Plate 7).[20]

With the waning of the middle ages and the end of the city's heyday two new sources of evidence for Salisbury's building history become available. The first street map of the city was published by John Speed in 1610, in a corner of his map of Wiltshire. Measuring only 11 × 9 cm it can hardly be relied upon for total accuracy in matters of detail, and each of the little houses, so carefully drawn, must represent two or three houses in real life. Nevertheless it provides a useful comparison with the much more detailed and accurate map of Naish a century later. If the two maps are to be believed the seventeenth century witnessed few changes in Salisbury, as indeed we might expect from the demographic evidence presented earlier. The city in 1600 was confined almost entirely within its original thirteenth-century boundary, the only exceptions lying along Castle Street outside the gate, along the north side of Fisherton Street, on the rampart near Winchester Gate and along Exeter Street south of St. Ann's Gate. Most chequers were lined with buildings on all four sides, concealing empty spaces in their centres. Only in the prosperous New Street chequer were these spaces marked out into gardens, or perhaps orchards, since most contain a single, symbolic tree. In Speed's map the Market Place is dominated by a pillory, the rows seem to consist of groups of buildings around the square, and St. Thomas's Church, with a substantial spire, seems to take a full part in the affairs of the Market Place instead of being tucked out of sight. By 1700 a little suburban development was taking place, notably along the south sides of Fisherton Street and St. Ann Street and outside the eastern ramparts, as well as some infilling along the rows in the Market Place. But at the same time houses seem to have been lost. Three of the northern chequers no longer contained buildings on all four sides, St. John Street and Exeter Street had lost most of the houses along their western side abutting the Close wall, and the cluster of buildings between the successive Winchester Gates had dwindled to a single line.[21]

The second new source of evidence in the post-medieval period comes in the form of reports by travellers of the state of the city at the time of their visits. Leland's verdict, dating from about 1540 and the earliest worth mentioning, has been often quoted: 'Ther be many fair streates in the cite of Saresbyri, and especially the High Streate, and the Castel Streate ... The market place in Saresbyri is very fair and large and welle waterid with a renning stremelet; in a corner of it is domus civica [council house], no very curius pece of work but stronly bueldid of stone.' The water channels, the Cathedral and the size of the Market Place seem to have been the features which impressed travellers most, and these noble feats of engineering provided a striking contrast to the squalid way in which, from the seventeenth century, they were maintained. Celia Fiennes, almost a native, commented on the dirt in *ca.* 1685, and her sentiments echoed those of John Evelyn, writing in 1654: 'The market-place, with most of the streets, are watered by a quick current and pure stream, running through the middle of them, but are negligently kept, when, with small charge, they might be purged and rendered infinitely agreeable, and made one of the sweetest towns; but now the common buildings are despicable, and the streets dirty.' Rather more than a century later there seems to have been little improvement: 'The churchyard,' wrote John Byng in 1782, meaning the cathedral close, 'is like a cow-common, as dirty and as neglected, and thro' the centre stagnates a boggy ditch.' The architecture of Salisbury was a matter of personal taste: Pepys (1668) thought the city, 'a very brave place,' but Cosmo de Medici (1669) found it, 'both in point of materials and structure, like those of the other cities of England.' To Louis Simond (1810) Salisbury was, 'a little old city, very ugly,' whilst for J. G. Kohl (1844) it was, 'one of the few English towns in which one may still luxuriate in antiquities and antiquarian recollections.'[22]

Our attempt to equate Salisbury's history with its present-day appearance now arrives at something of a paradox. Up until the eighteenth century the surviving fabric is as we might expect: the period from about 1450 to 1600 is very well represented, with fewer survivors from earlier medieval times and a distinct paucity of seventeenth-century buildings (Figure 12). But when we reach the eighteenth century Salisbury has many new buildings and reconstructions on display. 'During the 18th century the town acquired the predominantly Georgian aspect which to some extent it still retains,' is the verdict of a recent survey. And yet these alterations and improvements were achieved at a time when Salisbury was slithering down the league table of English cities and incapable of regenerating its population without the help of immigrants from the countryside. In the words of a contemporary (writing in 1801), 'It is remarkable, that there has only been one house, on a new site, added for many years. Salisbury has now fewer houses and inhabitants, than it had one hundred years ago.' What, therefore, was happening to Salisbury, that, without seeming to stir from its

Building Survival

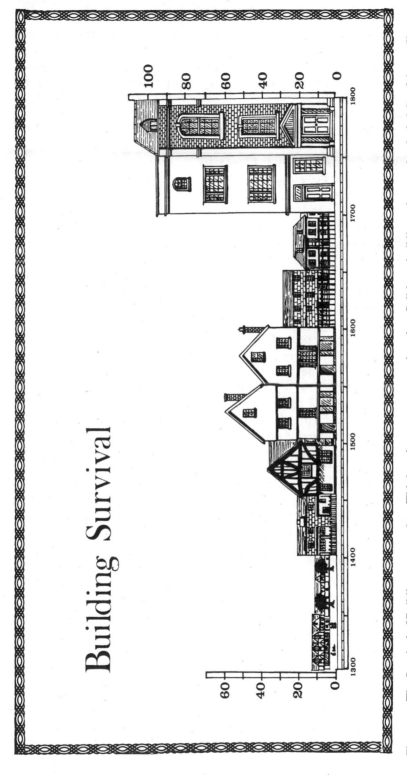

Figure 12. The Survival of Buildings, 1300–1800. This imaginary street scene, based on Salisbury buildings, denotes, by the height of the rooflines, the number of buildings in Salisbury which survive from each fifty-year period (or have only been demolished since *ca.* 1960) according to the inventory by R.C.H.M. 1980.

post-medieval lethargy, it could be reworking its fabric into a new style and leaving its mark for us to admire?[23]

The answer to this paradox probably lies in the changes in social structure which affected all towns at this period. To the eighteenth century belongs the segregation of urban society into the fashionable squares and terraces of the wealthy and the incipient slums of the poor. Many of the towns which grew prosperous during this period expanded into spaciously-planned suburbs of Georgian housing and found their medieval street patterns swept away by developers. Cities became divided, socially and geographically, between rich and poor. At Salisbury, however, not visited by the new-found wealth of its counterparts, the tendency to make radical changes and polarise the city into good and bad areas could not be carried out. Salisbury had to settle for more modest improvements, a new house here and there, a new front on an old house, two old houses knocked into one. And although the cumulative effect of these alterations was to change the character of the whole city, lack of funds prevented Salisbury's citizens from carrying out the wholesale destruction of their medieval heritage in their enthusiasm for civilised living.

Nevertheless, it is possible to detect subtle changes during the eighteenth century which were affecting areas of the city, even though no new roads were being built and no expansion was taking place. The window tax returns of 1706 despite their shortcomings give a very rough indication (based on the number of windows) of the size of houses in each chequer, and from these it is clear that no part of the city, outside the Close, was reserved for mansions and, conversely, no areas consisted exclusively of poorer housing. Although there was a slight preponderance of smaller houses in some of the chequers furthest from the Market Place and in the area immediately south of Milford Street, the overall impression is of a good mixture of large and small throughout the city. But by the end of the century, from the evidence of surviving buildings, it is clear that money had been spent unevenly on improvements and redevelopment and that, whereas some areas of the city exhibit a large number of eighteenth-century buildings, in other places they are relatively few. In the St. Ann Street and Exeter Street area, lying on the southern fringe of the city, much eighteenth-century work may be seen, and considerable changes were taking place at the same time in Castle Street, the city's northern exit. Along New Canal smaller houses were replacing the medieval merchants' opulent halls; but few have survived, having themselves fallen prey to the opulent merchants of our own generation, the chain stores. And in the north-eastern chequers, between Milford Street and St. Edmund's Church, a number of eighteenth-century houses remain. But elsewhere in the centre of the city, in the High Street and Market Place area, there was less in the way of wholesale rebuilding; indeed, after the damage by fire to the Council House in 1780 the area of the Market Place now occupied by the Guildhall was cleared of a number of houses and shops and these were not replaced.[24]

The overall impression of a centrifugal force, drawing people from the centre to the edges of the city, is supported by comparing the population figures of the three city parishes in 1700 and 1801. During the century, when the total population rose by about 450, St. Edmund's parish, including the northern end of Castle Street and the north-eastern chequers, gained 400, and St. Martin's parish, which includes the St. Ann Street area, gained nearly 200; but St. Thomas's, the parish which takes in High Street and the various rows in the Market Place, showed a loss of 150. There are signs too of an increasing social rift. Many of the new-built houses of the eighteenth century, as represented by those that survive, were reasonably large and well-to-do, and a number clearly supplanted two or more older houses. At the same time the pressures of commerce were taking over some of the buildings in the city centre formerly used as dwelling-houses. Towards the end of the century the population began to rise once more and by 1795 very nearly half the total population was classed as poor and eligible for relief. Many poor families, according to a commentator of the time, were by now sharing houses. By 1800 the medieval city was too small to accommodate the commercial needs and private aspirations of all its citizens, and it was at last time to break the bounds which had contained it for nearly six centuries.[25]

Suburban Salisbury

In order to understand what has been happening to Salisbury since 1800 we must return briefly to the world of statistics. As we have already noted, between 1800 and 1900 the city's total population more than doubled, and since 1900 it has doubled again. During the same period the number of inhabited houses has increased eightfold, from about 1,500 to over 12,000, and the area incorporated within the city's boundaries has shown a thirteenfold increase, from fewer than 120 to more than 1,450 hectares. As a result the density of occupation has fallen from between five and six people per house in 1801 to a little under three in 1971, and from over 170 people per hectare on occasions (St. Thomas's parish in 1811 and St. Edmund's parish in 1841) to a current average of slightly under 24 overall. Two parishes bordering Salisbury showed rapid gains in total population during the nineteenth century: Fisherton Anger increased sixfold, from 865 in 1801 to 5,149 in 1891 and Milford more than ninefold, from 419 in 1801 to 3,989 in 1891. The city's other neighbours showed far less dramatic rises during the same period and two – Stratford-sub-Castle and Laverstock – actually declined. And as Salisbury's population gradually encroached on the surrounding countryside the city's boundaries were repeatedly redrawn – in 1835,

1904, 1927 and 1954 – until its autonomy was lost with local government reorganisation in 1974.[26]

The process of expansion has been haphazard, depending on the laws of supply and demand, the whims of individual speculators and the decisions of elected committees (Figures 13–16). Nevertheless there have always been certain considerations which have affected the siting of new houses. Excessively steep terrain, such as the Avon valley north of the Devizes Road, is unsuitable, as is low-lying, floodable ground such as Harnham water meadows. It is easier and cheaper to build alongside existing lines of communication than to create new ones, especially where mains services have already been installed; hence ribbon development along main roads is a common feature of nineteenth- and early twentieth-century housing. A developer must be able to acquire the freehold of the land which he proposes to develop, and so he must find an owner willing and able to sell him his land. Finally, developers of recent years have had to satisfy the planning authority that new buildings will not spoil their surroundings. The development of Salisbury, therefore, though for the most part unplanned, has been influenced by the topographical, legal and aesthetic constraints placed upon it.[27]

Suburban living began among those from the middle and upper ranks of Salisbury society who saw themselves in the role of country gentlemen. Between 1820 and 1860 a number of quite elegant houses in spacious grounds were planted on the approaches to the city (Figures 13, 14). Cliff House, East Harnham, of 1825, is no more, but the Paragon and Llangarren House (now part of the Old Manor Hospital) survive in Wilton Road; Bemerton House and Milford Hill House, on opposite sides of the city, also date from this period. For those of more modest means the 1850s saw the first batches of Victorian villas. Glenmore Road, built alongside the newly-opened London Road cemetery, and Park Lane, connecting Castle Road and Stratford Road, retain some of their character, though surrounded now by housing estates and, in the case of Park Lane, adjacent to a football ground. Similar houses proliferated along Wilton Road, and rejoiced in names such as Belmont Villa, Lucerne Villa, Alexandra Villas and Parian Place. A few years later Victorian mansions began to appear on the city's wooded eastern backcloth, first on the Elm Grove estate of 1864 (where 'The Mount' and 'Landscape View' evoke the appetites of their purchasers), then in the Fowlers Hill area and, after 1880, Manor Road and its neighbours. To walk along these roads now, luxuriant in their shrubbery, and to see the blend of original mansions – now mostly divided or put to institutional use – and newcomers – the modern-movement 1930s house in Manor Road, the discreet block of flats in Elm Grove – is to sample the attractions of spaciousness and vista which drew the Victorians here, but led them to build their homes on a scale which few can now afford to maintain (Plate 8).[28]

Ostentatious living was not the only motive for building new houses.

A railway station was a great filip to suburban development, especially in compact, close-built cities such as Salisbury where the stations themselves could only be accommodated in the suburbs. So it was that Windsor Road and Windsor Street were built at the same time as their neighbour, the Great Western Railway. And largely because of the presence of the railway stations Fisherton's population increased by over 2,000 in the twenty years from 1861 to 1881 (Plate 9). Such rapid growth is reflected in the many terraces of small town cottages which are concentrated to the north-east of Devizes Road (Gas Lane and its neighbours) and south of Fisherton Street (Dews Road and North, South, East and West Streets), all within a few hundred yards of the stations. Less well known are the railway cottages (appropriately called Waterloo Road) which remain as a legacy to Salisbury's first railway station, at Milford, now the Tollgate Road industrial estate. The cottages remain, smarter now than ever, even though the railway has long gone.[29]

A third form of suburban development, which lay somewhere between the railway-workers' cottages of Fisherton and the pretentious villas of Milford Hill, began when a large area of land to the north of the city belonging to the Wyndham family was put up for sale in 1871. Gradually between that date and the first world war all the segment of land between Castle Street and London Road was built over, with terraces of small villas marching up the hill, back alleys, semi-detached and detached houses, and one fine, tall terrace overlooking a playing field (Plate 10). Here was in effect an extension of the city chequers, built to house a new kind of citizen, the lower middle class.

By 1900, therefore, Salisbury's development had been concentrated in three areas. To the west of the city, in Fisherton, ribbon development had taken place along Wilton Road, and blocks of land had been sold off piecemeal for speculative building. Comparison between the tithe map of 1843 and a modern street map shows that the tracks and hedgerows of agricultural Fisherton rapidly became the streets and boundaries of a flourishing suburb. Secondly, in Milford, to the east of the city, the former pattern of small closes erratically dividing the hillside left its legacy of an idiosyncratic and irregular suburban landscape. Thirdly, to the north of the city, but much closer to the centre than the other suburbs, a more systematic approach was possible, which combined a fairly high density of housing, but retained, in its artificial street plan, a pleasing variety.[30]

The period from 1900 until the outbreak of war in 1914 saw further development in those areas – Wilton Road, Devizes Road and the former Wyndham estate – already exploited by the Victorian housebuilder, as well as several forays into virgin territory south of the city (Figure 15). Ribbon development occurred along the Downton Road, and a new estate was pegged out opposite the Alderbury Union Workhouse in Coombe Road. The incentives for moving to this estate were probably the same as those which had attracted colonists to the Fowlers

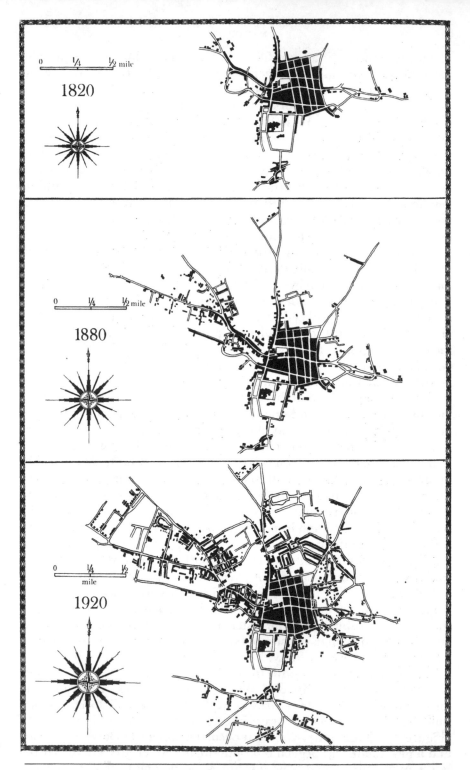

Figure 13. Salisbury, *ca.* 1820. Apart from ribbon development along Fisherton Street (to the west of the city) virtually no suburban expansion has taken place. Existing

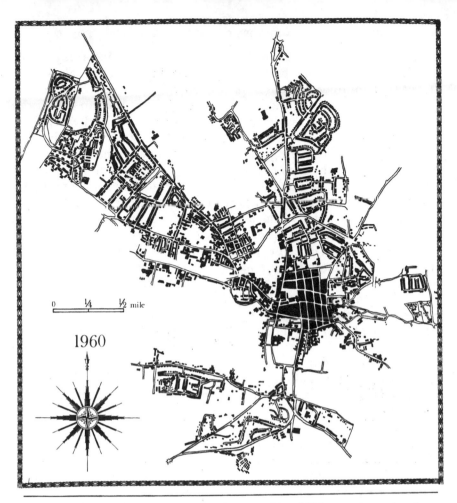

1960

settlements at Milford (east), East Harnham (south) and Fisherton Anger (west) are shown.

Figure 14. Salisbury, *ca.* 1880. Suburban expansion has taken place principally on the western approaches to the city – Wilton Road and Devizes Road – and south of Fisherton Street. Isolated villas have appeared on Milford Hill (east) off Castle Road (north) and London Road (north-east) and development has begun on the Wyndham estate (immediately north of the city chequers).

Figure 15. Salisbury, *ca.* 1920. Extensive building work has taken place on all sides. To the north the Wyndham estate occupies most of the land between the southern ends of Castle Road and London Road, with further expansion imminent. To the east large houses have proliferated on the hillside and a housing estate has been commenced on the north-east. To the south building has occurred along the Downton, Coombe and Netherhampton Roads. And to the west infilling has taken place in Fisherton's existing residential areas and building on the Pembroke Park estate (in the fork of Wilton Road and Devizes Road) has begun. The loop of Macklin Road, the first council housing, is clearly seen.

Figure 16. Salisbury, *ca.* 1960. Like the sails of a windmill Salisbury's suburbs continue to push further from the historic centre. To the north-west the Pembroke Park estate has been capped by developments at Westwood and Bemerton Heath. The Paul's Dene and Stratford Road estates flank the city's northern approach, and housing at Laverstock and West Harnham has attached itself to previously independent villages on the city's east and south-west periphery.

Hill and Elm Grove area in the previous century. According to the prospectus the Coombe Road development had a great deal to offer: 'Already a number of houses have been built and are occupied by tenants, and speculators and investors are invited to take up the various sites, there being a great demand for moderate sized houses by those looking for high and healthy positions for family residences in close proximity to the city.' The great war brought a halt to housebuilding in Salisbury, but as the grim conflict wore on there came a new determination to manage housing differently when peace eventually returned. The city council responded quickly to a circular from the Local Government Board in July 1917, which proposed that councils should draw up plans for government-subsidised local authority housing schemes. Within six weeks of receiving the circular a new committee was sitting, under the chairmanship of the mayor, and soon negotiations were under way for the purchase of sites in outlying parts of the city. The end of the war found this committee haggling about prices with various landowners, and finally in March 1919 a bargain was struck with Mr and Mrs Chubb of Bemerton Lodge for land south-west of Devizes Road, to be purchased at £325 per acre on condition that it was surrounded by a six-foot-high fence and was not used for either a school or a hospital. Another site, in Wain-a-long Road, Milford, was acquired shortly afterwards, and the council instigated a competition to decide the best layout for its new council houses. The Housing Committee brought enthusiasm and dedication to its work, endeavouring not only to solve the problem of overcrowding in the city, but also to help to provide work to alleviate the chronic unemployment faced by returning (especially wounded) servicemen. After a good deal of Whitehall bureaucracy over the exact specification and cost of the houses, the stonelaying ceremony for the first council house took place at the Devizes Road estate on 9th September 1920 and three- and four-bedroomed houses sprang up in a large loop, which the council soon decided to christen 'Macklin Road' in honour of its chairman, Sir James Macklin. By June 1921 42 houses were ready for occupation. Macklin Road today is reminiscent of the textbook 'garden-city' concept of town planning, with its carefully irregular siting of thoughtfully-designed houses, and still, 60 years on, the estate proclaims the pride and idealism with which it was planned (Plate 11).[31]

· Macklin Road was the first of a number of council housing schemes which were to provide the homes for Salisbury's heroes between the wars. By August 1921 the first of fourteen council houses at West Harnham, built by the Salisbury Rural District Council, were let to tenants, and other developments by the city council rapidly followed. Wain-a-long Road (1922), Waters Road and Stratford Road (1924), Butts Road and Hulse Road (1929-1930) and large parts of the Pembroke Park estate (between Devizes Road and Wilton Road) belong to this period. At the same time the overcrowded, airless courts which were hidden inside the poorer chequers were gradually emptied and demolished. A survey of the city in 1919 found 153 houses unfit for habitation and 400 occupied by two or more families (Plate 12). One of the worst examples of overcrowding was cited by the Town Clerk to the city's Member of Parliament in 1922: 'In one house in a Court containing only two bedrooms one is occupied by the tenant, his wife and five children, the other by a lodger, his wife and three children.' Most of the condemned houses lay in courts, such as Toones Court, Jefferies Court and Peniston's Court, which are now only memories; but one example, Finch's Court in Winchester Street, is still standing, though no longer inhabited (Plate 13).[32]

The inter-war years also witnessed further private-sector housing, notably on the Pembroke Park estate and in the Moberly Road area north of the Wyndham estate. Since the second war both private and local authority housing have burgeoned yet further into the surrounding countryside, continuing the process of suburbanisation (Figure 16). But despite, or perhaps because of, the care with which our generation monitors every new development, Salisbury's post-war development has largely followed the pattern set between the wars and earlier. The chalk spurs which divide the river valleys have seen further exploitation for housing, so that the outermost houses on the Westwood estate are a full two miles from the Market Place. Just as the rural villages of Fisherton and Milford were engulfed by Salisbury in the nineteenth century, and East and West Harnham were overtaken in the first half of the present century, so now it is the turn of Laverstock, Alderbury and Wilton to find themselves in 'a particularly close relationship' with the city. And whilst the external boundary has been expanding along fairly predictable lines, the process of infilling and renewal has continued apace in the historic city and the older suburbs. There is nothing particularly unpleasant about the mantle which Salisbury has built to surround it, but neither is there anything remarkable. Were it not for the ever-present Cathedral spire lurking somewhere in the distance, suburban Salisbury could be anywhere.[33]

In introducing this chapter we spoke of the contribution which each generation must make to the ever-changing townscape of Salisbury. Of course it is too early to assess what impact the mid twentieth century will have had on the city, or how, looking back in 200 or 500 years' time, the vestiges of our civilisation will be judged. Perhaps in the paragraph which some historian will write about us there will be praise for the way in which we have handled the city's expansion and for some of the more imaginative council housing schemes, and perhaps some of our architecture will be carefully preserved as monuments to our culture. On the other hand we may come in for censure for the wanton destruction of city-centre buildings, or derision for the way in which we pretend that a concrete supermarket is still the row of medieval houses that were demolished to make room for it. But this is for the future; our concern is with the past.

CHAPTER THREE

Working

An old joke, sometimes commemorated by an inn-sign, describes society in terms of 'the five Alls.' Mankind falls falls into five categories: the rulers – 'I govern all;' the clergy – 'I pray for all;' the lawyers – 'I plead for all;' the soldiers – 'I fight for all;' and the labourers – 'I pay for all.' Since it is human labour that has underpinned everything that Salisbury has achieved no history should proceed very far before it turns its attention to the city at work.

Mistery (part one)

It does not really make any difference whether I live in a town or a village. I wear the same clothes, eat the same food, drive the same car and enjoy the same rights in the country as I would in the town. I pay rates and taxes to the same authorities, from whom I expect to receive the same services. I happen to work in a town, but if the building in which I work was transferred to a village, it would not make any difference to my work. In a nutshell I have lost touch, along with the rest of my generation, with the essential differences which made towns develop as towns and villages develop as villages. Size and topography apart towns and villages have become almost interchangeable. But this confusion is of quite recent origin. A century ago there would have been no need to make the point that most villages existed to exploit the land around them, which provided most villagers with their means of support. The size of a village was limited by the number of mouths which its territory could be persuaded to feed, and the village economy was directly related to its inhabitants' skill at rearing livestock and growing crops. Towns, on the other hand, had little in common with villages. They were the focal points in the countryside, where specialists could gather to make and market the occasional necessities of the villagers' lives; where entrepreneurs could buy, process and sell the surpluses and by-products of the countryside; and where administrators could govern, tax and sit in judgement over a landscape of villages. In a world where most people were villagers, the town-dweller was a special kind of person, living by his wits and by the skill with which he practised some esoteric art. Townspeople were craftsmen and tradesmen; the craft or trade which they mastered was known as their 'mistery.'

As we embark on our survey of the 'misteries' of Salisbury, the industries on which the city has depended, it will be helpful to begin in the same way as we began the previous chapter, by drawing together as much statistical evidence as we can, so as to discover the relative importance at different periods of various industries, and the range of interesting occupations which the city has encompassed. The familiar problems of incompleteness and bias are again present in the evidence, as in most historical statistics; very few women are listed, poorer trades are sometimes under-represented, journeymen employees are not usually included, and little indication is given of the status and relative wealth of the various occupations. What the sources do portray, however, are the men of moderate means, the small businesses and the family firms, which seem to have formed the backbone of Salisbury's economy (Figure 17).

Salisbury's Workforce

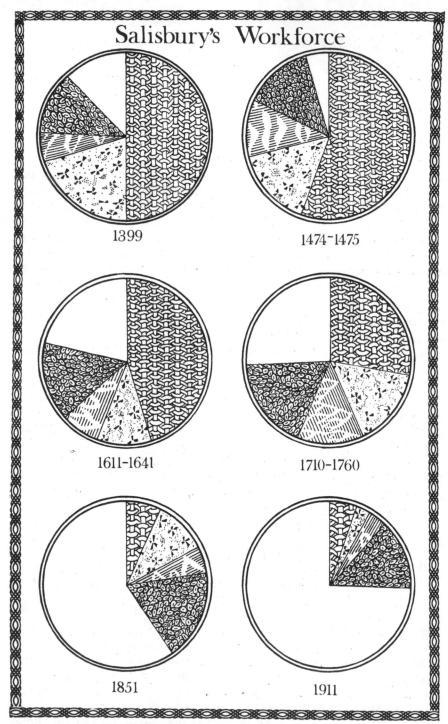

Figure 17. Salisbury's workforce. The proportion of citizens engaged in four key industries, from samples of various dates, 1399-1911, is depicted. The industries (clockwise, from top) are textiles (woven pattern), leather (stippling), metalwork (broken lines) and food and drink (cereal grains). The segment left blank represents other industries. Sample sizes are as follows: 1399- 222; 1474/5- 252; 1611-1641- 241; 1710-1760- 498; 1851- 2,906; 1911- 6,086. Sources of these data are described in chapter three, notes 1 and 2.

Apart from a number of occupations mentioned in a document of 1306, the earliest listing of a significant number of tradesmen comes in the ward lists of 1399/1400 (see appendix one). The occupations of about 200 inhabitants (about 20% of those listed) are given, without any apparent bias, and since the lists probably include every householder in the city at the time this is a particularly valuable roll-call. Forty years later, in 1440, an entry in the first city ledger describes a meeting attended by representatives of nineteen guilds embracing no fewer than 39 crafts and professions. And an entry of 1474/1475 lists the members of eleven of these guilds, 252 names in all. No satisfactory sources exist for the sixteenth century, but at the beginning of the seventeenth century the guilds were reorganised into 35 trade companies, and a register was kept of the members of each, except the two most influential groups, the weavers and tailors. This most interesting register, which survives among the city muniments, seems to record not only the names of those citizens who in 1612 paid for the incorporation of the trade companies, but also everyone who joined the various companies from their inception until about 1640, a total of nearly 800 names. The only drawback is the absence of the weavers and tailors, who are thus an unknown quantity at this period, but this deficiency may be remedied in part by examining the stated occupations in the series of wills proved in the court of the sub-dean of Salisbury, whose jurisdiction extended over the city parishes. The years 1611 to 1641 yield a sample of 241 and thus may be used to check the register of trade companies.[1]

After the civil war and commonwealth period the sources available for this kind of study become more prolific. Wills again prove useful, with more than 400 named occupations occurring between 1660 and 1710. From 1710 to 1760 the records of apprenticeships to Salisbury masters may be used to give a sample of nearly 500 tradesmen, and thereafter poll-books, directories and census data are all available. The careful analysis of occupations given in the 1851 census report marks the first attempt to chart the city's entire workforce, employees as well as employers, and makes an interesting comparison with the trade directory of 1855, which, by listing only businesses and gentry, is more akin to our earlier sources. Thereafter the methods of recording employment have become more sophisticated and more diverse, but the great changes which have taken place in the nature of industry and the types of work done make comparisons rather difficult.[2]

Having identified and collected these various data and placed the more important alongside one another (Figure 17) it is possible to detect some of the ways in which Salisbury's economy has shifted during the centuries of its existence. The most striking trend is the decline of the textile industry. During the medieval period textiles, including all the processes from fleece to finished garment, seem to have accounted for between 50% and 60% of the city's workforce. The development of the cloth manufacturing industry probably took place largely during the fourteenth century – in 1306 only one webber (weaver) is identified as such in the list of citizens, but by 1399/1400 precisely half of our sample of 200 names worked in wool, mostly as weavers, fullers or dyers. In the fifteenth and sixteenth centuries the proportion may have been a little higher, and probably remained above 40% until the civil war. As late as 1669 it was claimed that 8,000 men, women and children depended for their employment on the Salisbury clothiers, but this comes from an untrustworthy source (the notorious Dr Pope, whom we discovered embroidering the foundation legend) and must be regarded as an exaggeration. A more realistic estimate is found in a petition of 1718 by the weavers' company against illegal wool exports, where it was claimed that at least 2,000 people (about 30% of the population) were dependent on the Salisbury woollen industry. Our analysis of wills and apprenticeship records suggests that between 25% and 30% were so employed in the later seventeenth and eighteenth centuries. By 1819 this proportion had dropped below 10% and so it has remained. In fact most people involved in the clothing trade in Salisbury since 1810 have been merchants and retailers with very little manufacturing taking place in the city.[3]

The remaining categories into which we have divided Salisbury's workforce form two broad groups, those which were peculiarly town crafts and those which were essential to life anywhere and so could be found in town and village alike. Or to put it another way, the first group comprised the specialists, whose products were distributed over a wide area, whilst the second group consisted of the providers, who catered mainly for the needs of their fellow townspeople. No single group of specialists has ever achieved the same dominance in Salisbury as the medieval clothworkers. But the workers in leather, who seem to have comprised between 10% and 20% of the city's businesses for much of its history, present a somewhat analogous picture. Like the clothworkers they were concerned with a by-product of the pastoral rural economy, which had to be treated in various ways before it could be converted into items of clothing and other useful products (Plate 14). So we find tanners and dubbers (leatherworkers) mentioned in 1306, and a considerable number of tanners and skinners (14% of the total sample) in the list of 1399/1400. Thereafter the treatment of raw leather (a rather unpleasant and anti-social occupation to carry on in the middle of a populous city) is gradually overshadowed by the crafts using finished leather. In 1612 the company of shoemakers, curriers and cobblers enlisted more than twice as many men as the company of tanners, and between 1660 and 1710 the wills of boot- and shoemakers comprised nearly 9% of our sample, compared with fewer than 3% engaged in the processing of raw leather. As late as 1851 shoemakers still formed nearly 8% of the male working population. Leather had many other applications, including gloves, hats, harness and parchment, each with its mistery, whose craftsmen figure in our lists. William Sprott, hatter, and

Robert Fromond, parchmenter, are two of the very few citizens to be given both surnames and occupations in the catalogue of 1306, and the company of glovers, parchmentmakers and collarmakers was one of the largest of the trade companies to be formed in 1612.

Apart from leather Salisbury's specialists worked mainly in metal or wood. As a group the metalworkers may have constituted about 10% of Salisbury's businessmen until the last century, but by the time of the 1851 census they had fallen to 5% and have probably continued to decline. Goldsmiths, ironmongers and a needler were at work in the city in 1306, and had been joined by braziers, cutlers, a pinner and a spurrier by 1399. In 1612 the company of armourers, cutlers, smiths and iron-mongers ranked fourth in size of the city companies, and the misteries of the pewterers and braziers, the plumbers and pinmakers, and the wiredrawers were represented by three separate companies. The eight-eenth century saw the heyday of the Salisbury cutlery industry with no fewer than 9% of our sample of apprentices choosing this as their career. About the same time trades such as clockmaking and gunsmithing, which involved mechanical skills, began to make an impact alongside the more traditional workers in pewter, tin and brass. Craftsmen in wood seem to have accounted for between 5% and 10% of businesses throughout the city's history until the present century. In a city built largely of wood it is likely that many of these workers were carpenters employed in the construction industry. Carpenters, wheelwrights and coopers were not, of course, exclusively town specialists, and could be met with in many smaller places around the countryside; but the joiners, who seem to have set themselves apart as a woodworking elite, were more of an urban speciality, and, as we shall see in due course, their furniture made something of a reputation for Salisbury. In 1612 their association, the company of joiners and wheelers, outnumbered the carpenters by 21 to thirteen members, and among eighteenth-century apprentices 24 chose the mistery of joinery compared with eleven car-penters. A separate company served the interests of coopers, sieve-makers, bellows-makers and turners.

The tradesmen who we have termed 'providers,' because their live-lihood was largely derived from consumers within Salisbury, are pri-marily those concerned with food and drink. Taken as a whole this sector has probably always comprised between 10% and 20% of the city's workforce, nearer the lower figure in the medieval period and at the present day, whilst nearer the higher figure between 1600 and 1900. A third or more of these workers have at certain periods been employed in what we would call the catering industry, as innkeepers and cooks – an indication of Salisbury's importance as a market and communica-tions centre. The remainder, until the seventeenth century, were mostly concerned with one of three staple foods, bread, meat (including fish) and ale. In the eighteenth and nineteenth centuries increasing numbers of grocers appear on the scene together with market gardeners and greengrocers. Spicers, cumminers and a garlic-monger were trading in the city in 1306, and the first of many apothecaries had made his appearance by 1399.

Besides the broad categories of workers which we have so far described there have been many throughout Salisbury's history whose work is not so easily categorised, many who have worked with their heads rather than their hands, and many who have not needed to work at all. The latter, those who when asked their occupation replied simply, 'gentleman,' or 'esquire,' seem to have gathered in Salisbury in increasing numbers from the seventeenth century onwards, forming more than one-quarter of those entitled to vote in the 1819 election, and only slightly fewer in the 1855 directory. Such a statistic, of course, exaggerates the size of the leisured class in Salisbury; in the first place our samples are biased towards the upper echelons of society; in the second place many who in the seventeenth century would have been proud to be called clothiers or joiners had by the nineteenth century shaken the dirt of commerce from their hands and preferred not to reveal the source of their wealth; in the third place our earlier lists rarely recognise gentry as such, and leave us guessing about the occupation or lack of occupation of many of their names, and so there is no realistic basis for comparison with the later period. Nevertheless, the fact that in 1855 there were at least 212 families in Salisbury purporting to lead an upper-class life of leisure, employing servants and demanding services, cannot be ignored as an important slice of the city's economic structure at that period. Among the professional classes, too, it is the recent centuries which have seen them flourish. The occasional attorney or chirurgeon (surgeon) is encountered before 1700, but by and large Salisbury managed until then without the professional and administrative men who in the eighteenth century perhaps formed 7% of the working population, had risen to 10% in the mid-nineteenth century, nearly 20% by 1911, and 40% at the present day. It is perhaps too early to chart the effect that this revolution is having on Salisbury's economic history, but this rise of the bureaucrat is bound to figure in local histories to come.

Our survey of occupations permits us to judge not only the importance of Salisbury's industries but also their diversity. The range of livelihoods which the city has supported is illustrated by the names of some of the city companies of 1612: the coopers, sieve-makers, bellows-makers and turners; the flaxdressers; the embroiderers; the ropers; the picture drawers and painters; the stocking-makers and stocking-menders. Later in the same century we find a bridlecutter, a limeburner, a musician, a coachmaker, a distiller of strong water, a patten-maker, a horner and a starchmaker. As Salisbury became fashionable in the eighteenth century an army of bodice-makers, mantua-makers, periwig-makers and staymakers set up in business. And Victorian shopping habits seem to have pulled in two directions – towards greater specialisation, as represented by the fishing-gear dealer, the music-seller, the taxidermist and the trunkmaker; and conversely towards diversification, where several different kinds of product could be found under a single roof. In 1855 we encounter, 'Robert Farrant, publisher of Salisbury & County Mirror, proprietor of baths, oil and colour merchant, soda-water manufacturer, wholesale and retail chemist and druggist,' and the redoubtable, 'Firmin Potto, "Haunch of Venison," wine and spirit merchant, and boot, shoe, patten and clog maker.'

A survey such as this is designed to pose questions rather than to provide answers. Inquisitive readers may now be pondering why the cloth industry came to Salisbury, how it was organised, what it produced and for whom, why it declined at the time that it did and why nothing took its place. And the data provoke a bevy of questions about Salisbury as a market centre – how wide was its influence and what was its relationship with its hinterland, whereabouts were particular trades carried on, how did the misteries uphold their standard of excellence, and how has the pattern of buying and selling changed during the city's history?

Cloth (part one)

In many parts of England where the remains of medieval prosperity may still be seen – from the Yorkshire Dales to East Anglia, the Cotswolds and the West Country – guidebooks are inclined to put it all down to wool, without explaining how or why the trade operated, or even that there is an elementary distinction between the wool trade and the woollen trade. Before we discuss the rise and fall of Salisbury's textile industries, therefore, we should attempt to discover what in fact those industries were, and how Salisbury was involved in all the various processes of cloth manufacture from sheep to ship.

The story begins on the chalk downlands of Salisbury Plain, which surround the city on every side except the south-east. The villages and farming units which had developed on Salisbury Plain during the Saxon and early medieval periods nearly all conformed to a pattern. A typical manor, as such units are described, comprised a settlement close to a river, with farmhouse, cottages and farm buildings, rich meadow land bordering the river, two or three large arable fields, divided into strips, carpeting the slope of the river valley, and an enormous tract of maiden downland extending perhaps four or five miles onto the plain. The work of the manor was concentrated on producing corn crops on the arable fields, and the quality and yield of the crops depended on the fertility of the fields. Sheep were reared primarily as a means of transferring the fertility of the downland soil – too thin itself to produce a worthwhile crop – to the arable fields, and this was achieved by grazing the sheep on the downs by day and folding them on the fields by night, where they could enrich the soil with their manure. The number of sheep was controlled and the position of the sheep fold in the fields carefully regulated, as may be seen from the surviving sixteenth-century customs of one such manor, Winterbourne Stoke, eight miles north of Salisbury: 'Our Custome is to Keep Fifty five Sheep to a Yard Lands upon the Feilds, Down and Commons of the Mannor ... Our Custome is that Everey Tennant is to keep a Ram to a Yard Land, and that the Tenants Lay A part of the feild Ground towards the Breeding of ten Lams to Everey Yard Lands ... Our Custom is that the Tennants' Foulds Goeth a Dead [i.e. penned] all over two of the Tennants' feilds once Every Year; and that the owner of Everey Yard Lande Must provide four Hurdles, and four Shores; also Everey Tennant to Carry his Hurdles which he Ought to Carry, Immediatly when the Common Fould is to Be Removed.' Of course the bountiful sheep was not only a producer of dung, and the income to be earned from the three by-products of sheep-and-corn husbandry – wool, mutton and skins – formed a vital part of the manor's economy. But it is likely that on Salisbury Plain they remained mere by-products throughout the medieval period, even though demand for wool may at times have tempted farmers to rear more sheep than they could properly accommodate within the sheep-and-corn regime.[4]

There is no way of knowing precisely how many sheep were grazed on Salisbury Plain during the medieval centuries. Much later, when enclosure and the floating of water-meadows enabled sheep to be reared more intensively, figures of 500,000 (1794) and 700,000 (1800) were estimated for the whole of Wiltshire. It has been suggested that the total may have reached one million around 1850. It is easier, in the medieval period, to discover the size of individual flocks, and from surviving accounts it is clear that many manors could support 2,000 sheep or more, often made up of two flocks, the sheep of the demesne (the manorial lord or his lessee) and the sheep of the tenantry. If we assume the average number of sheep per manor to have been rather fewer than this, perhaps between 1,000 and 1,500, and the number of manors farming on Salisbury Plain to have been between 150 and 200, we arrive at an approximate total sheep population of 150,000–300,000, much of whose wool was destined to find its way to Salisbury by one means or another.[5]

The medieval sheep which grazed on Salisbury Plain was a small, robust animal, with short, fluffy wool. Its ancestry was a mixture of the small, fine-woolled Soay sheep of prehistoric Britain and the white-faced, coarser-woolled sheep introduced by the Romans. It was much smaller than most modern breeds and yielded about half the quantity of wool, approximately $2\frac{1}{2}$ lb per animal. There is evidence that the large Wiltshire sheep-farming estates took a great interest in the quality of their sheep, both by removing inferior animals and by inter-breeding with superior strains from elsewhere. The type and quality of the wool was of course an important factor in determining the kind of textiles that might be produced from it, and Wiltshire wool was generally regarded as being of medium value, producing a woollen cloth of good, but not outstanding, quality. From two fifteenth-century lists of prices for different grades of wool it appears that Wiltshire wool was less highly regarded than wool from the Marches of Herefordshire and Shropshire, and from the Cotswolds and parts of Lincolnshire, but on a par with, or superior to, wool from Dorset and Hampshire, and most other parts of England.[6]

Until the late fourteenth and early fifteenth centuries many of the manors of Salisbury Plain were owned and farmed by a relatively few large landlords, including religious foundations such as Amesbury Abbey and noble and ecclesiastical magnates, such as the Bishop of Winchester and the Lords Hungerford. Because they owned a string of manors on various types of soil they could carry on their sheep-farming operations to a remarkably sophisticated degree. On the Hungerford estates, for example, sheep were continually on the move between manors, which might be 30 miles apart, less bleak and inhospitable manors being singled out as breeding-grounds from which yearling sheep were sent to replenish stocks elsewhere. This high degree of organisation extended to the collecting and selling of the wool, which seems to have been purchased in bulk, either for export by a foreign or large English merchant, or for the internal textile industries. Evidence from the accounts of Cistercian monasteries (including Stanley in north Wiltshire) shows that at certain periods their entire yield was sold annually to Italian merchants for export. From such large, monopolistic landlords as these there was probably little opportunity for Salisbury men to prosper. The demesne flocks, however, represented only a proportion (perhaps about half) of the sheep population of Salisbury Plain. The remainder was owned by the tenantry, who relied on the few shillings that their hundredweight of wool and dozen sheepskins might bring in to improve their lot in the village, perhaps by adding to their holding or making some small capital investment. After 1400 opportunities arose for the more enterprising tenant farmers who had amassed a little wealth, by these and other means, to take over the lease of the demesne farms, as the corporate landlords began to withdraw from direct farming operations. A new class of substantial farmers arose, drawn not only from the tenant peasantry but also from the former employees – the stewards and local agents – of the large estates and from the petty gentry. These demesne lessees rarely farmed more than a few nearby manors and so their wool production would not have rivalled that of the corporate landlords whom they succeeded, but their yield was far greater than that of the average tenant farmer, and on account both of their social standing and their business acumen they must have commanded a measure of respect from the wool-merchants with whom they dealt.[7]

Thus there were three tiers of wool producer – the demesne lord with many manors and a centralised means of disposing of the large quantities of wool which he produced; the demesne lessee who replaced the lord in the fifteenth century and operated a smaller, but substantial, sheep-farming business; and the small tenant farmer whose annual yield of wool amounted to no more than a few hundredweight. All three produced wool in two forms – the clip or fleece, which resulted from the spring shearing, and the fell or skin, which resulted from the autumn slaughter of surplus stock. The wool was bought either for export in its raw state or to be manufactured into cloth by the domestic textile industry. Until the mid fourteenth century most wool was exported, and there is evidence that Salisbury had from very early in its history its share of merchants engaged in the overseas wool trade. But by 1400, as we shall see presently, a flourishing cloth manufacturing industry had been established at Salisbury, as at many other places, so that in the fifteenth century finished cloth, rather than wool, was the principal export. It is therefore with the wool destined to feed the Salisbury looms that we are chiefly concerned. But here we are faced with a difficulty, because virtually all the evidence available to explain how the collection of wool from the producers was organised is concerned with the export trade and not the domestic market. We know, for instance, that there was a considerable export trade to Italy through Southampton in the fifteenth century which was able to by-pass the staple at Calais; and we know that Salisbury merchants in the 1370s were competing with Italians to buy the clip of Wiltshire wool. We can only assume that the collection of wool for the domestic market was organised in a similar way. If this was the case then a producer on a Salisbury Plain manor had the option of selling his wool in one of three ways. He could either come to an arrangement with a merchant, from Salisbury or another market centre, who might tour the area in person, but more often employed agents to do the rounds of the farms; alternatively he could strike a bargain with one of the itinerant wool broggers (brokers) who would then sell the wool in Salisbury market; or he could take his produce to market himself and obtain the best price he was able. Which of these methods he chose no doubt depended on various circumstances, including the amount and quality of wool he had to sell, his distance from Salisbury and the state of the market. But however the sale was effected it is likely that a large proportion of the wool grown on Salisbury Plain found its way eventually to Salisbury, and that somebody in the city stood to make money out of its arrival.[8]

The conversion of raw wool into finished cloth involved a number of processes employing specialised craftsmen, and it is to these – their status, organisation and premises in the city – that we must next direct our attention. It may be helpful at the outset to summarise the various stages in cloth manufacture, so that the place of each craft within Salisbury's great production line is easily seen. When shorn from the sheep wool is greasy, dirty, matted and tangled with burrs and the like. After a consignment of wool had been graded, therefore, foreign bodies had to be removed, water and detergents applied, and the fibres prepared by a method of brushing known as carding, which used either the prickly head of the teasel plant or a manufactured substitute. The wool was then ready for spinning, a process which, by a combination of pulling and twisting, at first using a weighted stick called a spindle and later a simple wheel, drew the fibres into a fine continuous thread. The thread, known as yarn, was next transferred to a loom, on which the lengthwise threads, the warp, were stretched. The medieval loom comprised a horizontal wooden frame incorporating two or more heddles to enable alternate threads of warp to be raised and lowered as a shuttle drawing the lateral threads, the weft, was passed between them. Narrow cloths could be made by a single weaver, passing the shuttle through the warp from one hand to the other, but broadcloth looms required two men sitting side-by-side, who threw the shuttle from one to the other. A comb, the width of the cloth, was used to beat the weft close together and rollers at either end of the loom were used to take up the finished cloth and feed the warp onto the loom. Raw cloth taken from the loom was known as 'say,' and was next passed to the fuller, who treated it with a solution of ammonia, often derived from human urine, and pounded it with hammers. The purpose of the former process was to remove oils added to the wool to assist spinning, and the pounding was intended to compact the fibres into a felt, plugging any gaps in the cloth left by the weavers. Originally fulling was performed by a man trampling on the cloth in a vat of stale urine or other alkaline solution, but by the later medieval period the process had been mechanised using stocks, or hammers driven by a horizontal rotating shaft driven by a water wheel. After fulling the cloth was stretched on racks, known as tenters, to dry, before undergoing the finishing processes of raising the nap – the loose fibre ends – with cards and shearing the face of the cloth evenly with a large pair of napping-shears. Finally the cloth was dyed, using a vegetable dye such as madder or woad and a mordant – usually alum – which made the dye fast. Where striped or patterned cloths were being produced dyeing took place much earlier in the manufacture – prior to spinning – and then the cloth was 'dyed in the wool,' as opposed to the single-colour method of 'dyeing in the piece.' Thus the medieval cloth manufacturing industry, as practised in Salisbury, may conveniently be divided into four compartments: spinning, including preliminary work such as carding; weaving; fulling, including finishing processes such as shearing; and dyeing.[9]

The evidence that we may use to reconstruct these processes in medieval Salisbury is patchy, but enough has survived to build up some kind of picture of the city's industrial life. It will be convenient to follow the progress of the wool in the order we have just outlined, and so begin with the preparatory work of washing, carding and spinning. This was women's work, and so – as has been the case throughout history – it has tended to go unnoticed. However we may assume that the ready supply of flowing water built into the city's design was put to good use for washing wool; and we know that the demand for teasels and cards was such that several thousands of each were imported through Southampton to Salisbury in a single year, and that cardmakers, who had practised in the city since at least 1379, were associating with other workers in metal and had formed a guild, which was certainly in existence by 1440. Female spinsters are mentioned in a list of 1379, and it is clear from the context that 'spinster' does not merely mean an unmarried woman. Much later, in the sixteenth century, when the woollen industry fell on hard times, the city council took steps to offer work to poor spinsters and a charity existed to relieve them. A legal document of 1461 mentions a certain William Coke, 'spyndeler,' who presumably made spindles. But in general spinning was probably so much a part of daily life that it was taken for granted and is reflected only incidentally in surviving documents. One such reference perhaps occurs in a legal enquiry of 1408, which heard that Thomas Baker, 'a common ravisher of women,' had broken into Margaret Hasilberie's house in Castle Street, raped her, and stolen various goods including 50 pounds of woollen thread and 50 pounds of wool. May we assume that the unfortunate lady was halfway through spinning a consignment of one hundredweight of wool when the crime was committed?[10]

The spinsters who fed the looms were probably as numerous as all the other clothworkers together and more widespread, as a certain proportion of spun yarn probably arrived in Salisbury along with, and from the same villages as, the raw wool. Salisbury had its yarn market near the present Guildhall, and here the weavers selected their wool from dealers, or from the industrious ladies of the city. The weavers outnumbered the other male clothworkers by a substantial margin. Nearly 300 masters and their employees attended a meeting in 1421, compared with 100 fullers, and in 1474 a list of craftsmen includes 66 weavers and 30 fullers. The proportion of men to masters in 1421 (207 to 81, or about $2\frac{1}{2}$ employees per master) is interesting, as it confirms the impression given by other evidence, that most weavers were small businessmen, maintaining their commercial independence although protected by the tutelage of their craft guild. The horizontal broadcloth loom, upon which most of Salisbury's cloth was woven, required two men to operate the shuttle, and an assistant was needed to keep them supplied with yarn. It is likely, therefore, that most of Salisbury's weavers in the fifteenth century possessed only one, or at most two, looms, and employed two or three men to work under them. But within this industrial structure it was nevertheless possible for a weaver to amass a considerable fortune. When Thomas Copter died in 1473 he seems to have owned all the northern end of Three Cups chequer fronting onto Salt Lane, and his property included two corner tenements and four cottages with gardens and racks for stretching cloths. Most weavers appear to have owned their own premises, and some, such as John Woton's tenement fronting onto Milford Street and Culver Street, were highly rated in the 1455 tax return. John Woton perhaps achieved a degree of affluence by trading, as he is known to have imported oil through Southampton in 1444. There was nothing in the city regulations or guild ordinances to prevent weavers from merchandising their cloth. Thomas Payn, who acted as a spokesman for the weavers' guild in 1440, appears fifteen years later as a witness to a dispute between members of the guild of merchants; William Pridy, another weaver, is known to have sold a large quantity of cloth to a Shrewsbury dealer; and Nicholas Shete, a Salisbury weaver, took John Christmasse, a London draper, to court in 1449 over a £20 debt. Weavers might also participate in other clothmaking processes. Edward Goodyer, a master tailor and prominent benefactor of the tailors' guild, who lived next to William Russel's house in Queen Street, appears to have begun his working life as a weaver; and John Durnford of Castle Street seems to have progressed from weaver to dyer. The ward lists of 1399/1400 seem to imply that weavers favoured the eastern side of the city – more than half the weavers recorded as such lived in Martins ward. But it would perhaps be wrong to regard any one part of the city as a weavers' colony, and certainly by 1455 most streets contained at least one known weaving family, with Endless Street (which is not in Martins ward) the most popular address. It is more likely that weaving, which did not require water power, did not create anti-social smells or pollution, and did not need to be carried on in or near the Market Place, was to be found in medieval Salisbury wherever the space was not required by other less amenable crafts. This point will be discussed further later, when we consider the distribution of trades in general.[11]

From the weaver the woven cloth was taken to the fuller, or tucker, as he was more commonly known, who in Salisbury seems to have been responsible not only for fulling but also for tentering, raising the nap and shearing. Like the weavers, the fullers had their own guild in the fifteenth century which, as we have seen, appears to have boasted about one hundred members (70 masters and 30 journeymen) in 1421. The ratio of employers to employed at this date suggests that many fullers worked alone, and there seem always to have been fewer fullers than weavers working in Salisbury in the fifteenth century. Whether formal or informal links between individual weavers and fullers existed is not known, but there may be some significance in the fact that Thomas Copter, the weaver referred to above, owned property which included tentering racks. Fulling itself, with the advent of water-driven machinery in the twelfth century, was no longer a job for the city chequers, and so, even though the fullers might live and have their workshops in the city, they must have taken their cloths to be fulled at fulling mills elsewhere. Such mills are known to have existed at Stratford-sub-Castle,

Ford, Milford, Harnham and Mumworth (Dairyhouse Bridge) as well as the town mill by Fisherton Bridge (from the sixteenth century) and many places further upstream and downstream. The present Harnham Mill dates from about 1500 and may have originated as a fulling mill (Plate 15). It probably occupies the site of an earlier fulling mill recorded at West Harnham in 1299. There is no evidence, however, that fulling mills were constructed to use the city's artificial water channels; indeed it is unlikely that they carried a sufficient head of water to make such use possible. A fifteenth-century visitor to Salisbury would nevertheless have seen plenty of evidence of fullers at work, in the form of cloths stretched on tentering racks wherever space was available. Fulling, no less than weaving, might be a prosperous business: William Hanleygh's will, of about 1400, besides giving details of some of his finishing tools – a press, a shears and twelve pairs of handles (frames to hold teasels), shows that he owned houses in New Street and at Old Sarum as well as his own dwelling in Gigant Street; and George Joce's property in 1431 included houses and shops with halls above, one of which, adjoining his own dwelling in Castle Street, he had let to a shoemaker. A third fuller John Colyngborn, may be the same as an importer of woad mentioned in the Southampton brokage book of 1439–1440.[12]

Salisbury's dyeing industry, the fourth and final manufacturing process we have to consider, presents something of an enigma. On the one hand references to dyers at work in medieval Salisbury are surprisingly few, so that we might conclude that dyeing was a relatively unimportant industry in the city. On the other hand evidence from various records kept by the port of Southampton shows Salisbury to have been the most voracious of consumers for the various dyestuffs imported through that city. Two dyers are identified in the earliest list of Salisbury citizens, that of 1306. By 1399/1400 twelve dyers are recorded in the ward lists, mostly grouped together in an area of the Market ward, which from other evidence is probably the western side of Castle Street and the Cheesemarket. A 'Diers guylde' is recorded in 1420 and recurs alongside the other guilds in 1440, but is not included among the eleven trades listed in 1474. Only three dyers are identified in the 1455 rental and one of these, John Durnford, is elsewhere described as a weaver. There are other incidental references to dyers, and of course the sparseness of evidence about medieval Salisbury makes arguing from silence a risky business, but it is strange that the dyers seem to have made no greater impact on the city's history. In the year 1443/1444 more woad was sent from Southampton to Salisbury (about 500 tons) than to anywhere else during the fifteenth century, except on a few occasions to London. Woad, along with madder and its mordant, alum, which also arrived in Salisbury in large quantities, were the principal dyestuffs used to produce most of the colours used in the native cloth industry, but virtually none was grown in England. In the fifteenth century, therefore, when the cloth industry was at its height, there were rich pickings to be had by importing dyestuffs, and Salisbury merchants were quick to realise the potential of such a trade. Besides the dyestuffs needed by the city for its own cloth such large quantities suggest that Salisbury also supplied dyers over a much greater area, and was probably of national importance as a market specialising in dyestuffs.[13]

Discussion of Salisbury's cloth manufacturing industry inevitably ends, as it began, with the merchant. We have seen that the merchant was there at the beginning, buying wool at the farm gate and bringing it to market for either manufacture or export, and because the various manufacturing processes were carried on by more-or-less independent craftsmen, there were opportunities for merchants to buy and sell at every stage. And it was the merchant who was there at the end, collecting the finished cloths, exporting them to France and the Mediterranean, and bringing back to Salisbury a bewildering range of goods, from the mundane and industrial, such as woad, alum and soap, to the exotic and luxurious, such as wine, honey and almonds. The true source of Salisbury's wealth, of course, was the labour at spinning-wheel and loom, fulling-stocks and vat, but it was the Salisbury merchant, with his forceful cosmopolitan ways, who ensured that the wealth thus created returned to the city, and it was he, rather than the craftsman, who grew fat on the city's success (Plate 16).

Salisbury's merchant class is typified in the imaginations of many by John Halle and William Swayne, two fifteenth-century merchants – bitter enemies and rivals – whose names are enshrined in two surviving buildings, the Hall of John Halle and the Swayne Chapel in St. Thomas's Church. Their well-documented quarrel in 1465, on account of which Halle incurred the wrath of Edward IV, has preserved the memory of Halle as a hot-headed, fearless autocrat, foul-mouthed and cantankerous, but with the ability to persuade his fellows that their city's honour was bound up with his own. Halle became a legend, both on account of his wealth and influence, and also as the champion of the city against the Bishop's domination, but despite the exaggerated hero-worship his fiercely competitive and self-centred determination were probably not untypical of the 'merchant-adventurer' attitude shared by others of his class. Fortunately there are other sources of evidence which enable us to present a picture of the Salisbury merchant without relying solely on the escapades of John Halle.[14]

Finished cloths had to be examined for size and quality by an official termed an 'alnager,' who marked the cloths he approved with a lead seal. In the fifteenth century many aulnage accounts have been shown to be unreliable, even fraudulent, but those of the late fourteenth century can be proved to be reliable and may be usefully compared with the ward lists of 1399/1400 (see Appendix one). The best and fullest account is for the year ending in November 1397, which includes the names of 292 men and women who submitted cloth to the alnager in Salisbury. All but 50 of these appear also on the ward lists, and so were presumably resident in the city. Salisbury residents accounted for nearly 90% of the cloths sealed, and their individual quotas ranged from 304 cloths (a standard cloth of assize was 24 yards long) to one-half a cloth, with an average per producer of about 24. In the case of about 25 producers their occupations are given in the ward lists, and they comprise seven weavers, seven fullers, five dyers, two mercers, a grocer, carpenter, hosier and brazier. It is clear therefore that at this rather early period in the city's manufacturing career there were many very small producers and merchants, for whom selling cloth was only a part of their business. More than a hundred men and women, in fact, submitted fewer than ten cloths each to the alnager. There were, on the other hand, over 30 producers or merchants who submitted the equivalent of one cloth each per week or more, and it was from their ranks emerged the John Halles and William Swaynes of two generations later. The thirty largest producers accounted for about 40% of the total number of cloths, and only two were not Salisbury residents. The top cloth producers were not necessarily the most highly rated citizens; in fact comparison of a list of the 30 largest producers with the 30 most highly rated residents reveals only four names in common, and nineteen of the top 30 citizens did not submit any cloths for aulnage during the year in question. This is clear evidence that by 1400 the textile magnates had not yet become the city's most influential class. One other conclusion to be drawn from the comparison of the aulnage and ward lists is that the cloth producers and merchants were not evenly spread throughout the city but were concentrated in Martins and Market wards, where they represented nearly 35% and 30% respectively of the total number of households. If our reconstruction of the ward lists is correct they were particularly numerous in Castle Street, Endless Street and Wyneman (now Winchester) Street.[15]

During the fifteenth century, although many small producers probably continued to market their own and other people's cloths, it was the trading activity of the large Salisbury merchants which enhanced the city's fame and prosperity, whilst establishing the merchants themselves as men of substance not only in the city but in a national and even international context. William Lightfoot was such a man, mayor of Salisbury in 1451 and one of its representatives in Parliament in 1455. The symbol of his success, his merchant's mark (which looks a little like an umbrella stand with wings), is carved on a column in the chancel of St. Thomas's Church, and so we probably have his money to thank for some of the church's fine perpendicular architecture. He owned at least three houses in the city, known as 'the Cheker' (in Endless Street), 'the Hynde' (in Winchester Street) and 'the Faucon' (in Crane Street), as well as garden plots and tentering racks near St. Martin's Church. 'The Faucon' survives as part of the present Church House in Crane Street; indeed he was probably the builder of the north range fronting the street, with its impressive arch sporting the original fifteenth-century oak gates (Plate 17). His wealth was derived from the export of woollen cloths made in the city to France and Italy, where he traded them for various commodities including wine, luxury goods and industrial products such as soap. The importing side of his business is better recorded than the woollen exports. In 1445, for instance, he made the mistake of purchasing a large quantity of Malmsey wine which, it transpired, had been stolen by pirates, and which he had to forfeit. In the previous year, as for a number of others, a record survives of all goods carried to him from Southampton. In February 1444 a waggon carrying 1½ tons of fruit arrived, followed a week later by a barrel containing twenty gallons of olive oil among a consignment of other goods for John Halle. Two weeks later a waggon brought four hundredweight of almonds, four hundredweight of rice and two hundredweight of dates. Later, in April and May, 250 gallons of wine, a half ton of alum and nearly a ton of wax arrived.[16]

William Lightfoot was a leading member of Salisbury's merchant guild, and his name often occurs in documents alongside other prominent merchants. One such, Thomas Freeman, illustrates two further facets of this fraternity. In 1434 he was found guilty of what amounted to piracy by capturing and robbing a ship, the 'Marie' of Lymington. Another merchant, Thomas Felde, showed similar maritime bravado by raiding a French ship as retaliation for a French attack on his own, and there are other examples, including John Halle, of Salisbury merchants owning and sailing their own ships. Thomas Freeman is also an example of a merchant with interests outside Salisbury, since in 1440 he was appointed controller of customs and subsidies at Southampton. Links of this kind between Salisbury and Southampton were to be expected in view of the close trading connection of the two cities, and a number of Salisbury merchants are known to have owned property in Southampton and vice versa. Salisbury merchants had similar links with London and Bristol, and trading interests with various foreign ports, in Brittany, Gascony and the Low Countries as well as the Channel Islands.[17]

The cosmopolitan nature of the Salisbury merchants' interests enabled them to offer in their shops in the city a bewildering range of exotic wares. Probably the best evidence of a sophisticated merchant shopkeeper's stock-in-trade comes in an inventory taken in 1542, as Salisbury's medieval heyday was drawing to its close. It is a list of the possessions of Thomas Hele, merchant of New Sarum, drawn up in consequence of his disappearance after admitting that he owed a debt of £500 to a London haberdasher. His assets were valued at £142.11.4. They included over a hundred different types of product on sale in his shop, ranging from soap to straw hats and from brown paper to treacle. Many types of cloth were represented, including fustians, says, 'rowsettes' (russets), worsteds, velvets, silks, satins, 'Salybery laces,' 'Northyn cottyn,' hollands and canvas. There were spices – ginger, dates, nutmegs, cloves and mace – and haberdashery – gold braid, cards, Bruges thread and Paris thread, Flanders pins and London pins – and strange delicacies – 'lycorys' and sugar candy. For fourpence you could have bought two pounds of rice (which was therefore 'tuppeny rice'), a yard of buckram or four straw hats. The most expensive fabric, at 3/4d per yard, was sarsenet, a fine silk, whilst russets cost between one shilling and 1/8d per yard, fustians and holland were under a shilling, and cheapest of all was a coarse 'bolt' (a type of burel) at a mere penny per yard.[18]

Cloth (part two)

Our description of the clicking and banging, the rubbing and splashing which made Salisbury wealthy in the fifteenth century does not tell the whole story. It remains to discover when and how the industry began, why Salisbury became a great manufacturing centre, and what led to its eventual decline. We have already noticed that, from the evidence of lists among the city records, the fourteenth century saw the emergence of clothworkers as the largest group of city craftsmen, and that they probably accounted for at least half the city's workforce until the sixteenth century, declining thereafter. Our estimates of the city's total population run along similar lines, and point to a quickly rising population in the decades after 1400 followed by a falling off between 1500 and 1550. It appears, therefore, that the evidence we have surveyed of Salisbury's woollen industry in the fifteenth century depicts a city at the height of its powers, the view from a plateau of affluence which was attained shortly before 1400 and lost shortly after 1500. We must now see whether other evidence confirms this impression.

The economic history of England during the three centuries between 1300 and 1600 was dominated by wool. Expressed in the crudest terms it was the story of declining exports of raw English wool counterbalanced by an expanding market for English manufactured cloth. At some time around 1400 cloth overtook wool, pound for pound sterling, and by about 1450 cloth had also overtaken wool, pound for pound in weight. The transition from wool to cloth was anything but smooth, and many erratic annual quotas cloud the overall trend, but it was real enough; it has been neatly calculated that 'in 1350–1360 cloth accounted for 8% of the trade and wool for 92%, whereas in 1538–1544 cloth accounted for 92% and wool for 8%.' A number of factors have been held responsible for this reversal, but the foremost was undoubtedly the vacuum in the market for cloth left by the collapse of the Flemish manufacturing industry in the 1370s, coupled with an advantageous trading position for the English cloth merchants, brought about by fluctuating prices, governmental controls and various theatres of war on the European mainland.[19]

So far as can be ascertained Salisbury's economy in the first century or more of its existence, from 1220 to about 1350, was not based on manufacturing industry. Like any market town, of course, it was concerned to satisfy its own population and that of its hinterland with clothing, and to cater for these consumers there had undoubtedly always been a modest band of craftsmen converting raw wool into finished garments. The importance of this domestic textile market is underlined by the large number of tailors (often more than 10% of the working population) who have inhabited the city throughout most of its history. The real source of Salisbury's wealth before 1350, however, and the impetus for its spectacular expansion, lay rather in its roles as a general market, and as a collecting centre for the wool of Salisbury Plain, prior to export through Southampton, Poole or Lymington. To what extent Salisbury ever achieved a really important place in the English raw wool trade must remain in doubt; scattered references attest to the existence of such a role, but the city's apparent failure to become a wool staple (in spite of having a 'Stapulhall' in St. Martin's Church Street) suggests that its importance in this trade was not on a par with neighbouring Winchester or Southampton.[20]

No precise date can be given for the start of Salisbury's manufacturing career in earnest; it was probably quite a gradual affair. But we may reasonably assume that it began later than 1353, when exports began to recover from the desolation of the black death. And it was well under way by 1400, when the city ward lists testify to an extensive industry. Southampton provides the clue for a more exact dating; until the 1370s or 1380s the city underwent a period of recession, aggravated not only by the black death, but also by a slump following the particularly bad harvest of 1370. Recovery came only with a revival of the Italian trade, conducted largely by Italian merchants, which began in 1379 and had reached record proportions by 1391–1396. It has been suggested that the main attraction of Southampton to the Italians was its ready access to Salisbury products, and if this was the case then we may assign with some confidence the burgeoning of the woollen industry in Salisbury to the years between about 1375 and 1390. If we are correct, then Salisbury's enterprise accords well with the national trend, which saw cloth exports double between 1382 and 1392.[21]

But there is a flaw in our argument. Closer examination reveals that although there was a national cloth boom in the 1380s and 1390s it was centred not on the towns and cities with a history of manufacturing and dealing, but on villages and rural areas, such as the valleys of the Cotswolds and the Bristol Avon. Indeed the competition from the growing number of rural clothmakers was the ruin of the older urban industries centred in cities such as Winchester and Bristol. Why, then, was Salisbury different?

The exodus of clothmakers into the countryside during the fourteenth century seems to have been a direct consequence of the water-powered fulling mill, which we have already described. During the thirteenth and early fourteenth centuries fulling mills began to appear along the West Country rivers, often alongside existing flour mills. By 1300 26 are known to have existed in the three counties of Wiltshire, Somerset and Gloucestershire. Faced with this innovation – perhaps the most important technological advance of the middle ages – the city fullers adopted a familiar stance. When it could no longer be ignored they legislated against it and continued their unenviable craft of stamping about in vats of stale urine. Those who were eventually persuaded that the fulling mill was a good thing, such as the Winchester fullers in 1269, discovered that their river, and city rivers in general, were too sluggish to operate the fulling stocks, and so the attempt to mechanise was abandoned. The decline of urban clothmaking, therefore, may be attributed on the one hand to an unwillingness to adapt to new technology and on the other hand to an inadequate power supply. But in Salisbury, it seems, neither of these problems arose. As a new city of the thirteenth century it was not hidebound by the accumulated regulations and traditions of centuries of clothmaking. Like a modern new town Salisbury, the Milton Keynes of the middle ages, was eager to accept and encourage technical innovation. It has been said that, 'New Salisbury is perhaps the clearest example of a large city that grew up with the fulling mill.' And, we might add, even if there were traditional clothmakers in the city who voiced their opposition to the new machines, the government of Salisbury, unlike the older cities, rested not with a conservative chamber of city merchants and craftsmen, but with the Bishop, whose own livelihood was not threatened by the fulling mill. Salisbury, therefore, took to the fulling mill rather more easily than its rivals. But the problem of power supply still had to be overcome. Some commentators have suggested that Salisbury's system of watercourses and large tenements was designed with the fulling mill in mind. But we have already noted that the city fullers do not seem to have used the water channels to drive machinery, and it is doubtful whether there was sufficient head of water, even when the channels were not clogged with refuse and mud, to have done so. However, Salisbury's natural rivers, it seems, could be so used, and at least five fulling mills were at work on the city's outskirts in the medieval period, to which the Salisbury fullers could resort.[22]

Tolerance and power were not, of course, Salisbury's only virtues. The existence of a vigorous wool trade in the centre of a major wool-producing region, the establishment of a rich market and a good network of road communications, the proximity of one major port – Southampton – and several lesser havens, such as Christchurch, Poole and Lymington, the presence of a rich aristocracy in the Cathedral Close and at Clarendon Palace to stimulate domestic trade and encourage the import of luxury items such as wine – all these factors served to encourage the cloth manufacturer. A weaver or fuller thinking of setting up business in Salisbury could also expect other advantages not shared by his country cousins. He would enjoy the rights and privileges which belonged to all citizens, including preferential trading arrangements with other towns and cities; he could purchase raw materials such as yarn, cards and dyestuffs practically on his own doorstep, and dispose of his finished goods in the same way; he could enjoy the social life afforded by the city, especially (from the fifteenth century onwards) the multifarious activities of his own craft guild; and finally he would find the spacious layout of the city and its running water supply most useful amenities for whichever branch of manufacture he wished to pursue.

Such were Salisbury's advantages as a clothmaking centre. We have already discussed at length the structure of the industry in the fifteenth century, but we should at this point say a word about the city's importance in the national context, and also describe the products and their destination. Salisbury at the beginning of the fifteenth century may have been the most important cloth manufacturing centre in England, but such assertions are probably not worth making, because each of the major centres specialised in different kinds of product, of various qualities and stages of completion, and for different markets. It will suffice to say that Salisbury in its heyday ranked among the greatest cloth manufacturers in England, and that it dominated its county, which was itself one of the wealthiest and most important. The aulnage accounts (see Appendix one) divided Wiltshire into two categories, Salisbury and the rest, and in the 1390s between 80% and 90% came under the heading of Salisbury, although this may include a considerable quantity of cloth marketed, but not made, in the city, or delivered to the city in an unfinished state. In the fifteenth century the same accounts reflect a growing industry in the towns and villages of west Wiltshire which gradually reduced the imbalance between Salisbury and its county, and eventually, in the sixteenth century, toppled the city from its pedestal.[23]

Unlike the plain, undyed broadcloths which the West of England industry in general was putting onto the market, Salisbury's products had their own idiosyncrasies. Two cloths of the flannel or kersey type were manufactured in unknown quantities, a plain broadcloth in a single colour, and a narrow cloth, probably also dyed a single colour, known as 'osete.' The latter, it appears, was so called because it was made by a single weaver on a 'one-seat' loom. But Salisbury's reputation was made not on these run-of-the-mill cloths, but on a special fabric known as a medley, or Salisbury ray. It is perhaps best to imagine this as equivalent to a modern tweed, a striped cloth of various shades on a single background colour. To achieve patterned cloth of this kind it was necessary to dye the wool prior to weaving, and to weave on a special loom. The looms used in Salisbury for this purpose, although basically broadcloth looms requiring two weavers, were not the full width of assize for broadcloth, and attempts in 1412 to legislate on the matter, so as to bring the Salisbury weavers into line, were strongly resisted in the

87

city, with the result that a deputation was sent to London with proof that the new requirements were impossible. Salisbury rays were not aimed at the luxury market, nor at the workaday peasant and labouring classes. They offered a good quality, attractive cloth in the medium price range, and it has been suggested that they were bought, 'by the middle classes, by the more prosperous peasants and artisans, or by the upper classes for their household servants and retainers.' Many, of course, went abroad, especially to Italy through Southampton, or to France (especially to Gascony, in return for wine), the Low Countries and the Baltic.[24]

Boom towns, as Salisbury undoubtedly was in the fifteenth century, do not continue for ever, and we are tempted to look for the first signs of decay so that we can begin to chart the city's decline. But in the case of Salisbury that is the wrong approach. The population and the extent of the woollen industry probably ceased to grow at some point in the fifteenth century, and because of this the city was overtaken and over-shadowed by other producers; but the population fell only slightly, and over a long period of time, and, as we have seen, there was no shortage of immigrants to take the place of victims in the plague years. Similarly, the numbers employed in the woollen industry seem to have fallen slightly, but still represented by far the largest group in the city. The Salisbury weavers achieved a new charter for their guild in 1562, which was revised in 1590; some at least of the city merchants were capturing trade from an ailing Southampton at the same period; and a new fulling mill was constructed at the Town Mill in the centre of the city shortly before 1562.[25]

The fifteenth-century boom which we have described, however, was based on a particular set of economic circumstances, which included a ready wool supply from the surrounding countryside, a convenient and successful port as an outlet for the export trade, a ready market in Italy with a lucrative import trade of luxury goods and dyestuffs in return, a demand for the kinds of cloth which the Salisbury industry was geared to produce, and a government policy which favoured the woollen trade. Any change in these circumstances which might occur beyond the city's control left it in a vulnerable position, and affected in particular the merchants, with whom the city's fortunes were so closely associated. When, therefore, the Italian ships deserted Southampton during the sixteenth century and the Mediterranean market was lost; and when in consequence Southampton slithered into a severe depression which led to its virtual abandonment by exporters; and when in the 1480s government embargoes on the import of woad dried up that lucrative trade; and when the demand for dyed striped kersey-type cloths was replaced by a demand for undyed broadcloth – the fragile framework on which Salisbury's economy depended was progressively shaken and damaged.[26]

It behoved Salisbury to adapt to changing circumstances, and indeed there were adaptations: merchants began to strengthen their links with the London market to compensate for Southampton's failure; some manufacturers switched to producing undyed broadcloth so as to compete with other producing areas; and the structure of the industry began to change, as the fullers came to be regarded as petty clothiers and became more involved in the marketing of their products. But these were relatively minor changes compared with the transformation taking place in the rural industry. In west Wiltshire the Tudor period of the sixteenth century saw the emergence of a new breed of capitalist clothiers, who controlled, to a greater or lesser extent, all the cloth-making processes. Such was William Stumpe, who converted part of the dissolved Malmesbury Abbey into a cloth factory, and such was James Terumber who, from humble beginnings, became a powerful landowner and respected benefactor in the Trowbridge area. These clothiers seem to have sprung from the ranks of the fullers, and the powered fulling mill was the key to their success. But for the weavers of west Wiltshire, living many miles from an important cloth market, they also played the role of merchant or broker, and from this vantage were able to control the weavers completely, supplying them with yarn in return for woven cloth, which was then fulled, taken to market and sold. A shrewd clothier, spurred on by the prospect of self-advancement, could bring innovation and business acumen to the industry, impossible under the old regime. But in Salisbury there was little opportunity for such a class of capitalist clothier to breed. From being the new city Salisbury had become a place of tradition, with strong craft guilds to safeguard the interests of the individual weavers and fullers, and a vigorous market in which these craftsmen could sell direct to Salisbury or London merchants. And so the clothiers who did emerge in Salisbury at the end of the sixteenth century, although they acquired influence and power in city affairs, were not to be compared with the giants of the west Wiltshire industry, and were overshadowed accordingly.[27]

As Salisbury approached the year 1600 its woollen industry had undergone a number of changes and had resisted others which occurred elsewhere. There had been periods of recession in the Salisbury industry, but these were common to cloth producers everywhere; there had been a slight decline in both the city's population and its manufacturing output, but these appear worse than they were because of comparisons with other more successful areas; and there was at last occurring the disappearance of the merchant class and its replacement by the clothier. Salisbury was no longer the most important woollen city in England, if indeed it ever had been, but the industry was far from dead. Later than most, but not quite too late, the city adopted the white undyed broadcloth to replace the obsolescent rays as its speciality, and in the course of the seventeenth century earned itself an international reputation for the quality of its products. 'The best white cloathes in England are made at Salisbury, where the water, running through chalk, becomes very nitrous and, therefore, abstersive. These fine cloathes are died black at London, and in Holland scarlet,' was the verdict of a not altogether unprejudiced commentator, John Aubrey, in about 1670. The mention of black-dyed cloth is probably a reference to its use in ladies' mourning garments, for which fine, good-quality cloth was preferred. So well was Salisbury cloth regarded that it suffered from imitations, and by the mid eighteenth century 'Salisburys' were being produced for export at Painswick in Gloucestershire.[28]

The change from coloured rays to white broadcloth and the emergence of the capitalist clothier in west Wiltshire and elsewhere did not completely undermine the medieval structure of independent craftsmen described at length in the previous section. The city council in the later seventeenth century admitted several hundred craftsmen as free citizens, including weavers, clothiers and clothworkers, and many were enabled to set up in business with the help of a loan drawn from funds administered by the city. The reorganisation of the guilds into trade companies after 1612 ratified the independence of the weavers as a company and created a new company of clothworkers and dyers. The interests of silkweavers, flaxdressers, linen-drapers, worsted-makers and milliners were also catered for by various of the trade companies. A picture of these independent craftsmen at work may be gained from probate inventories, which exist in considerable numbers for the seventeenth and eighteenth centuries. Amongst the equipment in the workshop of Nicholas Rose, a weaver, when he died in 1618, were, 'two Broad loombes, one narrowe Loombe, one warping barr ... one spinning turne, one ladder and some old craft things,' worth altogether £3.13.0. John Watkins' working tools in 1624 proclaim him to have been a shearman; they included a box of handles, four pairs of shears, four burling irons, a 'sheer borde,' four 'sheer hocks' [perhaps an early form of crook which made the shears easier to use], a pair of 'paring sheeres' and a 'hayr brysshe.' These and other tools were valued altogether at twelve shillings. Some idea of the number of clothmaking businesses in the city in 1720 may be given by a petition of that year objecting to printed calicoes, which carried 197 signatures. Another petition, two years earlier, claimed that at least 2,000 people in Salisbury were dependent upon the weavers.[29]

In choosing to concentrate on white undyed broadcloths as their speciality the Salisbury manufacturers fell victim to a series of events, beginning with the disastrous Cockayne project of 1614 to 1616, which by antagonising overseas customers crippled the export trade. This was followed by the thirty years' war in Germany and the English civil war, which played havoc with the international and domestic market places respectively. If these setbacks were not enough, the city suffered debilitating outbreaks of plague in 1604, 1627 and 1666 which impaired its resistance to its economic misfortunes. In consequence the city failed to respond to changing fashions and once again lost the initiative to its west Wiltshire rivals, who by 1630 were concentrating on a new cloth – medley – which was made from fine Spanish wool, dyed in various colours prior to spinning. Salisbury seems never to have followed this lead, even though by the end of the seventeenth century medleys had almost entirely captured the market for fine cloths from undyed broadcloth. By 1750 it was in the awkward position once again of manufacturing a high-quality, expensive product for which there was virtually no market.[30]

This was not, however, the end of Salisbury's career as a clothmaking centre. Flannels, soft loosely-woven cloths with a worsted warp (spun from combed wool), were probably made in the city throughout the eighteenth century, and seem to have been especially profitable during the period 1780–1810. The short-lived appearance of a new trade company, the woolcombers, at this time was no doubt connected with the success of the flannel industry. Three grades of flannel appear to have been manufactured – fine, low and serge – and these were used for clothing of various kinds and were widely exported. Other cloths to come out of Salisbury at the end of the eighteenth century included linseys (or linsey-woolseys), made of linen and wool, fancy cloths incorporating silk and Spanish wool, and marbled cloth, a coarser fabric of mixed dyes. One such mixture, known as 'pepper and salt,' according to Hatcher, was much in request for trousers. The city clothiers claimed a powerful advertisement in the person of Henry Wyndham, a Wiltshire member of Parliament who apparently cut an impressive figure at court dressed in a dark striped coat. 'What!,' exclaimed George III, 'Wyndham in a French coat?' 'No, please your majesty, it is not French,' replied Wyndham. 'What then?' 'It is a cloth made at Salisbury.' 'Then send me some of it!' It was probably as a result of this encounter that a Salisbury draper, Thomas Ogden, obtained the royal warrant as 'Draper to his Majesty' in 1786.[31]

The revival of fortunes in the city's textile industries between 1780 and 1810 has passed largely unnoticed by historians, whose gaze has rested largely on activities in west Wiltshire during the period. That Salisbury's importance as a clothmaking centre has been underestimated is hinted at by surviving Sun fire insurance records, which show Salisbury, at the very nadir of its fortunes between 1753 and 1771, still second only to Trowbridge among Wiltshire towns in the value of stock insured by clothiers and other textile workers. Indeed, the value insured at the four towns of Warminster, Devizes, Wilton and Chippenham altogether only just exceeds Salisbury's total, and Bradford too is well behind Salisbury. A Salisbury merchant in 1770 incurred the displeasure of his west Wiltshire and Somerset rivals by undercutting their lowest price for superfine cloths, and another, William Hussey, insured stock to the value of £5,000 in his Salisbury warehouse in 1754, a sum equalled by only one other Sun policyholder in Wiltshire during the period 1753 to 1771, and bettered by none. The period of prosperity towards the end of the century gave rise to several individual success stories. Edward Hinxman, carpet manufacturer and master clothier, served as mayor of Salisbury in 1784, and ten years later purchased the prestigious Little Durnford estate in the Avon valley north of the city. William and Robert Hutchings, who specialised in fancy cloths made partly from silk, operated a successful factory near St. Martin's Church, which subsequently became the National School. Henry Wansey, who claimed to have reduced the manufacturing costs of flannels by 10% through his pioneering use of machinery, was so busy in 1791 that he had to turn away orders. Among the West Country woollen towns Salisbury seems to have pioneered the use of machinery. The spinning jenny was successfully working in the city in 1777, thirteen years after its invention, and earlier than most of the west Wiltshire towns. Wansey in 1791 contemplated buying a steam engine – the first enquirer Boulton and Watt received from a West-Country manufacturer – and although he did not proceed with the purchase he, along with some of his fellows, were keen to introduce machinery of various kinds into the industry. As factories were put up for sale during the first decade of the nineteenth century the extent of mechanisation became apparent. Three engines, six jennies, three billies and reels were included in a sale in December 1807, and a further three carding engines, nine jennies, a wool mill and a horse-wheel with two shafts were auctioned in June 1808. A steam engine, purchased from Oxford in 1808, was offered for sale at a bargain rate in 1812.[32]

But mechanisation could not save Salisbury's textile industry. The application of steam power, which reduced manufacturing costs in the northern industrial towns, was not a success in Salisbury. Unlike the west Wiltshire towns, such as Trowbridge, which had a ready supply of coal near at hand in Somerset and a canal link with the coalfield, the cost of bringing coal to Salisbury was prohibitive. Coupled with this drawback there seems to have been no scope in the city for building large factories, either because space was not available or because investors could not be found. And thirdly, Salisbury's chief product, flannel, seems to have been susceptible from an early date to undercutting by northern towns, such as Rochdale. The directory listings of 24 clothiers in 1798 was reduced to thirteen in 1814 and three in 1830. By 1843, according to Hatcher, 'the articles made here are too trifling to deserve notice.'[33]

The Market Place

To jostle and bustle on a Saturday morning among the pushchairs and tourists, between the canvas-clad stalls selling parts for vacuum cleaners, washable fabrics, anoraks and vegetables, to fight one's way to the centre of the Market Place and join the queue for the best ice cream in the world, dispensed from a green and red van, to eat one's cornet on the Guildhall steps and watch the scurrying shoppers, the endless procession of cars changing lanes and the traffic lights, as the price of carrots is broadcast among the lime trees in an anguished shout and a scent of chips floats across on the breeze – simply to be there, and by one's presence to re-enact the weekly ancient pantomime, is to experience a sense of vibrant history, an impression of unquestioning permanence. The cast may change but the plot remains the same. That at least is the impression, but perhaps such immutability is a fraud. Let us go back a couple of generations. 'The beasts tied up to the wooden railings, the calves with great eyes of terror straining at their ropes, the sheep and pigs penned within hurdles, the bleatings and bellowings and squealings; horses, their manes and tails stuck full of porcupine straw ornaments, and bright coloured streamers falling over their eyes, being run up and down; the rows of covered carriers' vans, drawn up at the edge of the causeway, the stalls, the cheap jack, the drovers in their dirty linen coats shuffling about; the shifting, loitering crowds, the gossipings and chafferings – these are things that seem to defy change.' But in the seventy years since these words were written nearly all of it has changed. As we approach the subject of markets and fairs in Salisbury, therefore, we should be alive less to the aspect of continuity than to the likelihood of changes which have taken place, not only changes of appearance but more especially changes of attitude to the market, changes in function and changes in the market's importance, both within the city and in the world outside.[34]

We must first decide what a market is, why it exists and how it differs from a fair. A market has been defined as, 'an authorised public concourse of buyers and sellers of commodities at a more or less strictly limited and defined place at an appointed time.' A fair also conforms to this definition, and indeed is a type of market, but differs in its time scale. Whereas a market is appointed to be held on one or more days each week a fair is an annual event and may continue for several days or even several weeks. Their origins, too, are different. The commercial aspect of fairs seems to have arisen in response to the practical needs of catering for large numbers of people gathered to celebrate a religious festival or to take part in an administrative or judicial assembly. In time the commercial possibilities of such gatherings outweighed their original purpose, which was often forgotten. Markets, on the other hand, were an adjunct of urban living, an answer to the problem of feeding those who did not produce their own food, and the means whereby a ruler could control his subjects' trading activities. Since both market and fair required control, to ensure their smooth running and to protect customers and honest traders, it was normal to seek authority to exercise that control from the Crown, in the form of a royal charter; and since the administration of a market or fair might be an expensive business, the charter usually permitted the organiser to levy tolls and dues from traders attending. As an important and regular part of town life the market usually affected the town's topography, being held either in a widened street or in its own market place. Accommodation for the infrequent fairs was naturally more makeshift, and fairs might be held, not only in the market place, but in the churchyard, in the church itself, or in the fields outside the town. Some fairs, especially sheep fairs, were held at unpopulated downland landmarks, such as Weyhill near Andover, Yarnbury near Wylye and Tan Hill near Devizes. At markets, and fairs held in towns, certain regulations were necessary to ensure that the owner of the market was not cheated of his revenue, either by bargains being struck away from the open market, in the town's hostelries or outside the town on the way to market, or at times before or after the permitted term of the market. Revenue was derived not only from tolls, the tax payable by the seller when goods were sold in the market, but also from various dues charged on entering the town, or passing over bridges, and on the use of a stall or pitch in the market place. Certain categories of trader might be exempt from some or all of these charges or might pay at a reduced rate. In return for these various charges – from which a handsome profit might be made – the market owner had to organise the setting-up and dismantling of the market, monitor the quality of the goods being sold, ensure that weights and measures were accurate, and provide adequate measures for sanitation and refuse disposal. He was also concerned to detect cheating of all kinds, the sale of stolen property, and the forbidden practices – quite acceptable now – of forestalling, regrating and engrossing, the buying and reselling of goods at a profit without adding to their value. As a consequence of these various duties of supervising the market, the owner had also the responsibility of holding special market courts, known as pie-powder courts, at which offenders might be fined, or placed in the common gaol, the pillory or the stocks, which were usually on public view in the market place.[35]

The downland fairs may have been as old as the hillforts in which they were sometimes held, and marketing, along with defence and administration, may have been an important function of hillforts in later prehistory. It is possible, therefore, although there is no evidence, that Old Sarum was in use as a fairground long before it fell into disuse at the close of the Roman period. But formal recognition of existing fairs and markets and the proliferation of new ones sanctioned by royal charter was a feature of the early medieval period, from the Norman conquest to the black death in the mid fourteenth century. Between 1200 and 1350 nearly seventy charters were granted for the holding of markets and fairs in forty separate places in Wiltshire alone, some of which have continued to be successful market towns, such as Chippenham and Devizes, but others have declined to become small villages, Wilcot, Upavon and Hilmarton, and one – Abradmere – can no longer be identified at all. This large number of market towns is explained by the needs of an increasing population living in an age of poor communications. Such conditions favoured small local markets and large occasional fairs. When population and economy went into reverse after the black death in the fourteenth century many smaller markets disappeared, and perhaps as many as two-thirds were lost between the thirteenth and sixteenth centuries in England as a whole. In Wiltshire 22 markets were still functioning in 1588, but only sixteen in 1656. A resurgence in market trading at the end of the seventeenth century revived several dormant market towns in south Wiltshire – including Wilton, Hindon, Warminster and Downton – but the whole open market system was under attack both from improvements in road (and later canal and rail) communications, and from private dealing away from the market place. The nineteen Wiltshire markets remaining in 1792 had fallen to nine by 1888, and the losses included Amesbury, Hindon, Mere and Wilton. Fairs, too, were suffering in the same way, although in decline they proved more resilient than markets. The 42 Wiltshire fairs of 1792 had become 29 in 1888, the funfair element continuing after the business had gone elsewhere. The great sheep fair at Yarnbury was held for the last time in 1913, a casualty of war.[36]

Salisbury's markets and fairs should not be examined in isolation, but in the context of the rise and fall of marketing generally, as described above, and in relationship to the city's neighbours. It may be helpful to begin our discussion of Salisbury market by establishing a chronology with these wider considerations in mind. Both fairs and markets were being held in New Salisbury before the city's royal charter was granted in 1227. The Bishop, who owned and stood to profit from both, obtained permission for a Friday market in 1219 and an August fair in 1221. A market was an essential source of food for any urban community, as we have seen, and we should not be surprised to find one taking place from the outset. The royal charter of 1227 confirmed the right to a weekly market, but altered the day to Tuesday, and ratified the August fair. A second fair, the October Michaelmas fair, was granted in 1270, and in 1315 both the Saturday market and a third fair, the Lady Day fair held during Lent, were permitted. Wilton and Old Sarum, the established market centres of the area, were justifiably aggrieved by their precocious neighbour, especially since unauthorised markets were being held every day in Salisbury in the thirteenth century, and it was not normal in any case for the Crown to sanction a new market so close to existing market towns. Their repeated protests ultimately led to a compromise in 1361 which restricted Salisbury to markets on Tuesday and Saturday and Wilton to Monday, Wednesday and Friday. Salisbury's market days have remained constant, but the number and dates of fairs have changed. The original August fair seems to have been lost during the medieval period in favour of an Epiphany or Twelfth-tyde fair in January; a Whitsun fair was held in the Close from the fifteenth century until as late as 1831, and this seems to have included on occasions a horsefair held within the Cathedral itself; and for a few years between 1491 and 1524 a fair was held at St. Edmund's Church, presumably around the patron's feast, November 16th. Apart from these last two fairs, which benefited the Dean and Chapter and St. Edmund's Church respectively, the profits from all Salisbury's markets and fairs were taken by the Bishop from their inception, and with a few interruptions, until 1785. Although nominally the Bishop was also responsible for the administration of the market, usually performed on his behalf by a bailiff or clerk whom he appointed, at certain periods of tension between the Bishop and the city the city council took control of a share of the government and profits of the market. For a few years on either side of 1500 the city appears to have leased from the clerk the right of receiving tolls as well as to have acquired permanent control of the stalls used by butchers from outside the city. From about 1570 part of the Michaelmas fair was held on the Greencroft and profits from this also went to the city. Absolute control of the markets and fairs by the city was agreed in 1784 and took effect in 1796, although after 1834 toll collection was farmed out to private collectors by tender or auction. By this time the cattle market, formerly held at Barnwell Cross, had moved into the Market Place, and in 1859 corn and some other merchandise was transferred to the purpose-built market house. The cattle market was moved first to a site in Castle Street in 1952 and subsequently to its purpose-built accommodation in Ashley Road in 1959. Although the three Bishop's fairs and the Dean's fair in the Close continued until the nineteenth century, by 1888 only the Michaelmas fair survived and has continued as a funfair to the present day.[37]

This in outline has been the progress of marketing in Salisbury. But its continued existence after $7\frac{1}{2}$ centuries should not blind us to the possibility that its function, organisation and purpose may have been continually changing. No written records exist from the earliest years of Salisbury market to give details of the tradesmen, wares and customers. But we may deduce a good deal from the descriptive names which have been used to designate parts of the Market Place and which, in many cases, are still in everyday use (Figure 18). If in our minds we empty the Market Place of its buildings and streets a large, flat, nearly rectangular open space remains, extending from Blue Boar Row to New Canal and from the modern Queen Street almost to the River Avon. With the building of the first encroachment, St. Thomas's Church, in the 1230s and the consequent eddying of the flow of traffic around its eastern and southern sides, the most sensible place to set up a market stall would have been in the area later occupied by the Poultry Cross, and in the first century of the city's existence, when informal markets appear to have been a daily occurrence, it was here that the market-men clustered. A forerunner of the present Poultry Cross, known as the 'Fayrecroys' or High Cross, had been erected here by 1307, and an early segregation into separate trades on each side of it may be reconstructed. To the north of the cross (now Minster Street) lay 'whelernrow,' the wheel-wrights' stalls; to the east were 'potrewe,' or 'bothelrewe' (now Ox Row) where crockery, bottles and pewterware were sold, and Butcher Row and Fish Row (which retain their names); to the south were Ironmonger Row (now the passage from Poultry Cross to New Canal) and Cooks' Row (probably in Silver Street immediately south of the cross); and to the west were Cordwainer Row (the shoemakers' stalls lying between Silver Street and St. Thomas's Church) and the poultry market (in Silver Street), which included fruit and vegetables. Most of these names date from the fourteenth century and suggest that by then it was possible to obtain most household goods and essential foodstuffs without straying more than a few paces from the Poultry Cross. Perhaps because of overcrowding, or abuses, or for reasons of hygiene, a number of changes took place in the early fifteenth century. A new cross, the Cheese Cross or Milk Cross, was built about a hundred yards north of the Poultry Cross, in the area still known as the Cheesemarket, and dairy products and greengrocery were transferred to the new site. Oatmeal corner (later part of Oatmeal Row, the modern name for the eastern side of Minster Street) is mentioned in the fifteenth century in connection with the Poultry Cross – by then so-called – and new, more sanitary, arrangements for butchers and fishmongers were introduced, whereby they were compelled to use the area between their rows and New Canal for the slaughtering and preparation of meat.[38]

Place-name evidence suggests, therefore, that the domestic function of the market – the foodstuffs and the household goods – were concentrated in the southern and western parts of the Market Place, adjacent, in fact, to the crossing of the two pre-existing main roads around which the city was built. The trades in this part of the market were enabling the city to survive by feeding and providing for its citizens, as well as offering specialist products and services to citizen and stranger alike (Plate 18). The remainder of the Market Place was given over to the bulkier agricultural and industrial functions of a market. The corn market seems to have occupied the whole of the northern part of the Market Place; similarly the eastern portion, from the base of Endless Street to the Bishop's Guildhall (on the site of the present Guildhall), was given over to the sale of wool and yarn, using first a large elm tree and later a stone cross as the focus. The area of New Canal, the southern edge of the Market Place, seems to have been used for the sale of wood and coal. Other commodities were bought and sold away from the Market Place altogether. The market for livestock, from at least the fifteenth century, was Barnwell Cross, remote from the Market Place in the south-eastern chequers of the city, but whether this was an original feature or a result of overcrowding cannot now be known. Other street names perhaps suggest specialisation away from the Market Place – such as Salt Lane and the now defunct Hog Lane, Cow Lane and Mealmonger Street – or adjacent to it – Silver Street and Cartern Street

SALISBURY MARKET PLACE
circa 1600

0   10   20   30   40   50 metres

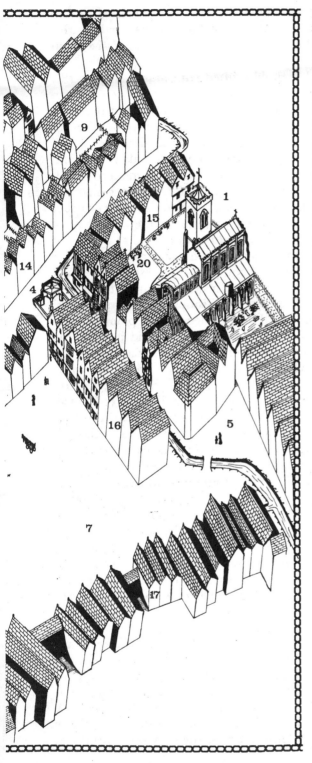

Figure 18: The Market Place. This isometric drawing of Salisbury Market Place as it may have appeared *ca.* 1600 shows in detail buildings which survive or which are known from illustrations. The possible positions of other buildings (based on later maps) are shown in outline. Particular buildings, rows and areas of the Market Place are denoted by figures, as follows: 1. St. Thomas's Church; 2. Bishop's Guildhall; 3. Council House; 4. Poultry Cross; 5. Site of Cheese Cross and Cheesemarket; 6. Probable site of Wool Cross and Wool and Yarn Market; 7. Corn Market, including stocks, whipping post and pillory; 8. Wood and Coal Market; 9. Mitre Chequer; 10. Pot (or Bottle) Row; 11. Butcher Row; 12. Fish Row; 13. Ironmonger Row; 14. Cooks' Row; 15. Cordwainer Row; 16. Wheeler Row (later Oatmeal Row); 17. Blue Boar Row; 18. Hall of John Halle; 19. Town Ditch (New Canal); 20. 3/5 Minster Street.

(Catherine Street) – whilst others known once to have existed can no longer be identified – including Chaffcorner, Sheep Street and Smith's Row. But, as we shall see in due course, such names should not be taken too literally.[39]

Our empty market place has rapidly filled with names (Figure 18). And the names, of course, were given to those structures which from an early date began to appear as permanent encroachments in the open space. The slow, evolutionary process whereby temporary benches removed after each market became benches known as shambles which were left in place from market day to market day, later taking root and sprouting wooden sides and roofs after the fashion of modern beach huts, and ultimately growing habitable upper storeys, must have occurred in too piecemeal and haphazard a fashion for us to reconstruct its progress. By 1455 over one hundred premises in the city, most of them in and around the Market Place, could be described as shops, but the word itself is imprecise and seems to have evolved along similar lines, from the 'beach hut' stages, through the workshop (its usual meaning in the post-medieval period) to our modern understanding of the word as any place of retail trade. By 1314 'shops' in the 'fysschamels' (fish-shambles) were sufficiently well-established to be a point of reference to the location of the Bishop's new Guildhall, and in 1368 the process of encroachment was given official sanction when the Bishop offered the citizens the right to build inhabitable structures on the Market Place in return for an annual rent of twopence per perch. The response to this invitation may have included three buildings, 31 Cheesemarket, 15 Minster Street and the western half of the Wheatsheaf Inn, Fish Row, which survive to the present day. By 1444/1445 there is mention of a 'pentyse' being repaired with boards; the name pentice or penthouse, of which a surviving but transformed example may be seen at Winchester, refers to a temporary stall attached to the front of an existing building on market days. A number of surviving buildings in the rows around the Poultry Cross may be dated on architectural evidence to the fifteenth century. Encroachment by shops reached its maximum extent in the seventeenth or eighteenth century; by now the rows to the south-west of the Poultry Cross had formed themselves into a chequer – Mitre Chequer – and the Bishop's Guildhall had become encased in shops, known as the Guildhall Chequer. The latter were demolished along with the Guildhall itself between 1785 and 1788 and no further encroachments have taken place since.[40]

Apart from the piecemeal development of shops the Market Place attracted a number of buildings which were necessary either for the regulation of the market or for the government of the city in general. St. Thomas's Church, the earliest official building in the Market Place, has already been described, and the four medieval crosses – the Poultry Cross, the Cheese Cross, the Wool Cross and Barnwell Cross – have been mentioned. The present Poultry Cross, the only one to survive, probably dates from the late fifteenth century, although it was re-modelled in 1852–1854 (Plate 19). It may be the third to occupy the site, as a predecessor (not the original High Cross) was allegedly built as an act of penance by a knight who had stolen the sacramental wafer and taken it home to eat with an onion for his supper. The Bishop's Guild-hall, the symbol of his supremacy over market and city, was prominently built at the eastern end of the Market Place early in the fourteenth century. The secular city government also had its administrative head-quarters in the Market Place, between the Cheesemarket and St. Thomas's Church; this first Council House, which perhaps dated from the reorganisation of the produce market in the early fifteenth century (discussed above) was superseded by an Elizabethan structure built on the site of the elm tree in front of the Bishop's Guildhall between 1580 and 1584. The building of a new Council House at this time seems to have been partly a struggling city's attempt to emulate its more pros-perous neighbours – many market houses were built at this period – and partly a symbol that the city council was gradually supplanting the Bishop's domain. When this Council House was damaged by fire in 1780 the opportunity was taken to convince the Bishop that it was time to demolish his Guildhall to make way for a new (secular) guildhall on its site as a replacement for the stricken Council House (Plate 20). The present building, a gift to the city by the Earl of Radnor, was completed in ca. 1794 and altered in 1829 and 1889. The remaining apparatus of the Market Place may be briefly described. In 1521 the city council, 'agreed that ther be a convenyent frame made in the market place to hang a bell, which bell rongen shal be warnyng for the nombre of the counsel howse, or for fyre, frayes or other assembles and ryottes.' The common weighbeam, at which all goods were weighed and the toll exacted, seems to have been positioned near the wool market in the sixteenth century and in later years was presumably kept in the Council House. A gaol formed part of the Bishop's Guildhall for those awaiting judgement, and for those found guilty of transgressing the market regulations justice was seen to be done in the stocks, pillory and whip-ping post opposite Blue Boar Row. To a habitual drunkard, John Selloway, in 1858 fell the distinction of being the last to occupy the stocks.[41]

Buildings and names tell part of the story of Salisbury's market; but much more can be discovered about its administration and day-to-day affairs from documents of various kinds preserved, for the most part, among the city muniments. Apart from the repeated struggles by the city council to wrest control of the market from the Bishop, with which we are not at present concerned, two themes recur in these documents – the need to regulate the times, position and quality of trading, and the need to safeguard the market itself by preventing clandestine selling and re-selling. A list of regulations made in 1306 divides the trading day into two parts: 'Before the Cathedral Church has struck the first hour of the day' no-one was permitted to purchase meat, fish or other provisions for eventual resale, but only the Bishop's servants, and those of the clergy and citizens for domestic use. If there was competition to purchase the same goods the Bishop's servants and then the Canons' took priority over the citizens. No trading was permitted before sunrise. After the first hour had struck buying was open to all. Further regulations of 1416 prohibited the storing for a future occasion corn, fish or meat remaining unsold after the ninth hour of the market. In 1521 it was agreed that, 'no corn be solde in the market on the market day bifore the houre of ix, nor noon [none] be solde after the houre of xii at the clokke.' As the market drew to its appointed close, therefore, it was a buyer's market and a hard bargain might be struck. In the early seventeenth century, faced with desperate poverty in the city, the forceful John Ivie was given official sanction to bend the normal rules of market trading. He described his dealings with the cheese-sellers: 'Then I tell them, "Try the most of your market; if you cannot sell as you would, come to me; if you will be reasonable I will buy it all for the use of the poor." They have come to me after sunset and entreated me to buy. I have then bought by candlelight above £20 worth at a cheaper rate than I could have the same cheese in the morning, by 4s, 5s, or 6s in every hundred.'[42]

The Bishop, as lord of the market, reserved the right to allocate pitches and stalls in the Market Place to those whom his bailiff licensed, and the city council was concerned with a reorganisation of the siting of the stalls in the early fifteenth century, which we have already described. Action was taken to prevent obstructions and nuisances: 'horses bringing victuals or other commodities to the city should, as soon as they should be unladen, be led by their drivers or others to the inn beyond the market and common street, lest they should be the occasion of hurt or annoyance to passers by.' Annoyance of another kind was proscribed by ordering that butchers should not slaughter beasts in the street in front of Butcher Row but behind the row, presumably in the less congested and better watered New Canal area. Furthermore, 'they should not carry about the foul parts or intestines of their beasts by day, but by night.' Fines levied against transgressors of the market regulations might be used for the benefit of the Market Place and the city in general, as in the case of the chandlers in 1556 who had, 'greatly offended the commons of this Citie in lewde and negligent servyng the same Citie of candelles unto theire great annoyaunces and trouble,' and whose fines were to be used, 'abowte the reparation and amendyng of the common house of office standyng nigh unto Crane Bridge ... as also upon the newe gravelyng and amendyng of the common market-place.' The chandlers' offence seems to have been that they were operating a cartel to inflate the price of candles; another common swindle was the use of short measures, as practised by the coal-merchants in 1518, when it was agreed, 'that a reformation be hadde agenst coliers for mysusyng of their sakkes, that is to say, that theire sakkes shalbe quarters and half-quarters and a mesur of tree be made at the costes of the Chamber for triall of the seid sakkes.' The vintners were similarly accused in 1583, and in 1607 no fewer than 28 tradesmen were fined for failing to submit their weights and measures to examination, a further five were found to be selling beer and ale in unlawful stone pots less than the standard, and two bakers were found to be baking light penny loaves. The provision of a common weighbeam was partly a response to the mar- ketmen's unreliable measures, and orders were made in 1614 and 1658 forbidding weighing by 'any other scales and weights then by those appoynted to be the publique and common weights and scales.' But there was more at stake than this, and when in 1629 the city council decided to proceed against a prominent citizen and councillor, Thomas Raye, 'for refusing to weigh such wool and yarn, as he buys in the markets, at the common balance,' it was not that they suspected him of fraud, but because by avoiding the weighbeam he was evading the toll due to the market on the goods he was buying, and thus attacking the principle of the open market.[43]

For the principle of an open market to succeed it was essential that trading in commodities proper to the Market Place should not be permitted to take place at times or places beyond the market's control. In particular the activities of the middleman were considered an un- welcome intrusion into the straightforward world of producer supplying consumer and were legislated against as far as possible. In Salisbury a regulation of 1306 aimed to outlaw the practice of forestalling – the purchase of goods from incoming traders before they reached the city – and regrating – the speculative buying and selling within the Market Place. In 1416 an order was made, 'that folk bringing victuals into the City for sale should not sell them in inns or secret places or before broad day, but in places ordained for the purpose.' Poulterers and especially rabbitsellers were singled out for condemnation in this respect. An attempt to control regrating of faggots was made in 1531 by fixing a maximum price of four faggots per penny, but in 1612, presumably because of profiteering by regrators at the poor's expense, an order was made prohibiting the forestalling, regrating or ingrossing of 'woode, faggotts, charcoal or seacoale,' except by the overseers of the poor. Three years later an informer brought a private prosecution against seven tanners and leathersellers, 'for selling leather in St. Edmund's, Salisbury, outside an open market or fair, before it had been searched and sealed,' and similar offences. At about the same period engrossers of wool, wheat, butter and cheese in Salisbury were also brought to trial. The illicit sale of fuel continued to worry the authorities, and as late as 1740 an attempt was made to enforce the rules of the open market: 'Whereas Jno [John] Warden sold and delivered Charcoal in New Street without bringing the same into the market & not measuring the said Coles there according to Orders given. I do as Clerk of the market suspend the said John Warden from carrying Coles till further Order & have accordingly taken his Badge from him.' But by the eighteenth century private marketing, which, encouraged by the structure of the wool trade, had formed a forbidden black economy during the medieval period and which had become a regular, but shady, practice in Tudor times, was now quite normal and accepted in agricultural and industrial circles and had already brought to an end many erstwhile successful markets. The development of shops which were open for business throughout the week had for centuries become an accepted part of life in a market town, and the inns, with which Salisbury was particularly well endowed, had also become centres of commercial life. Markets were no longer an essential concomitant of urban living.[44]

But if the ill wind of private trading and easier travelling had blown away many of the smaller markets from the English countryside there was nevertheless some good blowing in Salisbury's direction. The demise of the small town market gave a new impetus to those agricultural and livestock markets which survived in the more important centres. Cities such as Salisbury found that the decline of their produce market was more than matched by a widening and more productive hinterland. In 1673 a guidebook described Salisbury market as 'very considerable,' but it shared this distinction with Hindon, Warminster, Westbury, Devizes, Marlborough and Shaftesbury – to name only a few nearby towns – to all of which the same adjective was applied. But by 1798 its cattle market was being referred to as one of the largest in the kingdom, in 1888 a witness at an official enquiry declared that he believed it was one of the most convenient beast markets in England, and in 1929 a government report described the corn exchange as the most important south of the Thames. Salisbury's growth as an agricultural and livestock market seems to have coincided with the city council's ultimately successful attempts to wrest control of the Market Place from the Bishop. The fire which damaged the Council House in 1780 provided an excellent pretext for a renewed attack, and the Bishop was persuaded to accept a package of redevelopment which involved not only the demolition of his medieval Guildhall and its replacement by a new, more opulent building – the gift of a secular lord – but also the relinquishing of all his rights over the market. This change of ownership may have been significant because from an early stage the city council seems to have realised that the value of the market was less in the tangible figure raised by tolls and dues and more in the benefits which the existence of a market in the centre of Salisbury accrued to the city generally. The revenue from tolls was never large – usually between £20 and £100 per annum in the nineteenth century – and the most important commodities, corn and cattle, were toll free. As a government inspector commented in 1888, 'I can understand you having a good market if you have no toll.' But this was precisely the point, as his repeated interrogations of the mayor revealed: 'The whole thing is only a matter of £100 a year to you, is it?' 'That is one point, but it is a benefit to the town generally from the number of people that it brings here, and the money that they spend in the town.' Or again: 'If we do not encourage agriculturalists to come here and sell their stock and spend their money, they will go elsewhere.' In other words the market had been transformed from being the channel through which all Salisbury's trading income had to pass to being the carrot which was used to lure people into the city, so that they might spend money and conduct business here rather than elsewhere, even though much of that business was done away from the Market Place.[45]

The evolution of Salisbury's markets and fairs since 1790 may be pieced together from evidence of various kinds. A day book of the period 1796–1815 records the income from tolls and dues on sheep, butchers' stalls, the butter market and the two annual fairs. In 1797 the number of sheep sold at fortnightly markets ranged from 151 on 14th March to 1,989 on 26th September, with an annual total of over 21,000. The sheep market was seasonal, with most business conducted between May and November. Between fifteen and twenty butchers paid a quarterly rent of one shilling for their market stalls and 26 traders sold in the butter market on the same terms. The Lady Day fair in April and the Michaelmas fair in October, though similar in size, seem to have been rather different in character. At the former the majority of traders were concerned with some aspect of textiles – there were over 50 clothiers, as well as sellers of tick, flannels, hosiery, blankets and drapery – and most of the remainder were selling cheese or other foodstuffs. The Michaelmas fair, on the other hand, was largely given over to fruit (54 stalls) and cheese (51 stalls), with only thirteen clothiers, and few other trades. It seems also to have acted as a hiring fair as well as providing entertainment in the form of three shows and three peep-shows. Twelve years later another document reveals the extent of the corn market. The farmers and dealers, who paid a quarterly due of one shilling, were drawn up in six rows, each in his allotted place. A few paid 1/6d or 2/–, presumably for larger or more advantageous standings. 33 of the 85 pitches were occupied by Salisbury dealers, and they were mostly to be found in the fifth and sixth rows. The remainder came into Salisbury from surrounding villages, but, unlike the carriers (Figure 24), they did not converge on the city from all points of the compass in equal measure. No fewer than twenty came from the Nadder/Wardour Vale area and the villages around Shaftesbury, whilst the Wylye, Chalke, Bourne and upper Avon valleys were scarcely represented. That Salisbury should draw so much of its corn from the west is perhaps an indication that the old battle with Shaftesbury market for supremacy was going in Salisbury's favour.[46]

After the activities of the 1780s and 1790s initiative for improving the market seems to have passed in the nineteenth century from the city council to private individuals and businessmen. After 1834 the right to collect market tolls was let to contractors and repeated attempts were made to make the market more attractive to dealers by providing shelter against the elements. Various schemes were tried, including temporary awnings and a shed-like structure, and others were proposed – one suggestion was that if special flooring were laid each week the corn market could be held in one of the court rooms in the Guildhall. None of these ideas offered a real substitute for a purpose-built market house and by 1850 it was clear to many city tradesmen that unless the council grasped the nettle and provided covered market accommodation the market itself was in danger of extinction, as dealers took their wares by train to new markets springing up at railway junctions. Repeated petitions to the city council eventually, in 1854, resulted in a decision to erect a corn exchange and cheese market on the site of the former Council House, in front of the Guildhall. An architect was engaged and plans were drawn up but the project was overtaken by a new scheme, mooted the following year, which had the double advantage of offering direct railway connection between the proposed Fisherton stations and the Market Place whilst not encroaching on the open market square. The Salisbury Railway and Market House Company, sanctioned by Act of Parliament and with the blessing of the city council, opened the great wrought iron gates of its new market house, which lay on the west of the Market Place between the Cheesemarket and the river, for the first time on 24th May 1859. Success was immediate – farmers and dealers expressed their warmest satisfaction at the new arrangements; within nine months of the opening they were petitioning for more room because of overcrowding; and five years later trading had to be restricted to corn, cheese and wool because there was insufficient accommodation for provisions and general merchandise as well.[47]

The success of the new market house, which continued through the nineteenth and sporadically into the twentieth century, brought an obvious change of emphasis to the trading that remained in the open market. The minutes of an enquiry held in 1888 enable us to reconstruct a picture of market trading at that date and to view the progress of the Michaelmas fair. The Market Place was devoted primarily to cattle, and these were sold by two firms of auctioneers, each of whom had yards in the city in addition to their market trading, and one of whom was also lessee of the market (Plate 21). The principal cattle market was held on alternate Tuesdays, and the intervening Tuesdays were known as small market days. Much of the trade was in beef cattle which had been bred in Devon and fattened in Somerset. On market days they would be driven through the city streets, breaking the occasional shop window here and interfering with the occasional pedestrian there, to be tied in double rows in the Market Place, where they might number several hundreds just before Christmas. Sheep were also sold in the Market Place, but they were less important, and more were sold either in the auction yards, or at an annual fair held in July at the Butts outside the city. A small pig market, described as 'rather a nuisance', was held in New Canal. Apart from livestock the Market Place also contained, then as now, a variety of traders. Each brought his own stall, and they were set up in two long lines on either side of the diagonal path (still to be seen painted yellow through the car park) known as 'Milksops.' Vegetables, cutlery and some meat and fish were sold here, although most butchers and fishmongers occupied shops in Butcher Row and Fish Row and simply placed their stalls in the row outside their shops on market days. Further along, by the Poultry Cross, were a few stalls selling eggs, butter and gingerbread, and in New Canal stood market carts with baskets, although what they were selling is not stated. All this took place on Tuesdays; the Saturday market was very small by comparison, no more than a dozen stalls, mostly selling vegetables and fish. By contrast the Michaelmas fair had become the highlight of the working man's year, offering two days of drinking, feasting and dubious entertainment, to the great consternation of the Salisbury Temperance Association and the Superintendent of Police. Its serious purpose had largely disappeared and there was a general feeling that it was declining and would ultimately die; but it was stoutly defended by many leading citizens on account of the trade that it brought to the city: 'The system has been adopted ... of paying harvest money about that time, and they come in to settle up their accounts and to buy clothes, and that sort of thing; and this fair, to a certain extent, attracts them. They come in partly for business, and partly for pleasure. If the pleasure part of the fair were done away with, there would be no tie whatever between these people and the town for their custom, and they are just as likely to go elsewhere as they are to come here.' The fair began on Monday afternoon and continued until Wednesday evening, and many of the showmen had come from Weyhill fair, which was traditionally held during the preceding week. On Monday and Tuesday it stayed open until 11 p.m. and it was during the evening, and especially the last hour, that most intemperance occurred. In the words of a popular song, 'For miles all round both far and near, They come to see the rigs of fair, They'll get so drunk as Eli Brown, They'll roll and tumble on the ground.' (Plate 22)[48]

Salisbury Market Place weathered the upheaval of the early twentieth century virtually unchanged. A writer describing her reminiscences of the market in the 1920s speaks in terms which might have applied equally well a century earlier. 'Then the farmers and workmen and their wives milled about the streets regardless of the ways of modern traffic ... Gruntings, mooings and lowings floated in through the open door and mixed oddly with the rattle of change and whisper of notes ... Not till the next morning, when the straw and dung were hosed from the market-place, did the town once more belong to the townspeople.' The proceedings in 1929 were still presided over by two firms of auctioneers who erected temporary pens and sheds in the Market Place each week. The corn exchange was considered the most important south of the Thames, attracting about one hundred dealers and two hundred or more farmers each week. The city plied a notable trade in cattle, calves, sheep, pigs, wool, poultry, eggs and skins as well as wheat, barley and oats. But the seeds of change were beginning to germinate. The motor lorry was replacing the drover and the horse and cart, and the vacated stabling was occupied by cattle auction yards. Agricultural produce, which was increasingly being sold in sale rings and auction yards away from the Market Place, was beginning to attract the bulk purchaser, such as the agents for west Wiltshire bacon factories and Southampton shipping lines. And the Saturday market for shopping and general goods was beginning to stage a revival, to such an extent that it continued into the evening in Butcher Row, by the light of paraffin lamps. It was even beginning to acquire the brashness of a tourist attraction: 'They'd be taking money from the crowd for all this junk but people didn't mind 'cos they'd had an evening's entertainment,' was the verdict of one pre-war market trader. The aftermath of the second world war has accelerated the changes. Since 1952 livestock has no longer been sold in the Market Place, and the Salisbury Railway and Market House Company was wound up at the end of 1965, a few years after celebrating its centenary. The open market remains, but – chameleon-like – it has changed its appearance again and now offers only food and household goods. The Michaelmas funfair remains, too, a mish-mash of gaudy electronic and mechanical razzmatazz calculated to provide an evening's unsophisticated entertainment. It may strive to appear modern, but it has not changed its nature in a hundred – perhaps seven hundred – years.[49]

Mistery (part two)

A few loose ends still remain to be tidied up before we can end our examination of Salisbury at work. We have dropped occasional hints about the way in which specialist tradesmen may have favoured one part of the city rather than another and we should perhaps approach the question more systematically. We have mentioned the various trade guilds and companies which existed in Salisbury without properly explaining the part they played in working life. And we have identified several crafts, such as cutlery and joinery, for which Salisbury was renowned, and which were more than ordinarily important to the city's economy. They too, together with some typical town crafts, deserve a rather fuller description. Many other tradesmen, who do not warrant separate treatment here, will appear later, when we discuss such topics as travel, government and social life.

A late-medieval visitor to Salisbury might have found, if he had bothered to inquire, that in the course of exploring the city he had wandered from Mealmonger Street into Wineman Street (at the point where it met Bellfounder Street), past Smiths' Row into the Market Place, where he would have seen Wheeler Row, Ironmonger Row, Cordwainer Row, Pot Row and Cooks' Row (as well as the still-familiar Butcher Row and Fish Row), before continuing along Carter Street and leaving the city by Tanner Street. The survival of a few such occupational street names to the present day, including Guilder Lane, Salt Lane (where the salters traded), Silver Street (moneychangers or silversmiths) and Love Lane (prostitutes), as well as the knowledge that there were once many more, reinforces an impression about historic cities that until quite recently their craftsmen were neatly arranged like goods in a supermarket. It has also led to the invention of false etymologies to explain streets with no obvious meaning, such as Brown Street (wrongly associated with the Brownists, an early Baptist sect – in fact the name is much older) and Gigant Street (which probably has nothing to do with the tailors' giant), as well as the absurd explanation of Rollestone Street that it refers to a method of transporting building material to the Cathedral. Street names must not be ignored as a source of information about the positions of tradesmen in the city – many of them are older than the earliest lists of names and addresses – but away from the descriptive rows of the Market Place they can be very misleading. Bellfounder Street was indeed near a bell foundry (see below), but Culver Street probably had more to do with pigeons – the usual meaning of culver in place names – than with culverts, and Tanner Street, as we have already seen, was probably originally known by the name which it now once again bears, St. Ann Street. But even if the original, or a very early, form of the name exists, there is still a problem. Streets were commonly named after individuals who lived in them or built houses in them – Ivy Street and Scot's Lane are examples which have survived, Nuggeston and Duynescorner are ones which have been lost – and since Salisbury streets were acquiring names in the thirteenth and fourteenth centuries at the same time as many men were taking as surnames the name of their occupation, who can possibly say whether, for instance, Wineman Street (now Winchester Street) was so called because vintners traded there, or because a man who had acquired the surname Wineman (perhaps from his father's or grandfather's occupation) was associated with the street? Chipper Lane is another example; it may refer to its use by market-men or 'chapmen,' but it may just as well have been named after someone called Chipper, whose family had once been market-men. And then even if we accept that some streets and rows were originally named after the occupations carried on therein, the question remains as to how long these occupations persisted in their namesake streets. Evidence from the fifteenth century suggests that, with the exceptions of Butcher Row and Fish Row, street names no longer referred to their occupations. Mealmonger Street was also known as Milkmonger Street (now Greencroft Street), so clearly by then the city had forgotten which product the occupants were supposed to be selling. In 1455 its residents included two saddlers, a dubber (leatherworker), a mason, a clerk and a tailor who had bought his house from a weaver. The list of inhabitants of the whole city in 1455 includes details of very many changes in ownership or occupancy, and in the case of eighteen properties it has been possible to establish the trade of both former and current occupant. Of the eighteen only two passed between members of the same trade, a further five between members of related trades, such as draper to merchant, fuller to weaver, weaver to tailor, whilst eleven underwent a total change of use, from fishmonger to chandler, ironmonger to shoemaker, dyer to sawyer, and so on. If this small sample is typical of fifteenth-century commerce, then there is little point by this time in using street names as a guide to occupations.[50]

There are, however, other sources that we may use. The 1399/1400 and 1455 lists of inhabitants, supplemented by various snippets of information from other documents of the period, give a very rough indication of where certain trades were practised. A similar list of 1667 gives more precise addresses, but the occupations have to be supplied from other sources (see appendix two), and a Victorian directory (we have chosen the 1855 issue) offers a further basis for comparison.

As we have already discovered, Salisbury in the years around 1400 was a city devoted largely to the production of woollen cloth, and the various craftsmen of the woollen industry made up a large proportion of the city's workforce. Each craft was not restricted to a single area – indeed weavers and fullers were scattered all over the city – but a certain pattern may be detected, which hinged on the line of Endless Street and Catherine Street, bisecting the city into eastern and western halves. We have already noted that most weavers lived to the east of this line, and they were particularly numerous in the south-eastern corner, around St. Ann Street. The fullers, on the other hand, straddled the line, and many of them lived in the northern part of the city, either in the Castle Street area or the north-eastern chequers near St. Edmund's Church. The dyers, of necessity because they needed the river, were concentrated west of the line, in the St. Thomas's Church, Cheesemarket and Castle Street area. The tailors lived all over the city but the merchants and especially the drapers were mostly to be found west of the line, living near the Market Place or in New Street or Castle Street. The leather-workers exhibit a similar vague pattern. Those concerned with the processing of raw leather, such as skinners and tanners, were mostly living in the south of the city, in either New Street Ward or Meads Ward (the High Street, New Street, St. Ann Street area), whilst those concerned with the manufacture of leather goods, the shoemakers, parchment-makers and bookbinders, for instance, preferred to work near the Market Place or the High Street area. The sample of food-sellers is too small to draw proper conclusions, but it is clear that there were butchers trading in the Butcher Row area and probably fishmongers in Fish Row, and there is a very noticeable concentration of inns fronting the High Street. Individual metalworkers may also be located, but they are too few for any discernible pattern to emerge.[51]

From the 1667 list it is possible to be rather more precise. The days of the individual fullers have now passed and they no longer appear. But weavers are still found in many parts of the city, the greatest concentration lying in one chequer north and three chequers south of Milford Street – Swaynes, Trinity, Rolfe's and Barnards Cross (Figure 11). Significant numbers also worked in the St. Ann Street area, the northeastern chequers and the Castle Street–Chipper Lane area, but there were very few next to the Market Place or in the New Street–High Street area. The majority of tailors and nearly all the drapers lived west of the Endless Street–Catherine Street line, the tailors appearing to be especially fond of High Street, whilst the drapers had formed a small enclave in Oatmeal Row. The clothiers, who seem to have replaced the fullers, were well scattered around the city, including concentrations both in the south-east (St. Ann Street) and north-west (Salt Lane–Chipper Lane), but they were less numerous in the chequers south of Milford Street. The locations of the leatherworkers had changed little in two centuries, although tanners had by now moved into Castle Street as well as congregating along New Street and St. Ann Street. The city chandlers, users of another animal by-product, seem to have established themselves in White Horse chequer, between Scot's Lane and Chipper Lane. Two noticeable concentrations of tradesmen were the butchers in Butcher Row and Three Lyons chequer (Queen Street), and the cutlers in the New Street–High Street–Catherine Street area. But the inns of Salisbury, formerly centred on the High Street, seem to have spread to most parts of the city, except the north-eastern corner and the chequers lying immediately south-east of Milford Street and Brown Street.[52]

By 1855 any grouping of tradesmen apparent from the earlier lists had almost entirely disappeared. The decline of a way of life based on the open market and the growth of a new way based on shopping had turned Salisbury into a city of shop-lined streets. In order of the number of businesses listed in the 1855 directory Castle Street was the most important shopping street (apart from the rows and streets surrounding the Market Place) followed by Winchester Street and Catherine Street, High Street and Fisherton Street. In Castle Street you could choose from seven shoemakers, six butchers, four bakers, three tailors, two drapers, a whitesmith, a cutler, an ironmonger and a goldsmith, but only in Butcher Row could it still be said that a particular street was devoted to a particular trade.[53]

The geographical grouping of crafts in Salisbury, therefore, was not so precise as street names would have us believe. But there were other ways in which the citizens could exhibit their natural human tendency for like to associate with like. The medieval guilds, or misteries, of Salisbury fulfilled this kind of need, and, although we have already mentioned their existence in a number of contexts, it remains to consider in a little more detail their history and functions. It is perhaps easiest to summarise the history of guilds as falling into three phases, each occupying about 200 years: 1220 – ca. 1400; 1400–1612; 1612 – ca. 1800. The guild merchant of Salisbury, as elsewhere, seems to have formed an integral part of city life almost from the outset, acting as a forum for tradesmen of all kinds (equivalent to a modern chamber of commerce) and participating to a certain extent in city government (hence the name 'guildhall' is applied to a building designed primarily for local government purposes). Around the year 1400, as Salisbury reached its peak as an industrial city, the artisans of the various crafts practising in the city began to form themselves into craft guilds, of which the largest were the weavers, the fullers and the tailors. The craft guilds did not replace the merchant guild, which continued to function as an association of merchants, in the more specific sense of the word; both merchant guild and craft guilds (which numbered no fewer than 38 by 1440) survived until 1612, when a reorganisation took place. The long-awaited city charter of 1612 swept away most of the craft guilds and replaced them with a number of trade companies, each operating under its own written constitution, which combined a series of general regulations with more specific provisions appropriate to each trade. The trade companies flourished in the seventeenth century but waned in the eighteenth and by 1800 the few that remained were obsolescent.[54]

The guilds and companies had two main functions: a social and religious function; and a commercial and professional function. The former was more pronounced before 1612, the latter thereafter. Conviviality was probably in most cases the original reason for a guild's establishment. There was no need for it to be more than a club for people who shared a particular interest. But because in the medieval world there was no sharp distinction between social life and religious life one of the chief activities of a social club was to worship together and pray for the souls of departed members. The reformation dealt this kind of guild organisation a severe blow. In the professional sphere the guild offered the possibility of controlling who and how many might set up in business in a particular craft by operating what was in effect a closed-shop; the training of apprentices could be organised; standards could be set and a price for the job fixed; and lines could be drawn to demarcate one craft from another. The guild was, therefore, a two-edged sword: it could ensure a high level of competence and raise the standard of workmanship; but it could also become a cartel to maintain high prices and act as a brake on all forms of initiative.[54]

To see the medieval guilds at their most impressive it was necessary to be in Salisbury at festival time. Midsummer, which was the eve of St. John the Baptist's day, was celebrated with processions and feasting, and a few weeks later the local saint, St. Osmund, was commemorated in the same manner. Special occasions, such as a royal visit in 1496, might also bring out the scarlet and crimson robes, the mace and insignia, and all the paraphernalia of civic pageantry (Plate 23). Such processions set off in well-ordered dignity with everyone in his place: '... Toukers and Shermen, Wevers with the Pagent, Tailours with the Pagent, maister the maire with his brethren, the Armed men next, Marchaunts with their felyship, Two constables with ther felyship.' Alone of the guilds the tailors have preserved the detailed instructions for celebrating the midsummer festival: 'Also on Midsomers day ... the stewardis of the Maisters shalle praye alle the brethren, the prest and the mynstrell, to go with the lyght of the jornemen to Seynte Johnnys hows at aylewater brigge and fro that place the jornemen to go by-fore the maisters, to oure lady Churche, [and then] ... to the halle of the Maisters throw the hyge-strete godely togeder yn rewle, forth by the Crowne, and so forth over the pament of the Market to the halle of the maisters, the jornemen afore the maisters, and thanne the jornemen there for to have a drynkyng yn the moste godely wyse by the avys of the wardeynes and stewards above rehersed.' The most impressive part of this carnival would have been the going of St. Christopher, the tailors' benevolent giant, who is now comfortably installed with his confrere, Hob Nob, in Salisbury Museum. 'The day that thou St. Christopher shall see, That day no harm shall happen unto thee,' was perhaps the mood of Salisbury at festival time. Such protection the guilds tried to afford to their members long after they could no longer take part themselves. Two surviving bede-rolls (lists of deceased benefactors for whom prayers must be said) are probably typical of many that once existed. A bede-roll of the merchants' guild dating from 1420 instructs members, 'ye shall pray for all the souls whose names here follow, the which sometymes were cytenzens in the cyte of New Sar' and in ther lyves gave any goodis mevable or onmevable as londis or tenementis to the Mayer and comnalte of the sayd cyte.' The tailors had many souls to pray for: a typical example was, 'Wyll'm Harrhold the wch gave unto the ffratrnite off Johne the Baptiste xii s. in redy money.'[55]

These various activities, which may rightly be seen as the forerunners of today's masonic and friendly societies, were augmented by other concerns, which would now be identified with trade unions or professional bodies. The tailors in 1479 drew up various regulations which ordained that, for instance, no apprentice should serve fewer than seven years, no stranger or alien should be taken as apprentice, and no member could set up shop in the city without the sanction of the guild's wardens. In 1563 they sought legal advice about the entry fines they were entitled to charge strangers who wished to set up business, and three years later they reached agreement with the skinners, 'that no brother or master of this occupacion (i.e. the tailors) shall use the craft of skynnenege, or ffurrenge of any kind of garment for man or woman, upon payne of vi s. viii d.' Evidently it was the furring of garments by one tailor in particular, Anthony Lambert, that had annoyed the skinners, and he was specifically forbidden to do so, on pain of a forty shillings fine. After 1612 the ordering of trades for the good of the tradesmen and for the good of the city in general became the uppermost concern of the trade companies, and rather eclipsed the jollifications of the old guilds. Many of the regulations which were framed in the years 1612-1615 and reiterated in 1675-1676 still have a familiar ring to anyone who has tried to run a society. They concern membership, procedures at meetings, officers and subscriptions, but alongside the protocol there are many rules which relate to particular problems. Apprentices figure large – not only who was eligible, how long they must serve, and how they could graduate to become master craftsmen – but there was also the problem of discipline: '... if anye apprentice of anye free brother or sister of this Company shall behave himselfe stubbornely towardes his M'r or M'rs or dame and shall refuse to be corrected by them, then everye suche apprentice shall be brought before the wardens of this Company at theire Hall there to receave such reasonable corre'ccon as by the said wardens shall be com'anded to be laide upon them.' That was the lot of the errant shoemaker's boy. The barber-surgeons liked to clothe their mistery in mystery: 'None to divulge the secretts of the Companye (penalty five shillings 1st offence; ten shillings each offence afterwards).' They also had an arrangement with the city council to improve their knowledge of surgery: '... the Wardens of the Company ... may have the body of any condemned person within this Cittie after he shall have been executed, accordinge to their judgement to make an anottomy thereof.' But other leftovers were in less demand, and the butchers were on no account to, 'empte the Bellies nor cast any intralls of any Beefes, muttons, veales, lambes or hoggs into the Towne ditch of this Cittie or over ffisherton Bridge except it be in the currant or shower of the river or els in the usuall place downe the staires appointed for such purposes ...' The bakers had special rules about bakers' dozens, the shoemakers about the types of leather to be used for boots and shoes, and the butchers were forbidden to kill pork in the summer months, between Shrove Tuesday and Michaelmas. Much of this was to the common good, offering both consumer protection and public hygiene, but other aspects, including the restrictive practices, the monopolies and the xenophobia, found themselves out of tune with the eighteenth-century mood, and like the concept of the open market, succumbed to the pressure of new trading practices. Any trade company members who lingered into the nineteenth century were regarded as objects of curiosity, as in a newspaper report of 1842: 'The usual procession was held, first the Mayor and Corporation, then came the Joiners' Company, viz, the Master and the beadle, the only remaining members, the first bearing the Company's banner, 115 years old, and the latter wearing the Company's livery, a suit of clothes which first met the light some 212 years ago.'[56]

Finally in this long and wide-ranging chapter it is appropriate that we should try to enter the world of a few Salisbury craftsmen, whose skills were either typical town crafts or were noted Salisbury specialities. We have chosen a bellfounder, a joiner, a cutler and a tobacco-pipe maker.

John Barbur, who died in 1404, is the earliest Salisbury bellfounder to be known by name. As the administrative centre for many hundreds of medieval churches the city was well placed to develop a bellfounding industry, and Salisbury bellfounders supplied the needs of most of south Wiltshire and adjacent parts of Dorset and Hampshire from about 1380 to 1700. Although identification is not certain in every case, John Barbur's bells may still be found at four places in Dorset, two in Wiltshire, two in Gloucestershire, and one each in Hampshire, Oxfordshire and Rutland. At Chitterne on Salisbury Plain a bell carries the legend 'IHON BAR BUR ME MADE'. John Barbur's house lay on a prestigious site on the corner of what is now Guilder Lane and Milford Street, and to the north and east, in the area between Guilder Lane and the city defences, he had his workshops, with a passageway and a gate leading out into Milford Street. He seems also to have owned other houses in the same area. When this part of Salisbury was given over to the inner ring road in 1971–1972 the opportunity was taken to excavate part of the site, and the remains of what was probably John Barbur's foundry were discovered. A large pit, two metres in diameter and still over one metre deep, lay near the site of a furnace, along with other pits and what may have been a working floor. Stake holes at the bottom of the large pit must once have held a centre post. Various shaped boards, 'strickling boards,' would have been rotated around this post to produce the very smooth surfaces required for the clay moulds from which the bell was to be cast. Fragments of moulds, both for bells and for smaller items, such as cooking vessels, were found inside the pits. John Barbur referred to himself as a brazier rather than a bellfounder and it is clear, both from the archaeological finds and from his will, that he also made copper vessels of various sizes. His wife survived him by four years, and his two sons, Peter and John, probably both followed their father's calling, Peter inheriting the Salisbury business and John perhaps moving to Shaftesbury. The Barburs were a wealthy family – Alice Barbur, John's wife, possessed at least five gold rings and a wardrobe of sumptuous clothes – and in death John was a generous benefactor, leaving various items to his employees, his business associates, the poor of the city and several religious foundations. From his will we may guess that John Oates, John and Richard Peccham and Humfrey the founder all worked for him, as well as a servant girl, Alice. He numbered among his friends and associates some of the most important citizens, and he had his own seat in the north aisle of St. Edmund's Church.[57]

Humphrey Beckham, our representative of the joiners' company, was an interesting character. We find him shortly before his death in 1671 living in a small rented shop somewhere in the city, perhaps in the Catherine Street area. The accommodation was mean, the workshop fronting the street which contained his tools, his grindstone and finished woodwork for sale, a kitchen behind and upstairs two bedrooms. In one of these he stored other pieces of finished work, and in a 'clossett' hung two flitches of bacon with his supply of cheese. Two sheds behind the house contained the raw materials of his trade, his timber, which was worth more than all the possessions in his house put together. But despite an apparently frugal existence in his old age Humphrey Beckham was neither poor – he owned three houses and land in the city which he let to tenants, and he invested large sums of money – nor was he uneducated – his possessions included books and, most unusually, five pictures. In his kitchen and front bedroom were two examples of his work – carved wooden chimneypieces – and doubtless much of the furniture was also of his own make. Humphrey Beckham lived to the age of 83 – a remarkable achievement in the plague-infested Salisbury of the seventeenth century – and died exactly 50 years after he had first held the chamberlain's office in the joiners' company. As a penalty for his longevity his later years were bereft of most of his family; his wife and daughter and brother John were dead, but another, 'dearly beloved brother, Benjamin,' was still alive, and it was to him and a grandson, Humphrey Hillary, that he left most of his property. Evidently he continued to work at his trade until his final illness, as he was still employing an apprentice in 1671. When he died one of his own chimneypieces was erected as his memorial in St. Thomas's Church, which he served both as sidesman and in a more professional capacity as repairer of broken pews and furniture. The carving may still be seen in the south aisle, proclaiming 'Humphrey Beckham . . . his own Worke.'[58]

Because of this inscription Beckham has been labelled as a boaster by subsequent generations. But it was no part of his will that such a memorial should be erected, and in any case he had every reason to be proud of his achievements. The story goes that his parents had been clothworkers and he was destined to follow their trade but for his childhood dexterity as a sculptor and carver. Because of this his father apprenticed him to a Salisbury painter and woodcarver, from whom he learnt the technical skills of the craft, which he supplemented with the primitive artistic flair to be seen in his surviving works. Other members of the family also became joiners, at a time when the craft of furniture-making in Salisbury was attaining new heights. In the hands of the Beckhams and others like them the skills of precise jointing and fine decoration replaced crude planks-and-nails furniture, and a distinctive style of joinery evolved which, like Barbur's bells, was to be distributed all over south Wiltshire and neighbouring counties. The pride of the joiners' company was their own hall, in St. Ann Street, which survives and is now owned by the National Trust. The richly-carved wainscoting, the carved chimneypiece and the elaborate warden's chair are no longer in place, but six grotesque carved mannikins, possibly the products of a Beckham imagination, may still be seen from the street holding the first-floor windows in position (Plate 24).[59]

In seventeenth-century Salisbury the name of Beckham would have been a by-word for fine joinery. The Beckhams' equivalent in another of Salisbury's specialist trades, that of cutlery, was perhaps the Braithwaite family. Humphrey Beckham and Christopher Braithwaite were of the same generation and must have known each other well. Like joinery, the craft of cutlery was making a name for Salisbury in the early seventeenth century, and two of its pioneers were William and Thomas Braithwaite, both active in 1620. Christopher, who was still alive 40 years later, probably learnt the craft from these two men, who were presumably his father and uncle, or father and grandfather. Unlike their later counterparts, specialising in scissors and penknives, these early cutlers seem to have been concerned mainly with weapons. When in 1612 the various trade companies were formed, the armourers and cutlers were grouped together as a separate mistery within the smiths' company, and when Edward Paley, cutler, died in the following year he left a shop full of swords and daggers. Two Braithwaites were trading as cutlers in Salisbury in the 1660s – Christopher, by now an old man, and one of his sons, John – and they probably both worked from the same, or adjacent, premises, in the High Street, or New Canal area. Both died in the plague year of 1666, the son shortly before the father. If it was the plague that took Christopher, then history had dealt an ironic blow, for only five years earlier John Ivie had published his account of a previous plague epidemic, that of 1627, in which he commended Christopher Braithwaite as having distinguished himself as one of the last two city constables who remained at their posts to assist him in his gallant attempt to maintain order in a city paralysed by anarchy, pestilence and panic. Braithwaite's role then had been, 'to carry out the infected persons to the pest houses and to help order the unruly bearers and a multitude of rude people, which were like both night and day to ruinate the whole city.' He was, of course, well equipped to lay down the law, as few would argue with a man whose shop was an arsenal of swords and firearms. When civil war came he sided with Parliament, and in 1645 made a present of six muskets to Cromwell's cause, worth 30 shillings each. So forceful a character bred truculent sons, two of whom set up in business as cutlers in Marlborough. The ageing father clearly sensed the problems that might arise when they divided his estate, as he added a note in his will: 'And I doe desire that my soons doe not goe to law but to agree.'[60]

The stock of John Braithwaite, Christopher's son, at the time of his death in 1666, testifies to the family's interests. He was making not only edged weapons, such as swords, rapiers, halberds and pikes, but also their successors in modern warfare, muskets and pistols, as well as armour and various kinds of knives. His workshop also contained the tools of his trade, including a grinding stone, an anvil, three vices, bellows for the forge and a press. The premises which father and son probably shared – father as owner and son as tenant – were also occupied by other craftsmen, including a wiredrawer and a silkweaver. Christopher Braithwaite employed a servant, Stephen Gibbs, who after his master's death appears to have bought the premises and set up on his own account as a swordcutler. Whether or not Christopher had amassed a fortune from his craftsmanship cannot be known. Apart from his Salisbury premises he owned land at 'Rogburne,' which is presumably Rockbourne in Hampshire, but most of his wealth was tied up in loans to other cutlers, including one of his surviving sons, Francis, working in Marlborough. With the double bereavement of 1666 the Braithwaite name seems to have been lost to the Salisbury cutlery industry, but the industry itself prospered; indeed the late seventeenth and eighteenth centuries saw it reach its peak. The Braithwaites continued to work in metal at Marlborough for two more generations at least.[61]

Our final craftsman, like John Barbur, but unlike Humphrey Beckham and Christopher Braithwaite, worked at a trade which was not a Salisbury speciality, but which could be found in towns and cities everywhere, and which catered mostly for local needs. Clay pipes were smoked all over Wiltshire, mostly during the three centuries from 1600 to 1900, and many of those now dug up in the county were made either in Salisbury or in Marlborough. Pipemaking was not a particularly prestigious occupation, and, although it demanded considerable skill and experience, no great outlay on tools and materials was required, and the product was never highly valued. A pipemaker's workshop needed only the raw material – pipe-clay – a mould, a vice or press, rods and stoppers to form the hollow bowl and stem, a knife to trim excess clay from the mould, and a die stamp to impress the maker's name. The moulded pipes had to be fired on a kiln, but in a town such as Salisbury where several pipemakers were at work, firing was probably a joint venture. Over three centuries the shape and size of pipes changed not only with the fashion but also in response to changing smoking habits and technical developments within the industry. The sequence of pipes turned up in Salisbury gardens illustrates these changes: they range from very small early pipes of the first half of the seventeenth century – when tobacco was a new-fangled and expensive luxury – through the larger but still rather crude heel pipes of the years before about 1700, which often carry a maker's name or device on the stumpy heel beneath the bowl, to the more sophisticated large spur pipes of the eighteenth century, with the maker's name stamped on the stem, and the mass-produced fancy designs of bowl – heads, wineglasses, acorns, even chamber pots – which were produced in London and elsewhere by large manufacturers in the nineteenth century.[62]

Joel Sanger, whom we have chosen as our example of a pipemaker, was at work in Salisbury from about 1710 until his death in 1750. Solomon Sanger and John Sanger are also recorded as pipemakers, around the year 1700, and so they probably belonged to an earlier generation of the same family. Joel's pipes illustrate the early eighteenth-century fashion of producing pipes with a large bowl – because tobacco was cheap – and a long narrow stem, and making them cheaply for a mass market. In the course of his career he used at least four different moulds for forming the pipes; some pipes he polished, in the seventeenth-century style, others he left unpolished to speed up production. Unlike the famous Gauntlett family of Amesbury in the seventeenth century and the Sayer family of Wellow in the eighteenth century, he was not aiming to satisfy the market for elaborately-finished luxury pipes, but to provide a serviceable, workaday pipe which would soon be broken and need to be replaced. His workshops were in Brown Street, and he owned land there besides, which included houses, shops, cellars, a malthouse and brewhouse. There is no mention of a kiln in his will and so he perhaps shared that facility with another pipemaker, of whom there were probably half-a-dozen or more in the Salisbury area in the 1720s and 1730s. But by 1750, when he died, snufftaking was replacing pipe-smoking as the fashionable way to take tobacco, and the clay pipe industry was in decline. It has been suggested that after 1750 there were never more than two pipemakers working in the city at any given period. His sons chose not to follow him into the business: one was apprenticed to a collarmaker; the other is variously described as a soap-boiler, a tallow-chandler and a common brewer, and so perhaps occupied his father's malthouse and brewhouse.[63]

Our survey of Salisbury's industries began by counting heads and has ended by looking at individuals. We have started to edge away from the idea of the city as a great machine or a huge animal, which was our theme in the previous chapters, and are moving towards a city made up of thousands of characters, each of them with a story worth telling. This is the theme which we shall develop in the final chapter of this book; but before we reach that stage we must examine two other facets of the city's economic history, its communications and its government.

CHAPTER FOUR

Travelling

Trading cities depend on a constant coming and going, an ebb and flow through their gates which is as natural and as essential as breathing. If the channels of communication are blocked the city suffocates. Salisbury has nurtured many lifelines. A new bridge here and there, a commission to improve the river, turnpike roads, a canal, a railway tunnel, a new bus station, a multi-storey car park. These are the inducements which bring the traveller to the city, and take the city's products to the world.

Early Roads

When Salisbury itself embarked on the momentous journey from Old to New Sarum at the beginning of the thirteenth century there already existed three distinct, yet complementary, road networks. By choosing its new site well and by diverting existing routes to its own benefit the new city became the centre of communications; but the imprint of the earlier roads on the landscape has been so deep that most of them can still be traced, some still functioning as modern highways, others remaining only as farm tracks or parish boundaries (Figure 19).

Before any roads existed, of course, there were rivers, the most ancient highways of all. But the role of Salisbury's rivers as carriers of goods and people has been very limited, and for the long distance traveller they have proved to be more of a hindrance than a help. Apart from the difficulty of knowing where to cross them, in winter when they were in full spate they could turn the local tracks in the valley floor into impassable quagmires. Any system of roads in an area like Salisbury, where several rivers converge, would be bound to be governed by these natural obstacles.

The serious traveller – animal as well as human – will always take the line of least resistance. The watersheds between the river valleys of Wessex offer the easiest going because they are dry and for the most part have been shunned by the farmers who have since prehistoric times cultivated the valley floors and sides. Ridgeways, as these watershed roads are known, have from prehistory linked to form trunk routes across England, although their distinction from other roads is not one of age, but of function. The modern Devizes road (A360) and Amesbury road (A345), which flank the Avon valley north of Salisbury, are two ridgeways still fulfilling their ancient purpose. The new Alderbury bypass (A36), south-east of Salisbury, is successor to an honourable tradition of ridgeways picking a route along the watershed between the rivers Test and Avon. All the other watersheds in the Salisbury area have their ridgeways, and all are mentioned as thoroughfares in Saxon charters, but they are no longer used as roads. The most important of these lost highways ran along high ground between the Rivers Nadder and Ebble westwards from Salisbury to Shaftesbury. It formed part of the great west road which fell into disuse in the eighteenth century when a valley road was turnpiked. It remains only as a pleasant walk.[1]

Ridgeways are sensible roads, the roads of countrymen attuned to their landscape, their use governed by their usefulness as trade routes. They were designed by no-one, cost nothing to maintain, and belonged

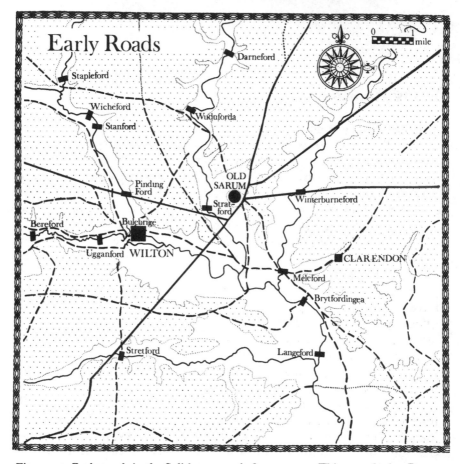

Figure 19. Early roads in the Salisbury area before *ca.* 1200. This map depicts Roman roads as a continuous line, roads believed from documentary sources to have been used in the Saxon period as a dashed line, and a few other roads conjectured to have been in use before *ca.* 1200 as a dotted line. Place names containing the element -ford are also shown, if the name is recorded before 1200, and the earliest known form of the name is given. The stippled area denotes land above 76 metres.

to everyone. Planned roads, on the other hand, were the prerogative of the invader. The Roman invasion of Britain brought a new network of roads to the Salisbury area, laid out along new – and mostly straight – lines, and fulfilling a new purpose, the government and exploitation of a conquered country. The Roman roads, however, though they were the work of innovators and engineers, did not ignore the existing pattern. Just as the Salisbury area had been a focus of prehistoric communications, so it became the centre of a Roman road network, which radiated from a settlement or settlements near the hillfort of Old Sarum. Two of the existing ridgeways – the Amesbury road (A345) and the Grovely Great Ridge (now a woodland track) – were incorporated into the Roman road system, besides three entirely new roads, south-west to Dorchester, east to Winchester, and north-east to Silchester (near Basingstoke). All these roads took a straight course as they approached Old Sarum, regardless of rivers and unsuitable terrain, and it might be expected that they would fall into disuse once Roman government was no longer there to repair them. But Roman roads were built to last – often, in fact, they were built more solidly than was strictly necessary – and so when Old Sarum again rose to prominence in the eleventh and twelfth centuries considerable remains of a thousand-year-old road system still led from its gates in every direction.[2]

The third network of roads which existed before 1200 was the most extensive and the most frequented, although also the most elusive. This was the system of local roads and tracks, linking hamlet to village and village to town (Figure 19). Most of the roads which we use every day, if the truth be known, would have been as familiar to our Saxon, and perhaps our prehistoric, ancestors, as they are to us. But roads do not easily yield up their age. Only those referred to in documents or place names can be given dates, and even these may be much older than the earliest reference to them. Roads in the Salisbury area which are mentioned in Saxon charters fall into two categories, valley roads and 'portways' or market roads. By the time of the Domesday survey in 1086 the valleys of south Wiltshire were thickly populated with farming villages, and it is most likely that roads linking these villages ran along each side of the valleys, as indeed they do today. A road running from Wilton to Wylye along the south bank of the River Wylye is mentioned in a Saxon charter, as are roads running west from Wilton on either side of the River Nadder, and another running south beside the River Avon from Amesbury to Alderbury, and perhaps on to Downton and the New Forest. There must have been many other valley roads, including an important route east from Wilton via Fisherton and Milford to join the ridgeways at Alderbury and the London road. Other roads headed towards Wilton across country, including a highway running north from Damerham in Hampshire which probably crossed the Ebble near the Roman ford at Stratford Toney, and another connecting the Avon valley with Wilton. Such roads, known perhaps as 'Wiltways,' were taking men and the works of men to market in Wilton long before the first stone was laid in New Sarum.[3]

The names of settlements along the valleys of south Wiltshire provide many clues to the Saxon and medieval road network, especially where they point to the existence of an early fording-place (Figure 19). The suggestive name 'Stratford,' which often denotes a Roman ford, occurs twice, at Stratford Toney on the Ebble and Stratford-sub-Castle on the Avon. Charford, on the Avon south of Downton, is recorded as the site of a battle in AD 519 and Britford, also on the Avon a mile below Salisbury, seems to have its origin in the period of Saxon colonisation. Many other fords are enshrined in Saxon place names or occur at the end of the Saxon period in the Domesday survey. These fords are variously described as 'long,' 'deep,' 'stony,' or 'hidden,' or marked by some distinguishing feature, such as an elm tree, a wood, a post, or a mill. Barford, a name which occurs in two places, seems to mean 'Barley-ford,' or 'a ford shallow enough to carry across a load of corn,' and of particular interest is 'Pinding ford,' in South Newton on the Wylye, which seems to mean 'a ford created by building a dam.' There must have been many other fords in use across the rivers of south Wiltshire by the time of Domesday, but their names are not recorded. Some would have served important roads, others (such as Landford, which probably means 'ford of the lane') would have been used by local roads and trackways; perhaps some had fallen into disuse and been replaced by better crossing-places, others may only have been passable at certain times of the year, others crossed rivers so insignificant that in the summer you could leap across them. But wherever there are fords there must be tracks leading away, and the existence of so many named fords at so early a date is evidence of an extensive Saxon road network.[4]

No traveller enjoys wading across rivers. If he can avoid wet feet, either by going a different way, or by using a bridge, he will do so. Thus the man who can afford to build and maintain a bridge holds the key to the road network and the traffic using it. The right of the Bishop to make and alter the roads and bridges leading to Salisbury was written into the city's grant of privileges in 1227. And so the need to build bridges in order to attract travellers into and through the new city was anticipated in the original conception. There was perhaps more than a glance in the direction of Wilton, where the Bull Bridge over the Nadder was already enticing travellers using the Nadder/Ebble ridgeway to make Wilton their crossing-place instead of continuing to a ford at Britford or further downstream. Salisbury took note of Wilton's success, and in 1244 Bishop Bingham replaced 'Aegel's ford' across the Avon with a fine stone bridge – Ayleswade or Harnham Bridge – which is still in use. Throughout the medieval period his action was remembered as the turning point which brought Salisbury supremacy over its neighbours (Plate 25). 'The chaunging of this way was the totale cause of the ruine of Old Saresbyri and Wiltoun. For afore this Wiltoun had a 12. paroch chirches or more, and was the hedde town of Wileshir.' So wrote Leland in the 1540s.[5]

To understand why Harnham Bridge made such a difference we must try to discover which were the most important trade routes in the medieval period. The earliest map of England to mark roads, which dates from about 1360, shows a route from London to Exeter and beyond – by way of Winchester, Salisbury and Shaftesbury – as one of the five principal roads of southern England. Opinions differ as to the exact course which this road would have taken in the Salisbury area before the move from Old to New Sarum, but it is clear that the Nadder/Ebble ridgeway was used and probably also parts of the Roman road from Winchester to Old Sarum. The intervening river system had to be crossed either at Stratford-sub-Castle and Wilton, Fisherton and Wilton, or further downstream, in the Britford or Downton area (Figure 19). After Harnham Bridge was built there was no doubt about the route – the road from Winchester passed through Clarendon Forest, over Milford Bridge (another medieval structure which has survived), into the city along the modern Milford Street (which was then known as Winchester Street), out of the city along Drakehall Street (now Exeter Street), over Harnham Bridge, and straight up onto the ridgeway. At the end of the medieval period, perhaps with the emparking of Clarendon or the building of St. Thomas's Bridge over the Bourne near Laverstock, the route through Clarendon fell into disuse and the name 'Winchester Street' was transferred to the road which now bears its name, entering the city at Winchester Gate. The second great trade route from Salisbury in the medieval period was the road leading to Southampton. At the height of Salisbury's prosperity in the fifteenth century one-third of all commercial traffic leaving Southampton was heading for Salisbury. The favoured route seems to have been through Romsey and Whiteparish, entering the city past St. Martin's Church and along St. Ann Street. The road continued, as it had before Salisbury existed, through Fisherton to Wilton and ultimately to Bristol, but its importance as a through route west of Salisbury seems to have dwindled as the city became established, and by 1675 it was omitted from the first detailed survey of main roads.[6]

By 1675 also the time-honoured attitude towards roads, that they would last for ever without any maintenance, had worn very thin. Heavier carts led to deeper ruts, more feet meant more potholes. But as the roads became worse so the need for them became greater, and in the seventeenth century, for the first time since the Romans, people began to care about their roads. When we return to roads it will be to a system organised by surveyors, commissioners and turnpike trusts.

Down to the Sea

Salisbury, the English Venice, knew better than most cities how to use its rivers to its best advantage. It was, after all, the allure of the rivers which had contributed to the abandonment of Old Sarum; and it was the rivers which had dictated the form the new city would take. The rivers provided drinking water for man and beast, a plentiful supply of fish, water for cleaning, sanitation and irrigation, water to drive mills and to use in the various processes of an industrial city; rivers could be used too in place of walls, to act as barriers or boundaries, and as highways, the most ancient highways of all (Plate 26). Unfortunately, although the bountiful rivers of Salisbury could be used in all these various ways, they could not satisfy all the demands placed upon them simultaneously. The needs of the fisherman, who strung nets across them, or the miller, who dammed them with weirs, or the carter, who built bridges over them, were considered more important than the needs of the boatman. Added to these man-made difficulties it is the nature of rivers to flow in one direction only and to vary in depth according to the season and the terrain through which they run. In fact, apart from the Severn and the Thames and a few Fenland waterways, it seems that in the medieval period most rivers, including the Salisbury Avon and its tributaries, presented more obstacles than opportunities to potential navigators (Figure 20).

The River Avon, which unites near Salisbury with the Nadder, Wylye, Bourne and Ebble to flow southwards to the sea at Christchurch, is not in its natural state a navigable river for any but the slightest of sea-going vessels. Salisbury's attitude to the river as a means of communication seems, until the seventeenth century, to have been ambivalent. The overland route between Salisbury and Southampton appears always to have been preferred by the Salisbury merchants, since, although water transport was theoretically cheaper, the natural and man-made difficulties along the Avon outweighed any advantages the river might offer. A right of passage fifteen feet wide had, nevertheless, to be maintained according to ancient custom along its course, and a commission of sewers existed in the Elizabethan period and later to see that this was maintained. It is a nice measure of the city's attitude to this right that in 1606 when a churchwarden of St. Martin's parish was required to visit Ringwood in connection with the commission he went on horseback by road to Ringwood and once there hired a boat to inspect the river.[7]

River navigation was one of the many activities to which the 'ingeniose' men of the seventeenth century turned their attention. With hindsight it is obvious that Salisbury never wanted to be an inland port; the enthusiasm of the few to make the Avon navigable only made a temporary impact on the many, and soon the city reverted to a half-hearted indifference. The first enthusiasts were John Taylor and John Ivie. In 1623 John Taylor demonstrated that the river could easily be made navigable to Salisbury by rowing his wherry from London to Christchurch and thence (behind a flotilla of swans) firstly to Ringwood, where a fanfare of trumpets welcomed him, then to Longford, where he was entertained by Lord Dundalk, and finally to Salisbury, where he passed unobtrusively under Fisherton Bridge one Friday night and lodged at the King's Head Inn. But despite publishing an account of his experiences and listing the benefits a navigable river would bestow on the city, it seems that his only reward was a new vessel, donated by Lord Dundalk, to replace his, 'tattered, wind-shaken, and weather-beaten boate.' John Ivie, the intensely practical and compassionate mayor of Salisbury, was advocating at about the same time a plan to raise money for a navigation scheme by imposing a tax on tobacco. This scheme and

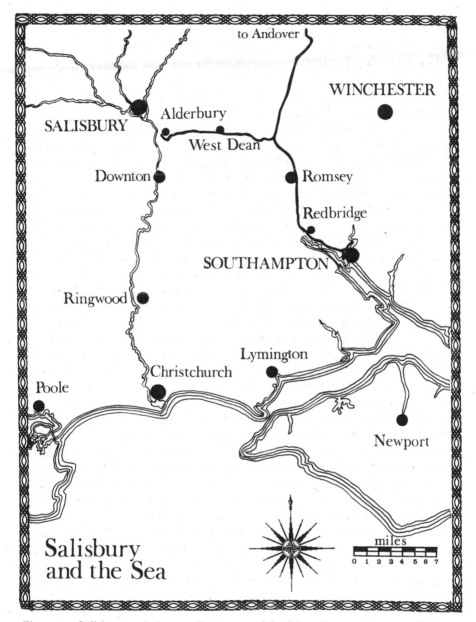

to Andover

WINCHESTER

SALISBURY

Alderbury

West Dean

Downton

Romsey

Redbridge

SOUTHAMPTON

Ringwood

Lymington

Christchurch

Poole

Newport

Salisbury
and the Sea

miles

0 1 2 3 4 5 6 7

Figure 20. Salisbury and the sea. The course of the River Avon to the sea at Christ-church, and the lines of the Salisbury and Southampton Canal and the Andover Canal are shown.

another a few years later both came to nothing. It needed an Act of Parliament, in 1664/5, and a further ten years' delay before the first practical steps were taken to make the Avon navigable.[8]

The enthusiast in 1675 was a man of the greatest influence in Salisbury, no less a figure than the Bishop. Seth Ward, besides being one of the few Bishops of his century to win the respect and love of the city, was himself an accomplished scientist and scholar. He brought to the navigation scheme his wealth and his good sense, with which to combat the natural obstacles; human objections he crushed under the weight of his considerable influence. The city appeared to endorse the scheme, and for a while the corporation, the neighbouring gentry and the citizens were all caught up in the general enthusiasm. But less than eighteen months after the Bishop had dug the first spit the project ran out of money. Several benefactors had died, others had defaulted, and 'lack of incouragement hath for a time sunk the undertaking.' An observer in Longford Castle was moved to poetry at the prospect of, 'Poor Avon ... How art thou of Auxilliarys bereft .... Like the Church Cripple at her gates th'art sett, having not mett with the Apostles yet.' A number of 'apostles' eventually came to the river's aid – in 1685 a syndicate of three offered to make the river navigable in exchange for the profits accruing from the scheme; in 1699 a new Bill was presented to Parliament in respect of the river navigation; in 1724 and again in 1729 a new generation of councillors tried to revive the project; finally in 1771 repairs were carried out following a new survey of the river, but these were quickly abandoned.[9]

From contemporary maps (including one drawn by the original surveyor for the project) and from a survey in recent years of the surviving remains, it appears that quite extensive works were carried out during the period 1675–1730. These consisted chiefly of small sections of canal built to circumvent obstacles in the river, including three quite long cuts between Salisbury and Downton. A pound lock of the period still remains in good condition at Britford, just below Salisbury. For short periods these efforts did indeed render the Avon navigable as far as Salisbury; the memory of barges struggling their way upstream was still alive at Downton in the 1730s. Such traffic had included 25-ton barges by 1685 and the temporary success prompted an elaborate list of regulations and charges, which could only have added to the navigators' problems. But failure was imminent, and despite all the excuses that could be made – the vagaries of the river itself and harassment by riparian landowners – it is quite clear that the navigation failed for two very simple reasons. Nobody wanted to look after it, and nobody wanted to use it.[10]

At the end of the eighteenth century Salisbury suffered from a serious outbreak of history repeating itself. By 1770 a number of newly-built canals in the Midlands and North were proving their worth and it was time for the city once again to consider whether it needed a navigable link with the sea. A canal between Salisbury and Southampton, it was argued, could reduce the city's annual coal bill by £3000 and would enable building materials and other heavy goods to be brought to the city far more cheaply and easily than hitherto. A committee of gentlemen met to consider the proposal, and acted with caution. Not content with the figures provided by the scheme's instigator, Mr George Yalden Fort, they demanded a more detailed survey of road traffic between Southampton and Salisbury, while at the same time seeking estimates for two lines of canal to Southampton and, as an alternative, the restoration of the Avon navigation. Once the survey, which lasted a year, was complete the gentlemen met and decided upon a route, but events beyond their control conspired to prevent a start being made and this project was abandoned. A second proposal, made by an entrepreneur in 1774 for an independent canal, also came to nothing.[11]

Nearly 25 years elapsed before the project was taken up again. The stimulus came not from Salisbury, but from one of the most extraordinary incidents in the history of canals. In December 1792, when the so-called 'canal mania' was at its height a meeting was summoned at Devizes to discuss a scheme to link Bristol with 'the interior parts of Wiltshire' by canal. The meeting was in fact a decoy to divert attention from shady transactions planned to take place in Bristol on the same day, but the ploy was so successful that Devizes found itself awash with Bristol speculators competing to sink their money in hypothetical canals. Out of this turmoil came a plan to link Bristol and Salisbury by a canal through Devizes and this in turn renewed interest in the Salisbury and Southampton Canal. Other canal schemes were mooted – from Salisbury to Andover, Andover to Basingstoke, Basingstoke to Winchester, Winchester to Southampton, Southampton to Andover, Andover to Devizes. For neither the first nor the last time the communications of southern England were in the melting-pot.[12]

At first Salisbury professed little regard for these goings-on. In fact its citizens were not greatly interested in a canal which would only pass through the city on its way to somewhere else. Only four Salisbury men attended a meeting at Christmas 1792 to revive the Salisbury and Southampton Canal, compared with at least 40 from Bristol and 30 from Southampton. But as the possibility of a through-route receded and the Bristol subscribers began to lose interest so Salisbury became more enthusiastic. By October 1794 the city had more potential shareholders than anywhere else, and they had between them subscribed over £50,000. Six months later the Act enabling the canal to be built passed through Parliament.[13]

What happened next is best forgotten. The canal, as envisaged in the Act, was to consist of three sections: from Salisbury via Alderbury, West and East Grimstead, West and East Dean to Kimbridge near Romsey; along the Andover Canal (already built) via Romsey to Redbridge; and from Redbridge via Millbrook and Northam to Southampton (Figure

20). The straightforward part from Alderbury to Kimbridge across open country was soon begun and several miles were completed satisfactorily. But the two tunnels which were essential if the canal was ever to be a commercial success, at Alderbury and at Northam near Southampton, were beyond the engineering capability of the well-meaning but incompetent contractor. In 1798, with the Northam tunnel incomplete and the Alderbury tunnel not even begun, the money ran out. The threats and accusations were followed by nature's unkindest cut, a surge of water along the River Dun in February 1799, which poured into the canal and destroyed gates and bridges. The canal was bankrupt, and its two intended termini were left high and dry. No-one could be found to risk more capital in so ill-fated a project, nor was the damaged and unfinished canal in any position to raise revenue from non-existent traffic. A final attempt to patch up the canal into some kind of working order was made between 1800 and 1804, and for a few years it was open to any traffic prepared to put up with its shortcomings. By 1808 this had ceased and the canal fell into disrepair and disrepute. The lesson of history, that for Salisbury 'the world runnes on wheeles' had been learnt a second time.[14]

Turnpikes and Stagecoaches

Stuart Salisbury was an important road junction, the hub from which six of the principal roads of the kingdom radiated. Of the cities of southern England only London, Exeter and Bristol could boast so many. From Oxford and Poole, Marlborough and Exeter, London and Southampton the waggons travelled across the downs to enter Salisbury by Winchester Gate or Castle Street Gate or over Harnham Bridge. Other less important highways led to Winchester, Blandford and Bristol. And interlocking with the main roads were innumerable tracks and lanes and byways, so that wherever the traveller wandered in south Wiltshire he would always find a turning which led to Sarum. Alongside the carters, merchants and messengers who arrived in Salisbury on business came less welcome guests. The 42 vagrants apprehended and sent on their way during 1630 testify to the cosmopolitan character which the city's road network earnt for itself. Five had come from Ireland, five from Wales, four from Yorkshire, four from Kent, two from Lancashire, and eight from the London area.[15]

An example of the travelling that a Salisbury man of affairs might expect to undertake during a year is provided by the diary of Thomas Naish, Sub-Dean of the Cathedral. In 1708 his ecclesiastical and family duties took him to London twice, to Bristol, Blandford, Yeovil, Wells, Minterne near Dorchester and Orchard Portman near Taunton, besides repeated journeys between Salisbury and his two livings near Sherborne. During two weeks in March his itinerary included Salisbury,

London, Salisbury, Bruton, Wells, Corton Denham (near Sherborne) and Salisbury, a total of nearly 300 miles. Most of his travelling, which during the year totalled more than a thousand miles, took place between March and November. So high a mileage, by eighteenth-century standards, took its toll, for on 4th October he noted in his diary that, 'My horse died of the frett.' Thomas Naish gives no other clue to his means of transport on these journeys, but in his youth he records that he walked from Oxford to Salisbury and was 'much fateagued.' He and his family made occasional use also of stagecoaches, as in November 1707 when he took the Exeter coach from Salisbury to London, and in 1726 when his wife and daughter made the same journey by 'flying coach'.[16]

The complicated life of Thomas Naish was not of course typical, but he does represent the growing number of administrators and tradesmen who were making frequent and regular use of the roads around Salisbury. The pressure which such traffic imposed on the roads was felt most acutely in the city itself, for here the roads converged and funnelled their cargo of waggons and horses through the narrow city streets. Constant pounding by wheels and hooves blended the road surface and the detritus of urban living into a fetid slime, which was quickly deposited, by the action of further wheels and hooves, in the street channels, causing them to become blocked. The channels filled with stinking liquid and overflowed across the streets, so lubricating another layer of slime.[17]

By 1670 the city streets had become so offensive that the city council took steps to oversee and coordinate the work of the parish surveyors who were lamentably failing in their duties as highway authorities. For 65 years, from 1672 to 1737, the city and the parishes struggled with the problem of road repair, spreading gravel and stones, flattening ruts, dredging watercourses, repairing bridges and railings, and removing rubbish. But every year when the surveyors made their report the same pattern of squalor emerged, as the most offensive streets were singled out for special comment. From the regularity with which their names occurred it is clear that certain streets were suffering worse than others from the increase in traffic. The streets which lay between Winchester Gate and Harnham Bridge, and which were therefore used by traffic on the London to Exeter road, fared particularly badly – Brown Street, Culver Street and Winchester Street were especially unpleasant. In 1734 one surveyor, more forthright than most, summed up the city's predicament: 'I do present the Highways of the Parish of St Thomas being in a ruinous condition; as likewise in a sad Nasty pickle, for want of removing the Dirt.'[18]

The arrangement of 1672 was failing because it lacked both the means to carry out repairs effectively and the power to compel householders to dispose of their rubbish in a public-spirited fashion. When by 1737 conditions had become so bad that the city fathers could no longer ignore them, they very sensibly realised that prevention was better than cure. Instead of filling in the ruts they decided to take steps to see that the conditions which caused the ruts were not allowed to occur. Accordingly an Act of Parliament was obtained in that year to transfer to the corporation responsibility for all the problems connected with the city streets, including road surfaces, drainage channels, refuse collection, street lighting and security at night. A new rate levied by directors of highways took the place of the old highway rate levied by the parish vestries. The newly-appointed directors approached their task with enthusiasm, and quickly embarked on a programme which included repairs to road surfaces, re-routing watercourses, removing trees whose leaves blocked the channels, substituting brick-arched bridges over watercourses for the previous rotting planks, filling-in open gutters, and fencing off certain short cuts used by waggons to the detriment of the roads. Inmates from the workhouse were set to work clearing weed from the watercourses, a contract was drawn up for the unenviable job of cleaning the town ditch, and two dust carts were purchased to operate a well-regulated collection service twice weekly throughout the city. Within a decade Salisbury became a much pleasanter place for both traveller and resident.[19]

Placing the roads in the care of a responsible body invested with statutory powers was very typical of the eighteenth century. At the time of Salisbury's big clean-up the most important country roads were receiving similar treatment from newly-established turnpike trusts, which were empowered to collect tolls from travellers in order to finance road improvements. The chalk highways of south Wiltshire were perhaps more resilient than roads elsewhere, and consequently the turnpike movement came rather late to the area. By 1750 roads in the Warminster, Devizes, Marlborough and Chippenham areas of Wiltshire had been turnpiked, but it was not until 1753 that the first trust was set up to repair roads leading out of Salisbury. As might be expected the city's two most important arteries – the London and Southampton roads – were the first to receive attention. Thereafter the next ten years witnessed a flurry of turnpiking, as one by one each of Salisbury's main roads – to Romsey, Blandford, Shaftesbury, Wimborne, Mere, Warminster and Devizes – received the attention of an Act of Parliament (Figure 21). The decisions taken during the 1750s and 1760s, the routes adopted or omitted, the battles between competing trusts, the success of certain roads and the failure of others – these have been the eighteenth century's legacy to the modern road pattern. Today's driver travelling between Salisbury and Bath uses the A36, a route adopted by the Fisherton Turnpike Trust in preference both to the old road across Salisbury Plain via Chitterne and Edington (now impassable), and to the alternative valley road through Wishford and Stockton (now minor lanes). The success of the modern A30 road to Shaftesbury via Barford and Fovant reflects the failure of the trust which turnpiked the old

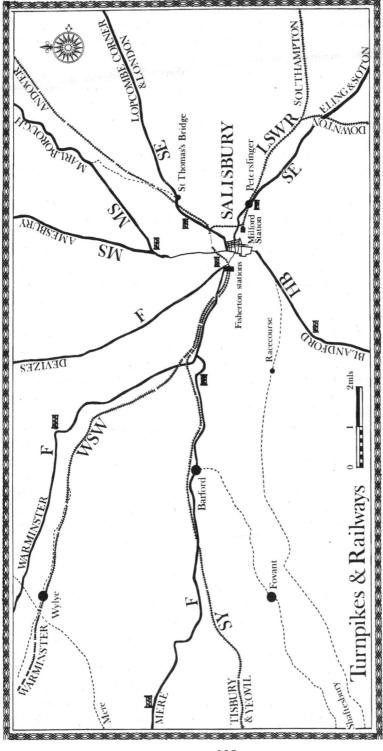

Figure 21. Turnpikes and railways in the Salisbury area. The principal turnpike trusts converging on Salisbury are shown as a thick unbroken line; their continuation into the city is shown by a thin unbroken line. Other trusts are shown by a dashed line. A gate symbol depicts a turnpike gate. Key: F – Fisherton Trust; HB – Harnham and Blandford Trust; LSWR – London and South Western Railway; MS – Marlborough and Salisbury Trust; SE – Sarum and Eling Trust; SY – Salisbury and Yeovil Railway; WSW – Wilts, Somerset and Weymouth (later Great Western) Railway.

ridgeway road past Salisbury racecourse and over Whitesheet Hill, and the substitution, by another trust, of the easier valley route.[20]

The first of the Salisbury trusts, known as the Sarum and Eling Trust, offers a good example of a well-run and efficient turnpike. Except in the depths of winter and at harvest time gangs of men were employed laying stones on the road surface, digging ditches and culverts, erecting milestones, signposts, gates and railings, straightening roads and easing gradients. One traveller in the 1760s was so impressed with their work that he described the Southampton road as having, 'more the appearance of an elegant gravel walk than of a high road.' Not everyone was so pleased, however, and a number of habitual travellers in the early years of the trust took exception to the appearance of gates and tollkeepers barring their way. Many instances of damage to gates, violence to keepers and toll evasion are recorded, including one notable occasion in 1756 when a hunting party passed through Alderbury gate and, 'did peremptorily refuse to pay the Toll due.' In the light of this the trustees made the sensible suggestion that for the future the tollkeeper should not open the gate until the toll had been collected. Controlling as it did the two most important roads out of Salisbury – to London as far as Lopcombe Corner, and to Southampton as far as Eling near Redbridge – the trust took tolls from many regular road users as well as the casual traveller. Within its first year it had reached a composition or 'season-ticket' arrangement with one firm of Southampton waggoners and three years later announced a scale of annual charges for various categories of road user. The trustees also took over responsibility from the corporation for certain city streets, including Winchester Street, St. Ann Street and Exeter Street, and for maintenance of these roads they received an annual fee from the city's highways directors. After the first ten years of the trust's existence, when much of the capital work had been completed and the roads had been placed on a sound footing, interest among the trustees began to dwindle, so that many meetings were abandoned without a quorum. Attention now passed to road improvements west of Salisbury, and these were largely in the hands of the Fisherton or Wilton Trust.[21]

The Fisherton Trust held its first meeting at the Deptford Inn near Wylye in April 1761. By their Act of Parliament its trustees took responsibility for three main roads: the Warminster road as far as Heytesbury (the modern A36); the Mere road as far as Willoughby Hedge near Hindon (the A30/B3089); and a ridgeway road across Salisbury Plain towards Devizes (now partly the A360). These roads formed the basis of Salisbury's links with the important manufacturing towns of west Wiltshire and east Somerset and with the city's agricultural hinterland. Both for their engineering works and for their tollhouses the Fisherton trustees won the admiration of their elder neighbour. The fine series of cast iron mileposts which still regulate the A36 breathe a little of the trust's elegance.[22]

Better roads meant easier travelling, and easier travelling meant more traffic. When the plague raged in 1625 it was felt sufficient to curtail the single Salisbury carrier's movements by preventing his waggons from entering the city. Sixty years later, shortly before Christmas 1684, the victims of a severe snowstorm in the Salisbury area comprised five West Country carriers and their retinues, a servant from Newton Tony and a shopkeeper from Broad Chalke. By 1770, however, nearly 6,000 wheeled vehicles annually (or more than sixteen per day) were passing through Petersfinger gate on their way to or from Southampton. Nor was it only goods vehicles to be seen trudging their way across the plain along the ribbons of white. The turnpike movement enabled a much greater revolution to take place in the field of passenger transport.[23]

When Thomas Naish took the Exeter coach in 1707 he was using a means of transport which had been familiar in Salisbury for at least 50 years. By 1750 'machines' were leaving Salisbury regularly each week for London, Exeter and Bath. Slowly and with great trepidation these early stagecoaches passed along the pre-turnpike dirt roads. A summer journey from Bath to Salisbury in 1754 took a whole day: 'We set out at nine in the Salisbury Machine: arrived at the Weymouth Arms, at Warminster, between twelve and one. We dined there, and set out at a quarter past three, and arrived at home at Sarum, about half an hour after seven.' Coaches between London and Exeter stopped overnight at Salisbury, and at least one in 1754 made an unscheduled stop when it overturned in the River Bourne at St. Thomas's Bridge, nearly drowning its passengers. Such mishaps were by no means uncommon until the turnpike trusts set to work. But as the roads improved so the stage-coaches proliferated. The six coaches per week between London and Salisbury in 1763 had become 24 in 1773 and 52 in 1795. The once-weekly service between Salisbury and Bath in 1750 had become a twice-weekly service from Gosport to Bath by 1770 and a daily service by 1800. In 1773 it was estimated that over 200 passengers travelled between Salisbury and London every week.[24]

The first half of the nineteenth century witnessed the flourishing and demise of the stagecoach network in England. In Salisbury it was a curiously muted flourish. South and west of Salisbury four roads competed for the West Country traffic and a fifth (through Amesbury) by-passed Salisbury altogether (Figure 22). No single Exeter road, therefore, developed after the fashion of the Bath road. And although in 1830 coaches ran daily from Salisbury to ten destinations all over southern England the number of coaches on the all-important London road had scarcely increased since 1800. Nevertheless, the traffic represented by these coaches, and the trade they brought to coaching inns such as the Black Horse and White Hart, should not be underestimated. A survey carried out in 1839 estimated that on the London route alone (which was served by seven coaches per day taking an average of eight passengers) an annual total of over 37,000 passengers was carried. A further

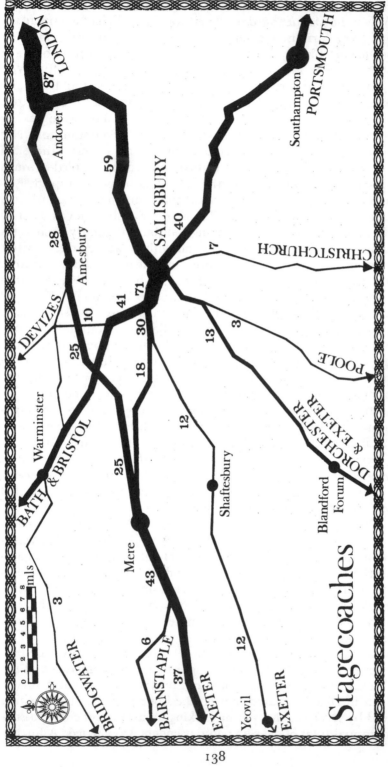

Stagecoaches

Figure 22. Stagecoaches operating through Salisbury in 1839. The number of coaches traversing each road is denoted by the thickness of the line. Numbers placed alongside roads relate to the number of coaches per week in each direction. Only coaches passing through Salisbury or Amesbury are shown.

14,000 passengers could afford the luxury of a private carriage. The Southampton road, with four daily stagecoaches and two private carriages, attracted another 40,000 passengers.[25]

Such to-ing and fro-ing along the roads of Salisbury was not to last. Elsewhere in Wiltshire the metalled road was already giving way to the iron road and it was not long before the stagecoaches running through Salisbury likewise succumbed to the attractions of the railway. The turnpike trusts, which for the most part had grown to depend on revenue from the long-distance traffic they had helped to promote, discovered that they could barely survive into the railway age. Income from tolls on the Fisherton Trust's roads slithered from £3,215 in 1838 to £2,441 in 1845, £1,849 in 1851 and £757 in 1860. Similar, if less dramatic, stories were repeated by the Sarum and Eling, and Harnham and Blandford Trusts. Every time a new railway line was opened these trusts' fortunes dipped accordingly (Figure 23). And although a few rural trusts, such as the Marlborough and Salisbury or Kennett and Amesbury, could remain unscathed because they faced no direct railway competition, the overall pattern of decline spelled the end of the turnpike. Gradually, after about 1860, as their enabling Acts of Parliament expired, the trusts sold off their tollhouses, their boards, gates and posts, and were absorbed into local authority highway boards (Plate 27). And the main roads, their task for the time being completed, lapsed into a state of dormancy, until they should be required once more.[26]

Railways

Old men in the 1840s still remembered the fiasco of the Salisbury and Southampton Canal, a project swept along on a tide of imagined prosperity and very soon swept away by the realities of nature and economics. If their memories were good they might have recalled that one of the desperate measures employed to make the Alderbury terminus work was the construction of a wooden railway, nearly 600 metres long – the earliest railway in the Salisbury area – and that a half-serious suggestion had been made in 1803 that an iron railway might be built along the Avon valley to connect Salisbury with Pewsey Wharf. Salisbury was justifiably suspicious, therefore, of early railway schemes which announced that they would link the city with Southampton, Bristol, London or Exeter, especially as the most credible, a line to Southampton, would follow precisely the same course as the embarrassing canal. Consequently proposals in 1834 and 1837 to bring railways to and through Salisbury were greeted with rather less enthusiasm than they deserved, and the city lost any initiative in the railway stakes that it might have used to its advantage. By 1844, therefore, when everyone realised that railways were viable, indeed essential for their future well-being, the city's negotiators found themselves dealing with a jungle

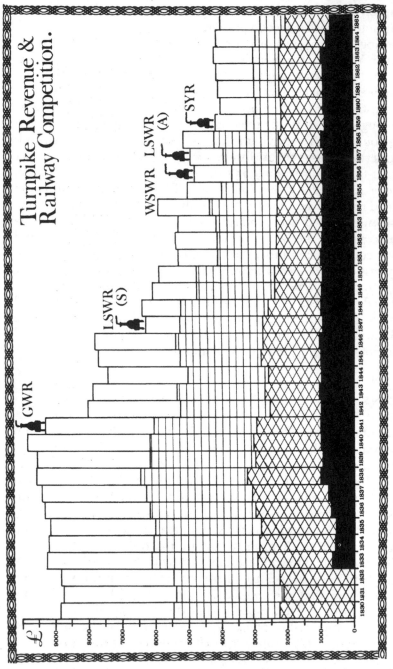

Figure 23. Turnpike revenue and railway competition. The annual revenue of each of Salisbury's principal turnpike trusts, 1830–1865, is shown in this histogram. The years of opening of railway lines are depicted by locomotives. Reading from the bottom of the graph the trusts are: Marlborough and Salisbury (solid); Harnham and Blandford (lattice); Fisherton (horizontal lines); Sarum and Eling (open). Abbreviations of railway companies are as follows: GWR = Great Western Railway (London–Bristol); LSWR (A) = London and South Western Railway (Andover–Salisbury); LSWR(S) = London and South Western Railway (Southampton–Salisbury); SYR = Salisbury and Yeovil Railway; WSWR = Wilts, Somerset and Weymouth Railway.

of competing railway interests, each concerned only to outdo their opponents and see a quick return on their investments. One such company with whom the city flirted in 1845 was the abortive Manchester and Southampton Railway, whose deputy-chairman, Mr Walkingshaw, typified the haughty Victorian cynicism of the railway tycoons. After first expressing his willingness to take the line near Salisbury, 'always bearing in mind the grand principle of the shortest and most direct route from Southampton to Manchester commensurate with the greatest amount of public accommodation that such a line could afford,' within a month Salisbury was offered only a branch line from Collingbourne Ducis.[27]

The first railway to reach Salisbury was the London and South Western's line from Southampton, which opened to passengers on 1st March 1847 (Figure 21). A goods service had begun a few weeks earlier, and the sight of, 'an engine scampering along, dragging after it from twenty to thirty wagons,' produced an effect along the line which was described as, 'mingled amazement and terror.' The opening was celebrated by a regal dinner at the White Hart Hotel, after which various speakers extolled the great advantages which the railway would bring to the city. Speech after speech reflected the city's opinion about itself, a place of faded commercial glory only now being given an opportunity to restore itself to its former pre-eminence, to become, 'the Manchester of the south.' It was, as the newspaper commented, one of the happiest evenings ever passed in Salisbury.[28]

Salisbury's first station, at Milford, was built to be a terminus, and it is clear that, whatever railways may have existed on paper, no company in 1847 was prepared to begin building a line to serve the sparsely-populated area west of Salisbury. The city council became exasperated as one scheme after another was proposed and sanctioned by Parliament, only to become just another move in a gigantic chess game played out across southern England by the railway companies. Works were begun and then abandoned, deadlines passed without completion, boardrooms were split and enabling Acts were allowed to lapse. In three successive years, 1853-1855, the city council petitioned Parliament to speed the rate of progress on various railway construction works, and one of the proposed lines - via Tisbury to Yeovil - was saved only by the action of a syndicate formed locally, who took over the entire project, obtained Parliamentary sanction and set to work. In the words of the directors who assembled in 1856 in pouring rain to turn the first sod: 'We have had so much cold water thrown upon us before that a bucket or two extra can make no difference now' (Plate 28).[29]

Despite the antics of the speculators three railway lines eventually arrived in Salisbury between 1856 and 1859 (Figure 21). The first of these, the Wilts, Somerest and Weymouth Railway Company's line along the Wylye valley from Warminster, was opened in June 1856. This company, an offshoot of the Great Western Railway, with whose network it connected, used a broad gauge track, and the trains terminated at a station in Fisherton. First impressions were favourable, although the newspaper reporter could not resist a sly reference to the company's procrastination: 'The permanent way, in consequence of the length of time which has been occupied in its construction, is now thoroughly consolidated, and this, together with the peculiar mode of laying the rails on the Great Western line, causes the propulsion of the train to be unattended with that oscillation which is so unpleasant on some of the narrow gauge lines.' Less than a year later, in May 1857, after nearly a decade in the making, a direct line to London via Andover and the Bourne valley was opened. Like the Southampton line, this terminated at Milford, with the added complication that London trains had to approach the station in reverse. In addition to providing a faster connection with the capital, it was hoped that this line would open up to Salisbury a new hinterland in north Hampshire, which included the important Weyhill fair.[30]

The most interesting of the Salisbury main lines was that of the Salisbury and Yeovil Railway Company, opened in May 1859. This company, born out of fifteen years' frustrations over the London and South Western's indecision, had begun work in 1856 allegedly with a bank balance of £4.2s.4d. On the verge of bankruptcy, its shares being given away, the project was about to be abandoned when the company succeeded in raising financial help on very favourable terms from their old adversary, the London and South Western, who now once again had an interest in extending the line westwards to Exeter. So successful was the smaller company's financial arrangement that it rewarded those shareholders who remained loyal with an annual dividend which eventually rose to $12\frac{1}{2}$%, a feat, according to the company's historian, believed to be unexampled in railway history.[31]

The Salisbury and Yeovil built their station at Fisherton, adjacent to the Great Western terminus. It was clearly desirable, therefore, that a line should be built connecting the Fisherton stations with Milford, on the opposite side of the city. Such a line involved building a tunnel and engineering extremely tight curves, but the work was put in hand nevertheless and completed in time for the opening of the Salisbury and Yeovil Company's line in 1859. At the same time the London and South Western abandoned Milford as a passenger station – which had recently been damaged by fire – and joined the other companies in Fisherton, where their new station was, 'a most commodious building with a glass roof over the platform which is one of the longest in England.' The events of 1859 had important implications for Salisbury. Although the full benefits could not be enjoyed until the Yeovil line was extended to Exeter and the Warminster line had been converted to standard gauge the city now had the makings of an important railway junction, standing at the crossroads of two lines of national importance – from London to Exeter and from Bristol to Southampton. The city council was quick to realise this potential and resolved in the same year to approach the London and South Western with a view to the company establishing its railway works in the city. Sadly – or perhaps mercifully – the proposal came to nothing. However, the effect of the railways on the Fisherton area of the city was very marked. All around the stations rows of cottages sprang up, Fisherton became almost a railway town, and Fisherton Street became one of the busiest and most important streets in the city. Indirectly, too, the events of 1859 led to the blackest day in Salisbury's railway history – 1st July, 1906 – when an express train failed to negotiate the tortuous curve of the connecting line between Fisherton and Milford and ploughed off the track as it passed through the station and over Fisherton Street with the loss of 28 lives.[32]

The Fisherton stations, although more convenient than the original terminus at Milford, were still over half a mile from the economic heart of the city, the Market Place. And whilst intending passengers were expected to walk along Fisherton Street, the railway's more important cargoes of corn, cattle and cheese were felt to need a connecting line of their own. All that remain now of the Market House railway are a few brick arches in the central car park and a small river bridge behind the library. During its lifetime it was never a very great success, but its opening in 1859 was a symbol of a new spirit of optimism and confidence in Salisbury's future which the arrival of so many railways had engendered. The line was built and owned by a private company although throughout its career it was worked by the London and South Western and later the Southern Railway. After the first world war its usefulness as a market railway declined and it ended its days carrying malt and coal. It closed in 1964 with at least the distinction that it had been the shortest standard gauge railway in England.[33]

By 1859 Salisbury's network of railways was almost complete, and, apart from the Market House line, it has remained intact. Two branch lines – to Downton and Wimborne in the south, opened in 1866 and to Amesbury and Bulford in the north, opened in 1902 – have not stood the test of time so well. The Amesbury line closed in 1952 and the Downton line in 1964. Salisbury's railway history since the heady days of 1859 has been unremarkable. When in 1874 the broad gauge line to Warminster was converted to standard gauge the city became at last a true railway crossroads, as it was no longer necessary to transfer goods and passengers between trains on the different gauges. In 1902 the present station building was completed. Although it still cherishes a proud record of tidiness and good management, its days of glamour and excitement have long passed. No more are the streamlined profiles of the Merchant Navy and West Country locomotives to be seen taking water on their way to Exeter; no longer, does the Atlantic Coast Express pull in at noon on its majestic run to Padstow. But the line is still there, and the work of the Victorian engineers is still in daily use.[34]

Local Traffic

'And working people from the villages, who used to fill the carriers' cart, now ride by motor-bus. At about four o'clock in the afternoon of market day, one of the chief sights of a market town is the setting forth of those great fleets of buses ...' As an elderly lady writing in 1941, Edith Olivier had observed one of the quieter and more gradual revolutions of her lifetime, the passing of the carrier. Indeed, so gentle was the transition from horse and cart to country bus – a span of nearly half this century – that few people noticed how profoundly it was affecting everyone's habits and attitudes, both in Salisbury and in the surrounding countryside.[35]

Although common carriers' waggons were probably serving the city as early as the sixteenth century, the extent of the service provided by the Salisbury carriers is first recorded in the pages of the early Salisbury guides of the 1770s. Poor roads and rudimentary vehicles dictated that nearly half of the 30 or so carriers who then appeared in the city for the Tuesday market could not travel there and back in the space of a single day. Nor was there sufficient trade for every village to have its own carrier, as was to be the case a century later. The pattern that had emerged was of three classes of carrier: the long distance stage waggons travelling between London and West Country towns, such as those we have already observed caught in the snowstorm of 1684; the purely local carriers who arrived from nearby villages up to a dozen or so miles distant and returned on the same day; and the 'overnight' carriers, who rumbled into Salisbury on Monday night from such far-flung towns as Marlborough, Andover, Winchester and Poole, stayed overnight at their respective inns, and set out for home at nine or ten o'clock on Tuesday morning.[36]

This pattern of eighteenth-century carriers continued into the nineteenth century, and a comparison between the carriers' lists of 1774 and 1825 shows few changes. Long distance waggons were declining a little, presumably in the face of competition from the developing stagecoach network, and there were a few more local carriers serving the Wylye, Nadder and Bourne valleys. But it was the emergent railway system of the 1840s and 1850s which was to prove the catalyst for the carrier, as for so much else. Railways were bad news for the long distance carriers, and only those who operated routes not served by the railway or were prepared to become agents for the railway companies survived. The increase in freight traffic and travel generally, however, presented an opportunity for a new generation of village carriers to set up in business. From Fittleton and Wallop, Mottisfont and Martin, Ansty, Knoyle and Imber they clattered into Salisbury every Tuesday morning (Figure 24). By 1865 their numbers had trebled in forty years. Some villages had two, or even three, carriers, and a headcount in Salisbury Market Place on a Tuesday morning would by this time have numbered over

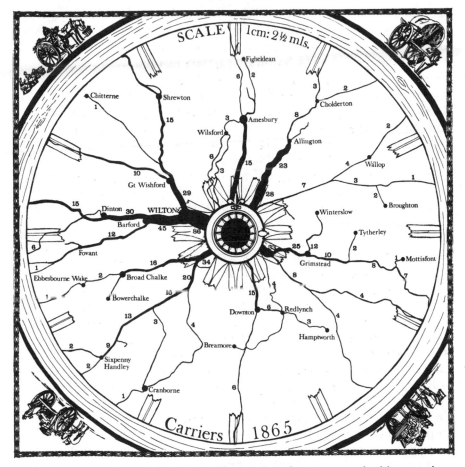

Figure 24. Salisbury carriers in 1865. The number of common carriers' journeys into Salisbury per week is denoted by the thickness of the lines and by accompanying figures. Most carriers operated once or twice per week, on Tuesdays only or on Tuesdays and Saturdays. The precise route taken by individual carriers must remain uncertain. (Source: Harrod, 1865.)

one hundred. About two-thirds attended the Saturday market as well, and a few came more often. If the number of carriers is an indication of a market's importance and sphere of influence, no Wiltshire town could rival Salisbury. Devizes came a poor second with 41 carriers, but, of these, nine were working the routes from Devizes to Salisbury.[37]

The village carrier formed the first tenuous link in a chain which brought even the remotest Victorian hamlet into contact with the world through the intermediary of a market town such as Salisbury. The service he provided was not ideal: 'The carrier stops at every inn,' wrote a critic in the 1870s, 'and takes a day to get over ten miles. The exposure in the carrier's cart has been the cause of serious illness to many and many a poor woman obliged to travel by it, and sit in the wind and rain for hours and hours together. Unless they ride in this vehicle, or tramp on foot, the villagers are simply shut off from the world.' Carrying, as a one- or two-day occupation, was often the second string to a villager's bow. Fifty-four out of 73 Salisbury carriers in 1889 were also engaged in other pursuits, such as farmer, shopkeeper or publican. It was, however, a valuable service he performed, taking the weight of heavy luggage and village produce, running errands and delivering messages, and offering lifts to those too young or old or ill to walk. Carriers were colourful individuals, and they brought a welcome idiosyncrasy to a tedious journey. Salisbury folklore has not quite forgotten the Coombe Bissett carrier, Mrs Ridout and her donkeys, who, trading under the rather optimistic title, the 'Coombe Express,'were to be seen every week enjoying the sustenance provided by a Harnham inn on their way home (Plate 29).[38]

The happy association between innkeeper and carrier came about not only through the latter's discovery that alcohol could be used as a remedy for most of the discomforts of the road. Many early carriers, as we have seen, stayed overnight in Salisbury, and so looked to the Salisbury inns for accommodation for themselves and their horses, and a safe repository for their carts. Their inn was their depot, and it became the practice of most of the day carriers also to adopt an inn for their arrival and departure. In the frenzied excitement and bustle of market day it was useful to have a fixed point where messages could be left and village people could rely on finding their means of returning home. No discernible pattern can be seen in the early carriers' choice of inns – indeed they might choose establishments such as the Sun in Fisherton Street which were quite some distance from the Market Place. But although the number of carriers increased in the middle of the nineteenth century, the number of hostelries they used did not, and certain inns close to the Market Place – such as the Chough and the Shoulder of Mutton – became very popular with carriers. By the end of the century a mere thirteen inns served over one hundred carriers, and a tendency for carriers from one area to congregate, usually at an inn on their side of town, is quite apparent. So it was that the majority of carriers using the Chough came from villages in the Bourne and Avon valleys north of Salisbury; the Shoulder of Mutton catered largely for the Wylye and Nadder valley men west of Salisbury; whilst the William IV and the Woolpack were the havens of those carriers who entered Salisbury from the south-east, and south-west respectively.[39]

The first world war brought to an end the carriers' heyday. The years since 1860 had seen little change in the number of carriers arriving in Salisbury. The longer routes had shown a decline in the face of improved rail services, but this loss was balanced by more frequent local journeys, particularly from the Winterslow, Downton and Amesbury areas. The war, however, was to jolt Salisbury into the twentieth century, so that by 1923 the carrier's cart seemed a strange throwback to a bygone age.

The motor vehicle had been forced to become reliable by the demands the war had placed upon it, and by 1919 it was an acceptable, almost commonplace, feature of the Wiltshire roads, which were themselves being improved to accommodate it. The war also provided the expertise needed to drive and maintain motor vehicles, so that the 1920s found no shortage of young men eager to set up in the motor bus or charabanc business. Until 1930 there were few controls over such operations, and with a little ingenuity it was possible to buy an old War Department lorry, convert it into a bus of sorts, and press it into service. Some operators were content to ape the carriers, whom they gradually drove out of business; others found new avenues for their vehicles, such as city services, long distance routes or seaside excursions. As in any free-for-all, there were winners and there were losers.

One of the winners was E. M. Coombes. His single bus, displaying the legend, 'Wilts and Dorset Motor Service,' began to run along the Woodford valley from Amesbury to Salisbury in 1914. His business was quickly acquired by a Sussex operator and he left for the war; but when he returned to find Wilts and Dorset flourishing he decided to start a new company, Salisbury and District Motor Services Ltd, to compete on the lucrative Salisbury to Wilton route. In 1921 he was bought out again, this time by Wilts and Dorset. Unlike most of the young hopefuls of the 1920s Wilts and Dorset succeeded because they rejected the carriers' mentality. They were among the first to realise the potential of three areas of bus operation, Salisbury city services, the expanding military townships of Salisbury Plain, and the longer journeys from Salisbury to to Southampton, Trowbridge and Bournemouth.[40]

Wilts and Dorset were not the only commercial success. During 1920 the firm of Tidworth Motor Services achieved a total of 24,000 miles plying between Tidworth, Salisbury and Andover. Lavington and Devizes Motor Services Ltd pioneered the long Salisbury-Devizes-Bath service and many other routes in the Devizes area from their depot at Market Lavington. Messrs Sparrow and Vincent (Victory Motor Services) began a successful coaching business in Salisbury in 1922 and between 1927 and 1933 offered Wilts and Dorset very severe competition on its city services. So fierce was the battle that in 1930 Salisbury City Council tried to impose a timetable on the companies to prevent bus-racing along Fisherton Street. Another successful business was established in the Bourne valley in 1923 trading as Silver Star Motor Services Ltd. From their first vehicle, a Ford Model T, their fleet quickly expanded to include two Rolls-Royce vehicles, and the gleaming silver bodywork of the impeccable Silver Star buses remained a familiar sight in Salisbury Market Place until the 1960s.[41]

Silver Star was an example of a bus service which had evolved from a carrier's business. Several carriers, including Hall of Orcheston and Whatley of Barford St. Martin, had purchased locally-made Scout motor buses before the first world war. By 1923 motor operators outnumbered the conventional carriers, who had declined from 124 to 39 since 1899. Throughout the inter-war years the carriers continued to disappear, or turn to motor operation. In 1947 a dozen remained, but by 1956 – when carriers appear in the directory for the last time – there were only three: Barlett to East Knoyle, Jarvis to Fovant and White to Netheravon. Nor was it a question of merely switching from horse to motor traction. Many of those bus operators who perpetuated the carrier's mentality of running into Salisbury from their own village once or twice a week were soon swallowed up by more ambitious neighbours or absorbed into the growing Wilts and Dorset network. Silver Star, which through determined and enthusiastic management survived until 1963, brought a certain panache and individuality which was the true legacy of the carrier. And it is still a pleasure to walk along New Canal on a Saturday afternoon and see a multi-coloured rank of private buses, from Winterslow and Tollard Royal, Newton Tony and Damerham, the last remnants of the carriers' centuries-old web of service (Plate 30).[42]

That one company should have emerged during the 1930s as the principal bus operator in the area was not surprising, since the 1930 Road Traffic Act, which controlled the licensing of buses, tended to favour the established companies and discourage competition. Salisbury City Council had never gone further than talking about a municipally-run tramway or bus service, and so Wilts and Dorset were free to establish lucrative city services as well as developing fast and frequent country routes along the valleys which converge on the city. One by one the competitors were taken over – Tidworth Motor Services and Bannister and Corp of Durrington in 1927, Andover and District Motor Services in 1930, Victory Motor Services (their fiercest rival) in 1933, Rowland and Sons of Castle Street in 1936 – and the company's tentacles stretched ever further. By 1936, as a result of takeovers and joint running agreements with neighbouring companies, Wilts and Dorset buses could be seen as far afield as Marlborough, Devizes, Bournemouth, Trowbridge, Weymouth, Shaftesbury and Andover. The resulting confusion of buses in the centre of Salisbury forced the company into acceding to requests for a bus station, which was duly opened for its own country buses in 1939. Wartime, which brought a huge influx of servicemen into the area, was Wilts and Dorset's finest hour. From all over the country buses of various hues were drafted into the fleet to help the company meet its swollen commitments. After the war came nationalisation, which brought under Wilts and Dorset's control most bus services in the Basingstoke and Andover areas. For a few years everyone travelled by bus, and buses were never so frequent as in the early 1950s (Plate 31). But slowly the bus passengers of the 1950s became the car owners of the 1960s, and the spiral of reduced services, fewer passengers and higher fares began. The decline of bus travel was also the decline of Wilts and Dorset. In 1964 control of the company passed to its larger neighbour, the Bournemouth-based Hants and Dorset, and although the Wilts and Dorset fleetname was retained until 1972 it has now become no more than a memory.[43]

The Motor Car

Travelling together – in stagecoach, train or bus – affords companionship and protection. When even quite a short journey was an occasion, fraught with danger and excitement, and when for nearly everyone their legs were the only form of transport they possessed, travelling tended to be communal and organised. Apart from carters, drovers, chapmen and others whose job it was to travel, the only solitary wayfarers were the very poor, who wandered homeless from parish to parish, and the very rich, who rode on horseback or in a chaise. The motor car revolution of this century, which has levelled social differences and transformed town and country in so many other ways, has also brought an independence to the traveller such as he has never known. With this new freedom has come control, and, unlike the earlier transport revolutions, it has been Salisbury's struggle to control rather than to encourage the motor car that has dominated the city's recent transport history.

From the first the motor car has manifested the unpleasant side of its nature. A complaint of reckless driving, 'to the great danger and annoyance of the public,' was made at Mere in 1902, and calls for licensing motors and improving the road surface quickly followed. By April 1904, after four months of compulsory registration, there were nearly 500 drivers in Wiltshire, running between them 168 motor cars and 229 motor cycles. Twenty-two motor cars and 40 motor cycles were owned by Salisbury citizens, with a further 25 cars and 21 motor cycles lurking outside the city in various parts of south Wiltshire. Five of the earliest cars in Salisbury belonged to doctors, seven to tradesmen of various kinds, including a chemist, an antiques dealer and Messrs Style and Gerrish, the departmental store. Most of the remainder were registered with motor engineers and dealers, who hired them to all and sundry. These local motorists, but more especially the London joyriders let loose on an unprepared Wiltshire countryside, made a thorough nuisance of themselves. The highway authorities disliked them because they damaged the roads; local villagers, such as Mr Targett of Idmiston who in January 1905 narrowly escaped being run down near his home, went in peril of their lives; and the motorists themselves suffered from their own or their vehicles' incompetence. St. Thomas's Bridge proved a particular stumbling-block: 'About six weeks ago,' wrote a motorist in July 1905, 'I was coming from Andover in my car and was thrown over this bridge owing to its narrowing the road. I may also state that mine was the third car which had collided with this same bridge in ten days. Towards the cost of erecting a warning triangle I am prepared to pay the sum of ten shillings when it is erected.'[44]

Everyone agreed that before the proliferation of the motor car the roads of south Wiltshire were in excellent condition. 'Splendid surface throughout,' was the accolade given to many of the roads radiating from Salisbury in a cyclists' guidebook of the period, and the best of all was the present A36 along the Wylye valley. Main roads were now maintained by the county council, who, finding that supplies of flint were dwindling, had taken to metalling them with stone brought by railway from Gloucestershire, Somerset and Shropshire. In Salisbury, however, where flints were still used in large quantities, the dust thrown up by the increased traffic moving rapidly along chalk and flint roads was beginning to become a problem. In summer the city streets were watered regularly, and in 1906 the city surveyor experimented by adding to the water 'Akonia,' a proprietary brand supposed to lay the dust much more lastingly than water alone. In the same year the question of spreading a $4\frac{1}{2}$inch-thick layer of tar macadam along Fisherton Street was discussed and rejected, but experiments were conducted with good pit gravel and other hard materials. Finally in March 1908 the city council took the courageous step of employing Taroads Syndicate Ltd to spread hot tar over eight streets at a cost of just under one penny per square yard. The experiment was clearly a success as it provoked an immediate petition from residents in Wilton Road asking that their road should receive similar treatment. In 1912 the city bought its own tar-spraying machine, and one by one the muddy brown of the city streets turned to black.[45]

The early motorists brought not only dust and danger to Salisbury. Here too was opportunity. By 1912 six firms of motor engineers were working in the city, and three of them – Arthur Edwards, Lowther and Sons and Rowland and Sons – had been in business for at least eight years. By 1925 the number had risen to 21 and by 1939 Salisbury could boast 30 motor engineers, as well as three coachbuilders, fourteen motor car garages, six car hire firms and four tyre dealers. In the early years Salisbury also had a more intimate connection with the motor industry and, had the first world war not intervened, the city might have rivalled Oxford and Coventry as one of the centres of motor manufacturing. Scout Motors Ltd, the brainchild of Albert Burden, a Salisbury clockmaker, built its first motor car in 1905. It was an immediate success and by 1912 the firm was producing two vehicles per week and employing 150 men at its Churchfields Road works. Not only cars but also Scout delivery vans, ambulances and charabancs appeared on the Salisbury streets and the firm gained a national reputation for reliability and good workmanship. Scout vehicles were exhibited at motor and agricultural shows, raced at trials and marketed with vigour: "How to fly. Purchase a Scout car. They simply fly up hills in top gear, and skim along the ground like a bird.' Sadly the tradition of craftsmanship and perfection which the clockmaker had extended to his manufacture of motor cars could not compete with the mass production of 'cheap' cars after the war and Scout Motors ceased trading in 1921.[46]

As the 1920s progressed motoring became no longer the prerogative of the very few. A traffic census in Milford Street in 1930 revealed that motors outnumbered horse-drawn vehicles by ten to one, and that two out of every five motor vehicles were private cars. Nearly a thousand cars, buses, lorries and vans passed along Milford Street every day, and traffic was beginning to strangle the narrow city streets. As if to underline the conflict between old and new the city council received a letter in September 1931 from Mr J. Coombs of Fovant protesting about the difficulty he had recently experienced in driving 70 head of cattle through the streets to market on account of the congestion from motor traffic (Plate 32). Congestion had become particularly bad on market days, not only because more vehicles came to Salisbury, but also because on those days the motorist was denied the only large open space in the city where he could park his car. Parking, and especially the informal way in which it was done, was seen by the chief constable to be at the heart of the traffic problem, and in 1931 he asked the city council to provide a car park. It was the first of a number of attempts during the 1930s to come to terms with the insidious motor car.[47]

Between 1932 and 1936 the motor car effected a profound change in what might be called the townscape of Salisbury. Much that is now taken for granted in any street scene originated in those five years, and has been only little modified since. The first car park was constructed – on the site of the present coach station – and the first car park charges levied. For the first time a decision was taken to demolish buildings – in Salt Lane – to make way for a car park. The first parking restrictions – in Castle Street – were imposed. The first one-way streets – Fish Row and Butcher Row – were designated. Traffic lights were placed at strategic junctions. Pedestrian crossings made their first appearance. Thirty mile per hour speed limit signs were erected at all the entrances to the city. And the first police patrol car was bought to ensure that they were observed.[48]

By 1935 the need for controls of this kind had become acute. The occasional mishaps of the early motorist had turned into a trail of injury and destruction. Road accidents occurred in three principal ways. In the countryside a combination of excessive speeds, inattention at junctions and poor road surfaces often spelled disaster. In the city motorists were travelling too fast along the main roads, especially those which had recently been widened and straightened. It was claimed that speeds of 50–60 mph were constantly achieved along the city's most accident-prone highway, Wilton Road. The third cause of accidents was a lack of road sense on the part of cyclists and pedestrians. Cyclists, who accounted for nearly half the casualties in 1934, were particularly vulnerable, and the introduction of speed limits and a highway code in

1935 seems to have made little impression on them. Between 1928 and 1937, when there were fewer than three million motor vehicles in Britain, the annual average number of people killed or injured on Salisbury's roads was 88. Forty years later the equivalent figure, at 209, had more than doubled, but the number of vehicles had increased six-fold over the same period. In 1934 the number of Salisbury casualties exceeded one hundred for the first time, and 1932 recorded the highest number of accidents. Thereafter speed limits, severer penalties and more rigorous policing succeeded in bringing about a reduction. But for those involved every serious road accident is a catastrophe and such statistics were no comfort to the victims caught unawares. As Edith Olivier observed in describing a rather unusual road accident involving an octogenarian lady and a charabanc: 'Little did she think that morning, when she left home in the quiet company of a psychological professor that, before night fell, eighteen fried-fish men would be responsible for her sudden death.'[49]

Besides the dramatic effect that the motor car has had on individual Salisbury citizens, it has also brought about a gradual erosion and transformation of the city itself. Because vehicles occupy a great deal more space than pedestrians, whether moving or still, the city has passively undergone a change of scale. The provision of car parks is an example of this change (Figure 25). In 1949 there were about 800 official parking spaces in the city, occupying most of one of the medieval chequers (Salt Lane car park), a large waste area just outside the original city (the present coach station) and the three most important open areas of the medieval city, the Market Place, the Cheesemarket and the Coal Market (New Canal). By the early 1960s the Central car park occupied an area immediately west of the city as large as four or more chequers, and was full of cars. By 1970 large parts of three more chequers had become car parks and the number of spaces had quad-rupled since the war. The accommodation of 3,000 large metal boxes, although it has been essential for Salisbury's survival as a real city, seems to have upset some indefinable equilibrium, which lay at the heart of Salisbury's character (Plate 33).[50]

The car in motion, no less than the car at rest, has affected the city's proportions. Early road improvements went hand-in-hand with ribbon development along the main roads, and were in response rather to the demands of an expanding city than to the needs of the motor car. Devizes Road and Stratford Road, for instance, underwent extensive programmes of widening and maintenance in the mid 1930s to meet the needs of housing estates springing up on either side of them. The first major road improvement designed for through traffic was the construction of a new Harnham Bridge in 1931–1932. It was, in its way, recognition that merely widening and strengthening existing roads would not solve Salisbury's traffic problem, and that the new means of transport demanded entirely new roads. The idea was developed at length after

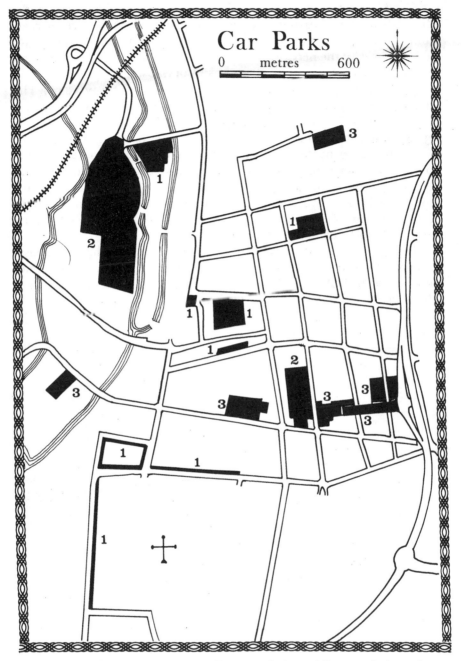

Figure 25. The growth of the car park. The map depicts public car parks in use by *ca.* 1949 (1); by *ca.* 1965 (2); brought into use since *ca.* 1965 (3). Some are no longer in use, and others have been altered or extended.

the second world war with plans for outer and central by-pass roads. Although neither was built at the time the modern city relief road (completed in 1976) clearly owes much to plans first published in 1949. In the same way the network of one-way streets introduced in 1964 and still in use was a response to the problem of Salisbury's gridiron street pattern which had hindered the flow of traffic for many years. The large-scale realignment of south Wiltshire's main roads, however, is a very recent development, and has concentrated on only two routes, the A36 Southampton to Bristol road and the A303 London to Exeter road. The first by-pass in the Salisbury area was built at Whaddon on the Southampton road in 1956–1957, but most roadbuilding activity has taken place since 1965, with by-passes at Amesbury (1969), Wylye (1975) and Mere (1976) on the A303 and Alderbury (1978) on the A36. Plans are in hand for far-reaching changes to the line of the A36 between Salisbury and Warminster.[51]

The urge to move, to arrive and depart, to see and exchange, is basic to human nature. It is no shame that Salisbury should trade on something so natural. As ever, Salisbury has itself to offer to the traveller. The allure is still there, the car park is full.

CHAPTER FIVE

Governing

Cities do not just happen. Their history is not simply a series of unforeseen events. Decisions must be taken and problems must be solved. Rules must be made for peaceful co-existence, and order must be created out of chaos. Somebody has to be in charge.

My Lord Bishop

As we left the Cathedral after the concert, Vivaldi's music still dancing in our ears, we found that a light mist had formed on the cool September air. The floodlit saints on the west front were there, as usual, to feast the concertgoers with one last encore. But tonight there was something more. At a point high above the Cathedral were converging the spires of other, spectral, cathedrals, as the floodlights projected their image onto the misty sky. And, looking back when we reached the car park, the effect could still be seen – a ghostly cathedral hung in the Salisbury sky, enveloping the city in its unreal mass. Perhaps this was how our medieval citizens felt as, for four centuries, the Bishop's spire cast a cold shadow across the city, demanding obeisance and frustrating autonomy. This book is not about Salisbury Cathedral, for that would be quite another story, but the presence of the Cathedral, with its Close, Canons and Bishop, has had certain effects on the city's history, and it is proper that these should be described.[1]

Town government evolved, like towns themselves, out of the manorial structure of the countryside; this evolution had been in progress for several centuries before Salisbury began. Of course in a town the conventional relationship between lord and tenant, governor and governed, could not apply. A villager's obligation to perform services on his master's land and to participate in the communal agriculture of the manor's open fields had to be translated into an urban equivalent, and this was known as burgage tenure. Instead of manual services the tenants, known as burgesses, paid an annual rent to their lord, who was normally the king, for a tenement, as well as sundry dues arising from their trading activities. Unlike their village counterparts burgesses usually enjoyed considerable freedom to buy and sell tenements, and greater mobility in connection with their trade. The conditions of burgage tenure varied from town to town, and the precise terms were laid down by charters granted either by the king or, if the town was not a royal possession, by its lord. Royal charters often granted particular privileges, or liberties, to towns, such as the right of townspeople to trade free of toll in other places. The effect of these liberties was to reinforce the differences between townspeople and villagers and lead to further innovations. Certain towns won the right to pay their rents and dues to the king as an annual lump sum, known as 'the farm of the borough,' or 'fee-farm', instead of as individual amounts from each citizen. This brought not only a measure of autonomy for the town, but also strengthened town government, since it became necessary to appoint officials to oversee financial affairs, and some kind of decision-making body to frame policy. Aldermen, mayors, chamberlains and clerks made their appearance and the range of responsibilities increased to include certain legal matters. Either by a gradual process of taking on new functions as circumstances required, by encroaching on existing functions of the lord, or by a formal charter of incorporation, many towns eventually became wholly or largely self-governing.[2]

Salisbury belonged to the Bishop. Like the other medieval new towns Salisbury was the speculative venture of a landlord, and the Bishop not only owned the soil on which the city was built, but also controlled the way in which it developed and the institutions which grew up within it. The first statement by the Bishop of his relationship to his citizens came in 1225, in a charter to the city, which established a conventional system of burgage tenure, at the normal annual rate of one shilling for a standard tenement. Tenants were permitted to sell, bequeath or divide their tenements, provided the recipient was not a corporate body, such as a religious house. Two years later, in 1227, the Bishop secured for the city a royal charter which granted various liberties, including the right to trade toll-free throughout the kingdom. To govern his new city the Bishop held a fortnightly court, presided over by his bailiff or steward, which had the trappings of the courts leet and baron held in rural manors. No court rolls of the Bishop's court survive until late in the sixteenth century, and so the day-to-day business transacted there in the early years must remain a matter for conjecture. But it is clear from rules drawn up in 1306 that it was responsible for overseeing all land transactions within the city, settling disputes over land ownership and between tenants, controlling all the trading activities which took place in the market and in the city generally, and administering justice in various criminal and civil matters. Although it was the Bishop's court and his officers presided, the citizens' right to appoint a mayor was recognised by 1249 and he took part in the court proceedings as a subordinate official. The Bishop's court continued, on paper at least, until 1835, and for most of its long history was held in the Bishop's Guildhall, on the site of the present Guildhall, although its power and influence were gradually eroded by the growing municipal administration (Plate 34).[3]

Scanty though they are, the surviving records of the Bishop's courts enables us to form an impression of their slide towards formality and trivialisation. In 1464 stern regulations about the price and quality of ale sold in the city were transmitted from the Bishop's court to the mayor. Habitual offenders might suffer imprisonment, 'at the discretion of the Lord Bishop, if he be present, and if he be absent, at the discretion of the Mayor, Steward or bailiff, if they be present, and otherwise at the discretion of the mayor.' Thus the Bishop and his officers, though taking precedence over the mayor, were willing to delegate their power to him when it suited them. A few years later the office of bailiff was filled by local gentry, such as the Earl of Pembroke, for whom it was probably a sinecure. The work involved in the office was then carried out by an underbailiff, who did not always command much respect from the mayor and corporation. By 1566, when records of the proceedings in the court baron begin, the business of the court had become largely formal and irrelevant. At the first meeting reported, in May 1566, only two of the four aldermen supposed to represent the city wards were present. They both reported that all was well, and their absent colleagues were placed in default. Another Bishop's court, the court of record or civil pleas, seems by 1600 to have been concerned mainly with cases of debt and distraint. After 1612, as we shall see, the rights of the Bishop over the city were greatly diminished, but his courts continued to be held in much the same way. A court baron held in August 1687 was attended by representatives of each ward and heard nine debtors' cases before the bailiff, the Earl of Pembroke. Thirty years later a typical court leet heard various grievances about citizens: in June 1718 the problems were a blocked channel in Exeter Street, a fish board placed in a passage between two houses, two thatched mud walls and a hovel which were considered a fire risk, an unlicensed beer-seller, the Bishop's failure to provide a pound in Love Lane according to custom, and Elizabeth Duke, 'for being a common scould and disturber of the neighbourhood in St. Martin's parish.' Many of these complaints might equally have been brought before other bodies in the city, such as the highway surveyors, the city council or the parish vestry. A pragmatic Bishop, such as Seth Ward in the late-seventeenth century, was aware that his court had become a mere talking-shop: 'But very many of those things which are inquirable and punishable at this Leete, are likewise, by vertue of the City's Charters so too, by the Mayor and Justices of Peace there, at their Quarter Sessions.' When the court of record came to be wound up in 1835 it had not tried a case for eighteen years, and the book of procedures had been lost.[4]

In the four centuries that separate the founding of the city from the charter of incorporation, granted in 1612, which gave legal force to the city's autonomous government, there is evidence of repeated disputes between the Bishop and the city over the extent of his jurisdiction and the role of the city's secular officials. Four episodes are particularly important. The first, which began in 1302, was a financial grievance. Under the terms of the 1227 royal charter the Bishop was given the right to impose a rate, known as a tallage, on his citizens whenever the king made a similar demand on the tenants of royal boroughs and manors. The Bishop tried to exercise this right, apparently for the first time, in 1302 and met with predictable opposition from the citizens. However, he won the ensuing legal action before the king and council, and the city was compelled to pay, with the concession that for the future Salisbury might renounce its charter, and so escape future tallages at the expense of losing all its liberties. The city's representatives, presumably as a face-saving exercise, agreed to renunciation in 1305, but the loss of the charter quickly plunged the city into economic and political chaos, and in the following year Salisbury made an ignominious surrender to the Bishop in order to retrieve its lost privileges. Over the next century-and-a-half only minor disputes seem to have occurred, but in 1465 personal animosity between two leading citizens, John Halle and William Swayne, spilled over into the council chamber and engulfed the whole structure of city government. Halle, who was mayor, and other councillors complained that the Bishop had sold to Swayne a piece of land in St. Thomas's Churchyard in order to build a house for his chantry priest. The council claimed to own the land and to have received rent from it, but could not prove its title, and the claim seems to have been very dubious. Nevertheless Halle and his colleagues chose to use this grievance to test the strength of the Bishop's grip over the city in general. Each side put its case to the king, Halle claiming that the city should be granted extensive powers of self-government, the Bishop protesting that for fourteen years the city had failed to meet its obligations to him under the terms of the 1306 reconciliation. Halle's forceful manner, far from carrying the day, landed him in prison. The issue then began to turn on the status of Halle as mayor, and in particular on the oath of loyalty to the Bishop which he and all mayors were supposed to swear on taking office. Eventually, after repeated petitions and counter-petitions, the king decided in 1471 that the mayor must take the customary oath to the Bishop, which probably began: 'You shall swere that ye shall wele and trewly serve our Soverayne Lord the King his eires and my lord the Bishop Richard, lord of the Cite of Newe Sar' and his successors in doying and beryng the office of mayraltie of this Cite while ye be in hit ...' Still the city refused, and it was not finally until 1474 that the mayor capitulated under the weight of royal displeasure and took the oath.[5]

The third and fourth episodes occurred in the sixteenth century, and, although both were sparked off by other matters, it was the wording of the mayor's oath and the acknowledgment of the Bishop's supremacy enshrined within it that were the real issues. In 1537 the Bishop angered the city by appointing an underbailiff not approved by the mayor and also by attempting to forbid certain traditional religious practices. In 1593 the immediate cause seems to have been a document from central government appointing tax collectors, which was addressed to the Bishop and 'to the mayor of the said bishop of his city of New Sarum.' But each dispute then reverted to the main issue, the Bishop insisting that the oath must be administered in full, the city claiming that this was no longer the custom. In each case the argument lost its force with the departure of the respective Bishops, through resignation in 1539 and death in 1596.[5]

The struggle by an oppressed people to be rid of a tyrannical ruler is a commonplace not only of history but also of the present-day world, and we are in danger of interpreting the city's disputes with the Bishop in a similar light. John Halle and those of his ilk may well have seen it in these clear-cut terms but the reality was not so simple. In the first place the successive Bishops who opposed the city were acting perfectly within their rights throughout the disputes. They owned Salisbury, and their lordship was guaranteed by the 1227 royal charter, without which the city could not function. Whenever the city challenged the legal status of the Bishop's lordship the challenge was bound to fail. Only a change in the law could threaten the Bishop. Secondly the city seems to have had little reason to complain about the way in which the Bishops exercised their lordship. By all accounts they were good landlords and just rulers, their demands for rents and taxes were reasonable and their administration was acceptably efficient. Thirdly there is no evidence that the city as a whole or the citizens as individuals fared worse because they were the Bishop's subjects than their counterparts in 'free' cities who paid a fee-farm to the king. Indeed they were to some extent spoon-fed by the Bishops, who secured for them additional privileges such as new fairs, for which as a free city they would have had to pay dearly. Nor was Salisbury involved in tiresome negotiations with the king's administrators over the level at which the fee-farm was to be set. And fourthly, whatever may have been the merits or otherwise of the Bishops' rule, there was nothing unusual in an ecclesiastical landlord clinging tenaciously to his ancient rights. Unlike a private magnate, whose heirs might sell off rights and privileges, whose line might die out and whose estates might be divided, the Church was a permanent institution and its bishops were under an obligation to maintain its possessions inviolate.[6]

The intransigent attitude of Salisbury's medieval bishops should, therefore, command our sympathy rather than our condemnation. Another aspect of the controversy which must be emphasised is that it was not a continual struggle between opposing powers, but an intermittent dispute spread over more than 300 years. So far as we can tell on admittedly incomplete evidence only four periods of prolonged open hostility occurred, lasting in total fewer than twenty years. There were other less serious disagreements at various times, but there must have been generations of citizens who voiced no complaint about the Bishop. Cordial respect, or at worst sullen indifference, greeted most Bishops most of the time. Rebellion, when it occurred, was usually a question of personalities – a militant mayor, such as the surly John Halle, matched against a resolute Bishop or a provocative bailiff. But there was also a political dimension. After the ignominious defeat of 1306 and with no legal basis to its claims the city could only hope to make headway against the Bishop when a reigning monarch seemed particularly friendly to its cause, or particularly hostile to the Church. It has been suggested that the reckless action of 1465 was prompted by a very comprehensive pardon granted to the city by Edward IV for various irregularities three years earlier. The king's sympathetic ear was, however, bent by the mayor's rudeness and the attempt failed. In 1537 the grievance coincided with Henry VIII's sweeping reorganisation of the English Church and so struck at the Bishop precisely as he was losing much of his power. This attempt achieved a small measure of success. Before the 1593 controversy the city had adopted the ploy of creating a sinecure office of chief steward of Salisbury to which it appointed in turn several senior politicians close to the queen who might use their influence on its behalf. This too was partly successful and paved the way for incorporation in 1612.[7]

A third area of possible misunderstanding about these disputes hinges on the meaning in this context of the terms 'city' and 'citizens.' Medieval cities, as we shall see, did not claim to be democratic communities, and it is difficult to know whether views expressed by the mayor and council reflected views held in the city at large. At the end of the tallage controversy in 1302–1306 it was claimed that the momentous decision to renounce the charter had been made by an unrepresentative minority without the concurrence of the citizens in general. This claim, however, may have been penned by the Bishop rather than the citizens, and so cannot be trusted. At the other end of our period an authentic voice from a group styling themselves, 'the middle estate of the said Citty,' has been preserved which dissociates them from any attempt to usurp the Bishop's lordship as 'hath bin heretofore unadvisedly attempted by others' (i.e. in 1593). But if the mayor and corporation were not entirely representative of the views of the city as a whole, neither could they be held entirely to blame for the actions of individual citizens. In 1450, during the Cade revolt, Bishop Ayscough was murdered at Edington by a mob apparently led by a butcher from Salisbury, but this sentiment, which could be regarded as the ultimate expression of rebelliousness, seems not to have provoked retaliation against the city nor to have been shared by the city fathers, who helped to pay for the next Bishop's installation and were outwardly friendly towards him. We should exercise caution, therefore, when we equate the views of the mayor with those of his citizens, and vice versa. And this leads to a further observation about the nature of the disputes, which we shall develop later. Had the city succeeded in freeing itself from episcopal control in the middle ages, and even when it did so in the seventeenth century, this victory could not in truth be described as bestowing freedom on the city as a whole; it was no more than the transfer of power from an individual – the Bishop – to an elite group, or oligarchy, of the principal citizens.[8]

And so we reach the heart of the matter. The disputes were not concerned with any real, or even imagined, gains to be had from emancipating the city from the Bishop, even though he, along with all kinds of other scapegoats, was probably blamed for the city's decline in the sixteenth century. The real issue was civic pride. Local government in Salisbury, as laid down by the 1227 charter, was conducted in a perfectly acceptable manner for a small planted town. But Salisbury had quickly outstripped similar foundations, and naturally aspired to the autonomous form of government which it found at work in places of equivalent size. It rankled that the mayor of Salisbury had no legal powers other than those granted him as subordinate to the lord of the manor, and the annual restatement of his subservience was an embarrassment and an annoyance. The sixteenth-century controversies were fuelled by words, not actions; the actual work of governing the city does not seem to have figured very often in, or been affected by, the debate, and only once is there a hint that the duality of government was proving irksome. Thus it was a political principle at stake, nothing more; and when in 1612 that principle was conceded its most important practical effect was simply to provide legal force to the status quo.[9]

The charter of incorporation in 1612 did not bring to an end the disagreements between Bishop and city. But now the boot was on the other foot, and it was the Bishop's turn to question the authority of the city government. Between 1630 and the outbreak of civil war a dozen years later the Bishop tried unsuccessfully to challenge the legality of the charter. It was perhaps a token protest, but it also gave rise to some petty aggravations surrounding the mayor and corporation's attendance in their allotted places at Cathedral services, which indicate the level of the dispute: '... thirdly, breaking of the locks of one of the seats of the forty-eight; fourthly, the commandment to leave open the doors and seats ...; fifthly, the sawing off one of the supporters of Mr. Mayor's seat.' One consequence of the civil war was that with the abolition of the episcopacy during the commonwealth the city was granted a charter which extended its jurisdiction to include the Close and made other changes beneficial to the city. This short-lived boon was followed by several decades of harmony under Bishop Seth Ward's benevolent tutelage. The last serious bout of soured relations came with his successor, the historian Gilbert Burnet. The issue in dispute had now left the theatre of local government altogether, and hinged on the political affiliations of the Bishop and citizens at Parliamentary elections. Burnet, an intolerant man, attempted to sway the voting in favour of whig candidates, and showed no mercy to those who disregarded his wishes. The recalcitrant clergyman suffered for his conscience: 'you and your father are two pert and sawcy persons, that have behaved yourselves very disrespectfully to me, particularly at the last election, in voting against me after you knew for whom I had declared myself, this I thought that no clergyman in my diocess would have done, and I take it very unkindly of you.' Sentiments of this kind did not make the Bishop at all popular in the city. In 1710 he preached a 'bad and offensive' sermon attacking the citizens, which was followed a few days later by the mayor and aldermen walking out of St. Thomas's Church as Burnet entered the pulpit.[10]

As with the earlier disputes it would be wrong to exaggerate these later disagreements or portray the city and Close in a state of constant warfare. Most Bishops were content to exercise the rights left them under the terms of the 1612 charter, which included their manorial entitlement to receive rents and market tolls, hold courts in the city as before, and exercise full jurisdiction over the Close. We saw in chapter three that the Bishop's interests in the market were forfeited at the end of the eighteenth century; with the reformation of boroughs in 1836 the remaining rights were lost, and the clergy's subjugation was complete. Writing a few years later, Hatcher concluded: 'But now their authority, save what a body of learned and pious churchmen must always indirectly exercise, is wholly swept away, and the Bishop himself is subordinate within the Borough, to the local magistracy.'[11]

But the importance of the Cathedral in the life of the city must not be measured only in terms of the power of its Bishops. Perhaps that noble spire is a symbol of the city's religious life, although in truth it has been their worship in the three parish churches, not the Cathedral, that has provided the citizens' spiritual food. The Cathedral's significance as a religious building has been rather as a seat of power and wealth for a wealthy, powerful institution, the Church. As an administrative centre for a tract of England which once extended from the Devon border almost to London the Close's economic importance to the city has been immense. Around the Cathedral lived the influential men of affairs who controlled this huge territory; their high standard of living offered employment to the townspeople and created a demand for luxuries which the city merchants and shopkeepers were delighted to satisfy. The huge machine which was the medieval Church required masons and vintners, glaziers and bellfounders, and a host of other service industries to maintain its buildings and priests in the performance of their duties. The supply of a single commodity, wine for the sacrament, seems to have kept many Salisbury merchants in business. And the Cathedral has always brought visitors to Salisbury. The line of inns fronting the medieval High Street, which we noted in chapter three, bears witness to the stream of messengers and pilgrims trekking into the city by reason of business or penance (Plate 35). No-one knows when the first tourist came to see the Cathedral; by the eighteenth century, when the first guidebooks were published, their numbers must have been significant. John Byng's account of his visit in 1782 illustrates the eternal priorities of the tourist: 'I was at Sarum in time for the hot rolls, and was receiv'd at the White Hart, civilly and attentively; there shaved, and dressed; drank coffee; and then went to survey the cathedral which I had seen before and of which I resumed my old remarks ...' Fourteen years later the sexton and the verger went to law over which of them was entitled to charge visitors a fee for showing them over the Cathedral. As travel became easier the number of tourists grew. No statistics were kept, but by the 1930s an annual increase was being noted, and in 1957 20,000 copies of a leaflet about the medieval clock in the Cathedral were sold in six months. It is estimated that 600,000 visitors saw the Cathedral in 1976.[12]

The relationship between Cathedral and city is a curious thing. If we may develop the analogy evoked in chapter one of the Cathedral as a beautiful woman, it is clear that her marriage to the city has been tempestuous and bitter. Out of the conflict has grown the city's respect and admiration, but no love – only indifference. A foreign visitor in 1811 recorded in his diary: 'We went to the morning service, and did not find a single person in the church except those officiating.' A century later W. H. Hudson saw a similar disregard in the eyes of the south Wiltshire villager. '[He] ... is extremely familiar with it as he sees it from the market and the street and from a distance, from all the roads which lead him to Salisbury ... But he is not familiar with the interior of the great fane; it fails to draw him, doubtless because he has no time in his busy, practical life for the cultivation of the aesthetic faculties. There is a crust over that part of his mind ...' More prosaically an annual report in 1935 noted: 'It is astonishing to find many intelligent folk living within easy distance who have never set foot within the cathedral.' Aloof she stands in her secret garden, enticing admirers the world over to visit her, but taken for granted by the city whose name she shares.[13]

Mister Mayor

The evolution of local government is possibly not considered by the general reader to be the most arresting of historical themes; but instead of skipping the next few pages it is worth reflecting on the overriding importance of an efficient system of government for the smooth running of a city and the maintenance of civilised life. To avoid the tedium of a dryasdust account of the development of obscure responsibilities we have chosen instead to select four short periods in the city's history, around the years 1420, 1620, 1800 and 1930, and to explore the state of local government during each. But two general points must first be made. Firstly, as might be expected, the growth of civic government is to some extent the corollary of the decline of episcopal government, and so some aspects of the story have already been discussed. Secondly, although this account is concerned with the mayor and corporation of Salisbury, it should be borne in mind that the city has contained other agents of local government, such as the guilds, trade companies, parish churches, trusts and boards, and these we discuss elsewhere in more appropriate contexts.

In the course of our discussion of the Market Place (in chapter three) we noted that a number of changes in the organisation of the market, including the appearance of the first Council House, took place in the early fifteenth century. It is to this period, when the city was at the height of its success, that we wish to revert for our first example of civic government in action. In the 1420s the activities of the city authorities were still dictated by the agreement reached with the Bishop in 1306, but, although Salisbury was still very much the Bishop's city, its recent spectacular growth was leading to a greater burden of responsibility falling on civic shoulders, and consequently new offices were created to tackle new problems. The city played a part in its government in five main ways. In the first place it exercised a certain measure of control and influence over trade and industry not only by supervising market traders but also by its contacts with the nascent craft guilds and by preventing public health nuisances. In 1418, for instance, 'it was ordained that keepers of pigs, geese or ducks should not suffer them to go out of their houses,' and arrangements were made at about the same time, 'that the common trenches running through the city should thenceforth be kept clear of dung or aught else unseemly.' Secondly there were various responsibilities imposed by central government, including the supply of armed men to fight at Agincourt, the internal defence of the land and the city, the collecting of taxes and the selection of the city's representatives in Parliament. The ward lists transcribed as Appendix one probably result from this tax-gathering responsibility. Thirdly there were ceremonial and religious duties to be performed. In 1420 they were still bound up with the guild of St. George, the old guild merchant out of which city government had emerged. On St. George's day the mayor and corporation joined in procession behind their emblem, the 'Jorge harnyssed,' to celebrate the patronal feast, and there is other evidence of involvement in pageants, processions, religious services, royal visits and the like. Fourthly, since a decision in 1406 that the city as a corporate body might acquire substantial land and property (thus overturning the prohibition in the 1227 charter), the civic fathers had begun to take on the role of landlords, and quickly found themselves administering a large number of properties throughout the city. Fifthly the principal officers of the corporation were required to participate in the Bishop's government by attending his court and, as we have seen, taking decisions by proxy in his absence.[14]

Modern local government consists of unpaid councillors elected for a fixed term, and salaried officers answerable to them, who are paid by the community at large through rates, taxes and charges. Medieval local government had far fewer responsibilities and so could operate much more cheaply. The principal officers were elected from among the medieval equivalent of the councillors, and were unpaid; indeed they could be fined for refusing to hold office. With very meagre sources of revenue the city council could employ few paid officials. By 1420 there were nine principal officers, elected annually – a mayor, two reeves, four aldermen and two serjeants-at-mace – and it is probable that this arrangement dated back to the city's first century of existence. Their duties are obscure, but it seems likely that the reeves' main concern was to collect the rents due to the Bishop and other financial matters, whilst the serjeants were concerned with law and order; each alderman seems to have had responsibility for overseeing affairs in one of the four city wards, and the mayor presided at council meetings and ceremonies and represented the city in the Bishop's courts. The office of mayor was a great honour in many ways, and not least because the civic year was named after the holder – 'in the time of John Beket ... in the time of William Waryn ... etc.' – but it was also an expensive business, and in 1420/1421 for the first time the mayor was voted £10 to recompense expenses incurred during his year of office. The lesser officers, supported it seems by a mixture of goodwill, salaries, perquisites and corruption, fell into three broad groups, concerned with law and order, money and ceremony. Law enforcement on the streets was in the hands of two constables, and other legal matters, such as inquests and some aspects of criminal and civil justice, were the concerns of two coroners elected by the city to be the king's representatives. A clerk of the city, later known as a recorder, first appears in 1411; amongst other secretarial duties he was responsible for drawing up and sealing the council's legal documents, and for his work he was paid a wage. Financial matters became more complicated after 1406, when the city began to acquire property, and so two chamberlains were appointed annually from 1408/ 1409, 'to receive the debts owing to the City, and to pay, do and discharge debts owing by the City, repairs of houses and all other the like matters touching the City.' At the same time auditors were chosen to oversee their accounts. The ceremonial side of the city's responsibilities, and the guild of St. George, seem to have occupied a chaplain, who also acted as the mayor's attendant. The mayor was paid by the council to give the chaplain board and lodging, and he also received a small annual salary. Minstrels were also employed, presumably to take part in the processions.[15]

Medieval city government fits uneasily into the categories – democracy, oligarchy, autocracy – which more recent political theorists like to use as expressions of approval or disapproval. The problem in Salisbury, as elsewhere, was to steer a middle course between the anarchy of an irresponsible mob and the totalitarianism of a selfish elite. Salisbury's rapid growth made the task more difficult; on the one hand the decision-makers had to take more momentous decisions, whilst on the other hand the large number of citizens made consultation prior to decision-making a cumbersome and uncertain business. In 1420 the old order, based on an annual meeting of all freemen or burgesses of the city to elect officers, was breaking down and being replaced by a standing committee of 24 leading citizens by whom and from among whom the mayor and principal officers were chosen. This could not be a democratic body, because only wealthy citizens had the necessary means to hold the principal offices, and once a man had joined the 24 it was impossible for him to avoid office-holding without incurring a fine. How one joined the 24 in 1420 is not clear, but it was probably by co-option rather than election. A few decades later a second body, the 48, had become established which shared in the decision-making and from which members of the 24 were recruited. An annual assembly, on November 2nd, attended by members of these two groups, elected officers for the coming year and debated matters of civic interest, and other assemblies of varying attendance were held at irregular intervals. Occasionally when a matter of unusual importance had to be decided, as when the assize of broadcloth was challenged in 1421, a special meeting might be called which was open to citizens who were not members of the ruling elite. To condemn Salisbury's rulers in 1420 as un-democratic would be anachronistic; they were attempting to govern the city in a representative way, using what was in effect a broadly-based oligarchy. Like any human institution their arrangements could bring out the best or the worst in those upon whom power was bestowed.[16]

The proud and prosperous city of 1420 had become by 1620 a place of squalor, poverty and plague. Newly liberated from the Bishop's control by the charter of 1612 a radically different form of local govern-ment might be expected. But on paper, at least, few changes were to be seen. The two-chamber system of government comprising the 24 and the 48 (now known as aldermen and assistants respectively) survived intact, and the former were still recruited from the latter. The traditional offices of mayor, recorder, chamberlains, serjeants-at-mace, constables and bailiff remained, and their holders continued to work in the areas of government – law and order, city properties, trade and public health – which had been mapped out centuries before. But scratch the veneer of traditional titles and historic functions and you would find that three underlying changes had occurred between 1420 and 1620. The first was a change in the *scale* of local government. Changing attitudes towards society and its problems prompted new legislation with additional re-sponsibilities for the city council. Poor relief, both by statutory means (rates) and by voluntary bequests (charities), was co-ordinated by the council, who organised the parish overseers, and administered various charitable funds. Apart from a small dole to poor citizens, other prac-tical expressions of help were attempted, including a workhouse, ap-prenticeships for poor children, and a pioneering co-operative scheme to buy food and brew ale in bulk for the use of the poor. In a less positive vein strenuous attempts were made to limit the number of claimants by deterring immigration into the city and by punishing vagrants. Other areas in which the city council became increasingly involved were the administration of justice through quarter sessions, the problems caused by the watercourses and their effect on the highways, and the more orderly regulation of trade through the newly established trade com-panies. The second underlying change which may be detected was in the *balance* of local government. One effect of the reformation had been to weaken the power of the city council's three rivals in government, the Bishop, the parishes and the guilds. We have already described the way in which the Bishop was eclipsed by the city in the late sixteenth century, and have suggested that the 1612 charter did little more than ratify the gains already won. The city's dealings with the parishes and the guilds display a similar shift of power, as the council sought to impose uniformity by overseeing the parish officers in the execution of their duties and by standardising the rules, membership and organisation of the new trade companies. The third underlying change was in the *attitude* towards local government. The decision-makers had become less representative of the city as a whole and more politically motivated. A symptom of this slide towards narrow oligarchy – a commonplace of urban government at the period – was the petition from 'the middle estate of the said Citty,' referred to above, which criticised the council's attempts to gain autonomy. And an illustration of the ruling elite's willingness to co-opt members without regard to established procedure is given by John Ivie when he was asked to become a justice: 'The recorder replied, "God's time is come, and we have need of one to sit with us and be in commission with us." "Gentlemen, I am sorry I cannot gratify your desire ... for that place is not for me, there being before me seven or eight which are more ancient in place." The recorder said, "We will dispense with that." '[17]

John Ivie, his circle of puritan friends, and their schemes to alleviate the city's problems, offer a good example of all three of these underlying changes – in scale, balance and attitude – which were manifested in Salisbury's government in the 1620s. This puritan group, which besides Ivie included Bartholomew Tookye, Henry Sherfield and John Dove – all at some time holders of the principal civic offices – was centred on St. Edmund's Church, and it was through their efforts that a presbyterian minister, Peter Thatcher, was appointed to the church in 1623. Their opponents in the council chamber were led by the city brewers and supported by the Dean and Chapter and the gentry of the Close. Their stronghold seems to have been St. Thomas's Church, which was firmly under the control of the Dean and Chapter and which several brewers served as churchwardens. At one level, therefore, we may detect a political struggle between the richer and more conservative parish of St. Thomas's and the poorer and more radical parish of St. Edmund's. The issue over which they were divided was poor relief. St. Thomas's parish and the liberty of the Close, under an agreement of 1599, were both required to subsidise the poor of St. Edmund's and St. Martin's, a requirement which they resented, and which led to their understandable opposition to any scheme which might involve more expense than the statutory penal workhouse for the idle poor. The puritan faction, on the other hand, peppered their idealism with religious zeal. 'It pleased God,' wrote John Ivie, 'to put it into my mind to give travellers some content; thus I began;' and then follows a description of one of several fund-raising schemes. Their cause was helped by the contrasting activities of two mayors: the puritan John Ivie, whose valiant stand to contain the plague in 1627 has won him continuing renown; and the brewer Robert Joles, who during his mayoralty in 1623/1624 committed several indiscretions, including a spectacular evening's drunkenness: 'as he was getting towards Mr. Harnes's house, he being at Gaunt's Kyve, which is the filthy miry ditch that runneth through the Greyhound, could not get over the bridge, but fell into the same gutter, and getting out with much adoe, thinking to go over the stupples [steps?], he walked through the river, and then went into Mr. Harnes's house at the back door.'[18]

Fortified by their religious convictions, John Ivie and his friends mounted a three-pronged attack on the causes of Salisbury's poverty. In 1623 they approved a scheme for enlarging the workhouse in St. Thomas's Churchyard and converting it from a house of correction into a training centre for the unemployed poor, to operate in conjunction with an apprenticing scheme for children under Salisbury masters. Secondly, in an attempt to beat the devil at his own game, they tackled the problem of drunkenness among the city poor not by closing the alehouses but by building and operating a municipal brewery. By this means they aimed not only to break the hold of their political opponents over the poor where they were most vulnerable but also to channel some of the money squandered on drink back into poor relief. The project, which was foreshadowed by a similar scheme begun in Dorchester in 1622, was never a commercial success. It operated efficiently and brewed large quantities of beer, but it could never overcome the opposition of the established brewers and never succeeded in repaying the loan raised to finance its construction. The third innovation seems not to have been copied from other cities but was the idea of Ivie himself. Following his organisation of storehouses to provide food during the 1627 emergency he developed the principle into a permanent city storehouse which bought food in bulk at favourable rates in the open market and sold it by a token system to the poor. Instead of a cash dole the poor were given special tokens which could be redeemed for food only at the storehouse and could not be used to buy drink. Like the brewery the storehouse was not a long-term success. Ivie himself blamed corruption and opposition from vested interests, but it has been suggested that the real reason for its failure was its inability to cope with fluctuations in the demands placed upon it. Nevertheless it was a bold scheme promoted by a group of men who brought a fresh approach to city government, extending its ambit and enlarging its power, motivated by a new and more compassionate political ideology.[19]

The tightly-wound mainspring of city government in the 1620s had nearly run down by 1800, and the excitement of newly-acquired autonomy had given way to a staid routine. Apart from a brief interlude during the commonwealth period new charters granted after 1612 had made little difference to the way in which the city was run. The most noticeable changes had taken place in the wake of the Council House

fire in 1780, so that by 1800 the mayor and corporation found themselves lords of the market in place of the Bishop and occupants of a new
Council House on the site of the Bishop's Guildhall. The city they
governed had changed, of course, but it had not overcome the problems
of poverty, industrial stagnation and social division which had spurred
John Ivie to action. In 1800 there was no John Ivie, although the offices
that he and his friends had held – mayor, recorder and chamberlain –
continued to function, and the old responsibilities, for law and order,
public health and poor relief, were still the council's main concerns.[20]

Surviving minute books and accounts tell us much about the business
which engaged the council, its committees and officers, during the year
1800. It was not perhaps a typical year – England was at war with
France, the king survived an assassination attempt, working-class anger
at food prices simmered and threatened to boil over into riot – but nor
was it particularly unusual so far as affairs in Salisbury at the period
were concerned. The city's common council met ten times during the
year, and two other meetings were abandoned without a quorum.
Attendance at council meetings, which were open to the mayor, recorder, 24 aldermen and 30 assistants (reduced from 48), varied between
25 and 42, and was usually nearer the lower figure. Although it was in
order to fine members who did not attend, the one meeting during the
year at which the matter was raised decided against penalising the
thirteen absentees. It is likely that a few members were not in fact resident
in the city. Before a common council could be held it had to be ordered by
the mayor and justices, although on two occasions only a single justice,
the chamberlain, joined the mayor to order the council. Routine business in council included approving changes in the tenure of city
lands, selecting suitable inmates to fill vacancies in the almshouses
administered by the city, paying bills and electing officers. The year
of office ran from November and most appointments were decided
in September. It had become common for aldermen to be excused
the office of mayor on payment of a £100 fine, and in a good year
up to £800 might flow into the city coffers by this means; but in 1800
the first nominee seems to have accepted the office and the council was
left in a difficult financial position. In making one appointment during
the year, that of John Hodding as Bishop's clerk, the council seems
to have overreached its authority; in 1805 the Bishop protested that
this was an invasion of his rights and the election was declared void.
Apart from routine business the council had particular problems to
resolve. The disgusting state of the privy on Fisherton Bridge was discussed in full council, and the responsibility for repairing damaged
arches over the New Canal watercourse was dealt with by the city lands
and highways committees. More important was the need to accommodate prisoners now that the gaol, part of the Bishop's Guildhall, had
been demolished; during 1800 the council secured an act of Parliament
which permitted the city to use the county gaol at Fisherton in return

for a contribution towards its upkeep. The management and financing of Trinity Hospital were also discussed, after a detailed report had been submitted by the city lands committee. And the councillors did not restrict their debates to purely local concerns; the king's deliverance from an assassin and Lord Nelson's victory at the Battle of the Nile were both made the subjects of congratulatory resolutions.[21]

Besides governing the city through common council and subordinate committees the mayor and senior aldermen also acted as justices of the peace, and presided at the city quarter sessions, which in 1800, despite their name, were held only twice, in January and September. Quarter sessions acted in both an administrative and a judicial capacity. They were concerned on the one hand with routine matters such as the supervision of freemasons' lodges in the city, ensuring that city officials had taken the requisite oaths of loyalty, levying a rate and paying the gaoler's and clerk's bills. On the other hand they were responsible for abating nuisances – which in 1800 ranged from inadequate guttering to obstruction of the highway with waggons and, 'one Pig running about Chipper Lane the property of John Nash' – as well as punishing more serious crimes. Offences which came before the justices in 1800 included selling short measures, regrating, keeping a disorderly house, assault and theft. A charge of what appears to be shoplifting – the theft of one pound of sugar, one pound of soap, one pint of brandy and a wine sieve – was found proven by the jury and the offender was sentenced to a year's imprisonment. By contrast an assault resulted in a fine of one half-penny.[22]

In view of the time spent by councillors discussing financial affairs and the princely fines demanded of defaulting office-holders, it is a little surprising that the city budget in 1800 amounted to no more than £420. So low a figure is explained partly by the existence of separate highway, poor and general rates levied by the city on a parochial basis – the poor rate alone reached a record £7,249 in 1800 – and partly by the absence of many of the services, such as education, housing and a salaried police force, which modern ratepayers take for granted. Much of the £420 was derived from the rents on city properties, and was spent on salaries, the payment of charitable bequests and miscellaneous items ranging from beadles' hats to firewood, lanterns and sealing-wax. Having failed to augment its income through fines the city council found that it had overspent in 1800 by more than £100 and had to call on the chamberlain to lend the city the deficit. Such years of crisis were common in the early nineteenth century, and the city finances were not helped by the activities of the chamberlain, George Maton who, when he died in 1816, was found to owe a personal debt to the city of more than £2,000.[23]

From an administration drawing to the end of its life – it was reformed in 1836 – we move forward to the year 1930, when the range of responsibilities undertaken by the city council was probably greater

than at any period before or since. During the intervening 130 years
Salisbury's population had more than trebled, and the city boundaries
had been repeatedly pushed further into the surrounding countryside.
One by one new powers were acquired, as Parliament responded to
social change by enacting more tasks for local government to perform.
In common with all the other dates we have described Salisbury city
council in 1930 had recently moved to a new home, having purchased
in 1927 an elegant mansion next to St. Edmund's Church, which is now
known as Bourne Hill. By far the largest expense during the year was on
education and council housing, each costing slightly over £30,000. The
housing budget contributed by the city's ratepayers, however, was very
small, as most of the money came from central government or from
rents. Road maintenance cost over £20,000, nearly half of which was
paid for by the county council; public health and the police force were
the two other major areas of expenditure, with much smaller amounts
(between £1,000 and £3,000) going on street lighting, the fire brigade
and the public library. At the bottom of the scale a host of miscellaneous
duties, such as rodent control (which cost £5 in 1930), flood prevention,
the mortuary and election expenses were paid from the public purse. In
all the city spent £137,000 on services during 1930/1931, of which half
came from rates and the remainder from government grants or the
county council.[24]

Policy was framed by committees and sub-committees, made up of
council members, which reported to monthly meetings of the full council. In 1930 there were more than twenty such committees, ranging
from the allotment committee and the publicity committee, which met
only once or twice during the year, to the most influential committees
– public health, watch, finance and general purposes – each of which
met more than a dozen times. A typical watch committee meeting considered a street collection, the chief constable's report, unsatisfactory
bus services, hackney carriages, fittings for a new police station, weights
and measures and arrangements for the infirmary carnival. The general
purposes committee dealt with road repairs and diversions, traffic control, street lighting, planning applications and telegraph poles, whilst
public health included slipper baths, infectious diseases, refuse disposal,
overcrowding and public conveniences.[25]

Rather than attempt to embrace all the city council's diverse responsibilities at this period it will be more satisfactory to concentrate on
a single item of business, and follow the decision-making process
through from beginning to end. In August 1929, following a promise of
government money to alleviate unemployment during the depression,
a Special Unemployment Grants Committee was established and met
to propose improvement schemes for the city which might qualify
for government aid. The most ambitious project involved the purchase
of land alongside the River Avon in order to construct a riverside walk
from Ashley Road, near the present cattle market, to Harnham. In-

cluded in this scheme was a proposal to buy a privately-owned road and tollbridge (now known as Nelson Road) which had been built across the river north of the city by Thomas Scamell in 1899 as a short cut between Fisherton and the Castle Road/Wyndham estate area (Figure 26, Plate 36). By the end of September 1929 the committee had discovered that the owners were prepared to sell the road and bridge to the council for £10,000 and recommended to the full council that the offer be accepted. A council meeting in early October considered the committee's recommendation and, despite criticism from some councillors that the price was too high and that the purchase of a tollbridge would do nothing to relieve unemployment, the motion was carried, with only three dissenting votes, that the offer should be accepted subject to a grant from the Ministry of Transport. The matter now passed out of the council's hands whilst approval was awaited from central government, and does not reappear in the committee's minutes until the following July. Meanwhile disquiet about the decision was voiced in a number of quarters. Not only was it felt that the council would be misusing the money by spending it in this way, but there were also more sinister innuendoes. The Salisbury Divisional Labour Party in December 1929 resolved: 'That this meeting ... protests against the proposed expenditure ... which would have the effect of improving the value of the land of a few individuals, and supports a motion ... that immediate steps be taken for the erection of baths, washhouses, the clearance of slums and improvements to the existing open spaces, which would benefit all the citizens.' The following month a letter in the *Salisbury Journal* claimed, 'Of course it is easy to see whose property will benefit now and in the future by the purchase of the toll bridge.' Salisbury Ratepayers Association pointed an accusing finger at Councillor Scamell, son of the bridge-builder and one of the trustees, and claimed that unless he were to resign because of his interest the sale would be illegal. By now the decision had taken on political overtones. Objecting to the Labour Party's accusations an editorial in the *Salisbury Journal* expressed a rather naive view: 'It cannot be emphasised too often that inside Salisbury Council Chamber politics are unknown. Practically every decision that takes place cuts clean across party politics.' Such an old-fashioned virtue came in for swift criticism from a correspondent – '[Salisbury] still prides itself upon what would be considered a reproach by any up-to-date city or town' – who then went on to compare unfavourably Salisbury's record for providing amenities with those of Labour-controlled city councils elsewhere. The Ratepayers Association directed their arrows at more personal targets, by suggesting that some councillors had no business ideas and appeared to base their claims on their prowess on the athletics field or with organisations unconnected with municipal work.[26]

By the end of January 1930 the political storm engendered by the decision had subsided and the matter was quietly forgotten for six

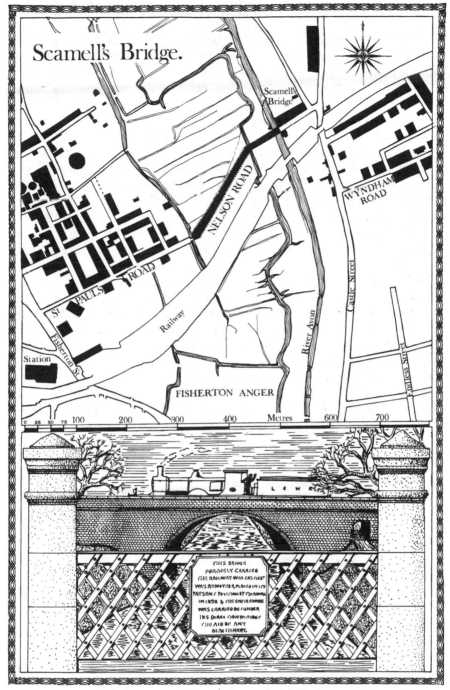

Figure 26. Scamell's Bridge and Nelson Road. The toll road and bridge were built in 1899 to connect new housing in the Wyndham Road area with Fisherton and the Railway Stations. The map depicts the extent of development *ca.* 1900. The illustration beneath the map is an artist's impression of the view southwards from the bridge, including one of the two plaques still in place on the bridge, which record its construction.

months. Criticism, when it eventually returned, was directed at the Special Unemployment Grants Committee, but its members were able to reply with total justification that they could not advance as fast as they would like because of vested interests on one side and ministerial controls on the other. Eventually in September 1930 the Divisional Road Engineer at the Ministry of Transport made his decision, which was that the asking price of £10,000 was too high, and that £6,250 was a realistic figure. The trustees disagreed, and in November told the council that the negotiations were at an end, but they soon relented, 'prompted by public feeling in the matter that it would benefit the city and would have been in accordance with their father's wishes.' In December 1930 the sale was agreed amid tributes and congratulations, but opposion was not quite silenced: 'I think we shall go down in history as the most extravagant council that ever represented the City of Salisbury.'[27]

The Scamell's Bridge affair was not, perhaps, the most important matter to be debated by Salisbury City Council in 1930; but it does bring into sharper relief some of the themes of local government which, for lack of evidence, we can only perceive dimly in the business of 1420, 1620 and 1800. Friction between individuals and cliques, the exploitation of molehills to make political mountains, the suspicion of vested interests and corruption, the tricks of passing the buck and judicious delay, the haggling over a fair price. These are the techniques of governing; and John Halle and John Ivie, Bishop Poore and Bishop Burnet have each in their time paid the toll to cross Scamell's Bridge.

CHAPTER SIX

Living

Do not discriminate against them because they are dead. Once they were alive. We may not know much about them, but they were real men and women, as real as we are now. Our problems were their problems, our pleasures and regrets were theirs. And so do not regard them as mere names, or puppets manipulated by the historian's strings. Try to think of them as people.

At School

Because we have all been to school we are apt to think of school as an inevitable part of our growth to maturity. Growth and maturity are inevitable, of course, but school, until the last century, was not the usual means of their attainment. In chapter three we discovered that for most of the city's history the majority of citizens were engaged in manual or craft industries. For such men and women schools were irrelevant; their education was by way of apprenticeship, and their training bestowed skills, insights and worldly wisdom unknown in a modern comprehensive. The history of formal education in Salisbury mirrors the changes in society and the growth of the professional and administrative classes. In our discussion we shall move from the medieval concept of school as a form of apprenticeship for a limited range of occupations, notably the Church, through the eighteenth-century idea of schools designed to turn out young ladies and gentlemen, to the Victorian reformers for whom education was a means of dispelling the vices of the poor, and culminating in today's educational panoply of school, colleges and evening classes for everyone.

Like other specialised trades and services of the medieval world schools were usually to be found in towns, and like the markets they served a large rural catchment area in addition to the town itself. Because medieval schools were geared chiefly to providing a supply of competent priests who would reinforce the hold of religion over society, it was the Church which established and controlled most medieval education. In view of this it would have been very surprising if a prosperous town and religious centre such as Salisbury had not also become a centre of learning. And indeed we find in medieval Salisbury every level of educational attainment, from the elementary teaching of reading and singing in the Choristers' School, through the study of Latin language and literature in the Grammar School, completed by a course in theology administered by the Cathedral clergy and even an attempt to found a university college. In fact the tradition of learning was not created by the new city's success, but was a legacy transferred from Old Sarum; one of the greatest of twelfth-century scholars, John of Salisbury, probably took his first lessons there, at a school which existed before 1091.[1]

The Choristers' School, although at the bottom of our educational ladder, was not an essential preliminary to the Grammar School. In fact at each level there was a good deal of overlapping between schools. There were fourteen choristers, chosen by the Dean and Chapter chiefly from boys of the diocese, and kept in the school from about the age of seven until their voices broke. From the fourteenth century onwards they were supported by rents from various properties and lived together in a house in the Close under the tutelage of a warden and a sub-master. The sub-master was mainly concerned to teach his charges to sing and read music, so that they could take part in services, but he was also required to supervise their grammar. The eccentricities of one master, Richard Southsex, which included a penchant for chasing poultry around farmyards and killing them with a sword, led to various complaints of embezzlement and immorality, as well as a dispute as to who was entitled to flog the boys. The choristers, too, had their moments. On 28th December each year, the feast of the Holy Innocents, it was customary for them to elect one of their number as the boy-bishop, who then presided at a solemn service in the Cathedral and received all the offerings made that day. But religious and musical duties apart the chorister schoolboys were required to attend the Grammar School and usually, when their voices broke, were promoted to the rank of 'altarist,' responsible for tending an altar in the Cathedral, which combined practical training for a clerical career with a continuing requirement to study at the Grammar School.[2]

The Choristers' School, although the best recorded, was probably not the only source of an elementary education in Salisbury. The city's two friaries would have included teaching in their ministrations, individual clergymen and free-lance schoolmasters probably took fee-paying students, and the city Grammar School, if, as seems likely, it was open to pupils who had not attended the Choristers' School, must have catered for a wide range of educational attainment. The Grammar School lay outside the Close, in Exeter Street near St. Ann's Gate, and it seems to have been identified with the city as well as the Cathedral. Nevertheless the responsibility for appointing a schoolmaster lay with the chancellor of the Cathedral, and it was through his negligence that the school sometimes failed to function. It existed in the thirteenth century and, like the choristers, may have been transplanted from Old Sarum. Between 1350 and 1470 a succession of schoolmasters is known, but thereafter the school seems to have disappeared. Its intake included, as we have seen, choristers and altarists, as well as the younger members of the vicars' choral – the next rung in the hierarchy of the Close – and probably fee-paying pupils from the city and elsewhere. The masters seem for the most part to have been minor clergy, and because they transferred to and from other grammar schools, we may assume that the standard of teaching was sometimes on a par with that available elsewhere.[3]

The student who had mastered reading and plainsong, and who had learnt the intricacies of the Latin language, was ready to embark on the study of theology. Theological training, like the Grammar School, was supervised by the chancellor, and seems to have taken place in a room next to the Cathedral library over the cloisters. The chancellor was supposed to appoint and pay for a lecturer who held a university degree in theology, but once again a rather half-hearted attitude was evident and sometimes no lectures took place. In part this may be explained by the presence of another institution in the city, De Vaux College, or the house of the Valley of Scholars, which in its early days had the trappings of a university college to rival Oxford. De Vaux College was established in 1262 by the Bishop of Salisbury, Giles of Bridport, as a home for twenty poor students studying theology and the liberal arts, with a warden and two chaplains, and supported by the rents from various properties in the diocese. Buildings were erected near Harnham Bridge and, although most were demolished in or before the nineteenth century, fragments of medieval work remain in the present De Vaux House and an adjacent building. The Bishop's intention was probably less to set up an institution to rival Oxford and Cambridge, than to cater for students who from as early as 1238 had resorted to Salisbury from Oxford. Nevertheless De Vaux College can rightly claim to pre-date the earliest Oxford college for secular scholars, Merton, by two years. By 1300 the possibility of Salisbury as a university city had waned, but De Vaux College remained until the reformation as a university college lying awkwardly more than 50 miles from the nearest university. Something of the careers of over one hundred students of De Vaux have been traced, and from these it seems that the typical student came from Salisbury diocese, was attached to the college but spent some time at Oxford where he obtained his degree before returning to Salisbury for ordination and one or more livings within the diocese. Not all students fitted this pattern and not all were theologians. Law and medicine might also be studied, although the diocesan authorities sometimes tried to dissuade students from these more lucrative occupations.[4]

The reformation brought to an end the Church's dominance in the field of education. De Vaux College was closed in 1542, and any teaching carried out by the two Salisbury friaries came to an end a few years earlier at their dissolution. But Salisbury also gained by these changes. The Grammar School, which seems to have lain dormant for seventy years, was revived in 1540 and moved into the Close. In doing so it strengthened its links with the choristers and quickly became identified as the Choristers' School and in due course as the Cathedral School (Plate 37). And a separate city Grammar School was begun in 1569, which we shall consider in due course. There were also changes in attitude, as the reformation coincided with the renaissance discovery of the classical world and its ideas of education as a civilising force. And so the schools which sprang up in Salisbury in the centuries after 1540 were no longer regarded as providing an apprenticeship for a life in the Church. That function returned to Salisbury only in 1860 when a Theological College was established in the Close. Meanwhile the emphasis turned to the equipping of young gentlemen and gentlewomen with the manners for a life in high society.[5]

Education in Salisbury from the close of the middle ages to the nineteenth century was provided by three types of school, a free grammar school, endowed charity schools, and private fee-paying schools. The establishment of a free grammar school, controlled by the city council, in 1569 was probably not the enlightened act that it may at first appear (Plate 38). On the one hand it seems to have been a political move in the dispute between Bishop and city, a counterblast to the Bishop's removal of the existing grammar school into the Close; and it also involved a piece of blatant deception, by which the city persuaded the exchequer that it should divert funds from existing schools at Trowbridge and Bradford-on-Avon to form the new school at Salisbury, on the grounds that the other towns had few inhabitants, and had 'small resort of gentlemen and merchants.' In fact, as we saw in chapter three, it was at precisely this period that the merchants of Bradford and Trowbridge were overtaking those of Salisbury in wealth and importance. Its inauspicious beginning may help to explain the Grammar School's rather mediocre performance over the three centuries of its existence. For a time it occupied a room in the George Inn, and was subjected to an investigation in 1608 on account of its decline. One cause of this decline was perhaps pinpointed when the school eventually moved into its own premises in Castle Street in 1624: 'The Scholehouse removed from the George because of the inconveniency of cominge to the schollers by the Taphouse and inne.' Rules drawn up by the city council a few years later make it clear that the school was intended for the children of poor citizens as well as the more affluent. The school was not in fact free; there was a quarterly charge of 7/6d per pupil, but this was waived in cases of poverty. How many poor children availed themselves of an education cannot be known, but by 1699 they were probably exceptional. In that year Thomas Naish recorded in his diary: 'I having observed a young lad of my parish to be very devout at the publick prayers of the Church, and inquiring who he was, I found his parents to be poor, and the youth not fit for work ... upon which I entered him at the free school in Salisbury under the tutelage of Mr. Taylor my worthy master.' The lad, Thomas Hibbert, went on to obtain his degree at Oxford, and subsequently became a schoolmaster and rector in Somerset. A century later the school came in for criticism again: 'We found upon inquiry that there has been little uniformity in the management of the school; and that from the change of times and inadequacy of the salary of the master far less benefit has for many years been derived from it than was contemplated by the founder.' But by now (1833) the school was in its death-throes. The Rev. Hodgson, appointed schoolmaster in 1804, grew old and the school grew old with him. By 1855 only seven pupils remained and the master visited the school briefly once or twice a week. When in 1864 he resigned the school boasted three pupils. Attempts to revitalise it continued for a few years, but without lasting success. The torch of learning had now passed into other hands.[6]

Between 1569 and the establishment of the earliest recorded charity school in Salisbury in 1718, an assortment of references to schools suggests that the free Grammar School had by no means a monopoly in the city. St. Edmund's Church provided a schoolroom, at various times in a storehouse, the east end of the chancel and over a vestry house. Teaching seems to have been carried out by the incumbent to supplement his stipend. Another school was begun in 1629 in part of the old Council House in St. Thomas's Churchyard. A Jacobite school in Salisbury was blamed for leading astray one young man who was executed in 1718 for treason. And two private schools in 1714 were vieing with each other over the wealth of their respective pupils.[7]

At least six endowed charity schools have existed in Salisbury, and all were established before 1760. A useful survey of charity education in Wiltshire in 1731 described three schools in Salisbury, educating between them two hundred pupils. Salisbury compares favourably with other Wiltshire towns, such as Devizes (86 pupils) and Bradford (75 pupils); many places, including Trowbridge, Warminster and Wilton, appear to have had no charity schools at this period. The three Salisbury schools, one in the workhouse, one endowed by the Bishop, and one in St. Edmund's parish endowed by subscriptions, aimed to provide a basic, practical education, which concentrated on reading and writing, and the basic skills of the woollen industry, spinning, knitting and carding. The children might be clothed by the charity as well as taught, but they were also expected to work, and the yarn which they spun was sold for the benefit of the school or their parents. None of these schools appears to have survived into the nineteenth century, but three others, established by individual bequests in 1718, 1726 and 1755, were still functioning in 1830, and one, the Godolphin School, survives to the present day. Talman's School, the latest of the three, was a typical charity school. The founder's intention was to provide instruction for eight poor girls of St. Thomas's parish for three years each in the arts of reading, needlework and the church catechism. He provided a house in High Street in which the school was held and in which the schoolmistress lived. She was not paid, but she could teach up to twenty fee-paying pupils in the house alongside the eight poor girls. The school seems to have functioned satisfactorily for about 80 years, from 1755 to about 1835, under the tutelage of only two mistresses, each of whom served about 40 years. Less typical was the Godolphin School, founded in 1726 for the education of young orphan gentlewomen, 'borne of parents of the Church of England and such as have some portion left them but not exceeding four hundred pounds.' The girls, aged between twelve and nineteen years, were to be taught to, 'Dance work Read write cast accounts and the business of Housewifry ... and shall be constantly obliged to attend the Service of the Church of England at all proper seasons.' The school was not in fact established until 1784, and from then until 1847 it occupied various premises in the Close, before moving to Milford Hill to escape a cholera epidemic. Prim and monotonous, the dull respectability of Victorian Godolphin was remembered with mixed feelings: 'Our day began with a Bible Class ... I think this was before breakfast. We repeated by heart I think three verses from the Bible, and if we even missed one word we lost a mark ... We learnt a "History in All Ages", with very long answers in small print ... The education was poor. We learnt Mangnall's *Questions*, I believe, and Mitchell's *Catechist*, and I rolled off answers and names such as quartz, feltspar, with no idea whatever as to what they were like or their uses. ... We walked out, mostly in pairs, every day, and the rest of the time was devoted to lessons which went on till tea-time, and I think the evening was spent in preparation work. Looking back, it seems to me we were always at it. Directly after dinner we lay extended on the floor with an old copy book under our heads for an hour, learning the lessons by heart which we had to say next day.'[8]

The Godolphin School in the nineteenth century had more in common with the host of private and dame schools which existed in the city than with the charity schools for the poor. These private schools existed in the seventeenth century, as we have seen, and became more numerous in the eighteenth century, although it is difficult to quantify the work they were doing until government reports and trade directories proliferated after 1800. The flavour of the pre-Victorian private academy, however, can be tasted from various sources, such as the prospectus of Mrs Voysey, whose establishment for properly educating young ladies was (*ca.* 1770) the King's House in the Close. In an attempt to, 'render them lovely to Society, and pleasing to themselves,' her charges were subjected to, 'experience the charming effects [of early rising], by being in School at *Six o'clock*, in the morning, during the Summer Months.' Besides an exacting curriculum, which included French and English, writing, arithmetic, music, dancing, drawing, geography and all kinds of needlework and embroidery, her pupils were to be, 'daily refreshed with intervals of cheerful recreation and agreeable exercise, whereby the task of Learning is blended sweetly with real pleasure and delight.' Teaching, though not a particularly highly esteemed profession in eighteenth-century society, was a suitable calling for the self-made man or woman, who discovered a talent for the arts or sciences and had the enthusiasm to pursue it. Such a man was Joseph Moon, teacher of the mathematics in Salisbury in 1791, who was remembered with affection by Henry Hatcher. As a servant boy his interest in geometry had led him to purchase mathematical instruments and compasses. When these dangerous weapons were discovered by the female servants he was thought to be contemplating suicide, but as a result his talent was recognised and he was enabled to study and become a teacher. 'Could he have conquered his shy and diffident temper,' wrote Hatcher, '[he] might perhaps have been better known ... Those who were acquainted with Mr. Moon, will long cherish his memory, and recollect with a mixture of pleasure and regret, his harmless oddities, his quaint yet ready wit, and his native kindness of disposition. He delighted in a pun, and sometimes his puns were good.' Henry Hatcher, the historian of Salisbury, was himself a schoolmaster in Salisbury for many years, commencing in 1823, and he recorded some of his feelings in letters to his friend, John Britton. He took a house in Fisherton, later moving to Endless Street, and began with ten pupils. In 1829 he wrote: '.., With half a hundred noisy and idle youths to superintend, it is not possible to give long and steady attention to anything ... However, there is one comfort: the trade of a schoolmaster is the best in point of profit that I have yet exercised, and I prefer solid pudding to empty praise.' Despite his boredom with Latin grammar he was impressed with the financial rewards – 'it will enable me to do something for old age or a wet day' – and like many similar practitioners he accepted his lot with gratitude: 'I am philosopher enough to think this the *summum bonum*.'[9]

Hatcher takes his place in the directories of 1830 and 1842 alongside many another schoolteacher. The 24 private schools listed in 1830 were scattered unevenly around the city. Castle Street was the favourite address, with no fewer than seven, as well as the free Grammar School; the remainder favoured the quieter peripheral areas away from the High Street and Market Place, such as the Close and the St. Ann Street area. Most schools were shortlived – only six of the 24 appeared in a similar list in 1822 and only three spanned the twenty years from 1822 to 1842. An incomplete survey of private education in 1833 recorded 236 pupils in nine schools, but was unable to collect statistics for another six, and seems to have ignored some of the small dame schools altogether. In 1851 a more accurate count discovered 25 private schools teaching a total of 408 pupils, over 60% of them female. This modest growth in private education, which has continued into the present century, was nevertheless outstripped by the development of schools for working-class children, and it is these which must next take the stage.[10]

Between 1780 and 1870 education ceased to be the exception and became the rule. This was no simple, sudden revolution, and its causes were many and various. The collapse of the old apprenticing crafts and their replacement by mechanical, factory skills, the shift from a scattered rural population to a frightening urban multitude, the sharpening of social divisions, the demise of an old morality, and the vices of a new condemned by an intolerant religion, the fear of a French revolution in England – to many people education seemed to offer a panacea. And Salisbury, though not affected to the extent of the new industrial cities, reflected in microcosm the turmoils and anxieties of the nation.

First to stir was the Church of England, in the person of Bishop Barrington, who arrived in Salisbury in 1782. Within nine months of taking office he had sent a questionnaire to each incumbent in preparation for his first visitation, asking among other things about the extent of education in each parish and the priest's role in preparing young people for catechism. The answers from the Salisbury parishes were not encouraging: the Rector of St. Edmund's replied that in his parish there was no public school, and as for religious instruction, 'The laudable custom is impracticable, unless the incumbent could afford to keep an assistant or two; but this the uncertainty and the smallness of the income will not permit of.' But this was the age of the Sunday school, the attempt to inculcate a mixture of learning, religion and respect for society into a child on the one day when that society was not exploiting his labour. In Salisbury the nonconformist Sunday schools seem to have fared better than those of the established church. By 1805, when its earliest surviving register begins, the city's Wesleyan Sunday school was attracting around 130 children to its morning and afternoon sessions. The school roll in the 1820s and 1830s fluctuated between 300 and 400 children, although truancy was rife. Teaching was carried out by unqualified volunteers, whose number rose from eight in 1805 to eighteen in 1836, thus permitting a very generous pupil-teacher ratio. The first aim of the Sunday school was evangelistic, not educational; in 1828 it was claimed that, 'the zealous and affectionate exertions of the Sunday School Managers have rescued many juvenile wanderers in the paths of vice and their minds have been deeply impressed with the truths of the Gospel of the Blessed God ...' The Wesleyan Sunday school was the largest and most successful, but it was not alone. In 1819 each of the three city parishes had a Church of England Sunday school, and there were at least four belonging to nonconformists. By 1833 over 1,200 children were attending seven Sunday schools in the city, and the nonconformist churches catered for three-quarters of them. There was also a Sunday school for children in the workhouse. Eighteen years later the numbers were similar, but nearly half now attended the Church of England Sunday schools.[11]

By 1851 Sunday schools were no longer the sole educational opportunity for most children; they had become an extra, offering religious enlightenment to the pupils and a peaceful Sunday morning to their parents. Some Sunday schools had developed into, or become associated with, day schools, and one, the St. Edmund's parish Sunday school, seems to have fluctuated between day-school and Sunday-school status. But a landmark in Salisbury's day-school provision was the opening of the first National School in the city in 1812, which quickly became established in a converted malthouse near St. Martin's Church. As originally planned, the school was to cater for deserving children nominated by subscribers to the project: 'Subscribers are earnestly requested not to recommend the children of parents who can afford to pay for their education; but at the same time, it is by no means to be understood, that those who with scanty earnings have meritoriously defrayed the expence of putting their children to school, should be excluded from the benefit of this institution.' The initial intake of 185 children had risen to 300 by 1814, 360 in 1819 and 1833, and then fallen slightly to a little under 300 in 1851. Not everyone was convinced of its value. The Rector of St. Martin's, who perhaps lived too close for comfort, wrote in 1819 that: 'The poorer classes have the privilege of attending the national school, which very much supersedes the want that exists within themselves.' The St. Martin's National School was intended to serve the whole city, as well as seven adjoining parishes, but it was soon complemented by other day schools. Between 1825 and 1850 both the other city parishes began their own schools, a Wesleyan School was held in a converted chapel in Salt Lane, a British School (for nonconformists) commenced in a new building in Scots Lane, and another National School (for Anglicans) was opened in Fisherton Anger. In the city (excluding Fisherton) by 1851 there were eight public day schools catering for over 900 children, which was the equivalent of almost the entire population of Salisbury children between the ages of five and ten.[12]

In the wake of this remarkable demand for education came a demand for trained teachers. The stern regime of drudgery, hunger and religious instruction which oppressed the fictional Sue Bridehead on her arrival at Salisbury Training College has immortalised the institution in literature, and Hardy's description, in *Jude the obscure*, was true enough to life. His own sister, Mary Hardy, had trained there in the 1860s, and, like Sue, had fallen foul of the authorities on account of her activities in the river. And a volume of reminiscences by former pupils, published four years before *Jude*, confirms to the letter Hardy's evocation. The Training College, established by Salisbury diocese in 1841 to supply female teachers to the church schools of the diocese and beyond, was complemented by a similar establishment for male teachers at Winchester, and together they set an example which was widely copied elsewhere. During the first twenty years of its existence, under the leadership of the redoubtable Mrs Duncan, numbers increased from one to 60 students, the college moved into the King's House in the Close, and the stamp of rigorous Victorian discipline began to be impressed on generations of young ladies. Classes were held in all the subjects which the students would be required to teach – English, history, geography, music, needlework, arithmetic, drawing, domestic economy and scripture, with more scripture added for good measure; they were also subjected to teaching practice, either in the model school which the college itself ran for a few years or in one of the local Salisbury schools. Students' attitudes and performance depended largely on their background – a day spent washing, mangling and ironing in the college laundry came as a rude shock to a young lady of genteel upbringing – and on their previous experience of teaching. Many had spent several years as pupil teachers before being sent to the college. Most looked back on their college days with a wistful mixture of respect, affection and discomfort (Plate 39).[13]

Salisbury Training College, along with its counterpart in the Close, the Theological College opened in 1860, were the sole representatives of higher education in the mid-Victorian city. In 1871, when the provision of education for all children was made a requirement, no fewer than 42 schools were at work in Salisbury teaching over 2,000 pupils at various levels of academic attainment. The majority were privately run by a single teacher, ranging in size from the Zillwoods' establishment in Bedwin Street (this run by a husband and wife) catering for 82 pupils, to Miss Snow in St. Ann Street with only two. Fifteen pupils were the average, and the schools were scattered all around the city, including Fisherton and the developing suburbs. But prolific though they may have been, these were not the schools which most Salisbury children attended. Four out of five went to one of the city's large elementary schools, run in most instances by the Church of England or one of the nonconformist denominations. The largest, St. Edmund's National School, with nearly 500 pupils, occupied purpose-built premises near the church, which in 1871 were only eleven years old (Plate 40). The pupils were segregated into boys, girls and infants, and each group was taught in a separate school room measuring about sixteen by six metres. A smaller classroom led off each, and the girls' school had a second classroom and a bonnet room. The teacher's house adjoined the school and its encompassing playground, and here a special room was provided as a 'retiring room for practising teachers,' where girls from the training college could recover their nerves between lessons. At St. Thomas's National School the arrangements were similar, boys and girls occupying separate floors and master's house and playground adjoining, but no infants were taught and the accommodation was slightly smaller. The original National School, near St. Martin's Church, was still functioning, and these three, together with Fisherton National School, accommodated more than half the city's schoolchildren. The remainder, if they were not at a private school, attended one of the two British Schools run by nonconformists, in Scots Lane and Dews Road, Fisherton, or St. Osmund's Roman Catholic School in Exeter Street, an infant school in Gigant Street, or, if they were particularly poor, a ragged school also in Gigant Street.[14]

As we approach the last century of Salisbury's schools, we find that, neither for the first nor the last time, factors other than the purely educational were at work. Financial, political and religious considerations all contributed to an unhappy episode, dubbed, 'the educational crisis in Salisbury,' which culminated in a debate in Parliament and has left its legacy in the pattern of schools which to some extent remains today. The scene was set by the passing of Forster's Education Act by the Liberal government in 1870, which envisaged the establishment of non-denominational board schools under the control of local school boards. The prospect of a board school in Salisbury was welcomed by the nonconformist faction, who went so far as to close two of their schools in an attempt to force the new school board's hand. But from its inception the elected school board was controlled by an Anglican majority, who sought repeatedly to supply the deficiencies in Salisbury's education by extending the existing church schools. A stalemate continued for eighteen years until the end of 1888, when the Scots Lane British (i.e. nonconformist) School failed to satisfy a government inspection and closed. Still the Anglican members of the school board were unwilling to entertain a board school, and under the patronage of the Bishop, John Wordsworth, they inaugurated the Salisbury Church Day School Association to fight the nonconformists' modest demands. Wittingly or unwittingly the Bishop seems to have provoked the displeasure of the parents of the closed British School by opening a room in his palace as a temporary school for their children – only 43 out of 236 chose to attend. During 1889 the dispute moved from its financial phase (with arguments about the higher cost of providing board schools, the ability of nonconformists to subsidise their own schools and the unfairness of rating nonconformists to pay for Anglican schools) into its religious phase (the quality of religious instruction in the various types of school, the meaning of the conscience clause in the Education Act which permitted nonconformist children to withdraw from lessons on Anglican doctrine, the status of parish priests in respect to board schools) and then escalated into a political phase. This point had been reached by September 1889 when the Liberal peer, Lord Fitzmaurice, wrote to one of the nonconformist leaders as follows: 'The manner in which the Liberals and Nonconformists of Salisbury have recently allowed the education of your town to be monopolised by the Church parties has been a source of great discouragement to many, as the evil of the example goes far beyond the limits of the district immediately affected. Mr Mundella [a former Liberal education minister], whom I have recently seen, has spoken to me very strongly on the subject.' A few weeks later a noisy and, by Victorian standards, acrimonious public meeting took place in Salisbury, addressed by another prominent Liberal educationalist, Lyulph Stanley, at which Bishop Wordsworth was given the right of reply. A rash remark by the Bishop was reported in the national press: 'Now as long as he was Bishop of Salisbury he would never allow board schools to be introduced into this town as long as he had a penny in his pocket (cheers and hooting).' Worse was to follow: a long series of letters between the Bishop and Mr Mundella attacking each other's conduct and interpretation of the affair appeared in *The Times* and eventually in March 1890 the conduct of Salisbury School Board in opposing the formation of a board school was debated in the House of Commons.[15]

As the dispute took its course the Bishop and the Anglican faction on the school board made a desperate, and ultimately successful, attempt to meet their responsibilities without resort to a board school, by building new church schools. Bishop Wordsworth was particularly eager to establish a boys' secondary school in the city, and he announced his intention in June 1889 to build and endow such a school. Although deferentially welcomed, his proposal came in for criticism at the public meeting already alluded to. He explained to that meeting that: 'They [i.e. the Bishop and his colleagues] did not want in any school of that kind all the roughest boys of the place – but they wanted to have rather a selecter class.' This was too much for the Liberal speaker: 'He had no patience with that middle class prejudice that would not allow a boy of the working classes to come between their nobility and the working classes. The school board system ... did more to break down these hateful class distinctions than almost anything else.' Undeterred, the Bishop's school was completed in April 1890, and along with three other new church schools – St. Mark's, St. Paul's Road and the George Herbert School – was dedicated at a ceremony performed by the Bishop to coincide with the diocesan synod. The church had won, and its victory held until 1924, but the Bishop's unease at the cost of his victory is reflected in his speech to the synod: 'You will not, I hope, think that I have been an unfaithful steward of the church's revenues in expending a comparatively large sum upon these schools. Nor will you consider that I am carried away by an idea when I ask you each in your own locality to do like work for the church, even if it be at a considerable sacrifice ...'[16]

The excitement of 1889 and 1890 was followed by a long period of stability. Salisbury City Council took over from the school board responsibility for the city's elementary education in 1903, and continued the state of affairs it inherited until after the first world war. In 1903 each of the six church schools – St. Thomas's, St. Edmund's, St. Martin's, St. Mark's, Fisherton and George Herbert – was divided into three departments, for boys, girls and infants. Most had around 500 pupils, fairly evenly distributed between the three departments, but Fisherton School was considerably larger and the George Herbert School, the former ragged school, was much smaller. Besides the church schools a small Roman Catholic school, St. Osmund's, provided a further 140 places, and was the only mixed school administered by the council. Each department was in the charge of a principal certificated teacher, whose salary amounted on average to £114 per annum, and they were assisted by nearly 60 other teachers of various levels of competence and twenty pupil teachers. Between 1903 and 1945, when the city handed its educational responsibility to the county council, the total number of schoolchildren receiving an elementary education remained fairly constant, around the 3,000 mark, and all but a few hundred lived within the city boundary. That boundary, however, was redrawn twice during the period, so that existing schools at East and West Harnham (in 1904) and Bemerton (in 1927) came within the city's ambit during the period.

Some reorganisation of the church schools took place in 1920 and 1926, and in 1924 the first non-denominational council school was opened, on a site amid new housing in Highbury Avenue, Fisherton. A second council school was built nearby, in Devizes Road, in 1940.[17]

Something of the flavour of school life during and between the two wars may be recreated from surviving school log books. The first war affected the teachers more than the children. At St. Martin's Boys School three of the five staff had left for military service by the end of 1916, to be replaced by female supply teachers. Two returned, and one subsequently became headmaster, but the third was killed in action during the final weeks of the war, and the news was sorrowfully recorded in the log book that Bertrand Young, after nineteen years at the school, would not be coming back. But there had been happier moments, such as the half-holiday awarded in December 1916 when it was learned that a former pupil had been awarded the Victoria Cross. The end of the war brought changes to the organisation of the school as well as to its staffing, and there was a chance to try out new ventures. An 'annual educational excursion' took place – in 1926 they visited the principal parts of London and made instructive visits to the Tower, Westminster Abbey and the zoo, for 10/6d inclusive. After beating Bowerchalke School at cricket on a July Saturday a fortnight later both teams and a few friends were invited by the headmaster to tea. Later in the year came the Christmas party, which was followed (and perhaps marred) by a full rehearsal of the chief items in the programme for the annual school concert to take place two days later. Boys aged between seven and fourteen years attended the school and were graded for teaching purposes according to attainments from standard one (the lowest) to standard seven. Classes might, therefore, include a considerable age range, so that in 1927 the standard five class consisted of one bright ten-year-old and two rather dull fourteen-year-olds as well as 26 other pupils in between. At the same period twelve-year-olds could be found in each class from standard three to standard six. Examinations in arithmetic and English took place in March, and oral and written examinations in the whole gamut of subjects taught rounded off the summer term. English set books in 1920 ranged from *Tom Brown's Schooldays* for standards six and seven, *Robinson Crusoe* for standard four, *Tales of the Fairies* for standard two, to *Alice in Wonderland* and *The Lost Pigs* for standard one.[18]

Meanwhile St. Martin's junior girls' school had other preoccupations. In November 1927 fifty-one girls were taken to the cinema to see 'Ben-Hur,' and by 1936 a 'Pet's day,' when children's pets were put on show in the school field, had become a successful regular event. An inspector's report of 1936 summed up the school curriculum: 'Careful training is given in the 3Rs, including clear articulation in reading and recitation and neat setting-out of the written exercises in English and Arithmetic. Good progress is also being made in needlework, drawing, physical training, singing, geography and history. An interesting series of visits has been organised to link up the work of the school with the simple geography, history and industries of the locality.' War, declared during the summer holidays of 1939, disrupted the curriculum for a while, but soon a certain normality returned, punctuated by frequent air raid warnings. Trenches had been built for the girls on Milford Hill, and they were frequently visited between 1940 and 1942. During the apprehensive spring of 1940 respirators were issued and checked, air raid practices were held and a gentleman from the Ministry of Information came to speak to the children about the dangers of idle talk. Also during 1940, and for much of the war, the school played host to evacuees from Portsmouth who came with their teachers, and at times formed as many as one-third of the school population. But the wartime spirit was maintained, and whereas in earlier less stringent days the school was closed if the lavatories were frozen (a frequent occurrence at St. Martin's in winter) when this occurred in January 1945 it was decided to keep the classes occupied and to allow children to remain at school if they wished, going home when necessary. The new heating system, installed during the same month, was not a success – indeed ten months later it was to prove disastrous, as it caused a fire which led to the school's permanent closure.[19]

The transfer of responsibility for education in Salisbury from the city to the county council in 1945 marks a convenient point for our discussion to close. It is too soon to offer a balanced assessment of the changes which have occurred since then, and the changes which, in 1982, are still in the offing. However, it is worth reflecting on the range of educational opportunity which now exists in the city, and how it has come about. The most marked expansion has been in the development of large secondary schools, with rolls of between 700 and 1,100, lying for the most part on virgin sites at the city's periphery. A reputable secondary school was, as we have seen, Bishop Wordsworth's aim, and between 1902 and 1927 his school provided secondary education for an increasing number of girls as well as boys. In 1927 two of the existing city schools, St. Thomas's and St. Edmund's, were reorganised into senior schools for boys and girls respectively, and in the same year a girls' grammar school, the South Wilts School for Girls, was opened by Wiltshire County Council. Bishop Wordsworth's School became once again a male preserve, and achieved public school status in 1936. After the war, with the implementation of the 1944 Education Act, new secondary modern schools were built, and one – Westwood St. Thomas – has subsequently become a comprehensive, and the largest school ever to have existed within the city boundaries.[20]

Progress in secondary education has been matched in other fields. The College of Technology, installed since 1963 in modern premises on the Southampton Road, fulfils a need which has been recognised ever since a Mechanics Institute was established in 1833; and its newer neighbour, the College of Art, was also anticipated in the nineteenth century, by a School of Art housed in Hamilton Hall, the gaudy polychromatic building in New Street, which was built in 1871 as a Literary and Scientific Institution. A public library was set up in the city following a referendum in 1890, nearly a century after Salisbury's first circulating library. In 1905 it moved into purpose-built accommodation in Chipper Lane, and seventy years later it has moved again, into a sumptuous modern building which hides behind the Market House facade. Another recent removal has been the Salisbury and South Wiltshire Museum. Founded in 1861 it was originally known, rather unromantically, as the drainage collection, on account of the items recovered during the removal of the canals which formed its original nucleus. After more than a century in premises in St. Ann Street it is now fulfilling its educational role in the King's House, a building which we have already encountered as both Mrs Voysey's academy and the diocesan training college.[21]

At Church

Salisbury is not a city of churches. Norwich and Bristol, Winchester and York, may have had a church on every corner, but Salisbury only began after the age of the tiny city parish was over. Apart from the Cathedral there are only three medieval churches in Salisbury, each quite different in character, and each seeming to reflect a facet of the religion which gave it birth. St. Thomas's, with one foot in the High Street and one foot in the Market Place, represents the civic face of medieval religion, the official church wrapped up in the city and its affairs. St. Martin's, older and wiser than Salisbury, tucked in its comfortable backwater at the city limits, represents the awe and mystery of medieval devotion (Plate 41). St. Edmund's, now an arts centre and no longer used for worship, with bright paint and spotlights, stage and curtains, represents the boisterous fun of medieval processions and earthy religious celebrations. To understand what churchgoing meant in the middle ages we must look at all three, and try to draw from their architecture and their archives something of the flavour of their worship.

Although they were all in being within 50 years of the city's foundation, the church buildings which greet us today are largely the result of Salisbury's fifteenth-century prosperity. Most of St. Thomas's Church was rebuilt after 1448, St. Martin's nave, aisles and chapels were reconstructed or built anew a few years earlier, and the surviving portion of St. Edmund's, the chancel, can also be dated to the early years of the fifteenth century. Two other survivors add to our knowledge of church life at this period: the churchwardens' accounts of St. Edmund's, which from 1443 record the day-to-day financial affairs of the parish; and the magnificent doom painting in St. Thomas's Church, which is a powerful statement of medieval theology at the end of the fifteenth century. From these pieces of evidence and by analogy with other places we can comment on what went on in the Salisbury churches, what were the religious beliefs underlying their activities, and how they were organised and paid for.[22]

The medieval church was both broader and narrower than its present-day counterpart – broader in the sense that it impinged on areas of human activity, such as local government and recreation, to which it is now largely alien, and narrower in that it was not greatly concerned with intellectual debate. The medieval worshipper attended church on Sunday to take part in a ritual, to listen to words in a language which he did not understand and to observe a ceremony which, in its subtler nuances, was for the most part lost on him. A list of the service books used in conducting worship at St. Edmund's in 1472 has survived, and includes missals, processionals, antiphoners, 'grayles' and other works totalling 52 volumes altogether. A brass lectern in the shape of an eagle, and contemporary with the list, survives at St. Martin's Church. Behind such a lectern, and dressed in one of the church's fine vestments, such as the 'Sute of white Damask wrought with eglys [eagles] of goolde,' stood the priest, reciting the Latin mass from his service book, and with the musical accompaniment, at St. Edmund's at least, of an organ, or pair of organs. But although the worship was rooted in tradition, there are signs that in Salisbury, as elsewhere, in the fifteenth century, changes were taking place. Seats for the worshippers had made their appearance at St. Edmund's by 1456, so enabling the priest to make his services longer and include, if he wished, a sermon or period of instruction. A fifteenth-century pulpit for this purpose, formerly in St. Martin's, is now in the Victorian church of St. Mark's. Also symbolising a desire to instruct the congregation is an item of expenditure in the accounts of St. Edmund's for 1474–1475, which records that seventeen pence were spent, 'in parchement for Seint Osmunde is story.'[23]

The regular Sunday observance of the mass was supplemented by the special occasions of the church year and by special services to mark landmarks in the parishioners' lives – christenings, marriages and burials. Each of the three city churches has preserved a thirteenth-century font, thus emphasising the importance attached to baptism. Weddings took place in the church porch and were followed by the nuptial mass inside the church. The door which opened into the church from the south porch of St. Edmund's was known as the 'wedding door'. When death was imminent the 'forthfare' bell was rung to signify that a soul was to 'fare forth' on its last journey. Its ringing summoned the priest to the deathbed to administer the last rites, and for this purpose in 1481–1482 the churchwardens of St. Edmund's spent sevenpence on 'a lantern bought for church use to be carried night and day with the altar sacrament'. Two years later a further eightpence was spent on 'one pound of wax bought for the light carried with the sacrament during the visitation of the sick'. The involvement of the church in the celebration of death accounted for a fair proportion of its income. As well as charging for the forthfare bell there was a fee for ringing a knell (when death took place) and at the burial service, a charge of 6/8d was made for burying within the church, and the mourners could hire from the church a cross, a candlestick and a black pall for the funeral service. The best cross and candlestick cost one shilling, the second best were fourpence. In addition it was customary for the church to benefit in the will of the deceased.[24]

St. Edmund's churchwardens' accounts have little to tell us about the major festivals which punctuated the weekly ritual, but it is clear that they were numerous and that each was celebrated in a special way. A payment was regularly made to boys who carried a banner in procession at Rogationtide, Whit Sunday, Trinity Sunday and Corpus Christi; veils were placed over the rood (crucifix) and the high altar during Lent, special lights were burned at Christmas, and the feast days of the various saints to whom altars in the church were dedicated were observed in distinctive fashion. The custom during Holy Week was to place the host (the bread and wine) in an Easter Sepulchre, or wooden model of the Lord's tomb. Here it was shrouded with two palls of cloth of gold and closely guarded by watchers until Easter Sunday, when with great ceremony it was elevated to the high altar for the eucharist service. Less appealing to modern tastes would have been the Whitsun ceremony at St. Edmund's of the 'Dawnse of Powles,' or 'danse macabre,' at which a large painting of a dancing skeleton was paraded inside the church, to remind worshippers of their mortality.[25]

The mysteries of atonement and incarnation, at the centre of Christian dogma, could not easily be impressed on the medieval mind through the vehicle of a dead, foreign language. Instead the church had recourse to symbols of various sorts, embedded in liturgy, architecture, stained glass and mural decoration. There are in England few more striking survivals of the latter than the doom painting over the chancel arch of St. Thomas's Church, which was painted at the end of the fifteenth century, covered with whitewash a century later, discovered briefly in 1819 and repainted to something like its original condition in 1881. Here is a medieval guidebook to heaven and hell, more vivid and direct than any theological treatise (Plate 42); as we gaze at it and try to understand we find that for once we are on an equal footing with the congregation for whom it was made 500 years ago. The painting occupies all the space above the chancel arch and continues down the spandrels on either side. In the centre, above the point of the arch, sits Christ in majesty, his feet resting on the world, a rainbow behind him. His hands are raised to display the wounds of crucifixion and behind him are the cross and the objects of his humiliation. His expression is solemn, just, serene. To left and right is the kingdom of heaven in the guise of a close-set thickly-populated medieval city, and beneath his feet, in a long line, are ranged the twelve apostles. John the Evangelist and the Virgin Mary kneel to his left and right. Emerging from a graveyard are naked souls, roused from sleep and helped to their feet by angels with trumpets. Some are being led into the eternal city, others are hauled down the opposite spandrel into the jaws of a terrible yawning monster, while a grimacing caricature of a devil points encouragement. The message of course is clear, direct and unequivocal, and the effect of staring at this 'permanently-exposed lantern slide', (in the words of one scholar) for a lifetime of Sundays is not hard to imagine. Familiarity leads the eye to search for details – there is a lady trying to bribe her way out of hell by offering the devil a pot of ale, below her a man endeavours to rescue two moneybags from the gaping abyss, a king and a queen and a bishop wait patiently in the queue for damnation. Even on the day of judgement the devil breaks the rules – he has one foot outside the painting, kicking over the tracery. By contrast with the nether regions heaven looks sturdy, comfortable, and lived-in, a pastiche of halos, wings and medieval architecture, with pious faces at the windows staring down at the apocalyptic events below.[26]

It is a fearful painting, preying on the guilt and insecurity of medieval life. The human response to the Church's superhuman threat, of course, was to take every possible precaution to avoid the fires of hell, including not only absolution during one's lifetime from sins committed, but also the protection of prayers for one's soul offered by later generations. Wills of the period frequently make financial provision for such prayers, either on the anniversary of the death, or at regular intervals, or for a limited period afterwards. William Kensyngton's will, made in 1437, is fairly typical. He left his body to be interred in St. Edmund's Church, with 6/8d for the burial, various bequests of money and plate to the Cathedral, the city churches, nearby village churches and the two city friaries. 'Also it is my will that a suitable chaplain should commemorate my soul, the souls of my family and of all the faithful departed for the space of a whole year; and that this priest should receive for his work eight marks ($£2.13.4d$) with bread, wine and wax.' If funds permitted more elaborate precautions could be taken to ensure salvation. William Swayne's munificence in building the south chapel of St. Thomas's Church after 1448 was partly inspired by selfish motives, in that he wished to establish a chantry for the benefit of his own soul and those of his family. In 1472 he appointed a chaplain, Richard Beton, whose principal duty was to perform a daily mass in the chantry for his soul, and subsequent appointments continued, if not to eternity as Swayne had intended, at least until the chantry system was abolished nearly 70 years later. Today's visitor to the chapel is still exhorted to 'Pray for the soul of James the father of William Swayne,' and 'Pray for the souls of William Swayne and Chrystian his wife,' by inscriptions on the beams of the roof. But few men could afford the luxury of so much prayer. A much cheaper alternative was to take a share in a chantry, by becoming a member of a fraternity organised for the purpose, or by sponsoring a chaplain through a trade guild. Each of the city churches had several altars or chapels sponsored by fraternities and guilds, and one, the Confraternity of Jesus Mass at St. Edmund's, is particularly well documented. By 1500 it had acquired (through the bequests of its former members) six properties in Salisbury which together earned twenty marks (£6.13.4d) in rent each year. Offerings and legacies collected during the year amounted to about the same, and so the confraternity had over £13 to spend on masses and services at their altar. The guilds, too, (as we saw in Chapter three) financed chapels and kept lists (known as bede-rolls) of the names of deceased guildsmen for whom prayers had to be offered. The tailors' bede-roll, which probably dates from about 1495, includes the instruction: 'Also ye shall p'y [pray] for all the soulis of all the brethern and susterne beinge quicke and dede & in speciall for the soulis of thes which wer speciall good doers in ther lyves. Also yowe shall praye for the soules that ar departede owt off this worlde.' Thirty-three names follow, and particular benefactions are noted.[27]

Whether we regard it as piety or superstition, such a trade had a number of practical implications for the medieval church and community. The first was the sheer number of clergymen employed to tend the altars, celebrate masses and pray for dead souls. A century before the period we have been studying, when chantries dedicated to individuals were especially numerous, a poll-tax return records that 68 priests of various kinds worked in the three city churches. The list of staff of St. Thomas's Church in 1432 makes impressive reading: 21 priest vicars, sixteen deacon vicars, eleven subdeacon vicars, nine chantry priests – 57 clergymen serving between 2,000 and 3,000 parishioners. A second consequence of the chantry trade concerned the relationship between the church and secular government. In chapter five we discovered that the city's ruling oligarchy, in its ceremonial and religious guise, was known as the guild of St. George; as such it maintained a chapel, probably in St. Thomas's Church, and acknowledged benefactions of property to the mayor and corporation by enrolling donors' names on its bede-roll. The link was strengthened by the mayor's chaplain, who was also the chaplain of the guild of St. George and seems to have served in St. Thomas's Church alongside other chaplains. This overlap between religious and secular institutions was extended in other directions, as is shown by a note in a city ledger of 1457 which suggests that council meetings were sometimes held in one of the city churches. Special seats were reserved in church for the mayor and corporation in the sixteenth century, and perhaps earlier; it is likely, too, that the important mayor-making ceremony was performed in church. A third consequence for the churches lay in the association between themselves and the powerful craft guilds. Two of the most important guilds, the tailors and the weavers, seem to have adopted St. Thomas's and St. Edmund's respectively as their guild churches, and so brought their wealth and influence within the community to bear on them, with the result that both churches gained spiritually and materially.[28]

Then, as now, much of the energy of individual congregations was spent on fund-raising activities in order to meet the salaries of clergy, to buy wax for candles and to carry out all manner of repairs to the fabric and fittings of the church. The three main areas of income in the fifteenth century – gifts, charges and social events – are annually represented in the surviving accounts of St. Edmund's Church. During the year 1473–1474, for instance, gifts totalling £16.6.4d were received by the church; nearly £5 of this was raised from various collections gathered at easter, whilst the remainder came in bequests, ranging from sixpence left to the church by Robert King, to 'the gift of Nichol Mason and others to the church works, £6.3.7½d.' Some benefactors stipulated what their money was to be spent on – 'the by quest of John Chapman to the new casting of the greete bell and to the reparacion of the stepull' – whilst poorer donors left cherished possessions in lieu of money – a towel or a brass pot – which were then sold for church funds. The most munificent gestures were made when a church was in trouble; after the chancel of St. Thomas's Church collapsed in 1447 the cost of rebuilding it, together with north and south chapels, was shared between the Dean and Chapter (who as rector were responsible for it) and various wealthy parishioners. In the south arcade of the chancel each bay seems to have been donated separately – on one capital is the legend: 'Jhon Nichol John Nichol John the founder of this peler [pillar] wt a part of this arche & Jhne [Johanna] the wif of the seyde John.'[29]

The principal charges levied by the church were in connection with the various ceremonies surrounding death and burial, and these we have already described. But St. Edmund's had three other sources of income which may also be considered under this heading: the profits from St. Edmund's fair, held in the churchyard; the sale of pardons; and pew rents. The practice of holding fairs in churchyards, although widespread, was not in general approved of by the medieval church authorities. This does not seem to have worried the churchwardens, however, who saw the fair as a source of profit for the church, and regularly charged, 'dyv's men' chese sellers which stode at the Church Walle,' or 'dyvers Tanners & other Craftesmen' havying & occupieng' stallis & stacions withyn the Wallis of Churcheyerd & withoute At Seynt E'mundes feyer.' The sale of pardons at the feasts of Michaelmas and the Annunciation brought into the coffers a few shillings each year, and during these feasts the church's relics were displayed, including various personal items which had allegedly belonged to Saint Edmund himself – a ring, a comb, a cruet and part of his shirt. Although the custom of charging rent for the right to occupy a particular seat in church has had a long history and has only died out in some places during the present century, a reference in the account of 1456–1457 to the receipt of 4/2d 'for assigning seats' is one of the earliest instances of the practice to occur anywhere in England, and points to an innovation which only became possible once permanent seating was provided in church naves in the fifteenth century. It was too good an opportunity for the churchwardens to miss, and by the end of the century between ten and twenty seats yielded a total income of around ten shillings each year.[30]

The most popular fund-raising events were probably the church socials, known as ales or scotales, which were held during the spring. Unlike the milk-and-water affairs which we have inherited from the Victorians, medieval scotales were boisterous drinking bouts which boosted church funds primarily through the sale of home-brewed ale at a profit. Although the revels may originally have been held in the church itself (to the dismay of the Bishop) this became impossible once fixed seating was installed, and by the fifteenth century St. Edmund's had its own Scotale House, also known as the taphouse, which was the medieval equivalent of a church hall. One male and one female parishioner took charge of the proceedings for each ale; members of the congregation were elected in turn, and were known during their brief term of office as the king and queen. Occasionally the churchwardens' accounts record the amount raised by the 'royal service' of men and women during the weeks of feasting. In 1469 four named couples raised nearly ten pounds, but a really good party season, such as that enjoyed in 1461, could yield more than all the church's other receipts put together. A second, equally irreverent, means of fund-raising took place at Hocktide, shortly after easter. It was an excuse for the men of the parish, equipped with a long rope, to catch and threaten to tie up any women or girls who happened to be passing unless they agreed to pay a small ransom to the church coffers. The modern equivalent – the sponsored walk – is far more tiring and much less fun. The financial side of scotales, Hocktide feasts and other social events was of necessity the main emphasis in the churchwardens' accounts, but was probably less important in the minds of their participants than the beneficial effect of fusing together the various strata of parish society in a common celebration of life. Even in the accounts there is an occasional hint of the real motives. In 1510, under the heading 'Collections at the feast of hokkis,' we read, 'And four shillings received and collected at the feast of hokkis from the gifts of various members of the female sex who gave to Church funds in order to protect themselves from being bound, as is the ancient custom at this time.' But further down the page is another entry, under the heading, 'Allocations of necessary expenses: ... And 3/4d spent on a dinner for the women on the day of Hockes.' So the church only made eightpence that day.[31]

The bittersweet world of late-medieval religion, in which fun was mingled with fear, gave way to something more serious and rational. If we leave behind the fifteenth-century church and move forward two hundred years, we find a very different kind of Christianity; and in order to glimpse this new religion we propose to attend morning service at St. Edmund's on a Sunday in June 1653.

The church which we are entering bears little resemblance to the St. Edmund's of today. Only the chancel and east end survive and these are now used as an arts centre. The nave, into which we are ushered by the sexton, extends westwards from the tower almost as far as the railings at the edge of the churchyard. Church attendance is compulsory, and so the nave is crowded with worshippers. Pews are fitted in everywhere, in long rows in north and south aisles and on either side of a central gangway in the body of the nave, around the pulpit, around the door into the quire and around the belfry. Pressure on space 30 years earlier led to the lengthening and narrowing of all the pews in the north aisle, and later a gallery was built over the wedding door, for 'such principall inhabitantes of the parish and others as want fitt seates in the body of the Church'. When in 1647 the font was removed by order of Parliament portable pews were immediately fitted in the vacant space. Folding seats have been fastened to existing pews and portable seats line the aisles and gangways. But pews are more than somewhere to sit: for the church authorities pew rents are one of the main sources of income; and for the parishioner his pew is his status symbol – a man's position in society is judged by his position in church. And so there are empty pews nailed up against intruders, and there are the vacant pews of absentees, where we, as strangers, are permitted to sit. Many pews are fitted with locks. Once a year the sexton summons the flock into church to decide who will change their seat, who will take on the pews of the deceased, who has just claim on a disputed pew, and who is behind on their pew-rent payments. Individual seats carry the idiosyncrasies of their occupants, who repair them and adapt them to their needs; and by noting empty pews the churchwardens can see at a glance who is absent from church today.[32]

The best seats are at the front. They are reserved for the city aldermen and their wives, and strict protocol has to be observed: 'the seate on the north side of the open passadge in the middell of the Churche is declared to bee the antientest seate, and the other opposite to it, the second and the third on the North ende of the auncientt seate, and the fowerth on the Southe side. And the lyke for the order of the pewes for their wives – And the Church wardens are to see them plased accordinglie on' the firste Sabothe daie of the nexte monethe.' Husbands and wives may have separate pews, or they may sit together with their children and servants. There are special seats for scholars, the youth of the parish, members of the weavers' company, midwives and mistresses. When new almshouses were opened in the parish, arrangements were made to seat the inmates in church: 'all the poore of the new Almeshouse and all other the Church Poore shall sitt in the Church according to former orders made upon fformes sett of purpose for them. And the Churchwardens are to see who are missing, and to keepe backe that weekes pay unles they can excuse it. And that the fformes may be knowen and not sate upon by others, there shalbe these wordes painted in great Red letters upon the fforme, *For the Poore*. Nevertheless old John George, and John ffudges, and Susan Beckett, and such others as have already used stooles may use their former places, if it prove not inconvenient.' Children in church could pose problems – in neighbouring St. Thomas's it was necessary to instruct occupiers of the front row of seats in the gallery, 'not to allow children to come in, to the annoyance of those that sit under,' and a few years later J. Boden was paid one shilling for 'washing the Chancell and taking out the names which the Boyes Rudely sett in.'[33]

All the mystery of medieval religion has disappeared. No more relics or images, no Latin mass, no doom painting. The walls are whitewashed and the only embellishment is a table of the ten commandments, the Lord's prayer and the creed. The eucharist has become a formal ceremony, and if we wish to take communion we have to notify the clerk in advance, receive a token and pay one halfpenny to defray the expenses of the bread and wine. After the service we have to give our tokens to the churchwarden. Even the wine is inferior: 'It is ordered that the Churchwardens shall provide Muscadine only for the wine at the Communions, and shall not provide any more Claret wine for that use.' But we have not come to be awed by a ceremony; we have come to be instructed by a preacher. John Strickland, M.A., B.D. has, in 1653, been Rector and Minister of St. Edmund's for twelve years. A staunch puritan, like his predecessor, he is in his early fifties, and during the civil war spent much of his time in London as a member of the Westminster assembly of divines, the religious power-house of the Parliament. At his best he is a vigorous orator with a powerful notion of God: 'I have looked into the Book of God to see whether God hath been wont, in former times, to bring in his people to repentance and reformation, by deliverances and mercies. For if God have never gone in such a way with a people heretofore, I should feare (that notwithstanding our many and wonderfull publick mercies wherewith God hath at present blessed our Land) we should have an after-clap, and be brought back again into the refiners of fire, and furnace of affliction, that our drosse (which is not yet severed from us) may be purged out, and our filthinesse depart from us, which is the way whereby God ordinarily prevailes with a people in that kind . . .'[34]

Our attention wanders, and we gaze out of the window. The medieval painted glass has gone, having offended the puritan conscience with its idolatry. The pew now occupied by one of St. Edmund's most respected parishioners, Francis Swanton, had previously belonged to Henry Sherfield, and he was responsible, in 1630, for a celebrated act of puritan iconoclasm. What Sherfield did was not in itself particularly remarkable. A church meeting in January 1630 sanctioned him to 'take down the windowe wherein God is painted in many places, as if he were there creating' the world ... for that the sayde window is somewhat decaied and broken, and is very darksome, whereby such as sitt neere to the same cannot see to reade in their bookes.' Despite a prohibition from the Bishop of Salisbury Sherfield was determined, and in October of the same year entered the church and set about the window with a pikestaff. In his efforts he broke not only the window but also the pikestaff, fell heavily to the ground, 'lay there a quarter of an Hour groaning,' and 'afterwards kept his House for a Month'. For his vandalism he was fined £500 by the Attorney General sitting in Star Chamber, and ordered to make a public penance.[35]

The severity of the punishment should alert us to a deeper significance in the act than the simple righteous indignation of a hot-headed parishioner; and the incident and its aftermath provide a nice example of religion touching many other areas of city life. On a straightforward theological level Sherfield was giving vent to his objections to what he saw as an erroneous and idolatrous medieval leftover. God was portrayed as 'a little old Man in a blue and red Coat', and the window's version of the creation confused the events of the various days. Certain worshippers had regarded the window as an object of veneration, and such idolatry had to be prevented. At his trial Sherfield – a lawyer – made good use of the Bishop of Salisbury's own published censures against such heresy. But there was also an issue of church authority at stake. The puritan caucus of St. Edmund's vestry was at pains to prove its independence from episcopal control; it had successfully appointed a puritan minister in 1623 against the Bishop's wishes, and this new act of defiance could be seen as another test of its independence. And we have already seen, in chapter five, that the radicals who controlled St. Edmund's at this period, and of whom Sherfield was a leading member, were not concerned with religious reform alone. Their enlightened social measures to reduce poverty and drunkenness were in 1630 foundering on the rocks of their political opponents, notably the church authorities of the Close. And the year 1630 also marked the beginning of the Bishop's campaign to win back some of the control he had lost to the city authorities in 1612. Thus Sherfield, as defendant, and the Bishop, as plaintiff, were engaged in a political, as well as a religious, battle; and when there is a battle, especially one such as this which brought Salisbury into national attention, then everyone takes sides. In the course of his career, as the city's member of Parliament and as its recorder, or chief executive, Sherfield had made many personal enemies. His trial offered many citizens an opportunity to complain about the radical oligarchy's brutal treatment of its opponents. One to have suffered was John Bowen, the sexton of St. Edmund's, dismissed from his job for insolence towards the puritan minister during the 1627 plague. Members of his family were the principal witnesses for the prosecution.[36]

It is a sad familiar story, reminding us on the one hand of how much wider than the walls of the church can be the consequences of what takes place inside, and on the other hand of how much narrower than the Christian ideal can be the motives which drive worshippers to religious acts. A more practical form of Christianity is probably uppermost in the minds of two members of the congregation which we have joined in 1653. Richard Grafton and James Harwood have just completed a term as churchwardens and have recently submitted to the vestry their accounts for the preceding year. Richard, a maltster who lives near the church in Three Cups Chequer, seems to be suffering from the sober regime of the commonwealth period. During a reorganisation of pews two years before he surrendered his former seat, worth £1. 3. od and moved to 'a littell Seat before for himselfe wife & Children & Servants five shillings'. James, on the other hand, improved his lot by renting the seat that had formerly belonged to Sir Giles Escott. Ten years later James was to become mayor of Salisbury. These two gentlemen handled an annual income and expenditure which averaged nearly 40 pounds. About 20% of this sum was raised from parishioners through pew rents and a further 40% by the offerings known as quarteridge payments or the quarter-book, which were successors to the former easter collections. Most of the remainder was made up from charges imposed for burials and gravestones. When the income proved insufficient to meet the expenses there were other ways of raising money. Sometimes items of church goods might be sold off, or an extra quarteridge rate might be levied. Naturally such a move was unpopular – when an attempt was made in 1650 to rate every parishioner at ten times the usual amount, the decision of the vestry was quickly reversed and a trebling agreed instead. This too seems to have failed as the income from the quarter-book was only marginally higher the following year.[37]

The 40 pounds or so thus raised was used for three main purposes, and each accounted for about one-third of the total expenditure. The two paid officials of the church, the clerk and the sexton, earned eight pounds and four pounds respectively. Then there were various day-to-day expenses which had to be accounted for, such as candles, communion wine, paper, small payments to the bellringers and for maintenance of the bells. And thirdly there was the maintenance of the fabric of the church itself. For many years the decrepit state of the building had caused concern. In 1638 the vestry ordered that Thomas Fort 'shall forthwith goe about the erecting of three Arch Pillars or Butteresses against the North wall of the Church, for the bearing up thereof sufficiently by Shrovetide, and for this he is to have sixty pounds'. But the job was harder than he imagined – four years later a further three pounds was allowed, 'uppon the Complaynt of Thomas ffort free Mason that the buildinge of three buttresses have beene to hard a bargayne for him & that hee is noe gayner by the worke.' Even after this work was complete the building still offered little protection against the elements. Among many patching-up schemes two of 1648–1649 are notable: '10 days sodering 147 holes & crackes in the leades over the 3 Iles at the West syde of the belfry 26s 8d;' and, 'Carpenter making three penthouses [presumably these were awnings of some kind] under the high windoe in the body of the Ch. to keep off the raine 2s 4d.'[38]

And now that we have come to consider the state of the church fabric we notice that many members of the congregation on this particular morning are showing considerable anxiety about cracks and bulges in the church walls. At a meeting three weeks earlier it was decided to remove one of the bells from the tower, and then on 19th June such was the vibration from the bells that the Churchwardens were ordered to remove them all from the tower except two. That was last Sunday. What was to happen next cannot be better told than in the words of the churchwardens themselves, written into their vestry book a fortnight later: 'Amongst the many Eminent Mercyes that the Inhabitantes of Edmundes parish have received wee may reckon the speciall providence of God whereby wee the Parishoners and our familyes were saved from Remarkeable and Iminent danger on the Sabbath day, being June the 26th one thousand six hundred fifty and three, when the Maior, and many other principall Inhabitantes of the Citty with a great Multitude of Godly Christianes weer mett at Edmundes Church for the Publique Worshipe of God. The walles of the Tower thereof were become ruinous, Broken, and ... onely not fallen. The maine pillars did bulge out, and sensiblely shake: the cleftes in the walles were seen to open and shutt with Ringing the Sermon Bell that day neither weer there any considerable Proppes under set to Support it, so that nothing but the very hand of God did keep the Stones and Timver from falling untill the next morning that his one people were all Secure at home, and then hee so sweetly Ordered the fall of the Tower that (albeit many workemen were about it that day) neither Man, Woman, nor Child, received any hurt therby ... When we Apprehend what danger wee were in though not sensible of it at that time, how sad an outcry would have bine made ... in our Citty ... wher almost every house would have suffered in the Death of so many if God had mingled our Blood with our Sacrifices that day ... wee cannot but Breake foorth into Praise and say as (Revelation the 19 first) Salvation, and glory, and honour, and Power unto the Lord our God ... And wee beseech our Brethren of this and the following Generationes by the Mercyes of God to present themselves living sacrifices holy, acceptable unto God in ther reasonable service of him, that day as long as ther shall bee one stone upon another in Edmundes Church and an Inhabitant left alive in Edmundes Parish...' (plate 43)[39]

From the miraculous deliverance of 1653 we move forwards again, another two centuries, and find ourselves in Victorian Salisbury in the year of the Great Exhibition, 1851. The rebelliousness of Henry Sherfield and John Strickland has borne fruit, and no longer is the religious life of the city dominated by Church of England orthodoxy. The visitor to Salisbury on a Sunday morning in 1851 has a choice of thirteen services to attend – five Anglican (the three city parish churches, the Cathedral, and St. Clement's, Fisherton Anger), three Methodist, two Congregational, a Baptist, a Catholic and a Swedenborgian. Between them these churches and chapels (excluding the Cathedral) can accommodate about 8,000 people, nearly three-quarters of the population, but on a typical Sunday morning only about half their seats are filled. Church attendance, therefore, is quite low, and on the Sunday morning in question – 30th March – only about one-third of the population has made it to morning service, one-in-five to the Church of England and one-in-seven to a nonconformist chapel or the Catholic church. At both afternoon and evening services a little over one-quarter of the population makes its act of worship; Anglicans prefer an afternoon service, and in fact only one Anglican evening service is held, whereas all the nonconformist chapels have their best attendance of the day in the evening.[40]

Our tour of the Salisbury churches in 1851 begins at St. Clement's, Fisherton Anger. Fisherton has doubled in size over the previous 40 years and will double again in a little over twenty years; consequently the church, 'a neat unassuming village church,' and the rector, 'a typical example of the old-fashioned village parson,' are a little out of place in this expanding suburb. Only within the last decade has the church orchestra, of violin, bass viol, clarinet, flute etc, accompanied by male and female voices, 'at times not very harmonious,' been replaced by a second-hand barrel organ, played by turning a handle and blowing the bellows with a foot pump. The church can seat 80 worshippers, but the average congregation at both morning and afternoon services is 67 adults and 80 Sunday schoolchildren, and so the children have to sit in the aisles. The Rector, Rev. H. G. de Starck, is precisely half-way through his 26 years of service in the parish, and his favourite recreation is fishing; he also enjoys standing at his front door, which faces the church, his long churchwarden's pipe in his mouth, and passing the time of day with any parishioners taking a short cut through the 'Church Field' (now the industrial estate). Plans are afoot to demolish St. Clement's and build a more commodious church, St. Paul's, on a site further north, near where new housing is taking shape. And in fact, after some 600 years, the last service in the church will take place in less than a year's time, 15th February 1852, after which most of St. Clement's will be demolished.[41]

The largest congregation this morning is to be found at St. Thomas's, where nearly 1,000 people are fitted into ungainly pews and galleries. The flamboyant painting of the last judgement is hidden under whitewash and the chancel is in a poor state of repair. The proceedings are managed by a curate, William Renaud, who will eventually become Vicar; when he does he will set about improving the fabric and restoring the chancel. The present Vicar, John Greenly, is a Minor Canon of the Cathedral, and lives in the Close. He has held his, admittedly unremunerative, post at St. Thomas's for nearly 30 years, and it is said that he never goes to his church unless it is to pocket a fee. Services take place three times on the sabbath, and as St. Thomas's is the only Anglican church to hold an evening service, the attendance is usually high, about 1,100. Such enthusiastic churchgoing carries its perils, however, as only four weeks earlier six youths aged between thirteen and seventeen years old had been convicted of indecently assaulting a lady member of the congregation as she passed over Crane Bridge on her way home from evening service. From the magistrates' comments such 'riotous assemblages of young blackguards' appear to have been quite a normal feature of Salisbury Sunday evenings.[42]

To St. Edmund's next, which we left in ruins. When the tower collapsed it was decided to demolish what remained of the nave, build a new tower, and rearrange the seating which had been in the nave in the chancel. The replacement tower, completed in 1655, carries an inscription 'PRAISE HIM O YEE CHILDREN' which cleverly conceals within it sufficient Roman numerals to total 1653, the year of the collapse. But 200 years later the church is once again in a bad state. The churchyard is a playground for children and a haunt of tramps and disreputable characters. The church is entered beneath an oppressive west gallery, stretching eastward some nineteen feet, the three-decker pulpit obscuring a little chancel tacked onto the old east wall in 1766. Near the pulpit stands a large box-pew – the Wyndham pew – with its own fireplace. Squire Wyndham, when he attends church, is preceded to his place by a footman, and when he feels that the sermon has continued long enough, he hints to the preacher by noisily poking his fire. But despite these distractions the church is well attended, with over 900 worshippers at both morning and afternoon services, and total accommodation for 1,250.[43]

St. Thomas's and St. Edmund's together claim nearly 80% of the city's Anglican community. But there remains St. Martin's, and of the three this church, in 1851, presents the most favourable impression to the visitor. Restoration was completed in 1849, under the Bishop's direction, and now the church boasts new seats, clean walls and ceilings, coloured glass in the east window and a splendid new altar-piece. The Rector of St. Martin's, William Wyndham Tatum, comes from a distinguished Salisbury family and owes his preferment to another, to which he is related. He has been incumbent for twenty years and will serve another twenty until his death in 1870. He is considered genial but eccentric, a man of great ability and widely-read, but who in later years will need the support of good curates, imported by the Bishop, to raise the tone of the parish. Church services are overrun by children, as the parish plays host to the city's National School, next door to the church, and together with the church's own Sunday schoolchildren, they account for nearly half the congregation of around 600, morning and afternoon.[44]

In order to understand the growth of nonconformity in Salisbury we must return briefly to John Strickland and the turbulent seventeenth century. After the restoration of Charles II Strickland, the presbyterian, was removed from his living at St. Edmund's, but remained in the city preaching dissent from the Church of England. At the same time a more radical group, advocating Baptist principles, had become established at nearby Porton, and drew support from a wide circle of south Wiltshire villages. Clandestine meetings were held in Salisbury and formed the nucleus of the original Baptist church, which separated from Porton in 1690. Strickland's preaching, too, led to the establishment of a church, of the denomination then known as Independent, but which later became associated with Congregationalism. By 1719 the Baptist community had its own chapel, in Brown Street, where it has remained, despite rebuildings at various dates, to the present day. The Independents opened a chapel in Salt Lane and their cause was successful for a time; but by the middle of the eighteenth century a rival group of Congregationalists, probably drawn partly from their own ranks, was flourishing at their expense. A Congregational chapel was opened in Scots Lane about 1767 and another, in Endless Street – the result of a disagreement among the congregation – in 1810. In 1815 the original Independent chapel in Salt Lane had been sold to the Methodists for use as a school.[45]

At the time of our visit in 1851, therefore, there are two Independent or Congregational chapels, in Scots Lane and Endless Street, and one Baptist chapel, in Brown Street. Between them they can accommodate over 2,000 worshippers, and the pattern of worship in each is similar. The best-attended service in each case is held in the evening. Endless Street chapel this evening is three-quarters full, but this is unusual, as the regular congregation has been joined by a contingent of reforming Methodists, whom we shall meet in due course. At Scots Lane and Brown Street more than half the seats are empty. The morning congregations at each chapel are smaller, but in each case they are boosted by large numbers of Sunday schoolchildren. Services are held in the afternoon as well, but these are mostly for children, and few adults attend. Scots Lane is without a minister at present, the pastor having retired through ill-health, and at Brown Street the Rev. John Wood Todd, D.D. is not entirely happy in his role as Baptist minister. His predecessor had left the congregation in a state of 'spiritual lassitude', and although the atmosphere improved when Todd arrived in 1847, morale has slipped again. In two years' time, at Christmas 1853, the congregation will gather to present him with a silver teapot in recognition of his services, and he will leave the Baptist ministry altogether, a disillusioned man.[46]

The other main strand of nonconformity represented in Salisbury in

1851 is Methodism. John Wesley himself preached in the predecessor of the present chapel in St. Edmund's Church Street, and described it as 'the most complete in England'. (Plate 44) It was built in 1759 and re-built in 1810. In 1851 a debt of £1,600, nearly half the cost of rebuilding, is still owing on the work. Another Wesleyan Methodist chapel was built in Mill Road, Fisherton, in 1832, and, together with a chapel in Wilton, the three form the nucleus of a circuit of 23 village chapels lying within a ten-to-fifteen mile radius of Salisbury. The Wesleyan circuit employs three full-time ministers and about 30 lay-preachers. Morning and evening services at St. Edmund's Church Street are generally taken by one of the ministers, but often in the afternoon, to a smaller congre-gation, one of the lay-preachers is given his chance to expound the gospel in the mother-church. To become a lay-preacher it is necessary to undergo a period 'on trial', and T. J. Davis, one such probationer coming to the end of his trial is engaged to preach on 9th March at Fisherton in the morning and Salisbury in the afternoon. A month later he takes afternoon and evening service at Wilton, and then he becomes a fully-fledged lay preacher. The chapel in St. Edmund's Church Street is a large building with a gallery, and can accommodate nearly one thousand worshippers. Two-thirds of the seats are designated to be rented for between 6d and 1/6d per quarter, although in fact fewer than half have a tenant. On a normal Sunday it is estimated that about 1,200 people attend at least one of the three services, and, taking an average over a normal year, the morning congregation is 600 and the evening congregation 900.[47]

But 1851 is not a normal year for Salisbury's Wesleyans. For the past decade the Wesleyan hierarchy at national level has come under fire from anonymous tract-writers calling for reforms in the structure and government of Methodism. Three ministers widely suspected to be the authors of the attacks were expelled from the movement in 1849 and proceeded to hold meetings all over England at which they propounded Wesleyan reform. The spirit of rebellion, which is presumably latent somewhere in the breast of every nonconformist, seems to have stirred among two groups of the St. Edmund's Church Street congregation, the day school and the tract society. At the school Mr. J. Mumford, the master, was a useful ally, since the school – a former chapel, as we have seen – was the ideal venue for meetings; and the tract society, which was formed in 1846, provided a nucleus of committed church workers who would drift into the new movement. Eight weeks before our visit the first quarterly meeting of the Salisbury Wesleyan Reform Com-mittee had been held in the school, and had resolved, 'to employ all its energies in correcting and removing the many abuses and serious evils which are alleged to exist in the present system.' One consequence of this meeting seems to have been that, by the time of our visit, about 200 members of the St. Edmund's Church Street congregation have deserted their fellow Wesleyans and resort to the Independent chapel. At the end of May the reforming group will hold a public meeting, at which 400 sympathisers will partake of tea, listen to six speakers and express their regret that the Rev. William Griffith, one of the three expelled tract-writers, is unable to be present, as advertised, because of a double-booking. In October they will find a venue for regular worship in a disused chapel in Wilton, and at Christmas they will hold an annual public tea meeting on the very same evening as the 'orthodox' Wesley-ans whom they have deserted. Next year they will build their own chapel in Milford Street, which will leave them with a large debt. They will rent their pews, make collections to pay the gas bill, drink a great deal of tea and hold fund-raising events organised by the bazaar com-mittee. They will, in fact, to the outsider, become indistinguishable from the body which they have left.[48]

Of the remaining congregations in Salisbury in 1851 we propose to say little. The Primitive Methodist chapel in Fisherton, erected about 1826, was the result of a similar split in the preceding generation of Methodists. All was not well here, either, at the time of our visit. The evening congregation, 162, was nearly 60 below average, and the num-ber of members in the circuit administered from Fisherton had begun to slide, from 579 in 1849 to 364 in 1856. A meeting in June 1851 will attribute the loss of thirteen members during the previous quarter to the unfriendly state of some members towards others. The Catholic community presents a happier picture. They meet in a handsome church, St. Osmund's, opened in 1848, and designed by a famous architect, A. W. Pugin, who had been converted to Catholicism during his residence in the city some years before. The Catholic faithful had never been numerous in Salisbury, but the cause had prospered through the patronage of a few powerful families, the Arundells, the Penistons and the Lamberts. The new church has a priest, Patrick Kelly, described as 'missionary apostolic', who celebrates mass every morning and ves-pers, benediction and catechetical instruction on Sunday afternoons. Unlike the other Salisbury churches, whose congregations for the most part live in the city, St. Osmund's draws its worshippers from all over south Wiltshire, and so the winter months attract a poorer attendance. On the day of our visit the morning service has a congregation of 145, 25 below average. Apart from the mainstream Christian denominations there has been from time to time a variety of more obscure sects meeting in the city, but only one, the Swedenborgian or New Jerusalem Church, seems to have existed in 1851. Their evening service, held in a chapel in Castle Street, attracts 55 worshippers.[49]

The service comes to an end, and the congregation stands in the aisles chatting until it is time to drift off home. 'Time, like an ever-rolling stream, bears all its sons away; They fly forgotten, as a dream dies at the opening day.' But the necessity of worship is a perpetual theme, and the human problems that sometimes stand in its way are nothing new. Our help in ages past may yet be our hope for years to come.[50]

In Trouble

On Monday 1st August 1842 an Irish family arrived at Mrs Bracher's lodging-house in St. Ann Street, near the Joiner's Hall. Margaret Easter, aged 35, her husband Charles and three young children, made their way in the world by begging, and they had come to Salisbury, for the second year running, to beg at the August race meeting. Their eldest child, a girl of about eight, was suffering from scarlet fever, and was so ill on Tuesday that Margaret took her to the Infirmary, where she obtained some medicine to treat the complaint. The other children, Charles and Mary-Ann, twins aged about two, were sturdy and boisterous. By all accounts their parents were kind and attentive to them, the father helping to wash and look after them, the mother still breast-feeding them even though they were now lively toddlers. Mrs Bracher, the proprietress, was not at home, and the lodging-house was in the charge of her niece, Mary. The house, although in a respectable part of the city, attracted a not particularly respectable clientele, and the other residents included a tramp and an orphan who both seem to have subsisted by begging. A fire burnt in the kitchen, which opened onto a yard adjoining one of Salisbury's courts, Pelican Place, and in the yard was a washing line, a communal privy and a tub of pigswill next to an earthenware pot for rainwater and a broken door.[51]

On Wednesday morning, 3rd August, the family breakfasted at about eight, and the twins were given bread and milk, The father then departed for the racecourse, accompanied by the orphan lodger, whilst Margaret stayed behind to look after their ailing daughter. At ten o'clock she enlisted the grudging help of another lodger, Elizabeth Jacobs, to administer the girl's medicine, as the twins were misbehaving. They became so troublesome that Margaret was alleged to have clasped her hands together in prayer and said, 'Oh what am I to do with my children? Oh my God, I wish my children were stretched before my eyes before night.' After this episode the other lodgers, most of whom were dozing in the kitchen, remembered her coming and going several times and suckling the twins. Between twelve and one o'clock she left them to play in the yard, fearing that they might burn themselves in the fire if left unwatched in the kitchen, whilst she apparently tended to the other child upstairs.

Soon after one o'clock Mary Bracher, the acting proprietress, happened to notice that the pigswill tub, which had been only half-full, was overflowing, and went to investigate. To her horror she saw the feet of one of the twins sticking into the air from the tub. She immediately roused the tramp, William Happy, from his sleep in the kitchen, and he was able to remove the child – it was the boy, Charles – and place him on the kitchen table, barely alive and covered in pigswill. Another lodger ran to summon Margaret from upstairs, and after repeated calls she eventually appeared and made her way slowly down, some six to eight minutes later. Seeing Charles she cried out, 'Oh Lord my child is drowned! Where is my other child?' and ran straight out into the yard. Nobody had told her where or how Charles had been discovered. In the tub she found the crouched figure of Mary-Ann just protruding above the surface of the swill. Margaret ran back indoors and while Happy the tramp was removing Mary-Ann's body she tried to revive Charles using the only means that occurred to her, by offering him her breast. As the room filled with people Margaret became hysterical and began to blame the other lodgers for not watching her children. She was noisy but tearless. She refused to run for the doctor and would not now touch her dead twins. For by then Charles too had died, despite several attempts to revive him. Doctor Fowler arrived, followed by Mr Winzar, a surgeon, and Thomas Blake, the superintendent of police. Margaret was arrested and charged with murder.[52]

We may use the case of Margaret Easter as an example of the working of law and order in Salisbury. Suspected murder, of course, is a relatively unusual occurrence, but the need to protect the citizen from all manner of crime and to safeguard the fabric of city life has been one of Salisbury's perennial concerns and deserves our consideration. It may be divided into four parts – the crime itself, the policing of the city, the administration of justice, and the punishment of offenders.

The nature of crime probably does not change much throughout history. In the first half of the nineteenth century in Wiltshire as a whole murder and very serious assault, including rape, accounted for about 2.5% of crimes tried in the county, whereas theft of all kinds accounted for over 70% and common assault about 11%. A list of criminal cases heard in Salisbury 600 years earlier, in 1249, includes an interesting assortment. Walter Tautre was accused of stealing from a clothes line, Henry Ode had fled after killing one of the cathedral clergy, a cobbler was accused of rape, a woman was acquitted of breaking into another woman's chamber and stealing money, two clergymen were alleged to have stolen a cloak and a brooch, and a woman claimed that she had miscarried after being struck by a man in the street. A fight in Minster Street in 1293 had fatal consequences for the attacker, William de Lavyngtone. His intended victim, William de Word, was knocked down from behind and struck on the face, but managed to draw a knife which he thrust into William de Lavyngtone's arm. The attacker died from this injury and William de Word was accused of his murder; however, as a clergyman, he could not be tried before a civil court and was handed over to the Bishop. A capital offence of another kind was alleged against Ann Bodenham in 1653. A clothier's wife in Fisherton, she was said to have talked of lucky and unlucky days, and of strange tales and things that might be done by cunning and wise people. On one occasion, as a maid servant approached her house, the door spontaneously flew open, and five spirits, in the guise of ragged boys, appeared at her call. She was said to have transformed herself into a cat. The justice of the day took its course, she was found guilty of witchcraft and executed. She was 80 years old.[53]

Other offences were of a less heinous nature. Offenders against the law of the market were tried in the Bishop's market court, or court of pie-powder, and we noticed a number of infringements of the rules of market trading in chapter three. The guilds, too, imposed rules of conduct on their members and could expel recalcitrant guildsmen. In 1575 the tailors decided to rid themselves of Richard Stevenson, 'for his great and notorious obstinacie and disobedience in refusinge to come to the wardens at theire commandment, and for his gevinge fowle and naughtie words to the officers, to the discredite of the authorite of the Wardens, and the charter of this companie.' Naughty behaviour of another kind invoked the wrath of the Church, as Thomas de Colne, one of the vicars' choral, discovered to his cost in 1231. An actor had complained to the Dean that his wife had left him, and had spent the whole night at Thomas's house. The Dean went to investigate and found that it was true. When asked what she was doing in the house, the woman replied that she had been having an affair with Thomas for more than a year and often came into the Close to him by night and day whenever he wished. The couple appeared before the Cathedral Chapter the next day and Thomas was relieved of his office, given three days to pack his bags and quit his house and a further week to leave the city altogether. His mistress was ordered to be whipped through the Close and out into the city.[54]

Examples of misconduct from all walks of life and all periods of the city's history could be multiplied, but to little effect. Society's response to the problem of wrongdoing is perhaps more interesting as it reflects the development of society itself, along with its changing attitudes and priorities. Had the deaths of Charles and Mary-Ann Easter in 1842 occurred ten years earlier no superintendent of police would have appeared on the scene, as a full-time, salaried, police force only came into being in 1836. The offices of constable, sub-constable and serjeant-at-mace had all existed from medieval times, and their role as servants of the corporation has been touched on in chapter five. But they were unpaid, appointed annually and their duties had become largely nominal. A more effective force, which had existed since at least the sixteenth century, was the vigilante body of watchmen set up to combat burglary and other perils of the night. In 1548 the watch, which seems hitherto to have been provided by private citizens, became chargeable also to the mayor and corporation and the city's innkeepers. A century later the watch was 30 strong, and included four junior members of the corporation (the 48), a constable and three sub-constables. In 1707 a scheme to impose a statutory responsibility for watching and street-lighting on the corporation failed, and it was not until 1737 that salaried watchmen patrolled the city streets.[55]

The arrangements for policing Salisbury at night, drawn up in 1737, have survived and may be briefly described. Ten watchmen were appointed at a salary of eightpence per night. Each was given a stave, a greatcoat and a lantern, and a nightly allowance of two-and-a-half candles. Their headquarters was the watchhouse, a rented shop in Fish Row. One of the annual constables was quartered here each night attended by a watchman who, in addition to his patrolling duties, was required to light the watchhouse fire. Each watchman had to report to the watchhouse at ten o'clock and was assigned a station, usually a street corner, where he had to stand all night. Every hour each watchman had to leave his station and walk a prescribed beat of one or two chequers, shouting out the hour as he went. The policing operation was under the control of the directors of highways, who were also responsible for lighting the streets and appointing a lamplighter.[56]

These arrangements continued, with slight variations, until 1836. Whilst they may have been sufficient to deter the nocturnal thief and drunk they offered society no protection against other forms of disorder. Nor were the honorific civic constables any match for the perils of riot, which became a persistent threat towards the end of the eighteenth century. In 1794, when fears of a French invasion and an English revolution in the French style were at their highest, troops of volunteer cavalry, drawn from the ranks of yeomen and gentlemen, were formed in towns all over England. A Salisbury contingent was one of ten such troops to be created in Wiltshire, and in 1799 it consisted of 67 men and three officers, of whom all but twelve lived in the city. The troop saw little action during the first 30 years of its existence, but in the dark days of November 1830, when desperate farm workers all over southern England rose to smash the machinery that had put them out of work and burn the ricks of the farmers who exploited them, then Salisbury panicked and the yeomanry drew its first blood. On 23rd November a running battle was fought along the London Road at Bishopdown on the outskirts of the city, and further action ensued at Alderbury and Pyt House near Tisbury. In little more than a week the rioting had ceased, but a scar remained, and fear of a repetition was one of the main reasons for the establishment of salaried police forces in many parts of England in the course of the next decade.[57]

Salisbury was the only urban authority in Wiltshire to form its own police force. The first appointments were made in 1836, and the force continued to operate as an independent body until amalgamation with the county constabulary after legislation in 1946. In Victorian times it was no paragon of a city police force, and was regarded as inefficient by government inspectors. The duties of policemen in 1836 were little different from those of the watchmen a century earlier, and consisted mainly of patrolling the city by night and apprehending drunks and malefactors. Eleven o'clock closing was to be enforced on public houses every Saturday, and on Sundays policemen were to report landlords who provided hospitality during times of worship. Hardly surprisingly, there were many instances of drunken constables appearing before the watch committee for summary dismissal. Thomas Blake, the superintendent of police who arrested Margaret Easter, had risen to his elevated position remarkably quickly. He joined the police force as a constable in September 1839, was made inspector the following April, and was appointed superintendent in November 1840 after his predecessor was asked to resign following disclosures that he had misappropriated funds. When Blake arrested Margaret, therefore, he had been a policeman for under three years. In his first twelve months as superintendent his force made 457 arrests, and he successfully applied for an increased salary. Morale in the force in 1842 seems to have been low, and on the day before the tragedy Blake had attended a watch committee meeting at which, following his complaint, one of his inspectors was dismissed for insubordination. The strength of the force was the subject of frequent revision in the early years, but usually hovered around twenty, mostly employed to work at night. Despite the government inspectors' criticisms Blake held onto his position for another fifteen years and did not resign until a chronic disease of the lungs forced him to retire in 1857.[58]

And so, on 3rd August 1842, Margaret Easter became an entry in the police superintendent's day book, and she would have been taken to Fisherton Gaol to await her hearing before the city justices. On the next day the coroner held an inquest on the bodies before a jury, and the jury requested that a post mortem examination be held in case the children could have been the victims of poisoning. The post mortem was held on Friday, two days after the deaths, and revealed that the cause of death was drowning and there was no trace of poison. The inquest returned a verdict of 'wilful murder'. Margaret appeared before the city magistrates and was remanded in custody until the following week. The next Thursday (11th August) the magistrates considered her case again and committed her for trial at the summer assizes which began on the following Monday. But before we see how her trial was conducted we should explain something of the history of justice in Salisbury.[59]

For much of the city's history justice has operated at three levels. At the local level the Bishop's courts were empowered to determine various civil and minor criminal cases from the founding of Salisbury until the nineteenth century. After 1462 the corporation also took on the responsibility of a separate commission of the peace for the city and so was able to hold its own sessions. As we saw in chapter five the corporation's power increased as the Bishop's declined, so that by the seventeenth century there was considerable duplication between their respective courts. Separate quarter sessions for the city continued after the reform of the corporation in 1836; in the first half of the nineteenth century most of their criminal business was concerned with various kinds of theft and common assault. In addition to its own jurisdiction Salisbury was from the fourteenth century the venue once a year for the county quarter sessions, an honour which it shared with Devizes, Warminster and Marlborough. In the course of time the judicial powers of the magistrates who met at quarter sessions were reduced, but there was a corresponding increase in administrative work, and from 1821 a second court apart from the main sessions sat to hear criminal cases. In 1888 the administrative functions of quarter sessions were largely taken over by the newly-formed county council. The most serious crimes were heard, not by local magistrates, but by circuit judges at courts of assize. The Western Circuit, which included Wiltshire, was inaugurated at the end of the thirteenth century and continued until the circuit system was abolished in 1971. Judges visited each county in their circuit twice in a year to hear and determine cases referred to them by lesser courts, to preside over civil (*nisi prius*) cases before a jury, to deliver (or empty) the county gaol, by passing judgement on all prisoners held there on remand, and to examine the county's magistrates. Salisbury was the principal assize town of Wiltshire, but from the nineteenth century onwards (and on some earlier occasions) Devizes and Salisbury alternated as venues for the Wiltshire assizes. In 1842 the summer assizes were held at Devizes; and so it was there that Margaret Easter was taken for her trial.[60]

The two judges, Mr Justice Wightman (who was to preside in the criminal court) and Mr Justice Creswell (who was to hear civil cases in the *nisi prius* court) arrived in Devizes on Saturday evening, 13th August, and were welcomed by the mayor. On Sunday they attended St. John's Church and on Monday the assizes began. In his opening address to the grand jury Mr Justice Wightman rehearsed some of the cases which would be heard, including several charges of sheep stealing, one of malicious wounding, and the most serious charge, wilful murder by Margaret Easter of her two children. He went on to congratulate the county on the good harvest and hoped that it would reduce the number of crimes committed on the pretext of distress.[61]

Margaret's case was not heard until Wednesday. Her indictment was for the murder of her son, Charles, by casting and throwing him into a tub, whereby he was choked, suffocated and drowned; and for the murder of her daughter, Mary-Ann, in a similar manner. The prosecution counsel called nine witnesses: Mary Bracher, the acting proprietress; the five lodgers who had been present on the day of the drama; John Perry, a gardener who lived nearby; Thomas Blake, the superintendent of police; and John Winzar, the surgeon who had conducted the post mortem. After interrogation by the prosecutor, Mr Slade, they were cross-questioned by Mr Bennett, the counsel for Margaret's defence. There was no conflict in the evidence presented by the lodgers and the lodging-house keeper. With one exception they seem not to have been particularly hostile to Margaret, whose qualities as a conscientious and attentive mother were not in doubt, but neither were they concerned to protect her. Elizabeth Jacobs was perhaps the exception, as she and Margaret seem to have argued on the night before the tragedy, when Margaret asked her to look after one of the twins and she refused. Her evidence, that Margaret had wished her children dead, was particularly damning. The prosecution was also able to set store by Margaret's delay in coming downstairs once told of the death of Charles, and her run to the tub to look for Mary-Ann although no-one had told her where Charles had been found. One witness suggested that the washing had been hung on the line in such a way as to obscure the tub from the kitchen, and the neighbour, John Perry, alleged that he saw Margaret in the yard at five minutes past one, where she looked at the privy (which was next to the tub) and then returned indoors. At the inquest he had said that Margaret had passed him in the yard carrying one child towards a door which led to the river, but on meeting him had turned back and returned to the house.[62]

The evidence presented by the policeman and the surgeon was more favourable to Margaret. The tub was produced and was found to be one foot eight inches deep; the children were two foot eight inches tall. There had been no trace of pigswill on Margaret's body or clothes, and no marks of violence on the children's bodies. There were other considerations in her favour. The tub was within five yards of the kitchen door and next to the privy, so anyone using it to commit a murder would have run a great risk of being heard and discovered. The boy had still been alive at the time of his discovery, when Margaret was upstairs. The only way from the yard to Margaret's upstairs room was through the kitchen, and only for ten or fifteen minutes were Margaret's movements unaccounted for. The broken door and rainwater pot next to the tub would have afforded the children a foothold if they had tried to peer inside the tub, and from this position they could have fallen in and drowned accidentally.[63]

Mr Bennett addressed the jury on Margaret's behalf and the judge, in his summing up, went through all the evidence, 'commenting on it in a most feeling manner and putting forward every point that could be suggested in its favour.' The jury retired to consider its verdict. Surprised murmurs echoed around the courtroom as the verdict of guilty was pronounced. The assize clerk asked Margaret if she wished to say anything before sentence was passed, but there was no reply. The learned judge put on his black cap and addressed the prisoner:

'Margaret Easter, after a most deliberate consideration of your case, the jury have found you guilty of a foul and most unnatural murder – the murder of your own unoffending offspring. By the law of God and man, you have incurred the fearful penalty of death ... For you there is no hope on earth. Cast, then, your thoughts beyond the grave, and endeavour to obtain from Heaven that mercy which is denied to you on earth. Nothing more remains for me to do than to pass upon you the dreadful sentence of the law, which is that you be taken from hence to the prison from whence you came, and from thence to a place of execution, and that you be hanged by the neck until you are dead; and may the Lord have mercy on your soul!'[64]

Margaret went back to Fisherton Gaol to await her punishment. In her case the gaol was fulfilling its traditional role, not in itself the punishment, but a mere cage where a suspect was held until judged and a convict held until executed. Like the Cathedral the gaol was one of the administrative buildings which Salisbury inherited from Old Sarum. From the middle of the twelfth century until about 1500 the county gaol was in Old Sarum Castle, but for the last eighty years of its life it had a rival somewhere in Fisherton Anger on the outskirts of Salisbury, and after 1500 this became the county's principal prison. There was also a prison within the city limits which belonged to the Bishop as lord of the city. It existed in 1246, but seems to have been transferred to the newly-built Bishop's Guildhall in the early fourteenth century, where it remained until 1785. Meanwhile the county magistrates decided in 1568 that they would build a new gaol. The first site they chose was at East Harnham, just across the river from the Bishop's palace. A hasty letter from 'Yo'r poore freude,' the Bishop, scotched this suggestion, and a site next to Fisherton Bridge was purchased. The present clock-tower between the bridge and the Infirmary incorporates some of the masonry from a later rebuilding of this gaol. As a result of delays caused by resentful ratepayers unaccustomed to so large an item of capital expenditure, Fisherton Gaol took ten years to complete. Old Sarum was plundered for stone, and a new two-storey building was erected, seventeen by nine metres, with seven small barred windows, inside a retaining wall seven metres high. For over two centuries this building was repaired and modified, altered and extended, and continued to serve as the county gaol until the beginning of the nineteenth century.[65]

Old Fisherton Gaol was an unpleasant place. A report of 1807 describes some of its faults. The brick floors were very worn and the walls needed whitewashing. The building was dirty and the ground floor cells very damp. These cells had wooden bedsteads, but upstairs the prisoners had no bedsteads at all. Four of the cells had been used for the past five years for storing ammunition. There was no bath or tub, no oven for fumigating clothes and no medical examination of prisoners on entering the gaol. The prisoners were fed $1\frac{3}{4}$ lbs of bread per day. There was no work for them to do and they were only let out of their cells into a small yard for an hour each day.[66]

Margaret Easter, as the date for her destruction approached, was spared this squalor. In 1822 a new gaol was completed at the bottom of Devizes Road in Fisherton and here, under the tutelage of a humane governor, she would have received kinder treatment. The bread ration was supplemented by a pint of oatmeal gruel night and morning and four ounces of meat from an ox-head on Sundays. Different categories of prisoners were kept separate, and Margaret was probably housed in a part of the prison adjoining the gaoler's lodging. She would have been allowed to walk in the yard for two hours morning and afternoon, and she would have attended chapel daily. Clean prison clothes were provided each week, there was a cistern with soap and towels in each yard, the cells were swept daily, the windows cleaned every month and the walls whitewashed each year.[67]

Margaret was to be executed by hanging from a drop erected in front of the gaol. Fisherton seems to have been the normal place of execution since at least 1610, when a gallows near the site of Margaret's gaol was included on a map of the city. Executions, by hanging or by military firing squad, also took place on the Green Croft in the seventeenth and eighteenth centuries; and at least two celebrities received the extreme penalty in the Market Place – the Duke of Buckingham for treason in 1483, and Lord Stourton for murder in 1557. Six years before Margaret's ordeal another vagrant, Henry Wynn, occupied the Fisherton death cell. Convicted on Friday, he afterwards confessed his crime, heard a sermon in chapel on Sunday, and received communion on Monday morning. At a quarter past noon he walked firmly up the steps to the platform. He said nothing to the spectators but asked the hangman to remove his cravat. Even before the executioner had finished adjusting the rope the prisoner gave the fatal signal and was launched into eternity without a struggle. Rain fell heavily throughout the morning and an unusually small crowd was assembled to watch the event.[68]

Execution was not the only punishment for serious crime meted out by nineteenth-century justice. Transportation, which became possible with the discovery of new lands for colonisation, was a slightly preferable alternative, although it was not a prospect to be welcomed. At Fisherton Gaol in 1826 Elizabeth Ogbourne, under sentence of transportation for stealing a five-pound-note, resorted to an unusual, and misguided, appeal for mercy. With a fellow-prisoner she concocted a letter, to be sent to, 'the Kings Most Royal Majesty Winsear Palys Ore eals wear London with Speed.' The fellow-prisoner gave her a glowing character reference: 'For indeade my Lord She is a Rale Beuty and She Bore a exclent Careter all except goin to prison ... so i ope your Majesty will Consider the young woman a lone as she and her Franes near a exclant good Careter and thay ear all respetale popel and i have Nown the young woman this teen years for she was prentes to Me 4 year and She all ways Beved with grate sovelty to Me and all my domestices and She was Greatly Admired by all the house...'[69]

Margaret's predicament evoked sympathy in more influential quarters. A week after her sentence had been pronounced the Devizes newspaper carried an editorial casting doubt on the jury's verdict, and suggesting that since there was no proof that the children were drowned by their mother she should be given the benefit of the uncertainty and reprived from the death penalty. Two letters, from 'A friend to justice to the poor,' and 'A lover of justice,' were printed in the same issue, both proclaiming reasons for believing her innocent. At the same time a memorial was prepared by a number of gentry and magistrates living in the Devizes area, including the town's Member of Parliament, which petitioned the Home Secretary on Margaret's behalf. On 22nd August the Home Office granted a stay of execution and commuted the sentence to transportation for life. But the petitioners were not satisfied with this. On 26th August they made a further appeal, and this received a curt reply: The Home Secretary 'has inquired into and carefully considered this case; and ... can discover no ground sufficient in his opinion to justify him in recommending the Prisoner to her Majesty for any punishment short of transportation for life.' However, another letter arrived three days later. The Home Secretary had communicated further with the judge who had presided at the trial, and Margaret was to receive a free pardon. The Devizes newspaper reported the news jubilantly and showered praise on the instigators of the petition. By contrast the Salisbury press carried a grudging comment: 'In the opinion of persons well qualified to form a correct and impartial decision on the question, there cannot exist a doubt of the woman's guilt. It is to be hoped that she will "go and sin no more." '[70]

On Monday 12th September, six weeks precisely since she had arrived in Salisbury, Margaret Easter walked out of Fisherton Gaol. She took with her sufficient money for her return to Ireland, but she chose instead to travel to Kent to work in the hop gardens. Her husband was there, with their only child. There is no record, nor, given the circumstances, is it likely, that she ever visited Salisbury again.[71]

In Hospital

It came home to me one day, when I discovered that I was talking to a man who in his youth had looked after the leeches at Salisbury Infirmary, how recent is the history of the medical care which we now take for granted. My concern in this section is to examine society's response to sickness, not only by caring for and attempting to treat the sick, but also by trying to prevent the occurrence and spread of disease. We have already brushed with this subject in chapter two, where we examined the effect of the watercourses on mortality and the effect of mortality on population. Now we must try to approach the subject from the point of view of the individual, to see how he fared at the hands of the medieval monk, the seventeenth-century quack and the Victorian surgeon.[72]

There were in medieval Salisbury two establishments which described themselves as hospitals. Both Trinity Hospital and St. Nicholas's Hospital are still in existence, and although nothing earlier than 1702 remains of the former, the latter retains considerable thirteenth-century work in its fabric. Both hospitals included provision for the weak and infirm, but neither should be regarded as hospitals in the modern sense of the word. St. Nicholas's Hospital lies on the southern edge of the city, next to Harnham Bridge; indeed an important part of its work was to maintain the bridge and oversee a small chapel, St. John's Chapel, provided for the use of travellers over the bridge. Its career as a place of refuge for the sick probably did not extend much beyond the first century of Salisbury's existence, and it is clear from the wording of a charter in 1245 that its patients were not the sick of Salisbury, who would have been expected to stay at home, but sick travellers, who were to be looked after, 'so long as their infirmity prevented them from going on their way.' Visitors were entertained in a church-like building, divided along its axis by an arcade, which probably separated male and female patients. The staff consisted of priests and lay-brethren, perhaps following the Augustinian rule, and apart from providing food and shelter, their principal contribution to the patient's welfare was spiritual, through prayer, hearing confessions and performing last rites. After about 1320 poverty seems to have forced the house to abandon its healing role, and the only sick encountered thereafter were probably members of the community who had succumbed to old age and infirmity.[73]

Trinity Hospital was a late foundation, the result of a private benefaction made in 1379, and it was intended primarily as almshouses for twelve permanent and eighteen temporary poor residents. However, provision was made to look after temporary residents who were ill, and the hospital claimed to fulfill the seven works of charity, which included comforting the sick, restoring the mad to their senses and delivering pregnant women. The standard of accommodation seems to have been high. From an inventory of 1418 it is clear that besides the beds in dormitories and solars there were enclosed cubicles in front of the altar, so that the bedridden could take part in the mass. The catering, too, seems to have been good. In the course of a week in May 1528 the residents were given beef and mutton on three days, bread, salt fish and stock fish, eggs and butter.[74]

In an age when the workings of the body were little understood and premature death was accepted as normal, society was less concerned with cure than with prevention, especially the prevention of epidemics. Leper hospitals could be found on the outskirts of many medieval towns, where victims were condemned to a lingering death of strict isolation. A Hospital of St. John at Old Sarum may have served this function, and at East Harnham a leper hospital is recorded at various dates from 1361 to 1620. A more serious problem was plague, and, although nothing is known of the effect of the 1348 black death on Salisbury, later epidemics are known to have occurred in 1477, 1579, 1604, 1627, 1643, 1665 and 1666 (Figure 7). With plague rampant elsewhere the citizens' first concern was to try to prevent it from spreading to Salisbury. Morgan Morse, the common carrier between London and Salisbury, was ordered to curtail his business in 1625. Extra watchmen were appointed to patrol the streets, city gates and ramparts to prevent strangers from entering the city, and all contact with Londoners, or any person or thing which had been in London during the previous month, was forbidden. In 1625 these precautions seem to have worked; but when they failed there were other measures which might be adopted to soften the plague's effects. In 1579 the mayor-making ceremony was transferred to St. Thomas's from St. Edmund's, because the disease was 'hot' near St. Edmund's Church. Public meetings and gatherings of all kinds were discouraged or prohibited. The tailors' company complied with the corporation's request not to hold their annual feast in 1625. Two years later the feast was again forbidden, but six tailors decided to hold it anyway. Within a week, noted the mayor, John Ivie, with grim satisfaction, five of them were dead. At other times the corporation was more understanding of the plight which its prohibitions imposed on tradesmen. In 1579 the landlord of the George Inn was forgiven a debt of £22.10.0 outstanding rent because no visitors were allowed into the city. The churches, which came into too close contact with plague victims for comfort, also took what precautions they could. Attempts to fumigate or purify the church seem to lie behind bills in the churchwardens' accounts for frankincense, rosemary, bay, sweet woods and juniper. The state of St. Thomas's Churchyard also gave cause for concern, and during the commonwealth period burials were forbidden for seven years, because, 'the openinge of Graves there Wherein dead have bine lately buryed, may be dangerous for infection.' When churchyards were full of the recent dead, recourse was had to the Greencroft and the Cathedral green as burial grounds.[75]

The dead were removed from infected houses by bearers especially employed for this unpleasant and dangerous task. In 1579 over-hasty bearers seem to have caused the burial of an infant sufferer who was still alive. In 1627 the bearers struck for a better wage, and were met by a volley of stones directed at them by an irate Mayor Ivie. Three days later he found them, much the worse for drink, dancing among the graves and singing, 'Hie for more shoulder work.' Ivie used his bearers not only to remove corpses, but also to take living, but infected, households to a 'pesthouse' which he had built in Bugmore, downwind and downstream of the city. Evicting the members of a plague-ridden family, very much against their will, was a revolting business. The Bull family resisted, and it was necessary for the bearers to break down their door. 'Then two of them went in and came out again immediately, and told me their lives were as precious to them as mine to me; they would not go in again; the house was so hot they were not able to stay there. For the smell of the house, with the heat of the infection, was so grievous they were not able to endure it ... It was a close house and but one little door to the street and a little window.' Mercifully the Bull family all recovered and were able to return to their home after the epidemic had passed.[76]

Plague apart, the plight of the individual sufferer afflicted with a painful or distressing illness, was unenviable. If funds permitted recourse might be had to a barber surgeon or apothecary, by whom quite extraordinary remedies might be dispensed. When his son suffered convulsive fits in 1723 Thomas Naish, the educated churchman whom we encountered in chapter four, 'hanged two wonts' [moles'] feet about his neck upon the pitt of his stomach, cut off alive, by which means we think that my son John was cured of the same distemper last Whitsuntyde ...' Fifty years earlier another churchman, Bishop Seth Ward, displayed a fanatical interest in quack remedies. 'He also delighted much in Fysic Books,' explained his biographer, 'which wrought the Effect upon him, which they usually do upon Hypocondriacal Persons, that is, made him fancy that he had those Diseases which he there found described, and accordingly take Remedies for them.' In his commonplace book the Bishop recorded many such cures. Gout was a particular problem: 'Take an old fat Cat, and flea [i.e. flay] it. draw forth the Gutts, then with a rolling Pin beat it wel, and so putt it all together into the Belly of a fat Gander with Pepper $\frac{1}{2}$ lb Mustard and Parsley seeds 4 oz sixpenny weight of Bole Armoniac, a good quantity of Wormwood, Rue and Garlick. Rost the Gander wel, saveing the greas. with it anoint the grieved part.' Evidently this did not work, as the Bishop crossed it through and substituted another concoction, which included red lead, olive oil, dog's grease, English honey, yellow wax, turpentine and stone pitch.[77]

But amidst such quackery one of Seth Ward's contemporaries in Salisbury stood out as a practitioner of a more professional bearing. D'Aubigny Turberville M.D. was the product of the union of the two noble West Country families enshrined in his name. As a student he became interested in ophthalmology and, after fighting in the civil war, he set up in practice in Salisbury. He numbered among his patients Princess (later Queen) Anne and Samuel Pepys. According to Walter Pope, his biographer and grateful patient, the presence of so eminent a physician in Salisbury was of great benefit to inns and private houses, 'insomuch, that one could scarce peep out of doors, but he had a prospect of some led by Boys, or Women, others with Bandages over one, or both Eyes, and yet a greater number wearing green Silk upon their Faces ... The Rendevouz of these Hoodwinkt People was at the Doctors House ...' Turberville's treatments included medicines, such as tobacco, lotions and surgery. He could cure certain types of cataract and remove diseased eyes completely. He was perhaps the first person to use a magnet to remove a foreign body lodged in the eye, and he displayed a lively curiosity about unusual complaints, which he reported in letters to the *Philosophical Transactions*. One patient was completely colourblind, but could sometimes read in total darkness; another, 'had no visible disease in his eyes, but could not see at all unless he squeezed his nose with his fingers, or saddled it with narrow spectacles, and then saw very well.' Turberville died in 1696 and is commemorated by an elaborate epitaph in Salisbury Cathedral. 'Adieu my dear friend,' wrote Pope, 'a rivederci, till we meet and see one another again, with Eyes which will never stand in need of a Collyrium.'[78]

Plague did not return to England after 1666, but in the eighteenth century smallpox took its place as the mass epidemic killer. In Salisbury severe outbreaks in 1723 and 1752 prompted vigorous debate about the merits and risks of inoculation and seem to have stimulated a more general interest in ways of treating and controlling the spread of the disease. In 1763 Viscount Folkestone, one of the city's Members of Parliament, who in 1752 was a bitter opponent of inoculation, purchased a house in Bugmore for use as a smallpox hospital. In the same year his uncle, Lord Feversham, left £500 for the establishment of a county infirmary within five years. The initiative was taken by the city council, who in 1766 advertised a public meeting to consider establishing a General Hospital or Infirmary, in or near the city. Viscount Folkestone had by this time become the first Earl of Radnor, and it was he who presided at the first and subsequent meetings. Such was the enthusiasm that within two months not only had an organising committee been appointed, but a row of houses fronting onto Fisherton Street had been purchased for conversion into a temporary hospital while a purpose-built infirmary was constructed on land behind. The project was to cater, 'for the relief of the sick and lame poor, from whatsoever county recommended,' and by the end of the first year the governors had devised a motto, 'the sick and needy shall not always be forgotten,' which has remained the Infirmary's watchword throughout its history. 1767 was a year of decisions and actions. The first staff were appointed in April, and in May the first patients were admitted. July saw the formation of a building committee, which in August approved the plans for an Infirmary submitted by John Wood the younger of Bath. On a memorable Sunday in September everyone involved in the project marched in procession with the civic dignitaries to the Cathedral for a service of thanksgiving, and then returned to the Infirmary site to witness the stonelaying ceremony for the new building, followed by a dinner in the Assembly Rooms.[79]

In a little under four years, on 17th August 1771, the new Salisbury Infirmary was complete and ready to admit its first patients. The makeshift accommodation which had served since 1767 was demolished to reveal, 'that great, comely building of warm, red brick,' which lay behind. Today's Infirmary is substantially the same as this eighteenth-century building, to which numerous additions have been made. As with the Market Place and the parish churches, therefore, a special effort is required to forget its modern connotations, in this case ambulances and intensive care, and place ourselves in the shoes of a sick eighteenth-century pauper as he hobbles up a flight of steps into one of the largest buildings ever to admit him. The entrance was on what is now the first floor, and here were the chapel, dispensary and apothecary's room, one large ward and an examination room ranged around a central staircase. Two large and two small wards occupied the upper storey, and in the basement, now the ground floor, were cellars, a kitchen, laundry, laboratory and pump room. To be admitted as a patient our pauper had to be recommended by one of the hospital's subscribers or benefactors, he had to present himself on a Saturday between 11 a.m. and 1 p.m., and he had to be of insufficient means to pay for his cure and support himself at home. Out-patients who came to the Infirmary for treatment and were caught begging in the city faced being discharged for misbehaviour. Like its medical predecessor the eighteenth-century hospital was also a reformatory, concerned with the patients' spiritual, as well as their physical, well-being; and so the ministrations of a chaplain and the provision of a chapel were integral parts of the treatment our pauper could expect to receive. The medical care was very limited, and consisted of herbal remedies, blood-letting, and hot and cold baths, including an apparatus for lowering the patient on a chair into cold water. An example may be quoted of a cure for bronchitis found in the prescription book of the Infirmary's first physician, John Tatum. After being bled and purged, the patient had to wait until full moon, when a pill was placed under his tongue and he was enjoined to remain silent for fourteen nights until the moon changed. However, the eighteenth-century physician knew his limitations. The real value of the Infirmary was that it offered the sick poor a chance to tackle their illnesses in a warm, reasonably comfortable environment, where they would be given better food and cleaner bed-linen than they could expect at home, and so would stand a far greater chance of recovery (Plate 45).[80]

The professional staff of the Infirmary in its early years consisted of two physicians and two surgeons, elected annually by the governors and unpaid, a matron, who claimed that, 'there is nothing from the kitchen to the garret but I understands,' a house apothecary and an unspecified number of nurses. Among the ancillary staff the porter was the most notable; apart from general handyman duties, including pounding concoctions in the great mortar, and tending the garden, he had to see that in-patients did not escape, and he was responsible for brewing all the beer and baking all the bread. About one hundred in-patients could be accommodated, originally on second-hand beds donated by well-wishers, but from 1776 on purpose-built light oak, sack-bottomed beds. Sometimes pressure on space meant that patients had to sleep two to a bed. Apart from rest cures and primitive medicines, more ambitious treatment was sometimes attempted. An electrical machine designed by Joseph Priestley was in use in the 1770s, and surgical operations might be undertaken after a conference of all the medical and surgical staff, but even as late as the 1830s operations averaged only about six per year. Some of the Infirmary's medical problems stemmed from unhealthy conditions within the hospital itself. Infested bedclothes, stagnant water and contagious patients resulted in an ever-present risk of infection, which occasionally turned into an epidemic – smallpox in 1790, malaria in 1828 and erisypelas in 1833. But despite these setbacks the Infirmary was respected and appreciated, and it continued to attract generous benefactions, legacies and subscriptions. It became one of Salisbury's most notable assets, and like the Market Place, helped the city to maintain a pre-eminent position in its extensive hinterland. To one observer the Infirmary was, 'the cord that draws and binds the city and the village closest together ... In numberless humble homes, in hundreds of villages of the Plain, and all over the surrounding country, the "Infirmary" is a name of the deepest meaning, and a place of many sad and tender and beautiful associations.'[81]

But in the annals of medical care it is not for the presence of the Infirmary that Salisbury is remembered, important and honourable though that institution's history has been. It is rather for the two private lunatic asylums, Laverstock House and Fisherton House, which in the Victorian period brought a greater concentration of psychiatric patients to the Salisbury area than to anywhere else in England outside London. Laverstock House, the earlier of the two, was probably operating as a private madhouse a few years before Salisbury Infirmary was built, and it continued as a psychiatric hospital until 1955. In 1779 it was purchased by William Finch, the founder of a dynasty of asylum proprietors which continued into the twentieth century, and under his son, also William Finch, it was catering for over one hundred patients in the early years of the nineteenth century. In 1813 William Finch junior opened a second establishment in the old manor house at Fisherton Anger, and by 1854, when Laverstock passed out of the Finchs' hands, Fisherton had become the larger of the two – indeed, with a licence for 214 patients it was the largest provincial private madhouse in England. It continued to grow rapidly, and from 1878 onwards its licence for 672 patients made it the largest private licensed house of all time.[82]

Most lunatics fell into one of three categories. They were either private patients, whose treatment and accommodation were paid for by relatives, friends, or from their own means; or they were paupers, too disruptive to remain in a workhouse, and so transferred to the asylum, where their keep was paid by their parish of legal settlement; or they were criminals, guilty but insane, who were maintained by the state. Both Laverstock and Fisherton strove to emulate large country houses, where private patients could enjoy comfortable rooms, a good standard of cuisine and recreations of various kinds. 'We believe the constant occupation of the mind in cheerful, harmless pursuits to be one of the most important points in the curative treatment of insanity' – was the philosophy which underlay their organisation. In 1841 Laverstock House was licensed for one hundred private patients and 50 paupers. By this time the demand for pauper accommodation in private madhouses was declining, as county asylums began to be provided by local authorities, and in 1851, a year before Roundway Hospital, the Wiltshire County Asylum at Devizes, was opened, Laverstock's pauper department was closed. Most other private madhouses reverted to the exclusive trade in private patients from the middle of the nineteenth century, but Fisherton House developed in other ways. It retained its pauper department, strictly segregated of course from the private patients, and began to attract large numbers of paupers sent by distant local authorities, such as Portsmouth and some parts of London, which had insufficient accommodation of their own. By 1859 only nineteen private licensed houses in England were still receiving paupers, and of these only three outside London took more than Fisherton. In addition an arrangement was made in 1850 whereby Fisherton House became an official establishment for criminal lunatics, transferred, for the most part, from the overcrowded Bethlem Hospital in London. Special criminal wards were built to house them, and the male attendants wore the royal insignia on their uniforms. By 1864 the total of criminal lunatics at Fisherton had reached 276, but with the opening of the purpose-built asylum at Broadmoor the number dropped rapidly, and by 1872 this function had ceased altogether.[83]

Evidence about conditions inside Salisbury's two Victorian asylums is confused and contradictory. For commercial reasons both houses tried to paint an idyllic picture of life inside, and each was the subject of an anonymous pamphlet extolling its virtues. The 'London reporter' who visited Fisherton House in 1850 was introduced to a patient named Card, a musician and composer who was said to entertain his fellow-inmates and the neighbourhood of Fisherton generally with the pleasing strains of his violin on summer nights, not infrequently accompanied by a lady singing in the distant garden of the female department. Card, when his condition improved, was allowed outside the asylum with an attendant. On one occasion an old friend accosted him and asked if he were coming out. ' "Not me," said Card, "I was never so happy in my life!" and then added, "if you knew all you would be glad to be with us." ' Against propaganda of this kind should be set a Lunacy Commissioners' report of the same year which named Fisherton House as one of three provincial licensed houses considered to be especially defective. In 1865 the commissioners complained that Laverstock House had, 'fallen into the hands of a new and non-medical proprietor, who apparently regards it as a money speculation only; and the comforts of the patients have consequently been neglected to a shameful extent;' and in 1883 they felt that inadequate oversight of nurses at Fisherton House was leading to rough handling of the female patients. Treatment, too, might appear cruel. The 'Rotatory chair,' in use at Laverstock in 1815, sought to induce vertigo, nausea, vomiting and prostration so as to take the patient's mind off his illness. But such cures, and the popular prejudices and fears with regard to mental institutions which were rampant among the Victorians, must not colour our judgement. There seems to have been a genuine desire not to resort to mechanical restraint and seclusion for the sake of convenience. Fisherton House pioneered the use of occupational therapy as early as 1829, and by 1847 various medical and surgical treatments were in use for mania, melancholia, epilepsy and paralysis. Several members of the Finch family attained recognition in their profession at national level, and one member by marriage, Dr Alfred Lush, became president of the Medico-Psychological Association in 1879. William Corbin Finch, in his report as resident proprietor of Fisherton House in 1854, claimed that his system of treatment was intended to give the patient, 'as much personal freedom indoors and out within the precincts of the establishment, as the nature of the case will permit, with due regard to his safety and that of others. To dissipate all past fears and apprehensions of the patient by kindness of manner and assurance of good will and intentions towards him ... with a view to secure the mental repose and confidence of the patient.'[84]

Salisbury had reason to be proud, therefore, of its medical institutions and the part they were playing in the development of medical care. It had far less to boast about in the field of public health and hygiene. In July 1849 cholera arrived in the city. Between 17th July and 10th September the disease claimed almost 200 lives and over 1300 new cases were received at the Infirmary. Sufferers were taken to the isolation hospital in Bugmore, 'a most miserable-looking place, of very limited dimensions,' which lay next to a sewage-ridden open stream, 'discoloured and offensive to the smell ... A place less adapted to afford a chance of recovery to those afflicted with disease could scarcely be selected.' A connection between poor sanitation and cholera was not universally accepted by medical opinion, but one Salisbury surgeon, Andrew Middleton, who became the champion of sanitary reform, was left in no doubt: 'I found the privy out by my nose. I looked about the yard, and at the top I found an open drain, and against a high wall this privy, in a ruinous condition, the fluid flowing over the yard. There were stepping-stones placed at intervals to enable one to get across it; and making use of them, I proceeded to explore this horrible receptacle of filth. [In the adjoining cottages,] I found the inhabitants in a most wretched state from poverty and sickness, covered with rags, and with scarcely a bed to lie on. In one room, – a very small one, – were two children dying, and another already attacked with cholera; one in a state of collapse.'[85]

Responsibility for Salisbury's drainage lay with the directors of highways, who maintained the street watercourses on a very inadequate budget. No-one was responsible for providing a supply of drinking-water, and recourse was had either to the watercourses or to wells, which often lay adjacent to cess-pits for sewage. Sewage was also channelled into the street watercourses. In many places the level of water in the watercourses was only just below street level, and so house drains had the greatest difficulty discharging into them. Sewage was in fact trapped in the drains or even driven back whence it came by the water in the watercourses. To clear this disgusting backlog the flow of water was interrupted by the closing of hatches for a period each day, thus permitting sewage to drain into empty watercourses and be flushed away when the flow was restored. Needless to say the watercourses and dependent drains were easily and frequently blocked, and then council employees dredged their contents into heaps which were left in the road pending collection. The beds of the watercourses leaked, and over the years the soil and subsoil of Salisbury had become an enormous, filthy, saturated sponge. As a result the water drawn from wells was often discoloured, pungent and offensive. Nevertheless such water was accepted as normal, even excellent. Middleton recorded a surprising instance of such acceptance: 'Some years ago, upon a well being sunk, the water yielded by it was of such colour and taste as to lead to the mistaken notion of a mineral spring having been discovered, – the truth was, a cesspool had been tapped.' The problems of drainage and water supply were even worse in the enclosed courts in the centre of chequers, and here the directors of highways had no power to make improvements, as there was no street frontage and the owners paid no highway rates. In the main these courts belonged to large landlords, many of them prominent citizens and councillors, who had no incentive to provide better sanitation for their tenants, but who were influential enough to prevent the council from interfering. Consequently an overcrowded population relied on a single source (the street watercourses) or adjacent sources (wells and cess-pits) for drinking water and sewage disposal. But because most of the disadvantaged lived in courts away from the main commercial streets and Market Place, and because when the water was flowing in the watercourses it appeared reasonably pure (since much of the sewage was bottled up in stinking drains until the flow was stemmed), and because the expense of making alterations would fall most heavily on the decision-makers themselves, there was little incentive to improve.[86]

After the cholera epidemic, in February 1850, the directors of highways commissioned a survey of the watercourses, and this was discussed at a meeting the following month, which the city's medical practitioners were invited to attend. Most favoured replacing the street watercourses with a network of deep drains, but such a scheme was rejected by the directors on the grounds of expense. So determined were they to ignore the medical advice, it appears, that the clerk did not even record the doctors' evidence and threw away a letter from Middleton, which had been read at the meeting. Instead work began on repairing a few particularly bad sticking-points in the watercourse system, and uncovering some of the channels which a few years earlier had been paved over in order to widen the streets for traffic. Opinion was divided on this subject; in the case of Catherine Street the directors prevaricated, and then flew in the face of a petition from residents asking that it should remain closed. Such tinkering with a dangerous and objectionable system incensed Middleton who, having failed to make his voice heard in Salisbury, took his complaint to Dr Southwood Smith at the General Board of Health. Battle commenced. Middleton tried to raise a petition to the Board of Health to send an inspector to Salisbury. He secured 60 names, including the Bishop, the Dean and Dr Fowler, Salisbury's most distinguished physician. But his efforts were surpassed by a much larger counter-petition signed by opponents of a drainage scheme. The directors of highways, for their part, hastily began to construct barrel drains in the eastern chequers fed by a pump in Greencroft Street. This was a clumsy attempt to forestall the government inspector, and it failed. The workmanship was not of the highest quality, as the highways surveyor admitted in evidence to the inspector: 'I have no map on a large scale exhibiting the courses of the sewers, and no system of levels. I took the levels in portions of 10 or 12 feet, calculating the gradients according to the fall; sometimes this was not very accurate ... The bricks at the bottom of the drains are laid dry; for one reason, to save expense. I have found that in course of time the interstices between the bricks in drains get filled up. The drains themselves may stop up in course of time; no doubt they will.' The directors themselves remained cheerfully oblivious to the problems of sanitary engineering: 'Being on the side of a hill, it was considered that the works were such as a bricklayer's labourer would be competent to carry out.' The pumps, which were crucial to the success of the operation, were manually operated, but no provision was made to employ anyone to work them. As one of the directors commented, 'I think it would be very seldom required to pay people to pump them, because people will use the pumps to get water, and when they do so, a little always escapes.' At other times, one assumes, the water was expected to flow uphill of its own accord.[87]

When the inspector, Mr Thomas Rammell, arrived in June 1851 – for Mr Middleton prevailed with the Board of Health – he was not impressed by the directors' maladroit scheme. Not only was it not working, leakage was causing flooding where there had been none before, and furthermore the pumps were illegal, as the directors of highways had no powers to spend money on water supply. Mr Rammell stayed for a week, and held his inquiry in the Assembly Rooms, since the mayor and councillors had effectively blocked his requests to use the Guildhall. At the end of three days' sessions he inspected the conditions in various parts of the city, and his observations are included in the report. In Bugmore Lane he found, 'a block of eight cottages – low lodging-houses – ... of two rooms each; and with the exception of one of them have no backlet, not even a window. They have no pump; the inmates get their water by sufferance from a public house, in St. Ann Street, about 10 minutes walk distant. They wash their houses and clothes with the water from the open sewage drain in front. There is not a single privy amongst all these cottages; as a substitute for one, the inmates have put up a sort of lean-to or wigwam, against the wall in the public thoroughfare facing their houses, which they have covered with various odds and ends, such as bits of matting, old saddles, etc. The seat or cross stick, overhangs the open sewer.'[88]

Underlying the inspector's visit, and the vehement opposition which attended him throughout, was an important principle which stemmed from the Public Health Act of 1848. This act enabled the General Board of Health, upon its inspector's recommendation, to compel local authorities to form a local board of health. If this happened the board of directors of the highways would disappear, and its powers would be transferred to the new board of health. This new board of health would derive its income from a general rate which, unlike the highway rate, would be levied on all property in the city, including the courts. In other words the slum landlords who packed the council would for the first time be compelled to pay for their drainage. Hence the council's opposition to the inquiry.[89]

The inspector's recommendations and conclusions endorsed the message which Middleton had been preaching. The subsoil should be dried out by the removal of the surplus water with which it was saturated; an efficient system of tubular drains should be laid to convey refuse to an outfall below the city; a fresh water supply, perhaps drawn from the River Bourne, should be inaugurated; and the provisions of the Public Health Act, creating a local board of health, should be applied to the city.[90]

With the publication of Mr Rammell's report at the end of 1851 Middleton had won a battle, but he had not won the war. Although a local board would now be set up it would consist of the same councillors, with the same attitudes and vested interests, as the board it had replaced. In 1852 he published a pamphlet, addressed to the inhabitants of Salisbury, in which he tried to justify his own stand, confound the objectors – mostly on financial grounds – to the adoption of a system of deep drainage, and place the debate on a moral and ethical footing: 'When certain causes of disease and death are clearly shown to exist, and their removal to be possible, even easy, it becomes *nothing less than criminal* not to take immediate steps for such removal, and for this reason compulsory measures ought to be resorted to, when nothing short of them will suffice.' When the report was published only five of the 24 councillors wished to adopt it, and memorials of protest were sent to the General Board of Health by both the city council and the directors of highways. It subsequently transpired that these were the work of the clerk, Matthias Hodding, a vigorous opponent of the inquiry, and not the considered views of the councillors. During 1852 Middleton and his supporters canvassed the council and eventually, at the end of the year, succeeded in convincing a majority of councillors that the recommended works should commence. By 1854 a waterworks had been completed and through the 1850s the work of building sewers and filling in watercourses continued. The average annual mortality dropped from 27 per thousand to twenty per thousand, cellars remained perfectly dry and the atmosphere became sweet. Looking back on his struggle in 1868 Middleton concluded: 'and I shall always be happy to plead guilty to any charge of having caused the destruction of the "English Venice," since by that destruction a "New Salisbury" has been created, and very many hundreds of human beings saved from untimely death.'[91]

It is not our intention to discuss at length the enormous changes and improvements that have taken place in medical care and public health during the last hundred years. Various factors have contributed to create the health services which exist today. On the one hand astounding scientific advances have revolutionised what actually happens and what can be achieved in hospital. The Burns Unit at Odstock Hospital and the Common Cold Research Unit at Harvard Hospital are examples of areas in which Salisbury has attained a national reputation. In addition medical facilities and establishments have proliferated, beginning with an isolation hospital at Old Sarum in 1911–1912, a sanatorium for tuberculosis sufferers at Harnwood in 1919, extensive alterations and additions to Salisbury Infirmary in 1937 and a wartime American military hospital at Odstock which was subsequently converted for civilian use. Thirdly there has been the removal of responsibility for medical services from local to regional level. With the growth of county administration certain medical functions, such as the school health service, midwives and health visitors, were fulfilled by the county council. When the National Health Service began in 1948 Salisbury Infirmary relinquished its independence and combined with Odstock and Newbridge (a geriatric hospital) to form Salisbury General Hospital, which along with other local hospitals was administered by the Salisbury Group Hospital Management Committee. In 1954 Old Manor Hospital (the name given to Fisherton House asylum in 1920) surrendered its company status to the Ministry of Health, and since 1974 all state hospitals in the area have come under the aegis of the Wessex Regional Health Authority. The fourth development is the consequence of the other three. It relates to the subtle shift of attitude towards illness, towards expectations of life and good health. The shortcomings of our modern health service are as nothing compared with the despair of the leper colony, the panic of plague, the dread of lunacy and the stench of an overflowing cess-pit.[92]

At Home

Forgetting the normal rules of civilised conduct it is time for us to enter doors marked private and peer in at strangers' windows. We should not imagine that our ancestors were any more willing to open their homes and their personal lives to public scrutiny than we would be, and so, like the voyeurs that we are to become, we must select with care the objects of our curiosity and try to catch them off their guard. Approaching in this manner the sources at our disposal we find three opportunities to investigate home and family life in Salisbury, and it is these that will occupy us in the course of the next few pages. Firstly by examining the inventories of possessions which were often compiled for probate purposes after a householder had died we are able to build up a picture of the typical contents of a middle- or upper-class Salisbury home at a particular period. Secondly by using the replies submitted to census questions in the nineteenth century we may discover where our Victorian predecessors lived and how they formed themselves into families. Thirdly we may focus on a single building and see how it has shaped up to being home through the centuries to a chain of Salisbury families.

Our first concern, therefore, lies with the furniture and fittings of the Salisbury home. If we had been invited to stay with friends in the city in 1700 what kind of bed would we have slept in, how would we have kept warm, in what would our food have been cooked, and how would we have eaten it? To answer questions like these we shall examine the evidence of a sample of nearly forty probate inventories, all made in Salisbury within a few years of 1700, and we shall pool the information they contain to reconstruct a composite home. It will not be typical of the city as a whole, however, because usually only the fairly well-to-do made a will which might require a probate inventory, and so our 'typical' home relates only to the wealthier strata of society.[93]

Rich people demonstrate their wealth in a variety of ways. In 1700 Salisbury's affluent citizens used their money for three purposes - either they spent it on a luxurious standard of living, or they invested it in their businesses, or else (in an age before banks and building societies) they lent it to other people. John Strong, gentleman, the richest man in our sample, tied up most of his money – more than £2,500 – in loans and property. Nearly half of the capital of George Godfrey, a successful milliner, was similarly invested, but his stock-in-trade accounted for only a little less. Elizabeth Viner, on the other hand, lived very well in a ten-roomed house containing over £180 worth of possessions – more than either John Strong or George Godfrey – but she had no other assets, and her value when she died was slightly below the average for the sample as a whole. By contrast William Jones seems to have been a miserly fellow; he lived in a single room which contained a mere £5 worth of furniture, including two rusty old pistols in an old box, but inside his coffer the executors found £36 worth of gold and silver and promissory notes owing him nearly £300. Quite humble craftsmen could make a respectable fortune, and a brazier, a currier and a maltster all rank near the top of our sample, with over £400 each to their names. Other businesses were not so lucrative – a pair of shoemakers could only cobble together £12 each to leave to their heirs, and both weavers left under £20. A kind of progression emerges in the cloth industry, from the two weavers to a clothmaker worth £36, a clothier worth £92 and a milliner worth over £1,000. The sample as a whole falls into three groups: an elite of ten, each worth over £300 and with substantial moneylending activities; a 'poor' group (though not poor by the standards of the city as a whole) of nineteen – half the sample – worth £30 or less, who had little to their credit apart from the contents of their houses; and an intermediate group of nine, whose capital was for the most part tied up in their businesses.[94]

Another index of the standard of living in 1700 may be deduced from the size of houses. Rarely are houses themselves valued in inventories but most are described room by room, and so it is possible to draw some conclusions from the number of rooms and the names given to them about the ways in which wealthy and more humble families organised their domestic lives. The most commodious dwelling in our sample contained fourteen rooms excluding cellars and outbuildings. It belonged to an apothecary, one of the intermediate group of nine described above, and at least two of his rooms, the bottlehouse and the distilling house, were given over to his concoctions. So large an establishment was unusual, although another six houses in the sample contained ten rooms or more; the commonest size, however, was three or four principal rooms, which catered for the vital ingredients of life – food, sleep and work. Every room-by-room inventory describes at least one bedroom, though it is never referred to as such, but always as 'chamber.' Most houses had one or two chambers, but William Eyers, the apothecary, had five, and Nicholas Staples, a slightly impoverished gentleman who lived in Butcher Row, had no fewer than six. A kitchen – but never more than one – is almost always present in the room-by-room inventories, and this served as the principal living room in the smaller houses. About half the examples also had one or more buttery or brewhouse, where a cheap, non-toxic beverage could be prepared in an age when tea and coffee were luxuries and drinking water was probably drawn from the muddy canal in the street. Equally common was a room designated 'shop' or 'workshop,' reflecting the artisan's normal practice before the industrial revolution of living and working in the same building. Two other rooms, the parlour and the garret, commonly recur in houses large and small. The parlour was the equivalent of the modern sitting room, and its furniture usually consisted of tables and chairs complemented by a well-stocked hearth. In the richer houses this room might show off wall-hangings, rugs, pictures and decorated screens, whereas in humbler abodes it doubled as an extra bedroom. Garrets, also described as cocklofts or lofts, were more properly spare bedrooms. Tucked under the eaves and usually unheated these poky attics often contained one or two beds with their accoutrements, but might also be used as storerooms. George Godfrey, the milliner, kept one of his three garrets as a bedroom – although it was also found to contain pots of honey – but the other two housed various raw materials for his trade, such as skins, horsehair and feathers. Rarely did a small house contain rooms other than those we have described, but wealthier residences might boast a hall or a dining room, or even a study. Large houses were sometimes equipped with cellars and various outbuildings, including sheds and stables. Only one of the houses in our sample had a wash-house.[95]

Let us now enter our composite house of 1700 and look more closely at its rooms and their contents. If the house belonged to a craftsman then it is likely that our entrance would be by way of his shop, which would occupy the room adjoining the street on the ground floor. The contents of the shop would vary, of course, according to the trade of its owner. In our sample we have a cook (whose shop contained spits and jacks and frying-pans), a butcher (knives and axes), a currier (hides and skins) and a saddler (saddles and bridles). Most tradesmen manufactured or prepared the goods they sold, but the milliner's shop was more akin to a modern retail department store, and contained a great variety and quantity of manufactured goods, including cloth, haberdashery, brushes, twine, looking-glasses, tobacco and even six gross of bird-calls. More typical was the shop of Edmund Mack, a brazier. He made pots and pans and kitchen utensils of brass, iron and pewter, and so his shop contained examples of his wares for sale, to the value of about £60. Because he lived in a small house with no separate storeroom he had to keep the remainder of his wares, another £50 worth of pewter, in his bedroom. His shop also contained the furnaces, raw materials worth over £90, and – in common with shopkeepers everywhere – a set of weights and scales. Craftsmen who lived in large houses might scatter the goods and tools of their trade in rooms throughout the house. John Weste, a plateworker, had thirteen rooms, including a shop, a ware-room, a hair-room (in which he kept tin, leather and hair), a workroom and a workshop over the cellar (containing his tools, wire, latten and plate) as well as two other premises in the city containing, 'goods of severall soartes belonging to the trade.' The weavers and clothworkers, who were still in 1700 active in the city in considerable numbers, also had 'shops,' but these were probably workshops for making rather than shops for selling. Unlike other shops, too, they were probably not at ground floor level, as weavers needed a large, light area in which to position their looms, and so preferred a first or second floor room with large windows. If they were concerned with the finishing processes of clothmaking as well as weaving they might also need tentering racks, and there is an example among our inventories of a clothworker who owned, 'four old racks and the ire gare [iron gear] belonging to them,' on Milford Hill, worth £14. 5. 0.[96]

Into the private part of the house now, which might begin with the kitchen, the parlour, the hall or the dining room, depending on the size of house and the status of its owner, and here we shall look first at the furniture. Apart from beds, which we shall discuss shortly, the most common items of furniture in the Salisbury house were tables and chairs. Nearly everyone had at least one table and the grander houses had as many as thirteen or fourteen. Most were simply described as tables (or table-boards, to give them their full title) but a few were further distinguished as having drawers or leaves, or as being oval or Spanish. Far more chairs occur than any other items of furniture in the inventories, each house having an average of about eleven. Nearly half were not described in any more detail, but about 80 were of leather (that is, the seat was covered with leather) and a further 80 had cane or rush seating. Heavy and cumbersome, many of the chairs described probably remained fairly well rooted to their places in the room, and there was a need in many households for a smaller, more versatile form of seating. Stools or 'joyned stools' (made with joints by a joiner) occur in more than half the inventories, usually at the rate of about six to a house. A few also boasted a form or settle. After providing somewhere to sit and something to eat from, the next most pressing requirement was for furniture in which possessions could be stored. Chests, coffers, cupboards and chests-of-drawers each occur in more than half the inventories, and trunks and presses are also very frequent. In 1700 the use of the chest (traditionally a box with a flat lid) and the coffer (like a chest but with a rounded lid) was giving way to the more convenient chest-of-drawers, and our sample catches the period when the two existed side-by-side in many homes. Chests, which are often described as old, become noticeably less numerous in our sample between 1705 and 1715 compared with between 1696 and 1705. Whereas chests and chests-of-drawers were primarily for the storage of clothes and linen goods, cupboards, presses (tall cupboards in which the shelves are enclosed by doors) and dressers, which are mentioned in six houses in our sample, were used for the storage of food and eating equipment.[97]

What we have so far described have been the furnishings necessary for even a quite mediocre standard of living in 1700, and consequently most of them recur in most inventories. About half the houses in our sample contained at least one other item of furniture, and the most common was a looking-glass. A clock and a close-stool box (commode) were other useful items occasionally found, and a few households adorned their floors and walls with carpets and hangings. Pictures, maps or 'cuts' (prints) hung on the walls of nine houses, but there were few other ornaments. There were, however, a number of miscellaneous items which may most conveniently be described at this point. Books, including Bibles and prayer books, were quite a common possession, and weapons, including a halberd, muskets, swords, 'birding-pieces' and pistols were all to be found. George Godfrey's glass cupboard contained Delft and china ware as well as glasses, and he was one of four owners of alarm clocks or watches. And James Greene, one of the wealthiest men in our sample, left a number of interesting luxury items, including a pair of silver buckles, a pair of silver spurs, four pairs of gold buttons, a silver-handled sword and belt with silver buckles, a pair of playing tables, a pair of virginalls, a silver-headed cane, three old pictures and a glass globe.[98]

Having explored the furniture and the downstairs rooms in our composite 1700 house we must now look upstairs at the sleeping arrangements. Most of the smaller houses in our sample possessed two or at most three beds, but the grander establishments might have as many as eight. Beds were usually to be found in rooms described as chambers, or less frequently in the garrets and cocklofts which we noted earlier. Richard Zelle and John Mills, who kept beds in their dining room and parlour respectively, were exceptional. Our ancestors of 1700 drew quite a clear distinction between the bed (which we should call the mattress) and the bedstead, the wooden structure surrounding and supporting it. Almost all the beds described in detail were made of either feathers or flock, and one inventory enables us to draw a comparison between them. Nicholas Staples had a number of beds in his house in Butcher Row, and when he died his executors valued them by weight. Feather beds, bolsters and pillows were reckoned to be worth between sixpence and tenpence per pound weight, whereas the equivalent stuffed with flock was valued at between $1\frac{1}{2}$d and 3d. The heaviest feather bed weighed 65 pounds and the lightest flock bed 35 pounds. And this distinction between beds in one household is reflected in the sample as a whole. The average value of a complete bed, bedstead and bedding which included a feather bed was around £4. 10. 0, but with an equivalent flock bed it was slightly under £1. The most expensive bed in the sample belonged to a widow, Elizabeth Viner, and was reckoned (with bedstead and fittings) to be worth £20. By contrast Priscilla Hellier's spare bed, including, 'one old flock bed and bolster, one pillow, one old coverlid and bed stead,' was worth a mere eight shillings. The bedstead itself was a complicated affair, and its constituent parts were often listed separately. The cord, which was strung tightly from side to side across the frame and the matting (or occasionally sacking) which lay on top of it are nearly always itemised. Upon these was placed the mattress or bed, and a valence generally hung from the sides of the bed to the floor. The most elaborate bedsteads, which we should describe as four-posters, included also a headpiece, tester (canopy) and curtains; but curtains were also a part of many beds which did not have testers, and so were presumably hung from the ceiling around the bed. For every bed there was, on average, one bolster, one pillow and one blanket. Like the beds themselves bolsters and pillows might be stuffed with feathers or flock, and if Nicholas Staples' beds were typical, a pillow weighed about seven pounds and a bolster a little more. Contrary to what we might expect a man's station in life in 1700 does not seem to have been reflected in the type of bed he slept on. Large houses had more beds, of course, but of the seven households which contained four-posters three were among the poorest in our sample. Feather beds and flock beds seem to have been owned by the richer and poorer elements indiscriminately, and there are four examples of feather beds supported by the most primitive type of bedstead, the truckle bed.[99]

Our survey so far has overlooked what many a householder would have considered the most important part of his home. The fireplace, with the mysterious ironmongery which accompanied it, has lost much of its significance in the modern world of gas and electric power, but in 1700 – as well as long before and long after – it performed the vital tasks of heating and cooking, and great care, verging on reverence, was lavished upon it. Smaller houses might rely on a single fireplace, in the kitchen, to provide a degree of warmth to the bedroom above, but most of the larger houses had several hearths. Despite incomplete evidence it is likely that all the dining rooms and nearly all the parlours in our survey were heated. About half the chambers seem to have had a fireplace, but only one garret was so fortunate. Fireplaces away from the kitchen were not generally used for cooking and so required the minimum of equipment; bellows, tongs and something to contain the fire were usually sufficient. But unlike the workaday kitchen hearth they might enjoy ornamental surrounds, and three of the larger houses boasted 'landskipps' (painted landscapes incorporated into the chimneypiece) in their principal bedrooms. At the time of our survey the fireplace was in the throes of a revolution which was transforming both the way it was designed and the way it was used. The exploitation of the coalfields of north-east England, and the transporting of coal by sea to the south coast ports at an economical rate, was of great importance to the town-dweller, who, unlike his country cousin, did not have a bountiful supply of free or cheap firewood on his doorstep. It is likely that until 'seacole,' as it was known, began to appear for sale in the city, most of Salisbury's fuel was wood or charcoal brought from neighbouring woodlands, especially the New Forest. Coal is more efficient than wood in terms of both its weight and its volume, and so involved less effort to carry and less space to store. Frequent references to fuel in the inventories suggest that many householders in 1700 stored both wood and coal, in the garden or outhouse if they had one, or else in the cellar. Coal, according to the inventory of Thomas Holmes, was worth £1. 12. 0 per hundredweight, compared with ten shillings for the same weight of wood faggots. George Godfrey, the wealthy milliner, adopted the curious practice of storing wood and coal in one of his garrets; he was perhaps taking a leaf from the book of a certain Mr Mintorne, a canon of Salisbury Cathedral in the sixteenth century, who was alleged to have discovered that in cold weather a thrifty way of keeping warm was to carry bundles of firewood up and down to his loft without ever actually burning them. The process of conversion from wood to coal is reflected also in the utensils employed to contain the fire within the fireplace. Logs were customarily burnt on the hearth and supported on either side by a pair of firedogs, usually of iron. Coal required less room and burned most efficiently if confined within a grate raised above the level of the hearth. Of 48 fireplaces in our sample 23 included grates or firepans (sometimes a synonymous term for grate) but no dogs, sixteen included dogs but no grate and nine included both. Thus rather more than half had been converted from burning wood to burning coal. As might be expected the changeover occurred first in the kitchen, where only three of the fifteen fireplaces described in sufficient detail were still burning wood. Two of these belonged to comparatively poor households and the third was owned by a maltster with copious piles of wood in his garden. By contrast about half the fireplaces in chambers and other rooms away from the kitchen were still designed for logs rather than coal.[100]

Meals were prepared in various ways in, above and beside the kitchen fire, which was rarely, if ever, allowed to die. Cooking in the fire could be achieved by pushing a gridiron (which occurs in nearly half the kitchens in our sample) among the burning coals or logs and standing a frying-pan on top; alternatively a skillet – a kind of long-handled saucepan with three legs – would support itself in the fire. Cooking above the fire was by means of a pot suspended from the chimney-breast by a long adjustable hook frequently known as a hanger or a pair of cottrells. For heating water a kettle, the commonest kitchen utensil in our sample, was hung over the fire. Roasting was the most important operation to be carried out in front of the fire, and this was the only form of cooking to have been mechanised by 1700. The meat was placed on a spit supported at either end by metal stands similar to firedogs which were known as andirons. High on the wall to one side of the fireplace the jack, a clockwork mechanism driven by a weight suspended on a chain, was connected by a cord to one end of the spit, causing it to revolve slowly in front of the fire. Beneath the meat on the spit was placed a dripping pan and nearby a basting ladle was ready for the cook to return the fat to the rotating meat. Three-quarters of the kitchens in our sample contained at least one spit, and most had several spits for different joints, which might be kept in a special rack. Two-thirds also had jacks, and in a few instances the chains and weights are listed separately. These, together with an assortment of knives, forks, ladles and skimmers, formed the basic culinary equipment in use in Salisbury in 1700. A few kitchens boasted more specialised utensils such as chafing-dishes (miniature grates for heating small quantities of food), saucepans, mortars, colanders and coffee pots. Kitchen equipment was manufactured in various metals, and we have already in the course of our survey entered the shop of the brazier, Edmund Mack, and found him at work making pots and pans in brass, iron and pewter. Other common materials were copper, which had to be properly tinned before use in cooking, and two copper alloys, bell-metal and latten.[101]

At this point, settled comfortably in front of the fire with the prospect of a good dinner before us, we have come to the end of our tour of inspection of a Salisbury house in 1700. We have not in fact seen everything. We have not visited the buttery where the brewing equipment was usually kept, nor the cellar where barrels and bottles were stored. We have not looked at the powdering tub, or silt, in which bacon was salted, nor examined the contents of the garden shed or the bottle-house where William Eyers kept a 'wheelbarrow, very old.' And we have not noticed some of the everyday items in the kitchen, such as the porringers (dishes), the trenchers (wooden platters), the candlesticks and the warming pan. But other items have been omitted because they were not there, and we, 300 years on, would find our visit most uncomfortable without them. The absence of electric power is obvious, but the ramifications of having to cook, preserve food and provide lighting and heating without it repay a moment's thought and help to explain some of the complexities and obscurities of our ancestors' possessions. The lack of basic sanitation, apart from the occasional cistern, which probably stored rainwater from the roof, and the 'washing cowl' found in four houses, would be even more difficult to come to terms with, and on reflection we should be more suspicious than ever about the suitability of water drawn from the street channels for any household purpose whatever. That it was a malodorous, gloomy, squalid world by our standards is not in question; but it had a certain dignity, and with it a well-wrought appreciation of the quality of simple possessions.

Despite our warning at the outset that probate inventories only reflect the standard of living of the upper and middle classes of society there is a danger that we may regard the foregoing survey as typical of the population as a whole. To redress the balance, therefore, we propose next to examine two of the city's chequers in some detail, in order to build up a picture of everyone, rich and poor, who lived there at a certain date. The date is 1871 and the chequers are Antelope (bounded by Catherine Street, Ivy Street, Brown Street and Milford Street) and its neighbour to the south, White Hart (St. John Street, St. Ann Street, Brown Street, Ivy Street). The area covered by these chequers extends from a corner of the original Market Place, in the north-west, almost to the limit of the historic city's development in the south, and is bounded by the old main road to Exeter on its west, the old main road to Southampton on its south, and lesser city streets on east and north (Figure 27). These two chequers almost certainly have a history of continuous, high-density occupation since the thirteenth century, and maps of 1611 and 1716 portray a virtually unbroken line of buildings along each frontage. Little new building has occurred here since 1871, and so most of the buildings which we see today were home to one of the families we are about to study. About one-third of Antelope chequer and part of the centre of White Hart chequer are now devoid of

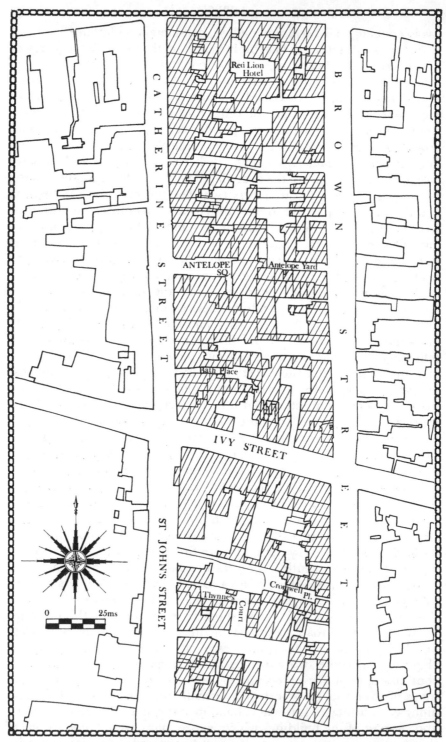

Figure 27. Antelope and White Hart chequers, 1879, derived from Ordnance Survey 1:500 maps.

buildings in the interests of the motor car. In 1871, by my estimation, 126 people lived in the area now occupied by the Brown Street car park. But in spite of widespread demolition parts of a dozen surviving buildings are at least 400 years old, and three of the inns, the Bell and Crown, the Queen's Arms and the Red Lion, are of fourteenth-century origin. In the ensuing discussion we shall look at this segment of the city in three ways: firstly we shall gather its whole population together and make observations about their ages, families, occupations and mobility; then we shall replace them in their houses and try to detect the richer and poorer neighbourhoods, the areas of specialisation and the functions of particular buildings; finally we shall cast backward and forward glances from 1871 in an attempt to see how the character of the area may have changed in the preceding three hundred and succeeding one hundred years.[102]

Everyone who slept in a house in Antelope or White Hart chequer on census night 1871 should appear in the census enumerator's return. Absent members of families on that night are therefore omitted, and temporary visitors included; unconscious mistakes and misunderstandings might arise between enumerator and resident, and deliberate errors might be introduced to conceal embarrassing truths or provide alibis. Nevertheless the nineteenth-century censuses provide the student with an unsurpassed view of the whole of society caught at a particular moment in its history. Our two chequers contained 548 people that night, 244 men and 304 women. This was about 6% of the total population of the city, excluding its new suburbs, in an area which was roughly 5%–6% of the city's total area. Apart from dwelling houses and shops with living accommodation the chequers also accommodated a disproportionate number of inns. The smaller establishments can be included in our figures, as they were run as small family businesses with few, if any, lodgers, but three large inns, the White Hart, the Red Lion and the Waggon and Horses (now the Churchill Rooms in Brown Street) must be omitted because they would distort our picture of family life. Before discounting them, however, we should take a brief look inside them. The White Hart, the grandest of the three, was under the supervision of a 35-year-old housekeeper, Jane Burch, with ten staff, and boasted among its visitors on this particular evening two American barristers, an elderly doctor from Clifton and a Member of Parliament. Most of the Red Lion's guests were commercial travellers. The hotels apart, we are left with 484 people living in 109 households, which works out at about four-and-a-half (two men and two-and-a-half women) per house. The imbalance of female over male is accounted for by two factors, the slightly greater life expectancy of women, but more particularly the prevalence of young girls in domestic service in the smarter homes. Thirty girls aged between fourteen and 33 were so employed, most of them under 21 and nearly all in the richer shopkeepers' houses in Catherine Street. Only five were Salisbury girls, and most of the remainder were sent by their parents from nearby villages to acquire a schooling in the polite society of the country town. Few families in this part of Salisbury could afford to engage more than one domestic servant. The largest households, with sixteen and twelve members respectively, were also to be found in Catherine Street. William Devereux, a draper, who lived at number 43 (now Ladbroke's betting shop) accommodated his wife, a sister, two young children, his six girl assistants, two apprentices, a domestic servant and two nursemaids, which was a fine achievement for a young man of 29. And James Best, landlord of the Bell and Crown on the corner of Ivy Street, sheltered a wife, six children under eight years old, a lodger, his ostler, a domestic servant and a nursemaid. These families were unusual, and it was comparatively rare to find more than six people in a house. Two-thirds of all the households had between two and five members, but apart from a few elderly widows in Brown Street, it was very unusual to live on one's own. Children of the householder living at home naturally accounted for a large proportion of the population, and nearly 40% fell into this category. Asher and Ellen Ratty, who lived in a now demolished house in Brown Street near the Queen's Arms, held the record with eight children, all under fifteen, but small families were much more common and few householders had more than three children living at home. Children of school age were more prevalent in the meaner Brown and Ivy Streets than in Catherine Street.[103]

Mere figures can never do justice to the little human stories behind them, and many colourful characters must have lurked within the doors of our two chequers. At 5 St. Ann Street, for instance, lodged Margaretta Coombs, described as 'an independent lady.' But how much of her independence remained is doubtful. She was 85 years old, blind, and accompanied in her lodgings by her neice, Sarah, and an elderly nurse. Other handicapped people included Harriet Nowlson, deaf and dumb from birth, who lodged in Brown Street with an attorney's clerk and his family, and Henry Topp, a deaf gardener of 61, whose wife, Ann, appears to have borne him a son when she was 47; in 1871 he was at school and living with them at their cottage in Bath Place, one of the courts off Catherine Street. In Brown Street lived a number of single-parent families, and it would be interesting to know how the neighbours regarded Susan Marvell of 7 Ivy Street (now a tropical fish shop), who had recently produced and was struggling to bring up her third illegitimate child, Bessie Ethel. Another unorthodox family lived in Thynnes Court (now incorporated into the White Hart). Jane Harris, aged 70, presided over an all-female household which included her two unmarried daughters, two illegitimate granddaughters, a lodger, Rosa Horne, and her two-week-old daughter, Edith. Rosa, like Susan Marvell and other unmarried mothers, had been in domestic service before her misfortune.[104]

Earning a sufficient living to support themselves and their Victorian families was a principal concern of the householders in our sample, and, although we have no means of gauging their relative wealth, we can discern the wide range of trades which were carried on in this small corner of Salisbury. Most of the master tradesmen which we can identify as such congregated in shops along Catherine Street. Old Salisbury specialities such as cutlery, joinery and cloth had by 1871 largely disappeared, but their influence could still be felt. William Beach, cutler, and Henry Borly, cutler and jeweller, were both prosperous enough to keep servants; the clothier's tradition was maintained by a young draper, with eleven employees, several tailors and, in Brown Street, no fewer than seven dressmakers and sempstresses. The joiner's craft was perpetuated by the carriage manufactory of Samuel Lewis, which stood in the very centre of Antelope chequer and employed nineteen men and five boys. After the various branches of the cloth trade, which occupied about one in five of the working population of our two chequers, the next most important activity was the preparation and supply of food and drink. Along the length of Catherine Street were three grocers, a confectioner, a baker, a butcher and a potato merchant, and elsewhere in the chequers was a dairyman, a cook and a seller of dried fish, as well as seven hotels and inns. Transport was another source of employment, especially for Brown Street and Ivy Street residents. They included two each of carriers, carmen, flydrivers and railway labourers, and a waggoner, bus driver and retired bus proprietor. Our sample, which shows that about three-quarters of adult men and women between the ages of fifteen and 60 were in employment, is rather too small to draw conclusions about most individual trades, which are often represented by only one or two individuals. But there were a mere handful of professional and administrative workers and very few of independent means. Nearly everyone worked in a manufacturing industry or in the retail, service or building trades. There was virtually no unemployment and very few empty houses.[105]

Surveying our crowd of nearly 500 Victorians, assembled as I imagine them in the Brown Street car park, it is impossible now to comprehend the reasons which brought them to Salisbury or the transitory and unpredictable length of their residence. Many of them of course were born in the city – precisely half, in fact – but that is not necessarily a sign of permanence, as nearly half of our crowd had not yet reached their 21st birthday. Of the 109 householders 45 were born in the city and a further 26 in the rest of south Wiltshire, but for the wives Salisbury was the native home to only twenty out of 65, and a further 27 were not even born in Wiltshire. The story of a well-travelled craftsman may be read in the family of William Wells, a master printer living in St. John Street. Aged 44 he was born in Norwich, and married a girl two years his junior from Swaffham in Norfolk. They must have settled in Swaffham for several years, as it was the birthplace of three of their children, aged sixteen, fourteen and eleven. They seem then to have moved briefly to Tewkesbury in Gloucestershire, where their ten-year-old son was born, but soon came to Salisbury, the birthplace of their youngest daughter, aged nine. The transient nature of urban Victorian society is reflected still more clearly in a comparison of the 1871 census with its predecessor in 1861. Of our 109 families only 35 had been living there for more than ten years. In other words, between 1861 and 1871 two-thirds of the houses in our sample had changed hands.[106]

Today's visitor to Salisbury is not usually encouraged to explore Antelope and White Hart chequers, although he may be familiar with them through the two large hotel complexes – the Red Lion and the White Hart – which occupy the northern part of each, or through the Brown Street car park. But having delved at some length into the private lives of their inhabitants a century or more ago we may be excused for taking a brief stroll around them to see what remains of their Victorian past. We shall begin at the northern end of Catherine Street, walk south as far as St. Ann's Gate, and return along St. Ann Street, Brown Street and Milford Street. Looking down Catherine Street today the impression is of a nearly continuous line of small shopfronts on either side beneath assorted eighteenth- and nineteenth-century upper storeys, and rooflines which sometimes betray earlier origins (Plate 46). It is not a prime shopping street – there are no supermarkets here – but it does contain a number of useful, individual shops which it is worth straying from the city centre to visit. From the Milford Street corner as far as Antelope Square (now the motor-cycle park) most of the buildings are older than 1871, and it is possible to equate what the census enumerator saw with what we can see today. A grocer, William Cripps, occupied the corner shop, and his neighbour to the south was a builder, followed by a chemist, a cutler, a tailor, a hosier, a saddler, Clapperton's bookshop and Elizabeth Brown's sweet shop. We have now arrived at the narrow passage which today forms part of Peter Dominic's wine merchants' building, but although modern in appearance the alleyway is marked on this site on a map of 1716. Proceeding southwards an ironmonger, another cutler, another grocer, a baker, a shoe-shop and another chemist would bring us up to Antelope Square, which is now, beside the motor-cycle park, the main pedestrian access to the car park. There was a way through here in the fifteenth century and later the Antelope Inn was built around it. By 1871 Samuel Lewis's carriage factory protruded across the square from behind the present antiques market. Further shops continued along the street to the south, including William Devereux's drapery store (the largest household in this part of Salisbury, as we saw earlier), a photographer, a hairdresser, a dyer and another grocer. At this point an elaborate late-Victorian row of shops, recently restored, has blocked the entrance to Bath Place, the first of four courts existing in 1871, but of which now only traces remain. Thirty-one people lived in ten small cottages ranged on either side of a narrow passageway at right-angles to the street, and the whole arrangement on the map looks suspiciously as if it was fitted into one standard medieval tenement. It is only a few metres now, past another saddler, a butcher and a potato merchant, to the end of Catherine Street marked by the Bell and Crown Inn.[107]

Our view of St. John Street, the southern continuation of Catherine Street, has changed very little since 1871. The imposing regency facade of the White Hart Hotel, with its grand portico, dominates the foreground, and timber-framed medieval buildings take us beyond, almost as far as St. Ann Street. Most of the changes which have occurred here have been inside the chequer, approached through a driveway beneath a modern extension to the hotel. Here in 1871, in the shadow of the great hotel, the nine cottages which made up Thynne's Court accommodated 32 people, including a charwoman, two laundresses, a gardener, an errand boy and twelve children, around a cramped and airless courtyard. A second court, Cromwell Place, which was approached from Brown Street, has also disappeared, but one wall remains with a story to tell, and can be seen from the hotel car park. Cromwell Place was quite new in 1871, but it was built on the site of a large medieval house, the Barracks, which was demolished a few years earlier. The surviving wall formed part of the south range of the Barracks, and two blocked mullioned windows may still be seen. The six cottages of Cromwell Place, together with four more fronting onto Brown Street, housed 35 people in the space previously occupied by a single large house. Returning to St. John Street a carpenter, a dealer and a printer (William Wells from Norfolk) occupied the houses adjoining the King's Arms, the ornate little classical building on the corner (now part of a newsagent's shop) belonged to a watchmaker, and Thomas Witt, master farrier, had his smithy around the corner at number 3, St. Ann Street, which has now, most appropriately, been renamed 'Welands.' Next door lived Margaretta Coombs, the blind but independent lady who we encountered earlier (her lodgings have gone) and then we arrive at the southern end of Brown Street. It is about one hundred metres from here northwards to the corner of Ivy Street; and in the cottages between these two points, if we include the adjoining Cromwell Place, almost one hundred people lived in 1871. Half of their 24 cottages survive, and, beginning with number 106, the householders' occupations were as follows: messenger, carpenter, dressmaker, painter, gardener (number 96, as 98 was unoccupied), cook, servant, plumber, sawyer, milliner and housewife. In Ivy Street there were few residential houses, and fewer have survived. The half-timbered building which is now a restaurant was occupied by a cook, and opposite lived the wayward Susan Marvell and her children.[108]

Precious little remains to be seen in the rest of Brown Street. After the Queen's Arms Inn and the adjoining dwellings, which in 1861 and 1871 housed a clutch of three elderly pauper women, nothing survives until the Waggon and Horses Inn, now known as the Churchill Rooms. The intervening tarmac has replaced the house in which Asher and Ellen Ratty brought up their eight children, the whole of another court – Antelope Place – and a row of large dwellings, which housed a master tailor, an attorney's clerk, a cutler, a cabinet maker, and W. A. Wheeler who, apart from his work as a printer's overseer, was a keen and useful local historian. Beyond the Waggon and Horses four small cottages, occupied by a tinplate worker, a cellarman and an elderly sempstress, bring us to the imposing corner shop, which belonged to George Surman. In 1861 George had worked here as a master cutler, but ten years later he had given up this declining industry and described himself as a shoemaker and leatherseller. The change was perhaps prompted by his sister, Louisa, who lived with the family and who worked in 1861 as a shoe binder. Their father, Charles, had gone blind soon after Louisa was born, and in 1871, an old man of 83, he was looked after in this house by his son and daughter. We turn the corner into Milford Street and pass the house of Walter Goddard, a young 'fly proprietor' (a fly was a light horse-drawn vehicle). The Oddfellows' Arms, which is next door, had both changed hands and names between 1861 and 1871. Formerly the Hope Inn, its curious renaming was perhaps the inspiration of its new landlord, Thomas Treadwell, who had probably moved here from Nottinghamshire. With a passing glance into the courtyard of the second large hotel in our chequers, the Red Lion, we return to the corner of Catherine Street and the end of our perambulation.[109]

Although we have now completed our survey of Antelope and White Hart chequers in 1871, it is possible to draw some comparisons with earlier and later periods. Both chequers lay in St. Thomas's parish, where it was the custom at the end of the sixteenth century to collect a donation every Easter from each parishioner. Some of the books in which these gifts were recorded have survived among the parish records, and they seem to provide a chequer-by-chequer directory of adult residents, distinguishing between husbands, wives, widows and servants. We shall look at the earliest surviving Easter book, that of 1574, and one of the last, for 1600, and, following their lead, we shall divide our area into three – White Hart chequer, Catherine Street, Antelope chequer apart from Catherine Street. For comparative purposes we shall also examine a modern register of electors (1981 for 1982), which, like the Easter books, should list all adult residents. In 1600 there were 227 adults living in the two chequers, 38 of whom were servants; this compares with 300 adults, including 27 servants, in 1871, and a mere 78 adults in 1981. Recalling the multipliers and population totals which we discussed in chapter two we find that the 1600 figure represents between 5% and 6% of the total population of Salisbury, about the same as in 1871. Thus the increase of one-third between the two dates does little more than reflect the general rise in the city's population. The disappearance between 1871 and 1981 of nearly three-quarters of the area's residents has been far more marked in Antelope than in

White Hart chequer, partly because of demolition – you cannot live in a car park – and partly because few people today choose to live over their shops. Comparison between the 1574 and the 1600 Easter books is difficult because one set of figures is incomplete, but there apprears to have been a modest increase (of the order of about 10%) between the two dates, probably achieved against the tide of the city's declining or stagnating total population. If we now look at the number of occupied houses in the two chequers we do not find a rise equivalent to the growth in population between 1600 and 1871. (A small rise in White Hart chequer could be more than explained by the demolition of the Barracks and its replacement by cottages.) Instead we find that the average size of household increased from about 3½ to about 4½. In 1981 this average has fallen again to slightly below the 1600 level. In both 1600 and 1871 the households in Catherine Street were considerably larger than those in the remainder of Antelope chequer. There is an unevenness, too, in the way in which the chequers filled up with extra people between these two dates. The overall increase, as we have seen, was about one-third, and the population of White Hart chequer grew by about that amount. But Antelope chequer, apart from Catherine Street, grew by only 13%, whereas Catherine Street grew by 50%. And if the number of servants is an index of prosperity Catherine Street's pre-eminence in 1871 was only a continuation of the status it already enjoyed in 1574.[110]

Nothing like the Victorian census returns exist for 1600, and so, although we know the householders' names from the Easter books, it is a laborious and uncertain task to discover their occupations and the size of their families. We are reasonably confident about the occupations of 27 of them, including three innkeepers, three joiners, two cutlers, two weavers, a spinner and a clothworker. Among the poorest residents Madalen Lewes, who lived in Brown Street, had appeared before the magistrates two years earlier, when she arrived in the city as a vagrant with her young son, Purnell, escorting a sick woman from King's Somborne in Hampshire. On that occasion she was ordered to make her way back to Romsey, the parish of her birth, but she seems to have returned. By contrast one of the wealthiest establishments in Catherine Street belonged to a feltmaker, Steven Talbot. So far as we can tell he was aged about 40 and had been married to his wife Sybil for eighteen years. They had five sons, from Steven, the eldest aged sixteen in 1600, to Zachary aged five. A daughter, Ellynor, had died in infancy. The family also had three male servants. It is tempting to read into the fragmentary evidence the familiar pattern of wealth in Catherine Street, moderation in White Hart chequer and poverty along Brown Street; certainly the pattern is present in the average contribution to the Easter offering. The Catherine Street residents put nearly 1/3d per household in the collecting plate, compared with a little under one shilling in White Hart chequer and eightpence in Brown Street. The pattern seems to emerge also in the size of those families which we have been able to trace. Eleven out of seventeen Catherine Street families seem to have had two or more children, and only six were childless or had a single child. In Brown Street and the rest of Antelope chequer another group of seventeen families provides a direct contrast – only six had two or more children, the remaining eleven had one or were childless. White Hart chequer, as usual, fell somewhere between these two extremes.[111]

Drawing together the threads of a conclusion about Antelope and White Hart chequers we must return to our theme of people in their place. We have tried to show that quite an ordinary – and probably fairly typical – corner of the city can be made to yield up the subtle variations which have existed in the status, mores and functions of its various parts. By freezing the picture at a particular moment we have been able to become acquainted with some of this variety, and to learn about the families who lived in the houses and walked the streets which we can see today. And although as families and as individuals their existence was temporary and insecure – a decade earlier two-thirds of the characters were different, after all – yet the homes in which they lived and the neighbourhoods with which they surrounded themselves were providing a sense of continuity. In terms of the good and bad areas, the residential and the commercial, the wealthy and the humble, very little changed between 1600 and 1871, and in adapting these chequers to our own needs we should do well to respect the centuries of humanity which have drained into their soil, and helped to shape their individuality.

The final approach to home life in Salisbury which we wish to attempt is by way of the history of a single building. Number 3/5 Minster Street is an imposing four-storeyed medieval house close to the Poultry Cross and adjoining the Haunch of Venison Inn; and it houses one of the longest-established businesses in the city, the jewellers William Carter and Son. By good fortune deeds survive which enable us to reconstruct an almost complete record of its owners and occupiers for the last 400 years. On architectural evidence the present building has been dated to the late-fifteenth century, and so it is unlikely to have been the first building on the site; Minster Street was probably crowded with houses at least a century earlier. It is an opulent building and reflects the wealth of the society in which its anonymous builder moved. He was perhaps a merchant, as the doorway between the hall and the principal bedroom is carved with an elaborate merchant's mark. The first re-corded occupier is one William Eaton, gentleman, who was living there in 1574, and who stayed on until his death, which probably occurred in 1599. He was married throughout this period, and the household generally included one servant, but after William's death his wife left the property, and for a few years the tenants or owners were Toby Hall and his wife, about whom we know nothing. The obscurity is soon blown away, however, by a most interesting document of 1612. By this time the house had passed to Robert Holmes on the death of his father, also Robert, and he was in the process of leasing it to a certain Robert Jole. Now we have come across Robert Jole before – he was the drunken mayor who fell into a gutter in chapter five. His fellow-aldermen described him as, 'beinge of a moste furious and fierye nature,' and many of them were so frightened of him that they, 'durst not come into the room to hym single ... for fear of beinge assaulted by hym.' Robert Holmes did not trust him either, and before relinquishing the house to him he drew up an inventory of all the fittings which he thought his lessee might possibly he tempted to remove, from the hangings on the walls to the glass in the windows and the bolts on the doors. From this inventory we can reconstruct the arrangement of the house in 1612. The ground floor comprised a shop with a partly boarded floor, which opened onto Minster Street, a kitchen approached through a door from the shop, and at the back of the house a second shop at a slightly higher level so as to accommodate a cellar beneath. Besides the usual cooking equipment and utensils (which are not listed, presumably because Robert Jole would have to supply his own) the kitchen also contained a lead cistern to collect rainwater via a long pipe from the gutter and a salt cupboard built into the chimney. From the kitchen led stairs to the main living area on the first floor, the hall and the principal bedroom. The hall was a long room, nearly eight metres from the window overlooking Minster Street to the back window facing the church; its walls were decorated partly with wooden panelling and partly with stained cloths proclaiming the monogram, RH, of their previous owner. The massive fireplace which warmed the room survives to the present day. The bedroom lay next to the hall and over the kitchen. On the noisy Minster Street side its windows were fitted with sliding shutters and, like the hall, it was richly wainscoted. The second floor was divided into four further bedrooms, less luxuriously appointed, but also with shutters on the windows overlooking the street. Two cocklofts in the roof completed the accommodation.[112]

Having taken these precautions to defend his property from the notorious Jole, the owner, Robert Holmes, found that his tenant did not wish to stay for long. Three years later, in 1615, Jole sub-let the house to a shoemaker, Richard Mason, and thus it began an association with the shoe trade which continued until the end of the century. Richard Mason continued to live in the house until his death nearly 50 years later, in 1662; for the first seventeen years he paid rent to Robert Jole – £7 per annum – but then negotiated the outright purchase of the property from the owner. During the following 30 years, from 1632 to 1662, the Mason family, including a son and four daughters, seem to have made no significant changes to their home, and a brief inventory made at the time of Richard's death enables us to put some furniture in the rooms which we have just described (Figure 28). Both the cellar and the small raised shop above it were used as storerooms and contained food, firewood and the shoemaker's raw materials; whilst the shop

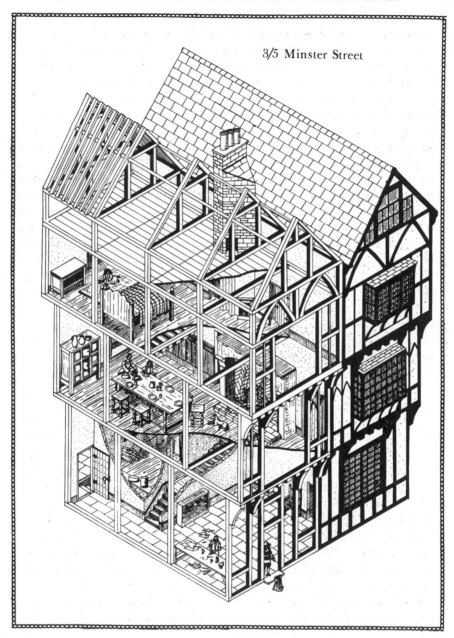

3/5 Minster Street

Figure 28. 3/5 Minster Street in 1662. An isometric drawing of the house and its contents as it may have appeared at the time of Richard Mason's death in 1662, using the room-by-room inventory attached to his will to reconstruct the approximate positions of his furniture and household goods.

opening onto Minster Street was full of shoes, earthenware and lasts. Upstairs the main living room, the hall, seems to have been sparsely furnished – a table, six stools and a cupboard – but the main bedroom next door contained all the comforts we might expect – a feather bed with all the accoutrements, three chairs, a rug, a chest, a spare bed, a small table and a warming pan. Three of the girls (one imagines, if they lived at home) slept in the large bedroom over the hall, since it contained three beds, whilst Henry the son presumably had one of the smaller bedrooms to himself. Another bedroom and the cocklofts seem to have been little used. Henry Mason inherited the house in his father's will and continued to live there. But he appears not to have had any children and was perhaps unmarried; so the house was a good deal too big for his needs. Accordingly he turned to his nearest relatives, cousins, also shoemakers, and their children, his nephews. When one of these nephews, Thomas Cooper, married in 1681, Henry divided his house into two and sold the newly-weds half of the ground and first floors, including part of the main shop, a cellar and the small raised shop, together with the hall upstairs, which was probably partitioned to create a bedroom. Henry continued to live in the remainder of the house until his death in 1688, but one month before he died he sold it to his cousin, Samuel Cooper. Meanwhile Thomas Cooper and his young wife had moved out of their share of the house, and had let it to yet another shoemaker, Ambrose Carter, who died there in 1691.[113]

It is at this point that the history of 3/5 Minster Street becomes rather complicated. The first division of the building has taken place – a relatively simple matter in a double-fronted house – and the practice of absentee landlords and occupying tenants has become established. From now on owners may change whilst tenants remain and vice versa. With the inventories of Henry Mason, 1688, and Ambrose Carter, 1691, we catch the last glimpse of what the house actually contained. It conformed very closely to the composite house of 1700 which we reconstructed earlier, and the main point of interest is the supply of shoes and leather which Henry was working on when he died: ten pairs of men's shoes, 27 pairs of small shoes, four bushels of ox hide, 22 upper leather hides, $3\frac{1}{2}$ other hides and so on. Between 1687 and 1741 the larger northern part of the house, which had belonged to Henry Mason, passed from a shoemaker to a bucklemaker, then to a clothier, a broadweaver and two more clothiers, father and son, but how many of these actually lived there is not clear. In 1741 a brazier or pewterer, Peter Tinham, was the occupant, and when he died in the following year he left in his will, 'a feather bed and all its furniture now used as such in my kitchen.' Ownership of the smaller southern part of the house was divided during this period between Thomas Cooper's two daughters, but it was later re-united and ultimately passed by inheritance to a certain Roger Rice of Bristol. One of its tenants was a widow who ran a grocery shop.[114]

Next in line to determine the house's destiny was Samuel Fawconer, who is described both as a shoemaker and as a hosier. The Fawconers were a long-established Salisbury family, and Samuel's pedigree has been traced back to about 1600 and forward to about 1900. He was already the owner of the Haunch of Venison Inn, which adjoins our property on the south, and in 1741 he negotiated the purchase of both halves of 3/5 Minster Street from their respective owners. He did not, however, convert the house back into a single dwelling, and it seems to have remained in single ownership but dual occupation for over a century. During this period it passed by inheritance through four generations of Fawconers, most of whom were Dorset clergymen. The last of the Fawconers to be associated with the property was James William Henry, a surgeon in practice at Wimborne Minster in Dorset and later at Broad Chalke. By his grandfather's will in 1802 he received the house, and his brother, a serving soldier, was given the Haunch of Venison. Falling on hard times in 1815 J. W. H. Fawconer mortgaged his share of the inheritance, and six years later the house was sold, and so passed out of Fawconer hands altogether. The occupiers during the 80 years of Fawconer ownership are of no great interest, but it is likely that in the early years Samuel Fawconer himself lived in the northern half, and the delightful name of one tenant, Solomon Sweetapple, is worth recording – he lived in the northern half and died around 1816. The house was sold twice, and its second purchaser, in 1834, was a Salisbury surgeon, William Henry Coates, who practised in Endless Street. When he died in 1852 or 1853 the house was put up for sale in two lots, and the final chapter of its saga began.[115]

Keeping tenants when owners change and keeping owners when tenants change has probably been the salvation of 3/5 Minster Street. This continuity has smoothed the passage from one phase of its life to the next and has militated against drastic changes which would have led to mutilation and possibly destruction. So the house was very fortunate that one of its tenants in 1853 was anxious to become the owner of the half he rented. William Carter was born about 1794 at West Anstey on Exmoor. Having learnt the watchmaker's trade (perhaps in Birmingham, the birthplace of his wife) he came to Salisbury as a young man of about 22 and set up in business in the southern half of our house in 1816. About four years later a son was born and was named after his father. In due course he too became a watchmaker and by the time of the 1853 sale had been working with his father for more than a dozen years. In order to buy his shop and home William Carter senior, now nearing 60, had to approach one of his colleagues, or rivals, a jeweller named Michael Phillips, for a twenty-year mortgage. William Carter senior had died by 1861, but the business was prospering. William Carter junior was master now, with two employees, and a one-year-old son, William Holderness Carter, who was doubtless expected to follow the family tradition. Once the mortgage had been repaid, in 1873, and third-generation Carter was growing up to his father's expectations, thoughts turned towards the northern half of the property. This had been bought in the 1853 sale by a draper from Wilton, Joseph Ward, but had remained for some years in the occupation of the Combs family, furniture brokers. By 1876 it was empty, and eminently suitable for William Holderness Carter as he reached manhood. In 1877, for the first time for nearly 200 years, the house was reunited, and we may speculate that the present shopfront, which extends across the whole width of the building, was constructed soon afterwards. Son probably took over the business from father in 1893, for in that year William Carter, now in his seventies, moved to a house in Exeter Street. William Holderness Carter, the son (and grandson of the founder) continued to live over the shop until 1911, when he moved to a house in Harnham Road, and a few years later to a more fashionable residence in Elm Grove. He died in 1926, but his widow, Bessie, who moved to Bedford and finally to Oxford, continued to own the premises for another 36 years, until her death at an advanced age in 1962. Meanwhile the business had passed to one of W. H. Carter's employees, Percy Holmes, who began to work for him in 1896. The present owner, Stanley Holmes, is his son, and has worked in the business for over 45 years. Upstairs there have been changes, and following extensions to the Haunch of Venison after the second world war, it is now possible to dine in the hall where Robert Jole, Henry Mason, Samuel Fawconer and William Carter have all dined. And in that dining-room we find the link which binds together 400 years and more of the history of Salisbury homes.[116]

Postscript: Endless Street

Now that we have travelled together through some three hundred pages I think that I owe you an explanation about Endless Street. I do not know whether any other English town or city boasts an Endless Street. I have never heard of another. But I think that most people who have even a passing acquaintance with Salisbury will associate this curious name with the city which forms the subject of our book.

But of course it is not just a distinctive name. There is more to it than that. Throughout this long exposition I have tried to convey an impression of the city's history as, on the one hand, a continuous thread of human endeavour passing through the loom of time and place and, on the other hand, as a seamless garment in which all aspects of the city's history are interwoven and interdependent. I hope that you, the reader, have come to realise, if you had not already thought of it, that a city's history is 'endless' in that its past extends into its present and its present will extend into its future; and that the subjects for study in a city are 'endless' in that they all merge into one another with no sharp boundary between such topics as population and money, housing and health, trade and politics, religion and justice. This is the end of the book, because this is the point at which I stop writing and you stop reading. But we have not really finished our journey through the history of Salisbury. That is an endless street.

Appendix One: Two Lists of Circa 1400

This appendix brings together two important, nearly contemporary lists which have not previously been published: an aulnage return for Salisbury of 27th November 1396 –27th November 1397 (Public Record Office E/101/345/2, transcribed here by kind permission of the Controller of Her Majesty's Stationery Office) and an undated roll of ward lists believed to date from 1399/1400 (Salisbury District Muniments WRO, G23/1/236 transcribed here by kind permission of the Chief Executive, Salisbury District Council). A major contribution to our knowledge about medieval clothmaking in Salisbury, which discusses aulnage returns at length, was published as this work went to press, and too late for me to give it due consideration (Bridbury, 1982, chapter 6).

The aulnage return, which contains 292 entries, is the fullest and most complete of several relating to Salisbury which survive from the late fourteenth and early fifteenth centuries. On the basis of these returns, which are the records of finished cloths sealed by the alnagers as being of the statutory assize (see V.C.H.4, 1959, 123-124), H. L. Gray calculated that Salisbury was the pre-eminent cloth producing city in England at this period (Gray, 1924, 30). His argument lost some of its force when E. M. Carus-Wilson, in an article published in 1929 (reprinted in Carus-Wilson, 1967, 279-291) demonstrated that many aulnage returns were wholly spurious. His conclusions were nevertheless quoted with approval by G. D. Ramsay (Ramsay, 1965, 19-20), and the returns were used by the authors of the *Victoria history of Wiltshire* (V.C.H.4, 1959, 124; V.C.H.6, 1962, 125). In 1962 A. R. Bridbury defended the authenticity of these early aulnage returns by comparing them with entries in the city ledgers and Domesday books (Bridbury, 1975, 34-35). The present comparison, which shows a close correlation of names with the ward lists, confirms that the 1396/1397 return is genuine.

The ward lists, described by A. E. J. Hollaender as a 'late 15th century roll of contributors' names with the sums contributed' (Rathbone, 1951, 81) have been extensively used by the staff of the Royal Commission on Historical Monuments (England) in their survey of Salisbury buildings, and have been shown by Mrs H. M. Bonney to date from 1399 or 1400 (R.C.H.M. 1980, xxvi, note 2). The lists contain 999 entries, of which two are wholly illegible. There is no indication of the purpose of the lists or the significance of the amounts entered beside each name. It is probably reasonable, however, to assume that they include all householders living in the four city wards (see above chapter two, note 4) and that the amounts give an indication of comparative wealth. If this is the case then they comprise the earliest directory of the city known to survive, and may be compared with the later lists of 1455 (Nevill, 1911) and 1667 (Nevill, 1910).

Individually the two lists printed here are of considerable interest, offering evidence about the woollen industry and other occupations in the city. But taken together they also help to gauge to what extent the cloths recorded under Salisbury and its suburbs in the aulnage returns in fact came from Salisbury producers and merchants, rather than being brought into Salisbury from other parts of Wiltshire and elsewhere to receive the alnager's seal. It should be borne in mind, however, that any conclusion drawn from comparison of the two lists must remain tentative: the lapse of two or three years between the lists should tend to reduce the number of matches, whilst the likelihood of homonyms increases the number artificially. The following, with this proviso, are some of the more interesting statistics that may be derived from the lists:

TABLE A: LARGEST NUMBER OF CLOTHS SEALED

Name	Number of cloths	Ward	Contribution
John Coscoumbe	304	Martins	20d
Thomas Eyr	142	Martins	3/-
Nicholas Hardyng	131	Martins	5/-
William Slegge	128½	Martins	2/-
John Notekyn	128	Market	16d
Walter Nandre	120	New Street	4/-
John Chippenham	109	Meads	2/-
Ralph Stille	108½	Market	40d
William Mede	102	Martins	6d
Richard Weston	99	Market	3/-
John Forest, sen.	94	Martins	8/-
Richard atte Heorne	90	Market	6d
Edward Purdy	88	Market	12d
William Walter	87	Martins	4/6
William Wil	83	New Street	2/6
Nicholas Bouklond	80½	Market	40d
John Magges	80	—	—
Robert Haselbere	80	Market	2/-
John Todeworthe	77	Martins	2/6
William Stout	75	Martins	2/-
John Baret	71	Martins	4/-
Thomas Wellis	67	Martins	12d
Thomas Northwode	65	Market	2/-
John Shute	62	Martins	12d
Stephen Kendale	62	—	—
John Ferur	60½	Martins	16d
William Woderove	60	Market	2/6
John Purdy	58	Market	12d
John Hoseman	54½	Martins	16d
John Moner	54	Market	13/4

TABLE B: HIGHEST CONTRIBUTORS IN WARD LISTS

Name	Occupation	Contribution	Ward	No. of cloths
John Baker	grocer	13/4	New Street	—
John Moner	—	13/4	Market	54
Richard Spencer	grocer	12/-	Martins	17
Thomas Castelton	—	10/-	Martins	32
George Meryot	—	10/-	New Street	—
William Warmwelle	—	10/-	Market	—
Thomas Bowyer	—	8/-	Market	—
Richard Leche	—	8/-	Martins	-
John Forest, sen.	—	8/-	Martins	94
Adam Teffont	—	8/-	Martins	33
Alice Cammel	—	8/-	New Street	—

John Nywman	grocer	8/–	New Street	—
Thomas Blechere	—	6/8	Market	36
John Nedler	—	6/8	Martins	51½
Robert Deverel	—	6/8	Martins	—
Edward Enefeld	—	6/8	Meads	—
Richard Juwel	—	6/8	New Street	—
William Pykard	—	6/–	New Street	—
Thomas Sexteyn	—	6/–	New Street	—
John Dokton	—	5/–	Market	—
Nicholas Hardyng	—	5/–	Martins	131
John Levesham	—	5/–	Martins	—
John Barbur	brazier	5/–	Martins	18
William Hul	—	5/–	Martins	—
John Chaundeler, sen.	—	5/–	Martins	—
John Edeshale	—	5/–	New Street	25
William Busshup	—	5/–	New Street	—
William Waryn	—	5/–	New Street	—
William Baly	—	4/6	Market	—
William Walter	—	4/6	Martins	87

TABLE C: NAMED OCCUPATIONS BY WARD (WITH % OF TOTAL HOUSEHOLDS)

Occupation	Market	Martin	New Street	Meads
weaver	7 (2.0%)	24 (6.8%)	6 (2.4%)	7 (20.0%)
fuller	3 (0.9%)	10 (2.8%)	2 (0.8%)	—
dyer	7 (2.0%)	1 (0.3%)	1 (0.4%)	1 (2.9%)
tailor	2 (0.6%)	5 (1.4%)	6 (2.4%)	—
mercer, draper etc.	5 (1.4%)	3 (0.8%)	2 (0.8%)	—
TOTAL	24 (6.8%)	43 (12.1%)	17 (6.7%)	8 (22.9%)

TABLE D: CLOTH PRODUCERS (NAMES ON AULNAGE RETURN) BY WARD (WITH % OF TOTAL HOUSEHOLDS)

Market	Martin	New Street	Meads	Total
105 (29.8%)	125 (35.2%)	30 (11.9%)	9 (25.7%)	269 (27.0%)

MISCELLANEOUS STATISTICS

1. 50 out of 292 (17.1%) names on the aulnage return do not occur on the ward lists.
2. 713 out of 6,942 (10.3%) cloths aulnaged (excluding narrow cloths) are to names which do not occur on the ward lists.
3. 23.9 cloths is the average per name. 98 names are above this average.
4. 2820½ cloths (40.6% of total) are aulnaged to names on table A above.

NOTE

I have added a running number to the entries in the ensuing lists. Numbers in brackets after an entry indicate the running number of the relevant entry/entries on the other list. The absence of such a number may be taken to signify that the name does not occur on the other list. Wherever possible I have expanded contractions and suspensions; I have occasionally resorted to ' ? or ... where the full form cannot be recovered without doubt. I have anglicised Christian names wherever possible. I am most grateful to Penelope Rundle of the Wiltshire Record Office, who has checked my transcript of the ward lists, and made many useful suggestions.

AULNAGE RETURN, SALISBURY AND SUBURBS, 27.11.1396-27.11.1397

1. John Forest, sen. 94 [479]
2. Robert Margery 75½ [262]
3. Richard Sharp 27½ [429]
4. John Hayward 21 [41/486]
5. John Magges 80
6. Richard Pridy 2½ [108]
7. John Ryngwode 3½ [317]
8. Thomas Yonge 16½ [680]
9. Thomas Bekhampton 4½ [612]
10. Reginald Wychford 5½ [257]
11. Walter Cok 11 [147]
12. John Notekyn 128 [129]
13. Thomas Castelton 32 [388]
14. John Anketille 53½ [93]
15. William Shupton 15 [119]
16. Agnes Carter 3½
17. John Shute 62 [496/685]
18. Walter Nandre 120 [772]
19. William Compton 32 [723]
20. Thomas Steor 26 [127]
21. Richard Fulham 43
22. John Reynald 13½ [734]
23. William Walter 87 [437]
24. Ralph Stille 108½ [135]
25. John Pope 48½ [201/251/600]
26. John Ruddok 44½ [731]
27. John Wroxhale 51½ [434]
28. Nicholas Hardyng 131 [436]
29. Nicholas Mendelond 8½ [33]
30. Richard Freok 32 [111]
31. Nicholas Melbury 47 [220]
32. John Todeworthe 77 [358]
33. John Moul 48½ [629]
34. John Stratford 41½
35. Richard Berde 21 [188]
36. John Parch 9½ [635]
37. William Fulham 43½ [700]
38. Thomas Gore 15½ [58]
39. John Hoseman 54½ [649?]
40. John Baret 71 [462]
41. Richard atte Heorne 90 [212]
42. John Ferur 60½ [594]
43. John Frye 33 [453/579]
44. John Chippenham 109 [739]
45. John Fovent, mercer 23 [112]
46. Thomas Foul 32½ [503]
47. Richard Chessam 21
48. Walter Babbestoke 1½ [753]
49. Henry Pretejohn 20 [679]
50. John Stoure 8 [264/412]
51. Roger Wodeford 10½ [843]
52. John Tulk 13 [323]
53. Simon Belch 28 [401]
54. William Westmour 44½ [722]
55. John Midlane 2½ [137]
56. Thomas Byshop de Wilton 32
57. Thomas Northwode 65 [118]
58. Thomas Wellis 67 [480]
59. Thomas Wake 1 [485]
60. John Fovent toukere 1½ [421]
61. John Coscoumbe 304 [432]
62. William Lamport 10½ [476]
63. John Nedlere 51½ [420]
64. William Nedlere 14½ [634]
65. John Purdy 58 [252]
66. John Hosyere 4½ [321/957]
67. Edward Purdy 88 [74]
68. William Wellis 17½ [513]
69. Edward Clerk 31
70. Richard Weston 99 [247]
71. Thomas Eyr 142 [615]
72. William Grym 4½ [478]
73. Robert Body 26 [325]
74. George Joce toukere 37 [126/131/735]
75. Thomas Hosebrigge 29 [492]
76. Robert Warwaelle 16½ [47]
77. Adam Waltham 18 [671]
78. John Elys 26 [242/941]
79. Robert Dibon 22½ [133]
80. William Dorsete 25½ [52]
81. John Fyssh 33 [528]
82. Thomas Slegge 46 [631]
83. John Wenchyng 7½ [754?]
84. William Stout 75 [531]
85. Cristina Foxes 33½
86. Thomas Stoke 32 [481]
87. Hugh Wyntebourne 24 [69]
88. Richard Dawe 2
89. John Dykere 8½ [690]
90. Ralph Cardmakyer 28 [35]
91. Stephen Bullok 41½ [29]
92. Margaret Godmanston 7½ [694]
93. Nicholas Joce 5½ [707]
94. James Burgeys 8½
95. John Stevenys 29 [497]
96. John Titchyng ½ [117?]
97. John Bole 2½

98. Cristina Handley 40½ [654]
99. William Woderoue 60 [249]
100. Hugh Toukere 17½ [128]
101. Nicholas Abyndon 21 [53]
102. John Gay 1½
103. Walter Ryngwode 3 [140]
104. Edward Boure 2½ [381]
105. Hugh Braban 6 [816]
106. William Wil 83 [921]
107. Thomas Mason 38 [246/296/526]
108. William Fysshere 27 [54/898]
109. John Stiward 7½ [716]
110. John Okford 8½ [291]
111. William Doggesay 6½ [83]
112. Nicholas Curteys 9 [844]
113. John Sloo 11½
114. Nicholas Hayward 14 [580]
115. Walter Gilmyn sen. 12½ [623]
116. John Chanslour 8
117. Richard Cove 2 [117]
118. John Bradeley 1
119. Walter Gilmyn 8 [623]
120. Godlefa Amale 21½ [762]
121. John Briston 22½ [19/765]
122. Walter Duyn 15½ [250]
123. William Penyton 8 [487]
124. Nicholas Toukere 32
125. William Tolous 27 [621]
126. Nicholas Frogge 24½
127. John London 1 [593]
128. Robert Redenham 14½ [813]
129. Simon Bont 8½ [205]
130. Richard Person ½ [454]
131. Richard Smyth 4 [105]
132. William Ferour 4 [482]
133. Hugh Taillor 1½ [245]
134. John Wotton 48½ [181/601]
135. Edward Dubber 8 [73]
136. Nicholas Weston 31½ [237]
137. John Lytle 37½ [241]
138. Richard West 3 [243]
139. Nicholas Laurenz 53½ [475]
140. Agnes Ballie 4½ [484]
141. John Dancastre 21 [748]
142. Thomas Serteyn 6½ [530]
143. William Moore 34 [378]
144. Henry Frere 18
145. Richard Sherman 29½ [686]
146. Johanna Suxhampcote 31 [75]
147. John Yweyn 5½ [940]
148. William Sopere 1
149. Walter Babbestoke 1½ [753]
150. Robert Forest 14½ [474]
151. Nicholas Norys 38 [632]
152. John Myrye 25½ [624?]

153. Roger Stapulford 28
154. William Isak 11 [911]
155. Adam Teffonte 33 [625]
156. John Wormynstre 13½ [648]
157. Thomas Hamme 19 [440]
158. Thomas Wheolere 7 [213/563]
159. William Purch 1 [228?]
160. Robert Stikeberd 4 [670]
161. John Forest 14 [520]
162. Agnes Holtis 1½
163. John Barnabe 2½
164. William Basket 12
165. John Whyte 42 [134]
166. Walter Dubbere 18 [82]
167. John Pynnok webbe 6 [572]
168. Thomas Blechere 36 [298]
169. Peter Corpe 2 [269?]
170. John Dyere 53 [189/441]
171. John Sloo 1
172. John Moner 54 [297]
173. Richard Boteler 24½ [562]
174. John Teukesbury 18 [511/616]
175. Robert Frye 2 [561]
176. Richard Bertevyle 33 [48]
177. William Boure 3½ [64]
178. William Slegge 128½ [595]
179. John Manyngford 14½ [263]
180. John Jakis 1½ [422]
181. Thomas Abbot 18 [304]
182. Nicholas Bouklond 80½ [138]
183. Henry Rook 9 [677]
184. William Dounyng 51 [267]
185. Stephen Kendale 62
186. Robert Cokelote 5½ [442]
187. John Umfray 7½ [266]
188. John Pymperne sen. 19 [672]
189. Robert Stonard 2
190. John Toryton 4 [597]
191. John Pymperne 11½ [672]
192. William Wyly 15 [113]
193. Henry Berwyk 10 [160]
194. John Sherbourne ½
195. John Grandon 6½ [397]
196. John Copper 14 [708]
197. Roger Fadur 22 [489]
198. John Oxstret 42 [92]
199. John Vyryng 11 [696]
200. William Pakeman 11 [657]
201. Laurence Lane 32 [721]
202. Adam Whyte 37½ [565]
203. John Bur 1½ [45/295?]
204. Adam Mareys 5 [120]
205. John Coliere 17 [146]
206. Robert Whytyng 17 [529]
207. John Wokyngham 14½ [505]

208. William Reynalde 27 [574]
209. William Mede 102 [550]
210. Edward Passewelle 52 [50]
211. Richard Gage 29 [592]
212. John Davy 21 [585/588]
213. Petronilla Gondy 40½ [788]
214. John Edeshale 25 [814]
215. John Spencer mercer 7 [47/837]
216. John Mate 1½ [348?]
217. Robert Bowyere 18½ [448]
218. John Pide 3½
219. William Saundres 53 [469/706]
220. Robert Hyndon 20½ [755]
221. Robert Haselbere 80 [248]
222. John Chamflour 4½
223. Thomas Jerveys 16
224. Geoffrey Parker 2 [217]
225. Robert Hooke 5
226. Benedict Lytle 2 [194?]
227. Thomas Boner 15½ [195]
228. Adam Strugge ½ [157]
229. Richard Pynnok 7 [895]
230. Agnes Lorde 1 [647]
231. Thomas Serteyn 2½ [530]
232. John Sexteyn 8
233. John Folsam 5½
234. John Horn 3 [589]
235. John Roude 3½
236. John Wyly 13
237. Richard Oseberne 1 [994]
238. Walter Mody 4
239. Thomas Kayser 25
240. Nicholas Coube (?) 2½
241. Walter Evesham 10 [608]
242. John Taillour 3½ [208/704]
243. Roger Pentrich 23 [675]
244. Peter Uphavene 2 [642]
245. Richard Dyghere 12½ [968?]
246. John Lety 4 [662?]
247. Thomas atte Nasshe 7 [664]
248. Richard Herberd 3 [742]
249. Thomas Farle 8½ [661]
250. Richard Pynnok ½ [895]
251. John Judde 5½ [165]

252. John Shapewyk 8
253. Robert Derby 13½
254. Henry Fayryeman 2
255. Walter Baron 1 [265]
256. Richard Spence 17 [433]
257. John Aleyn 3½ [191?]
258. John Chapur 1½ [584]
259. John Hardyng 3 [535]
260. Thomas Goodchyld 6 [838]
261. John Doly 11½ [599]
262. Thomas Dancastre 14½ [122]
263. John Vyncent 3 [447]
264. Thomas Yevele 2 [49]
265. Thomas Byston 9
266. Alice Hethis 16 [934]
267. Walter Dyere 24
268. John Mody 1½ [350/196?]
269. John Barbur brasyere 18 [369/564/826]
270. Thomas Couper 2 [464]
271. John Crystchurche 1 [368]
272. John Hewissh ½ [560]
273. William Ferour 12 [482]
274. Henry Sherley 10½ [303]
275. John Furmage 7½
276. William Katerton 3½
277. Thomas Tuchefelde 8 [219]
278. Henry Woderoue 15½
279. William Blauncharde 11 [222]
280. Richard Ywerne 20½
281. Thomas Redenham 6½ [276]
282. Richard Hert 23½ [277]
283. Stephen Meryot 4 [514]
284. Stephen Lychenard 13
285. Peter Toukere 10½ [130]
286. Robert Charlis 7 [153]
287. John Huggebody 1 [665]
288. John Wilkyn de Gloucet'shere 20 [60/456]
289. William Robyn 4 doz stricti [narrow cloths]
290. Thomas Dykere 2 doz stricti
291. Richard Noble ½
292. John Comfort 7 [462]

WARD LISTS, SALISBURY [WRO.
G23/1/236, 1399/1400]

Forum

1. John Caumbrigge dyere 12d
2. John But corveser 16d
3. Nicholas Russel 4d
4. John Spencer 4d [215]
5. Thomas Bakere 8d
6. John Lokyere 8d
7. Robert Skot glovere 4d
8. John Harnham 12d
9. Eva Fyfhyde 4d
10. Peter Bampton 4d
11. Thomas Artur skynnere 6d
12. William Wyght dyere 4d

13. John Eward corveser 4d
14. Peter Baron 4d
15. John Dovere spycer 4d
16. William Edmond 4d
17. John atte Wode 6d
18. John Swyft 40d
19. John Bristow 4d [121]
20. Richard Oword 40d
21. John atte Nasshe mason 6d
22. William Gilmyn 4d
23. Simon Blakhalle 4d
24. Thomas Bowyere 8s
25. William Baly 4s 6d
26. Laurence Dyere 4d
27. Martin Taillour 4d
28. John Tissebury 4d
29. Stephen Bullok 2s [91]
30. Thomas Frogge 16d
31. Richard Cory 12d
32. John Bullok dyere 4d
33. Nicholas Mendelond 4d [29]
34. John Murlawe dyere 12d
35. Ralph Cardmakiere 16d [90]
36. John Joce toukere 4d
37. Robert Polton barbur 4d
38. William Horn 6d
39. William Warmwelle 10s
40. William Ryver 40d
41. John Hayward 6d [4]
42. Nicholas atte Heorne 4d
43. John Wynterslewe 6d
44. Stephen Markham 6d
45. John Bour dyere 4d [203]
46. Roger atte Brigge 4d
47. Robert Warmwelle 6d [76]
48. Richard Bertevyle 8d [176]
49. Thomas Yevele 6d [264]
50. Edward Passewelle 12d [210]
51. Simon Lavyngton 4d
52. William Dorsete 6d [80]
53. Nicholas Abyndon 8d [101]
54. William Fysshere dyere 12d [108]
55. Thomas Fyport 4d
56. John Dokton 5s
57. Robert Blake 16d
58. Thomas Gore 8d [38]
59. Thomas Langeford dyere 4d
60. John Wilkynes 4d [288]
61. Walter Busshuppe 4d
62. Robert Fovent 16d
63. John Wollop' —
64. William Boure 3s [177]
65. Walter Titelyng 4d
66. Robert Bloode 4d
67. John Brutford 4d

68. Edward Bremmore 4d
69. Hugh Wynterbourne 16d [87]
70. John Durneford dyere 12d
71. Reginald Druwery 6d
72. William Lechur 8d
73. Edward Dubbere 8d [135]
74. Edward Purdy 12d [67]
75. Johanna Suxhampcote 2s [146]
76. Nicholas Dubbere sen. 8d
77. John Gilberd 12d
78. John Paxhulle 4d
79. Adam Wareyn 6d
80. John Pykard 6d
81. Ralph atte Wode 6d
82. Walter Dubbere 8d [166]
83. William Doggesay 6d [111]
84. John Noble 40d
85. Nicholas West dubbere 4d
86. John Drewery 40d
87. John Shupton 2s
88. Thomas Cake 4d
89. Robert Nyght 4d
90. Nicholas Smyth dubbere 4d
91. Henry Glovere 4d
92. John Oxstret 40d [198]
93. John Anketille 6d [14]
94. Walter Cobelere 4d
95. John Baron parchementer 4d
96. Robert Mason 4d
97. Johanna Melbrigge 4d
98. William Freok 4d
99. Reginald Grenehulle 4d
100. John Peeris webbe 4d
101. John Sterre 4d
102. John Gullok wheolere 4d
103. John Myldenale 12d
104. Alexander Cake 2s
105. Richard Smyth 6d [131]
106. Robert Latesmaker 4d
107. William Bayllif 6d
108. Richard Pridy 12d [6]
109. John Smyth glovere 4d
110. Robert Bakere 12d
111. Richard Freok 12d [30]
112. John Fovent 4d [45]
113. William Wyly 8d [192]
114. Robert Chyld 8d
115. John Sybely taillour 8d
116. John Evesham 6d
117. John Titelyng 4d [96?]
118. Thomas Northwode 2s [57]
119. William Shupton 6d [15]
120. Adam Mareys 6d [204]
121. John Stagard 16d
122. Thomas Dancastre 6d [262]

123. William Purvyour 6d
124. William Wrythe 8d
125. Edith Shuppestere 12d
126. George Joce jun 2s [74?]
127. Thomas Steor 8d [20]
128. Hugh Toukere 6d [100]
129. John Notekyn 16d [12]
130. Philip Toukere 4d [285]
131. George Joce senior 12d [74?]
132. Thomas Taillour 4d
133. Robert Dibon 6d [79]
134. John White 6d [165]
135. Ralph Stille 40d [24]
136. John Stille 4d
137. John Midlane 4d [55]
138. Nicholas Bouklond 40d [182]
139. Edward Taillour 4d
140. Walter Ryngwode 4d [103]
141. William Lyly bakere 6d
142. Thomas Doughton 20d
143. Richard Chesstur 6d
144. John Bythewode 4d
145. Robert Dyere 4d
146. John Colyer toukere 8d [205]
147. Walter Cok toukere 4d [11]
148. John Canyng 8d
149. Cecilia Ferour 6d
150. Alicia Spycer 4d
151. Simon Bradeley 12d
152. Henry Sheep 6d
153. Robert Charlis 8d [286]
154. Richard Knollis 20d
155. John Bottenham 3s
156. Thomas Stabbere 16d
157. Adam Strugge 8d [228]
158. Robert Stokbrigge 2s
159. Roger Tille cum soc' 12d
160. Henry Berewyk 40d [193]
161. Thomas Touker de Wilton 4d
162. Nicholas Yernmanger 4d
163. John Stabber 4d
164. Robert Hantot et Moone drapere 4d
165. John Judde 3s [251?]
166. Stephen Thorbourne 12d
167. Henry Rampayn & Gregory de Brutford 12d
168. John Compton de Wermester 6d
169. John Gust de Wilton 6d
170. William Webbe de Knyghton 12d
171. Thomas Shawe de Berford 6d
172. John Frost yernmanger 6d
173. Edward Prentys 5...
174 John Fendur 6d
175. John Ermynton 6d
176. Thomas Bereford 12d

177. Nicholas Mauncel 40d
178. William Fouler 6d
179. Thomas Dyere 12d
180. John Cotel drapere 6d
181. John Wotton lyndrapere 6d [134]
182. Thomas Toukere de Wilton 6d
183. Richard Goudchyne 12d
184. Laurence Purvyour & John Hamelyn 2s
185. William Clerk 6d
186. John Midnyght 6d
187. Robert Plai......merant 8d
188. Richard Berde 8d [35]
189. John Dyer de Der... 40d [170?]
190. ...John Gatecoumbe...
191. John Aleyn —
192. .....drapere —
.....
.....
193. ....ch.. 12d
194. Benedict Lytle 6d [226?]
195. Thomas Bouer 6d [227]
196. John Mody drapere 6d [268?]
197. John Shedde 2s
198. John Gillyngham 6d
199. .... Dale 12d
200. .... Taillour de Bradeley 6d
201. John Pope Jun 6d [25]
202. Thomas Merlawe 12d
203. John Pyk yernmanger 12d
204. Thomas Kayse 12d
205. Simon Bont 16d [129]
206. William Prymer —
207. John Kyvel et ⎫ 8d
208. John Taillour ⎭   [242]
209. John Webbe et ⎫
210. Henry Kaym ⎭ 12d
211. John Turnour 6d
212. Richard atte Heorne 6d [41]
213. Thomas Wheolere 8d [158]
214. Richard Bordmakyere 6d
215. Thomas Taillour 6d
216. John Ambesbury 6d
217. Geoffrey Parker 4d [224]
218. William Coupere 4d
219. Thomas Tuchefeld 6d [277]
220. Nicholas Melbury 40d [31]
221. John Botelmakyere 8d
222. William Blaunchard 4d [279]
223. John Selk 4d
224. Thomas Feraunt 12d
225. John Rankyn 4d
226. Alicia Brembeshawe 4d
227. Robert Tille 8d
228. William Purchas 8d [159]

229. John Kyng webbe 4d
230. William atte Wode 4d
231. William Conerbe [?] boucher 6d
232. John Weston 4d
233. William Clerk cook 8d
234. John Pruwer webbe 4d
235. William Teue webbe 4d
236. John Cosyn 6d
237. Nicholas Weston 12d [136]
238. John Rous 4d
239. John Durant motlemakyer 4d
240. Nicholas Mercer webbe 4d
241. John Lytle mercer 40d [137]
242. John Elys 6d [78]
243. Richard West 6d [138]
244. Henry Taverner 4d
245. Hugh Taillour 4d [133]
246. Thomas Mason 2s [107]
247. Richard Weston 3s [70]
248. Robert Haselbere 2s [221]
249. William Woderoue 2s 6d [99]
250. Walter Duyn 6d [122]
251. John Pope 8d [25]
252. John Purdy 12d [65]
253. John Sterk 4d
254. Geoffrey Tannere 4d
255. Thomas Morweyene 4d
256. William Braucey 6d
257. Reginald Wichford 4d [10]
258. Thomas Segere 20d
259. John Clyve tannere 16d
260. John Soryveyn 4d
261. John Shefford 4d
262. Robert Margery 4d [2]
263. John Manyngford 12d [179]
264. John Stoure 4d [50]
265. Walter Baronn 4d [255]
266. John Umfray 8d [187]
267. William Donnyng 8d [184]
268. William Haselbere 4d
269. Peter Coppe 4d [169?]
270. Peter Dawe 8d
271. John Peeris 4d
272. Ralph Lokyere 6d
273. Edward Brut 4d
274. Peter Cosyn 4d
275. John Wayte hosier 2s
276. Thomas Redenham 8d [281]
277. Richard Hert 8d [282]
278. Johanna Robynet 4d
279. John Milburne 12d
280. John Stodesbury 4d
281. William Parys skynnere 4d
282. Henry Pope 12d
283. Walter Bakere cum sociis 8d

284. Richard Broun 4d
285. Robert Roddene 4d
286. Thomas Davy 4d
287. John Heele workman 4d
288. William Chapur 6d
289. Thomas Hayward webbe 4d
290. John Strete 4d
291. John Okford 8d [110]
292. John Compton 4d
293. Edward Bakere webbe 4d
294. Reginald Woderoue 4d
295. John Bour kombere 4d [203?]
296. Thomas Mason 4d [107]
297. John Moner 13s 4d [172]
298. Thomas Blechere 6s 8d [168]
299. Gilbert Tannere 18d
300. Laurence Baker 6d
301. Roger Smyth 6d
302. Hugh Yernmanger 4d
303. Henry Sherley 4d [274]
304. Thomas Abbot 6d [181]
305. Philip de Shaftesbury 4d
306. John Momfort 6d
307. John Baker wolmanger 6d
308. Richard Short 4d
309. William Hulle 4d
310. John Parmynter de Wynchester 4d
311. John Palfreyman de Arundel 4d
312. William Osteler 6d
313. John Crop skynnere 4d
314. Andrew Plomer 6d
315. William Trybus 4d
316. Richard Coupere 4d
317. John Ryngwode 8d [7]
318. Richard Hen skynnere 4d
319. Martin Dyer 2s
320. William Elton 4d
321. John Hosyer 6d [66]
322. Robert Gudlyngton 20d
323. John Tulk 6d [52]
324. Walter Aleyn de Stokbrigge 4d
325. Robert Body 2s [73]
326. John Lake 16d
327. Thomas Grene fishere 6d
328. John atte Nashe fishere 6d
329. John atte Hulle portur 6d
330. Adam Dawbeney 20d
331. John Rolf taillour 4d
332. John Broun boucher 6d
333. Thomas Sherman 6d
334. Ralph Scryveyn 6d
335. Roger Capon 8d
336. William Wilton 12d
337. John Brewer boucher 4d
338. Henry Wynnepeny 16d

339. John Dene nappere 6d
340. William Ropere 6d
341. Thomas Brasyer 12d
342. John Braas 4d
343. William Plomer 6d
344. Simon Hosier 4d
345. James Smyth 12d
346. John Frankeleyn 20d
347. John Fox nappere 4d
348. John Mace 12d [216?]
349. William Staunton 4d
350. John Mody 6d [268]
351. Thomas Ropere 4d
352. John Paxton 4d
     summa totalis £15 14s 10d

Martinus
353. Eustace Taillour 4d
354. John Weye skynnere 4d
355. John Cary 20d
356. John Rede taillour 4d
357. Richard Mason corveser 4d
358. John Todeworthe 2s 6d [32]
359. Oliver touker & John Harnham 8d
360. Johanna Thorbourne 20d
361. John Wodewey spycer 4d
362. Edward Nasshe 4d
363. William Hoore 8d
364. William Cat wolmanger 4d
365. John Randolf 4d
366. Thomas Horn 12d
367. John Somerton 6d
368. John Cristchurche 4d [271]
369. John Barbur 4d [269]
370. Johanna Stikeberd 4d
371. Geoffrey Barbur 4d
372. John Blaneford 4d
373. John Saundres 6d
374. Henry Glovere 8d
375. Maud Tilles 6d
376. John Lange taillour 12d
377. Walter Sherle 20d
378. William Moore 8d [143]
379. Thomas Marleborgh 12d
380. William Clerk 6d
381. Edward Bour 6d [104]
382. Thomas Clerk webbe —
383. John Fryday de Curnebourne 20d
384. Walter Wolmanger 6d
385. Thomas Gogeyn 12d
386. John Wolmanger de Shaftesbury 8d
387. Thomas Balle 4d
388. Thomas Castelton 10s [13]
389. Philip Trubbe 12d

390. William Trubbe 6d
391. John Hoore 6d
392. Richard Stone 6d
393. William Barbur 8d
394. John Horsenayl 6d
395. Robert Ware taillour 6d
396. Robert Ferour 6d
397. John Grandon' 16d [195]
398. William Salle 2s
399. Walter Jurdan 6d
400. Thomas Wolmanger 4d
401. Simon Belch 6d [53]
402. Maud Grevys 4d
403. John Trym 4d
404. Peter Momfort toukere 4d
405. William Bryan 6d
406. Philip Dyere 4d
407. Walter Hauk 4d
408. Robert Ravyle 4d
409. Edward Serteyn 4d
410. John Pynch toukere 6d
411. Richard Grenefeld 4d
412. John Stoure 4d [50]
413. John Clerk 4d
414. Isabella Hunte 4d
415. John Edward 4d
416. Thomas Toukere 4d
417. William Bouklond 4d
418. Robert Meyre corveser 4d
419. Adam Dommere 6d
420. John Nedlere 6s 8d [63]
421. John Fovent toukere 6d [60]
422. John Jakis toukere 6d [180]
423. Robert Goylon 6d
424. John Wynnegod 6d
425. Master Richard Leche 8s
426. William Cassewelle 4d
427. John Saundris 4d
428. John Wattis 4d
429. Richard Sharp' 4d [3]
430. John Lomb 4d
431. John Croos 4d
432. John Coscoumbe 20d [61]
433. Richard Spencer grocer 12s [256]
434. John Wroxhale toukere 8d [27]
435. Isabella Colys 6d
436. Nicholas Hardyng 5s [28]
437. William Walter 4s 6d [23]
438. John Kendale toukere 4d
439. John Mog toukere 6d
440. Thomas Hamme 8d [157]
441. John Dyer webbe 8d [170?]
442. Robert Cokelote 4d [186]
443. Roger ser[vant of] Richard Leche 6d

444. Gilbert Skynnere 4d
445. Thomas Neraford 4d
446. John Levesham 5s
447. John Vyncent 8d [263]
448. Robert Bowyere 16d [217]
449. Gilbert Oword 16d
450. William Sure 4d
451. John Symond webbe 4d
452. Thomas Saundres 4d
453. John Frye webbe 6d [43]
454. Richard Person 4d [130]
455. Henry Dounton 4d
456. John Wilkynes 6d [288]
457. John Wrythe 4d
458. Robert Deverel 6s 8d
459. John Brasyer cum fratre [?] 8d
460. Roger Grateley 16d
461. Johanna Shupster 4d
462. John Comfort 4d [292]
463. John Baret 4s [40]
464. Thomas Coupere 4d [270]
465. Stephen Broun 2s
466. Robert Taillour 4d
467. Peter Berde skynnere 4d
468. William York webbe 4d
469. William Saundres 4d [219]
470. John Lange brewere 3s
471. Stephen Taillour 4d
472. William Chepman webbe 6d
473. John Buteler mercer 20d
474. Robert Forest 12d [150]
475. Nicholas Lauerenz 16d [139]
476. William Lamport 8d [62]
477. William Whyte 20d
478. William Grym 8d [72]
479. John Forest sen 8s [1]
480. Thomas Wellis 12d [58]
481. Thomas Stoke 8d [86]
482. William Ferour toukere 6d [132/273]
483. John Parys skynne 6d
484. Agnes Ballis 20d [140]
485. Thomas Wake 4d [59]
486. John Hayward webbe 4d [4?]
487. William Penyton dyere 6d [123]
488. William Clerk toukere 4d
489. Roger Fadur 2s [197]
490. Thomas Pentriche 4d
491. Nicholas Pille 4d
492. Thomas Hosebrigge 6d [75]
493. Thomas Scryveyn 4d
494. Edward Charlton 4d
495. Thomas Uphavene 6d
496. John Shute 12d [17]
497. John Stevenys 12d [95]
498. John Shaftebury 4d
499. Henry Belde 4d
500. Walter Taillour 4d
501. John Maynard webbe 6d
502. William Forster webbe tenentes infra 4d
503. Thomas Foul 12d [46]
504. Robert Peytresfeld in alia parte vici 4d
505. John Wokyngham 8d [207]
506. Nicholas Dol 4d
507. Philip Grym 4d
508. Edward Compton 4d
509. Thomas Rede 4d
510. Robert Lord 4d
511. John Teukesbury 6d [174]
512. Thomas Webbe 4d
513. William Wellis 6d [68]
514. Stephen Meryot 4d [283]
515. William Hardle 4d
516. John Coupere webbe 4d
517. John Durneford webbe 4d
518. Thomas Doupol 4d
519. Thomas Vyryng webbe 4d
520. John Forest junior 6d [161]
521. John Turvyle 4d
522. John Cappe 4d
523. John Wykham 4d
524. Alice Grym 4d
525. John Jurdan carpenter 6d
526. Thomas Mason webbe 4d [107]
527. John Vynter webbe 4d
528. John Fysh webbe 6d [81]
529. Robert Whytyng 6d [206]
530. Thomas Serteyn 12d [142/231]
531. William Stout 2s [84]
532. Thomas Dawe ...
533. Roger Smyth ...
534. William Spencer webbe ...
535. John Hardyng ...
536. Nicholas London ...
537. John Wynter ...
538. P.....lla Coupere ...
539. John Fontel carpenter ...
540. John Shorberde carp......
541. Richard Braundon' ...
542. Richard Sherburne ...
543. William Cole ...
544. John Smyth webbe ...
545. Robert Panyot ...
546. John Bremmore 4d
547. Nicholas Webbe 4d
548. Edward Webbe iuxta horsemulle 4d
549. Thomas atte Mulle 4d
550. William Mede 6d [209]

551. Thomas Wyot 4d
552. William Robard 4d
553. John Alsolyn 4d
554. Maud Ouewynes 4d
555. John Slegge 4d
556. John Fromond smyth 6d
557. John Cokelote 4d
558. William Skyle 4d
559. Simon Webbe 4d
560. John Hewissh 4d [272]
561. Robert Frye carpenter 8d [175]
562. Richard Boteler 2s [173]
563. Thomas Wheoler 4d [158]
564. John Barbur brasyere 5s [269]
565. Adam Whyte 8d [202]
566. William Sevyere 6d
567. John Conerbe 4d
568. William Sende 4d
569. Henry Smyth 4d
570. William Gillyng 4d
571. Thomas Tennere 4d
572. John Pynnok sen 4d [167]
573. John Palmere sen 4d
574. William Reynald 2s [208]
575. William Turrok 4d
576. William Swayn 4d
577. John Rayford 4d
578. Nicholas Gryndere 4d
579. John Frye webbe jun 4d [43]
580. Nicholas Hayward 6d [114]
581. John Symmes 6d
582. John Dykeman 4d
583. John Parson 4d
584. John Chapur 4d [258]
585. John Davey sen 8d [212]
586. Robert Carpenter 4d
587. John Gilmyn carpenter 4d
588. John Davy junior 6d [212]
589. John Horn 6d [234]
590. Walter Coppe 6d
591. John Hulle webbe 4d
592. Richard Gage 8d [211]
593. John London 4d [127]
594. John Ferur webbe 16d [42]
595. William Slegge 2s [178]
596. Benedict Godeshome 6d
597. John Toryton 4d [190]
598. Thomas Rede 2s 6d
599. John Doly 4d [261]
600. John Pope drapere 40d [25]
601. John Wotton 2s 6d [134]
602. Henry Whelere webbe 4d
603. Robert Benet 4d
604. Richard Stagard 4d
605. John Putton 4d

606. Robert Blakemour 4d
607. John Shereve 4d
608. Walter Evesham 6d [241]
609. John Purvyour 4d
610. Hugh Coupere 4d
611. Henry Hayward 4d
612. Thomas Bekampton 4d [9]
613. John Ragge 4d
614. Thomas Baldenale skynner 4d
615. Thomas Eyr 3s [71]
616. John Teukesbury 4d [174]
617. Roger Houwe 4d
618. Godfrey Carter webbe 4d
619. John Giffard 4d
620. Roger Tolous 4d
621. William Tolous 6d [125]
622. John Holewey 4d
623. Walter Gilmyn 6d [115/119]
624. John Mury tanner 16d [152?]
625. Adam Teffonte 8s [155]
626. Thomas Davy webbe 4d
627. John Leokere tanner 2s
628. Henry Bryan 8d
629. John Moul tenens infra 4d [33]
630. William Wollop 6d
631. Thomas Slegge 8d [82]
632. Nicholas Norys 12d [151]
633. John Coyfer tanner 6d
634. William Nedlere 20d [64]
635. John Parch 40d [36]
636. John Prydy & John Scot socius eius 8d
637. John Waltham 4d
638. John Tully 4d
639. James Swet 4d
640. Stephen Toukere 12d
641. John Montegew 2s
642. Peter Uphavene 6d [244]
643. William Coupere 12d
644. William Loord 6d
645. William Hul 5s
646. Yweyn Tannere 6d
647. Agnes Lordis 6d [230]
648. John Wermynstre 6d [156]
649. John Hogeman 16d [39?]
650. Henry Okebere 4d
651. Mathew Webbe 4d
652. John Hulle carpenter 20d
653. John Route 6d
654. Cristina Handle 8d [98]
655. William Busshel 4d
656. John Caundel clerk 40d
657. uxor William Pobeman 4d [200?]
658. Thomas Denham 4d
659. Richard Pympol 4d

660. John Motesfonte 6d
661. Thomas Farle 6d [249]
662. John Lecy bakere 16d [246?]
663. Richard Benet 4d
664. Thomas Nasshe 4d [247?]
665. John Huggebody 4d [287]
666. Robert Nyweport 6d
667. Thomas Lyonn brouderere 6d
668. Andrew Damarle 6d
669. John Waltham toukere 4d
670. Robert Stykeberd 4d [160]
671. Adam Waltham 6d [77]
672. John Pymperne 4d [188/191]
673. John Knyght webbe 4d
674. Robert Werburne 6d
675. Robert Pentrich 4d [243]
676. Robert Curteys de Curnebourne 6d
677. Henry Rook 4d [183]
678. William Gys 16d
679. Henry Preterjohn 6d [49]
680. Thomas Yonge 4d [8]
681. Nicholas Comine 8d
682. John Sampson 8d
683. Henry Taverner 4d
684. William Ynkepenne 4d
685. John Shute skynnere 4d [17]
686. Richard Sherman 2s [145]
687. Edward Fletchere 4d
688. John Chaundeler jun 4d
689. John Chaundeler sen 5s
690. John Dykere 2s [89]
691. Robert Taillour 4d
692. Thomas Plomer 4d
693. David Fyshere 6d
694. Margaret Godmanston 40d [92]
695. John Wyke taillour 4d
696. John Vyryng 6d [199]
697. John Monk 4d
698. Henry Chubbe 6d
699. Henry Gog carpenter 4d
700. William Fulham 16d [37]
701. John Payn taillour 4d
702. Matthew Farnhulle 8d
703. John Lacy 4d
704. John Taillour 4d [242]
705. Thomas Brid 4d
706. William Saundres 12d [219]
707. Nicholas Joce 4d [93]
708. John Coppe 8d [196]
     summa totalis £15 5s

Pratum

709. William Taillour atte Freren yate 4d
710. John Dygher passeger 12d
711. Thomas Messag' 16d

712. John Lymburner 16d
713. John Underwode corveser 4d
714. John Bakere 12d
715. John Penne 8d
[added between lines] John Harnham 6d
716. John Stuward dyghere 8d [109]
717. William Hogen 8d
718. John Sydenham 4d
719. William West 2s 6d
720. John Shereberd 4d
721. Laurence Lane 12d [201]
722. William Westmour 8d [54]
723. William Compton 8d [19]
724. Richard Derby webbe 6d
725. John Palmere webbe 6d
726. Thomas Coscoumbe webbe 16d
727. Robert Durant 40d
728. Stephen Barbour osteler 4d
729. Richard Stamford 6d
730. John Salesbury webbe 4d
731. John Ruddok webbe 16d [26]
732. Kyng Tannere 8d
733. Robert Stanleygh 8d
734. John Raynald 8d [22]
735. William Smyth webbe 4d
[added between lines] George Joce 8d [74]
736. Robert Tavel 4d
737. William Warman 6d
738. Edward Enefeld 6s 8d
739. John Chyppenham 2s [44]
740. Stephen Edyngdon 20d
741. William Lymburner 8d
742. Richard Herberd webbe 6d [248]
743. Robert Erlestoke 4d

Novus Vicus

744. Richard Peyntur 4d
745. William Cornewayle 4d
746. John Hillery skynnere 4d
747. John Stone 4d
748. John Dancastre dyere 8d [141]
749. William Mone webbe 4d
750. Alice Cammel 8s
751. Robert Sopere webbe 4d
752. John Mulman carpenter 6d
753. Walter Babbestoke 4d [48/149]
754. John Wenelyng 6d [83?]
755. Robert Hyndon 6d [220]
756. Henry Kent 4d
757. Walter Davy 6d
758. John Chedyngdon 4d
759. William Cokwilly 4d
760. John Fenel mason 6d
761. John Bedeford skynnere 6d

762. Godlefa Amale 4d [120]
763. John Solas carpenter 4d
764. John Marchel webbe 4d
765. uxor John Briston 6d [121]
766. Thomas Biston 2s 6d
767. John Wellis webbe 6d
768. Robert Lye carpenter 4d
769. Edward Fonteyn 4d
770. Cecilia Mossel 4d
771. John Kyngbrigge 2s
772. Walter Nandre 4s [18]
773. Walter Cook 4d
774. Richard Taillour 4d
775. John Heryng 4d
776. John Osteler de Georges In 4d
777. John Kyngesbury skynnere 4d
778. John Broun toukere 6d
779. John Barbur 4d
780. Andrew Shether 4d
781. John Dore pynnere 4d
782. William Stanys 4d
783. Michael Shethere 4d
784. John Ony corveser 4d
785. Robert Latener 4d
786. Thomas Stille 12d
787. Edward Clay 4d
788. Petronilla Gondy 16d [213]
789. Edward Compton 4d
790. John Nyweman hatter 16d
791. Reginald Glovere 2s 6d
792. Roger Cook 6d
793. Robert Hattere 16d
794. Nicholas Clerk 4d
795. Edward Barbur 8d
796. Walter atte Mulle 4d
797. John Chamburleyn taillour 4d
798. Richard Goldsmyth 20d
799. Alice Northam 4d
800. John Workman 4d
801. John Sadeler bakere 16d
802. Richard Wellis 4d
803. John Baker grocer 13s 4d
804. William Cokhulle pardoner 8d
805. John Stoke sadeler 4d
806. John Sherman s[ocius] Alex Moys 6d
807. John Kyng skynnere 4d
808. William Pykard 6s
809. William Curreour 4d
810. Richard Hurlebat 4d
811. Nicholas Bray webbe 4d
812. Geoffrey Peauterer 6d
813. Robert Redenham 16d [128]
814. John Edeshale 5s [214]
815. John Dyer taverner 4d

816. Hugh Braban 18d [105]
817. Thomas Holm 12d
818. Richard Irlond 4d
819. Cristina Hukkestere 4d
820. William Adecok 4d
821. Walter Taillour 4d
822. Walter Orm 3s
823. Walter Sadeler 4d
824. Henry Sherman 4d
825. John Berton' barbur 4d
826. John Barbur 4d [269?]
827. Robert Redyng 6d
828. George Corvesor 6d
829. George Sadeler 16d
830. John Noble 8d
831. William Fuystur 3s
832. Thomas Taillour 6d
833. John Yonge sadeler 4d
834. William Furbur 8d
835. Reymond Wyrdrawer 4d
836. Henry Goldsmyth 8d
837. John Spencer mercer 2s [215]
838. Thomas Goudchyld 6d [260]
839. Richard Barbur 8d
840. John Croos sadeler 4d
841. Robert Hamond 4d
842. Nicholas Goldsmyth 4d
843. Roger Wodeford 18d [51]
844. Nicholas Curteys 8d [112]
845. William Bowyer 4d
846. Isabella Cammel 20d
847. John Skympayn 4d
848. Isabella Taverner 4d
849. Robert Jakis sporyour 4d
850. Stephen Cornyssh 8d
851. Ralph Barbur 8d
852. Robert Felton goldsmyth 4d
853. Robert Fode 4d
854. Thomas Gardener hukster 4d
855. Alice Swynford broudester 4d
856. Philip Goldsmyth 16d
857. Robert Spencer fysshere 4d
858. John Crabbelane 20d
859. John Stoke 2s
860. John Goudale ferour 6d
861. Walter Gaude 6d
862. Bartholomew Skynnere 8d
863. Cecilia Marchel 12d
864. Thomas Marcel 4d
865. William Quyk taillour 4d
866. Thomas Paskere skynnere 8d
867. Richard Hillery skynnere 8d
868. William Sherewold 8d
869. John Drapere clerk 6d
870. John Ayleward Juyn' 4d

871. Alexander Moys 6d
872. John Juwel 4d
873. John Homes 6d
874. Robert Poole 16d
875. Robert Smyth 6d
876. Thomas Sexteyn 6s
877. Martin Yrmanger 10d
878. William Douk 10d
879. John Helyer yrmanger 6d
880. John Coor potecary 4d
881. John Mannyng boucher & Richard socius 8d
882. John Drew boucher 4d
883. John Wellis boucher sen' 2s
884. John Harold boucher 4d
885. John Wellis Jun 6d
886. John Frye boucher 6d
887. Robert de Grantham fysshere 4d
888. Edward Bur 4d
889. Robert Curtlyngotoke 2s 6d
890. John Spencer 4d
891. Margery atte Nasshe 4d
892. William Yrissh spycer 4d
893. Edith Daubeneyes 6d
894. Margery Cappestere 4d
895. Richard Pynnok 8d [229/250]
896. Martin Fysshere 6d
897. John Whitlok 6d
898. William Fysshere de Harnham 6d [108?]
899. William Barbur harpere 4d
900. Thomas Ferour smyth 4d
901. John Wyght taillour 6d
902. John Russel 6d
903. Hugh Yrmanger 12d
904. Walter Man 4d
905. Richard Helier 4d
906. William Hattere 4d
907. William Handle taillour 12d
908. John Parfyt 4d
909. William Purbyk skynnere 6d
910. Simon Tredynek 20d
911. William Isak 2s 6d [154]
912. William Hillery skynnere 6d
913. George Meryot 10s
914. William Doudyng 40d
915. Henry Bakere 8d
916. Hugh Stalbrigge 4d
917. William Portur taillour 20d
918. John Ovyns 2s
919. William Busshup' 5s
920. Nicholas Fysshere 4d
921. William Wil 2s 6d [106]
922. John Frogge & John Berde fyssheres 8d

923. John Drake & Philip socius eius 12d
924. Robert Wroxhale webbe 4d
925. Richard atte Mulle 4s
926. Hugh Portesham 6d
927. John Grey 8d
928. Richard Beele de Hampton 8d
929. Nicholas de Forde 8d
930. John Marchaunt 8d
931. Richard s. Thomas Chyld 4d
932. Thomas Chyld 40d
933. Thomas Cofford 16d
934. Alicia Hethis 40d [266]
935. Placidacius Deye 20d
936. Robert Axebrigge 8d
937. Reginald Sherman 6d
938. Richard Cove hosiere 12d [117]
939. John Goudale cardmakyere 2s
940. John Yweyn toukere 4d [147]
941. John Elis strengere 4d [78]
942. John Nywman grocere 8s
943. Robert Wolf 6d
944. John Biterley taillour 4d
945. John Bollok skynnere 6d
946. William Goudale cardmakyere 12d
947. John Founder brasyer 4d
948. John Hillery corveser 4d
949. John Preston 6d
950. Robert Chutel wolmanger 12d
951. John Edelof de Wymbourne 8d
952. Master Simon Leche 8d
953. John Brid taillour 4d
954. Richard Knyght 4d
955. William Waryn 5s
956. John Harleston 6d
957. John Hosiere 4d [66]
958. Robert Beryng 4d
959. Thomas Felde 4s
960. William Taillour 4d
961. Thomas Woode 4d
962. Nicholas Mauncefeld 6d
963. Isabella Fulham 12d
964. William Freond 8d
965. Henry Wermystre 4d
966. Richard Juwel 6s 8d
967. John Redenham webbe 4d
968. Richard Dyere 4d [245?]
969. Henry Godfray 12d
970. Geoffrey Boucher 4d
971. Simon Elyot 4d
972. Richard Benton curreour 4d
973. William Bray bakere 12d
974. John Berdene curreour 4d
975. Thomas Gerveys 20d
976. Walter Glasiere 4d
977. Gregory Gilberd 4d

978. John Grey curreour 6d
979. John Derby 4d
980. William Gylis 4d
981. John Brid juynour 8d
982. John Curreour 4d
983. William Avyn skynnere 6d
984. John Boket 4d
985. Thomas Flawener skynner 4d
986. John Berton cuteler 8d
987. John Hastere cuteler 8d
988. Robert Weye skynner 20d

989. Thomas Pidis 12d
990. Stephen Coole 6d
991. Richard Goude glovere 4d
992. John Hathewey 12d
993. William Blythe 6d
994. Richard Oseberne 4d [237]
995. William Cook 8d
996. Cristina Cook 4d
997. Reginald Cook 4d
     summa totalis £12 8s 2d

Appendix Two: Salisbury Tradesmen in 1667

The list of contributors to a royal aid and supply in 1667 has been used at various points in this history. It was printed by E. R. Nevill in 1910 (Nevill, 1910) and forms a most useful directory of householders, both owners and tenants, in restoration Salisbury. The list, as it stands, however, does not identify occupations, and the purpose of this appendix is to detail the occupations, derived from other sources, of the names on the list, wherever this can be done without too great a risk of error. Various documents among the city muniments have been examined, together with certain archival sources which have appeared in print and other printed secondary sources. These have been abbreviated in the list that follows, and the abbreviations are noted below.

The order of entries is the same as that in Nevill, 1910. Only tenants and owner-occupiers (usually signified in the original by the words, 'tenement ... in his own hands') are considered. At the beginning of the list for each street or chequer is given the percentage of applicable names in Nevill, 1910, which appear in this appendix. The remainder are omitted because it has not been possible to assign an occupation to them with confidence. Since the sources used in this exercise are mainly concerned with masters rather than journeymen it may be assumed that in general the percentage corresponds roughly to the proportion of masters to journeymen living in that part of the city, and so may be taken as an approximation of wealth of one area compared with another. Each entry includes, after the name and occupation, a summary of the sources used, with the date given in brackets, where this is ascertainable from the source. Where conflicts of evidence have arisen which cannot be satisfactorily resolved I omit the entry altogether; this is usually in cases where it is clear that several people of the same name were working in the city at different trades and it is impossible, without considerable effort, to decide who lived where. The abbreviations used are as follows:

1. Will proved in the court of the Sub-Dean of Sarum (W.R.O.)
2. Will proved in the consistory court of Sarum (W.R.O.)
3. W.R.O. G23/1/59
4. W.R.O. G23/1/117
5. W.R.O. G23/1/264
6. W.R.O. G23/1/250
7. W.R.O. G23/1/265
8. Swayne, 1896.
9. Rowe, 1966.
10. Haskins, 1912.
11. Baker, 1906.
12. R.C.H.M., 1980.
13. Williams, 1960.
14. Waylen, 1892.
15. Hatcher, 1843.
16. W.R.O. G23/1/71

NEW STREETE WARD 33/81 (41%)

Thomas Hellyard, haberdasher 1 (1668)
Henry Smyth, shoemaker 7 (1671) 1 (1679)
Thomas Sweetman, pinmaker 7 (1677)
Richard Deane, cooper 5 (1670) 1 (1673)
William Wilson, apothecary 1 (1705)
Nicholas Langley, clockmaker 1 (1674)
Henry Mussell, hosier 5 (1668)
Robert Paradice, milliner 5 (1668)
Robert Langley, watchmaker 1 (1668)
John Ashton, tailor 6 (1667)
Edward Spickernell, shoemaker 1 (1671)
George Knapton, grocer 5 (1668) 8 (1670)
Henry Gilbert, tailor 6 10 (1647)
Robert Blake, glover 3 1 (1679)
William Waterman, innholder 8 (1667) 1 (1707)
Hugh Dickery, vintner 2 (1667)
Henry Powell, cutler 1 (1680)
Henry Curryer, cooper 1 (1681)
John George, clothworker 5 (1664) 10
Thomas Woodman, blacksmith 1 (1671)
Thomas Cooper, shoemaker 5 (1668) 12 1 (1686)
Robert Roberts, shoemaker 7 (1671)
Christopher Wheeler, barber (1673)
John Langley, watchmaker 12 (1649)
Abraham Veale, saddler 1 (1700)
John Cuxey, tailor 3 6 10 (1657)
Robert Ellyott, tailor 6 (1668) 5 (1671)
Jesper Kelloway, turner 3
James Day, tailor 6 (1649)
Henry Mattershaw, cook 3 9 (1658)
Edward Fry, parchmentmaker 5 (1668)
John Mills, shoemaker 7 (1664) 1 (1698)

NEW STREET 14/35 (40%)

Christopher Wheeler, barber 1 (1673)
William Carden, shoemaker 5 (1667) 7 (1677) 1 (1679)
Abraham Veale, saddler 1 (1700)
William Cole, gent. 1 (1704)
Thomas Sturridge, glover 3 5 (1668) 1 (1693)
George Roberts, carpenter 5 (1664) 8 (1679) 10 (1680)
John Purchase, barber 1 (1681)
Peter Easton, corviser/currier 7 (1665) 7 (1671)
Thomas Crooke, currier/shoemaker 7 (1675) 10 (1677)
William Waterman, innholder 8 (1667) 1 (1707)

Allen Bell, tanner 1 (1674)
John White, carpenter 5 (1664)
Nathaniel Leversuch, currier 8 (1670) 10 (1677) 7 1 (1709)
Cornelius Cornwall, gardener 1 (1698)

DOLPHIN CHEQUER 47/120 (39%)

George Keevil, yeoman 1 (1696)
Jeffery Everatts, blacksmith 5 (1668)
Thomas Weekes, butcher 3 7 (1675)
Peter Matthewes, yeoman 1 (1678)
John Banister, wiredrawer 3
George Godfrey, pinner 3 (ratkiller 9 (1659))
Edward Wheeler, barber 3 1 (1674)
Abraham Wilson, cutler 3
William Dewe, tailor 6 (1645)
Christopher Willmote, wiredrawer 8 (1667) 1 (1694)
Mr Hackeman, yeoman 3
John Noyce, shoemaker 8 (1670) 1 (1670)
William Nashe, grocer 2 (1671)
William Courtney, bookseller/binder 5 (1670) 9 (1670) 8 (1685)
Nicholas Rowe, butcher 1 (1672)
Mrs Haskall, ironmonger (widow of Nicholas? 9 (1658))
Thomas Ovyatt, merchant 3
John Creed, basketmaker 5 (1676) 1 (1704)
William Prater, baker 8 (1667) 10 (1672) 1 (1681)
George Vowles, tailor 6 (1655)
Thomas Ryddall, innholder 5 (1664) 9
Henry Mattershaw, innholder
Thomas Raye, clothier 3 9 12
Edmund Mackes, brazier 8 (1679) 1 (1699)
John Joyce, apothecary 12 (1649)
John Flower, tailor 6 (1645) 10 (1658) 2 (1698)
Stephen Chubbe, tailor 6 (1648)
John Purchase, barber 1 (1681)
Thomas Boswell, cutler 3
Roger Bedbury, innkeeper 9 (1664)
Henry Gauntlett, baker 10 (1672) 1 (1695)
Samuel Appleyard, saddler 5 (1666) 1 (1670)
John Hewlett, tailor 3 6
William Chubbe, tailor 6 (1641)
Benjamin Jenkins, tailor 6 (1660)
John Shorey, joiner 3 1 (1690)
Henry Powell, cutler 1 (1680)

John Carter, horner 1 (1673)
Nicholas Card, shoemaker 7 (1669)
Joseph Mitchell, shoemaker 3
Thomas Cuttler, clothier 3 1 (1681)
William Penney, maltster/brewer 5 (1668) 1 (1704)
John Whitmarsh, innholder 8 (1670)
Thomas Meynety, carpenter 5 (1664)
John Curtis, carpenter 3 1 (1679)
Mr Tettershall, gent. 13

MR MUNDEYES CHEQUER 15/28 (54%)

James Harris, gent. 3
Edward Brownjohn, tailor 6 (1668)
William Collyar, yeoman 1 (1697) 12
George Clements, innkeeper 9 (1664)
Edmund Mackes, brazier 8 (1679) 1 (1699)
William Nash, grocer 2 (1671)
Humphrey Ditton, gent. 13 (1668)
John Fletcher, shoemaker 3 7 (1667)
John Cosens, blacksmith 8 (1647) 5 (1675)
George Hall, tailor 3 6 1 (1670)
Oliver Pope, tailor 8 (1667) 1 (1701)
Timothy Edwards, tailor 6 (1668)
Thomas Bennett, apothecary 5 (1675)
Henry Mussell, hosier 5 (1668)

SOUTH SIDE OF BUTCHEROWE 9/15 (60%)

Henry Harlocke, butcher 7 (1665)
John Searchfield, butcher 5 (1663)
William Indey, butcher 1 (1685) 13
Thomas Browne, butcher 3 7 (1666)
John Nicholls, butcher 7 (1676) 1 (1696)
Symon Marks, butcher 1 (1684)
John Weekes, gent. 14 (1645)
Walter Rice, butcher 7 (1674)
William Bryne, butcher (1665)

SOUTH SIDE OF YE FISHEROWE 4/12 (33%)

John West, bellowmaker 3 1 (1667)
John Ames, tailor 5 (1670) 6 10 (1660)
William Oburne, tailor 6 (1640) 1 (1676)
Morgan Newbury, shoemaker 1 (1667)

MARKET WARD 90/227 (40%)

Cornelius Smyth, innholder 1 (1668)
John Bennett, yeoman 1 (1677)

Henry Stokes, glazier 8 (1681)
Henry Gauntlett, baker 3 10 (1672) 1 (1676)
Anthony Pittman, glover 3
Thomas Sutton, clothier 3
Robert Hayter, shoemaker 3
Richard Jordan, shoemaker 7 (1665)
Thomas Lawne, papermaker 3
Henry Seward, grocer 9 1 (1703)
Walter Combes, barber 1 (1679)
Thomas Willis, shoemaker 7 (1675) 10 (1677) 1 (1682)
George Hughes, innkeeper 9 (1658)
Francis Pistle, silkweaver 5 (1664), barber 5 (1674)
Henry Mason, cordwainer 1 (1687)
Goddard Ellyott, grocer 9 (1666) 1 (1671)
Thomas Mitchell, shoemaker 3 1 (1673)
William Skeate, tailor 3 6
Thomas Browne, shoemaker 8 (1667)
Peter Williams, shoemaker 1 (1674)
Richard Phelpes, woollendraper 3
Walter Combes, hosier 12 (1649)
William Vyner (senior), innkeeper 9 (1657) 12
William Vyner (junior), linendraper 5 (1670)
William Clements, mercer/clothworker 3 9 1 (1701)
Thomas Batter, innholder 8 (1649)
Edward Mason, innkeeper 9 (1658)
Adam Draper, tailor 6 10 (1664)
Robert Greene, joiner 1 (1682)
Thomas Barlow, tailor 6
William Heeley, glazier 8 (1648) 1 (1695)
Edward Parker, baker 8 (1667) 5 (1668) 1 (1680)
Thomas Body, maltster 1 (1678)
John Cabbell, dyer 3 (1679)
Gyles Freeman, skinner 1 (1668)
Edward Irish, butcher 3
Edward Allen, butcher 3 1 (1675)
Matthew Harper, shoemaker 3 13 (1668) 1 (1687)
Henry Harlocke, butcher 7 (1665)
John Bowles, baker 10 (1672) 1 (1698)
Edward Martin, baker 10 (1672)
John Hewlett, tailor 3 6
David Lovedee, mason 1 (1667)
William Hall, grocer 3
Richard Harrison, hellier 13 (1672)
Henry Cooke, bellowmaker 1 (1676)
Ambrose Webb, tanner 1 (1677)
John Strickland, minister of St. Edmund's 8 (1655)

Joseph Antram, clothier 3 1 (1692)
Thomas Abbotts, bishop's bailiff 15 (1658)
Walter Bath, tanner 1 (1671)
Edward Doman, carpenter 5 (1678)
Thomas Snooke, innkeeper 10
William Snooke, yeoman 1 (1696)
John Snowe, parchmentmaker 12 (1649)
John White, carpenter 5 (1664)
Thomas Welch, yeoman 1 (1698)
Thomas Lambe, husbandman 1 (1678)
John Fowles, tailor 10 (1647) 6 5 (1670)
Robert Hill, shoemaker/bridlecutter 7 (1675) 10 (1677)
Robert Edmonds, clothworker 1 (1672)
Zachariah Wayte, carpenter 8 (1681)
Ralph Pasby, shoemaker 7 (1665)
William Hunt, schoolmaster 8 (1648)
William Jeffery, carpenter 1 (1669)
David Dee, pavier/sawyer 5 (1668) 1 (1680)
Andrew Hellyar, maltster 1 (1683)
John Stokes, hellier 8 (1648) 1 (1676)
Richard Emery, parchmentmaker 3
Thomas Hancocke, gent./brewer 14 (1645)
Richard Streete, weaver 3
Thomas Barnes, shoemaker 7 (1665) 5 (1674)
Peter Peirce, cordwainer 2 (1680)
William Vincent, shoemaker 3
Edward Fry, parchmentmaker 5 (1668)
Richard Emery, parchmentmaker 3
John Scranch, weaver 3 1 (1676)
Thomas Eyre, gent. 1 (1699)
William Antrum, parchmentmaker? 1 (1676)
Nicholas Farre, glover 5 (1663)
Allen Bell, tanner 1 (1674)
Stephen Smyth, tanner 1 (1673)
Thomas Smyth, tanner 8 (1647) 3 7 1 (1684)
Robert Whatly, weaver 3
Sir Wadham Wyndham, gent. 12

MR SWANTONS CHEQUER 6/19 (32%)

Maurice Greene, brewer 14 (1645)
Robert Townsend (junior), kerseyweaver 1 (1683)
Robert Townsend (senior), hellier 3
Thomas Noyce, shoemaker 7 (1666)
John Thatcher, surgeon 1 (1673)
William Foxe, parish clerk 1 (1677)

WHITEHORSE CHEQUER 18/44 (41%)

John Ivye, goldsmith
William Parsons, clothier 5 (1671)
Roger Knight, hellier 5 (1670) 1 (1691)
Richard Harrison, hellier 13 (1672)
George Nicholas, weaver 3
Robert Friend, chandler 3 1 (1670)
Philip Young, chandler 8 (1649)
Jonathan Smyth, gunsmith 5 (1663)
Andrew Roberts, innholder 3
John Whitmarsh, innholder 8 (1670)
John James, clothier 5 (1668)
Thomas Grist, chandler 3
Michaell Mills, tailor 6 10 (1659)
John Bampton, weaver 1 (1674)
William Gray, clothier 3
Andrew Roberts, tailor 3 1 (1668)
John Bugden, weaver 3
Robert Blake, glover 3 1 (1679)

THREE SWANNES CHEQUER 33/74 (45%)

Mr William Dove, clothier 3
William Clements, clothworker/mercer 3 9 1 (1701)
Bennett Cowslade, blacksmith 1 (1685)
Archibald Beckingham, innholder 1 (1671)
Thomas Smyth, tanner 8 (1647) 3 7 1 (1684)
Thomas Sandy, tailor 6 (1643, 1665) 10 (1664)
John Barnes, shoemaker 3 7 (1666) 1 (1703)
Francis West, bellowmaker 1 (1686)
Reignold Sewell, joiner 3
George Symes, innholder 1 (1681)
John Eastmont, shoemaker 2 (1686)
Henry Hammond, stationer 8 (1656) 1 (1669)
Alexander Williams, baker 10 (1672)
George Mills, shoemaker 3 7 (1666)
John Peasland, shoemaker 7 (1668)
John Powell, barber 3
John Powell, clothworker 10 (1675)
Thomas Tynham, pewterer 9 (1667) 1 (1686)
William Wansborough, grocer 1 (1674)
Henry Cole, glover 13
John Hancocke, apothecary 9 1 (1682)
John Phillipps, innholder 5 (1664)
Thomas Heyward, goldsmith 1 (1677)

Richard Durneford, innholder 1 (1680)
William Sanger, barber 1 (1694)
Thomas Taylour, weaver 1 (1688)
Robert Hunt, apothecary 1 (1678)
William Heely, glazier 8 (1648) 1 (1695)
William Ogbourne, flaxdresser 2 (1701)
William Woodman, blacksmith 3 1 (1668)
William Gawen, grocer 9
John White, carpenter 5 (1663)
Richard Greene, cooper 5 (1670)

OATMEALE ROW 6/12 (50%)

Nicholas Parsons, feltmaker 5 (1670)
John Priaulx, linendraper 5 (1664)
Joseph Stockwell, haberdasher 1 (1676)
John Slanne, silkman 1 (1688)
Henry Edmonds, tailor 6 (1675)
Thomas West, mercer 1 (1686)

GOALE CHEQUER 6/10 (60%)

Henry Edmonds, tailor 6 (1675)
Anthony Wilkenson, goldsmith 1 (1678)
William Hewlett, tailor 6 1 (1674)
Roger Penny, butcher 1 (1673)
Francis West, bellowmaker 1 (1686)
Richard Hillary, shoemaker 3 1 (1672)

PART OF THE BUTCHEROWE 12/23 (52%)

George Page, grocer 9 (1656) 1 (1673)
John Coleman, apothecary 5 (1674)
Thomas Shergold, innkeeper 9 (1666)
Charles Phelpes, confectioner 9 1 (1670)
Mr Ditton, clothier/mercer? 8 (1647)
Henry Mattershaw, cook 3 9 (1658)
Edward Penny, butcher 3 9 (1671) 7 (1676)
Thomas Marsh, cook 1 (1685)
John Carter, horner 1 (1673)
James Rowe, butcher 1 (1705)
Nicholas Staples, shoemaker 5 (1671) 10 (1679) 1 (1705)
James Greene, basketmaker 5 (1670) 1 (1700)

MARTIN WARD 16/61 (26%)

John Williams, weaver 3
William Crowcher, joiner? 11 1 (1671)
William Whatley, clothworker 3
John Crouch, cardmaker 3 1 (1669)
Robert Johnson, bricklayer 5 (1672)

Robert Edmonds, clothworker 1 (1672)
Widow Pennicoate, weaver (widow of Henry? 3)
John Conditt, weaver 3
Jeffrey Barnes, wheeler 5 (1664)
George Tynham, clothworker 3 8 (1667) 1 (1700)
Stephen Brownjohn, wheelwright 1 (1679)
John Symonds, shoemaker 5 (1671)
Henry Fricker, yeoman 1 (1667)
Richard Spaggs, weaver 3
Thomas Phillips, gent. 1 (1671)
Thomas Knight, weaver 3

MR ROLFES CHEQUER 19/57 (33%)

Simon Rolfe, clothier 3 9 (1666)
Simon Ranger, weaver 3
Christopher Turner, husbandman 1 (1680)
Richard Eaton, joiner 3
Edward Gennett, mason 8 (1648)
Edward Hall, parchmentmaker 5 (1668)
William Bayley, weaver 3
James Oakeford, yeoman 3
John Oakeford, carpenter 8 (1648, 1660)
George Evans, yeoman 1 (1677)
John Browne, kerseyweaver 5 (1670)
Richard Rowden, goldsmith/brazier 11 2 (1698)
Henry Lake, bricklayer 5 (1664) 8 (1687)
Richard Spagges, weaver 3
John Bishop, silkweaver 13 (1663)
Lancelot Davis, clothworker 3 1 (1667)
Maurice Hawkins, pewterer 7 (1676)
John Lucas, shoemaker 5 (1664) 1 (1696)
William Tanner (senior), weaver 3

TRINITY CHEQUER 15/62 (24%)

John Crowch, cardmaker 3 1 (1669)
Thomas Harris, starchmaker 5 (1664) 1 (1676)
William Antram, clothmaker 8 (1648) 3 1 (1669)
Nicholas Thomas, tailor 3 6
Richard Noble, yeoman 1 (1683)
William Staples, shoemaker 3 7 (1676)
John George, clothworker 5 (1664) 10
John Bishop, silkweaver 13 (1663)
Thomas Grafton, weaver 3
William Jennoway, parchmentmaker 3 1 (1678)
Maurice Warren, carpenter 5 (1668)

James Russell, tailor 6 (1659)
John Grady, weaver 3
Thomas Hibbert, hellier 1 (1681)
William Wickham, weaver 1 (1693)

WHITE BEAR CHEQUER 24/67 (36%)

John Godfrey, pinner 3
Nicholas Farre, glover 5 (1663)
John Gerrett, shoemaker 7 (1675) 2 (1683)
Robert Whale, ropemaker 8 (1648) 3 1 (1666)
George Tynham, clothworker 8 (1667) 3 1 (1700)
Walter Rice, butcher 7 (1674)
John Symonds, shoemaker 5 (1671)
Robert Freeman, carpenter 5 (1668) 8 (1682)
Robert Day, butcher 3
Walter Buckland, innholder 5 (1664)
John Gumbleton, innholder 1 (1670)
Robert Early, pewterer 3
Vaughan Richards, innkeeper 9 (1666)
Edward Kensington, coachmaker 5 (1672)
John Mathewes, tailor 6 (1663) 1 (1687)
Robert Shergold, shoemaker 5 (1669)
Francis Manning, innkeeper/baker 9 (1664) 10 (1672)
Anthony Carter, miller 6 (1648)
William Richardson, saddler 1 (1672, 1679)
John Fullocke, smith? 8 (1668, 1676)
William Prator, baker 8 (1667) 10 (1672) 1 (1681)
George Godfrey, pinner 3
Humphrey Beckham joiner 3 8 1 (1671)
Richard Myles, baker 5 (1664) 10 (1672)

THREE LYONS CHEQUER 24/26 (52%)

John Barrowe, innkeeper 10
Gerard Errington, gent. 1 (1677)
Paul Thatcher, grocer 1 (1678)
Christofer Legge, ironmonger 8 (1647) 9 11
Thomas Coleman, saddler 7 (1675) 1 (1694)
William Percevall, painter 3 8
Morgan Morse, carrier 8 (1656)
John Pride, blacksmith 1 (1670)
Christopher Samwayes, tailor 6 1 (1676)

Henry Peirce, shoemaker 7 (1666)
William Twinnyhoe, haberdasher 5 (1668) 1 (1691)
Thomas Haytor, cordwainer 9 (1666)
Richard Mineveh, milliner 5 (1668) 9
Edward Thomas, shoemaker 3 7 (1673)
John Naish, clothier 5 (1664)
Henry Harlocke, butcher 7 (1665)
Edward Penny, butcher 3 9 (1671) 7 (1676)
Anthony Wilkinson, goldsmith 1 (1678)
Symon Markes, butcher 1 (1684)
Henry Mattershaw, cook 3 9 (1658)
John Searchfield, butcher 5 (1663)
Mr Richards, musician 8 (1649)
Thomas Marsh, cook 1 (1685)
James Dyett, shoemaker 7 (1675) 10 (1677) 1 (1703)

BLACK HORSE CHEQUER 12/33 (36%)

Thomas Evans, innholder 3 1 (1667)
John Cosens (junior), blacksmith 5 (1675)
Gerrard Errington, gent. 1 (1677)
Benjamin Beckham, joiner 3 8 (1661) 1 (1683)
Richard Deane, cooper 5 (1670) 1 (1673)
William Symes, weaver/hairweaver 3 1 (1670)
Widow Bunne, hempdresser (widow of Richard? 3)
John Good, grocer 3
John Cuxy, tailor 3 6 10 (1657)
Robert Ford, tallowchandler 1 (1702)
William Cooper, silkweaver 5 (1674)
Mr. William Doves, clothier 3

MR SWAINES CHEQUER 13/38 (34%)

William Antram, clothier
Edward Thomas, shoemaker 3 7 (1673)
Widow Badgin, weaver (widow of Michael? 3)
John Small, weaver 1 (1680)
Edward Martin, baker 10 (1672)
William Tanner (junior), clothier 3
Roger Godfrey, butcher/cook 9 (1666) 1 (1676)
William Vincent, shoemaker 3
William Prewett, blacksmith 1 (1696)
James Fourt, clothmaker 1 (1681)
John Davis, clothworker 5 (1668)
Robert Johnson, bricklayer 5 (1672)
Nicholas Parsons, feltmaker 5 (1670)

GRIFFIN CHEQUER 13/40 (33%)

Thomas Thresher, bellfounder 1 (1674)
Henry Potter, limeburner 3 1 (1686)
James Greene, basketmaker 5 (1670) 1
   (1700)
Thomas Howse, butcher 3
Robert Keele, weaver 3
Richard Batten, mason? 8 (1651)
John Wimbleton, innholder 1 (1676)
Anthony Cooke, clothier 1 (1677)
William Morris, innholder 1 (1670)
Thomas Dawes, schoolmaster 16 (1674)
Widow Silvester, pinmaker (widow of
   Richard? 1 (1666))
William Payne, yeoman 1 (1686)

THREE CUPPES CHEQUER 9/38 (24%)

Thomas Powell, weaver 3
Thomas Taylor, weaver 1 (1688)
Thomas Batchelor, clothier 5 (1669)
Joseph Hill, weaver 3
Richard Grafton, maltster 1 (1674)
John Hillary, shoemaker 3
Alexander King, tailor 3 1 (1685)
John Barnes, shoemaker 3 7 (1666) 1
   (1703)
John Batt, tanner 3 1 (1680)

MR PARSONS CHEQUER 3/23 (13%)

John Willmote, wiredrawer 1 (1694)
William Percevall, painter 3 8 (1647)
Anthony Roberts, plasterer 8 (1654) 1
   (1690)

VANNERS CHECQUER 8/33 (24%)

Richard Vanner, tailor 6 10 (1669)
John Fishlake, baker 3
Abell Cooper, sawyer 1 (1672)
Hugh Smyth, parchmentmaker 3
Henry Wheeler, weaver 3
Humphrey Beckham, joiner 3 8 1 (1671)
Widow Pennicott, weaver (widow of
   Henry? 3)
Robert Roberts, shoemaker 7 (1671)

MEADE WARD: ST MARTINS CHURCH TO BELL CORNER 20/89 (23%)

William Romsey, sexton 11 (1660)
Mr Thomas Ovyatt, merchant 3

John Bowden, hellier 1 (1680)
John Nash, clothier 5 (1664)
Christopher Haveland, clothier 5 (1664)
Mr Horton, rector of St. Martin's 11
   (1664–1670)
Ambrose Curtis, aledraper 1 (1702)
Richard Hill, tanner 3 1 (1689) parish
   clerk 11
Thomas Batt, tanner 1 (1687)
Simon Rolfe, clothier 3 9 (1666)
Thomas Smyth, tanner 8 (1647) 3 7 1
   (1684)
Francis Frye, pinmaker 5 (1670)
Arthur Marshman, clockmaker? 8 (1676)
Augustus Knight, mason 8 (1648)
Samuel Bell, tanner 14 (1645) 3
Mr Henry Bacon, papermaker 3
Edward Barnes, yeoman 3 1 (1672)
John Skilling, blacksmith 1 (1679)
Nicholas Kimber, clothworker 10 (1675)
Mr William Haylocke, innholder 5 (1672)

CHEQUER BY BERNARDS CROSS 1/5 (20%)

John Laurence, yeoman 1 (1700)

THE NEXT CHEQUER 4/20 (20%)

John Bradford, weaver 3 1 (1691)
Thomas Biddlecombe, tanner 1 (1667)
William Samson, tanner 6 (1652)
William Porter, weaver 5 (1668)

MR DORRELLS CHEQUER 11/46 (24%)

Thomas Bennett, apothecary 5 (1675)
Edward Hall, parchmentmaker 5 (1668)
Mr John Fishlake, baker 3
Ephraim Moore, mason 1 (1699)
Thomas Swetman, pinmaker 7 (1677)
Richard Goddard, cooper 3
John Bawden, hellier 1 (1680)
William Walden, labourer 1 (1682)
John Bishop, silkweaver 13 (1663)
Thomas Collins, yeoman 1 (1685)
Henry Greene, tailor 6 (1643)

WHITE HART CHEQUER 9/30 (30%)

Thomas Willmote, barber 3 1 (1681)

John Bishop, silkweaver 13 (1663)
John Willmote, wiredrawer (1694)
Thomas Wilsheer, glover 3
William Cooper, silkweaver 5 (1674) 4
Richard Coleman, recorder of city 8
(1663)

Robert Grigge, parchmentmaker 5 (1663)
Richard Musselwhite, glover 1 (1705)
John Smedmore, innholder 5 (1664) 1
(1669)

Notes

NOTES TO CHAPTER ONE: NATIVITY

1. For example, Ordnance Survey 1:2500, Wiltshire sheet LXVI, 7, 3rd edition, 1926. 'In castro stabat urbs castrum stabat in urbe:' a rather ugly pentameter from a poem by Henry d'Avranches printed and translated by Torrance, 1959, 242,244 line 19. The excavations undertaken between 1909 and 1915 were summarised in interim reports. The Old Sarum model was displayed in Salisbury Museum until it closed its St. Ann Street premises in 1980. Quotation from Burnett, 1978,14.

2. For general discusssions of the role of hillforts see Cunliffe, 1978, 243-286 and Bradley, 1978,121-129. Detailed discussion of Old Sarum in prehistoric and Roman times by Musty, 1959, and Rahtz and Musty,1960; more recent summaries by Haslam, 1976, 47, and R.C.H.M., 1980, xxviii and 1. The siting of Roman towns is discussed by Wacher, 1975,17-35. Dorchester (about two miles from Maiden Castle) and Cirencester (about three miles from Bagendon) are examples of Roman town plantation near important existing hillforts. On the Roman road network see below, chapter four. The function of the *mansiones* and the working of the *cursus publicus* (or official transport network) are described by Chevallier, 1976. V.C.H.6, 1962, 52 suggests a settlement at Stratford-sub-Castle, following older writers, whilst Stone and Algar, 1955, have discovered evidence of Roman occupation on the site of the modern Pauls Dene housing estate, and their discovery was supplemented by Roman finds uncovered in a pipe trench dug in the area in 1957 (Musty, 1959). However, evidence of Roman occupation within the ramparts of Old Sarum was discovered during excavations in the north-east sector in the same year (Rahtz and Musty, 1960, 364-370). Two recent studies, Haslam, 1976 and R.C.H.M., 1980 do not discuss the issue. The battle of Searoburh, recorded in the Anglo-Saxon Chronicle, is discussed by Cowan, 1981, who suggests that it may have taken place in the area of modern Salisbury. R.C.H.M., 1980, xxix, following Bonney, 1969, 58, suggests that the absence of Old Sarum from a charter of 972 is an indication that no settlement took place until after this time.

3. The fullest history of Wilton is in V.C.H.6, 1962, 1-50. See also Haslam, 1976, 67-69. The relationship between Bedwyn, Ramsbury and Chisbury is noted by Aston and Bond, 1976, 58-60 and is the subject of a study by Keith Ray (according to Haslam, 1976, 49) as yet unpublished. South Cadbury is comprehensively described by its excavator, Alcock, 1972.

4. The text of the burghal hidage (as this list of forts is known) has been published by Hill, 1971, and there is a good recent assessment by Hinton, 1977, 30-41. I accept the arguments of Brooks, 1965, 75-79, that Cissanbyrig in the list represents Chisbury (V.C.H.6, 1962, 8 follows the older interpretation that it is Tisbury). Bredy in Dorset and Halwill in Devon are other re-used hillforts included in the burghal hidage: Hinton, *loc. cit.* It is tempting to suggest that Old Sarum may in fact have been the burghal hidage fort for Wilton, as is hinted in V.C.H.6, 1962, 52-53, but on present evidence this suggestion cannot be sustained. The hidage assigned to Wilton, 1400, implies a line of defences 1925 yards long (4 hides = 5½ yards) which is approximately 550 yards

longer than the iron age rampart of Old Sarum (where this calculation has been made at other burghal hidage forts the figures correspond much more closely: Hinton, 1977, *loc. cit.*). A distance of 1925 yards, on the other hand, would nicely encompass the extent of Saxon settlement at Wilton suggested on Haslam's plan (Haslam, 1976, 91), and traces of Saxon defensive work have been discovered at the western entrance to the town, near Ditchampton (notes in *Wiltshire Archaeological Magazine*, vol. 66 (1971), 191 and *Wiltshire Archaeological Magazine* vol. 67 (1972), 175-176). Wilton was successfully defended by Alfred in 871: V.C.H.6, 1962, 8; the battle is mentioned in the Anglo-Saxon Chronicle. Numismatic evidence for the consequences of the sack of Wilton is discussed by Dolley, 1954. Minting seems not to have resumed at Wilton before the accession of Cnut in 1016. South Cadbury offers an interesting parallel, where minting was transferred from Ilchester in 1009/1010, but the moneyers returned to Ilchester after 1016 and by 1019 minting at Cadbury had ceased: Alcock, 1972, 196-197. At Old Sarum the moneyers seem to have stayed on.

5. It has recently been suggested (R.C.H.M., 1980, 2) that traces of walls found in 1957 (Rahtz and Musty, 1960) may belong to Ethelredian fortifications of the early eleventh century. That the borough of Sarisberie is assessed separately from the Bishop's manor of Sarisberie at Domesday (V.C.H.6, 1962, 51) is an indication that the former was distinct from the latter and was not involved in farming the Bishop's lands. The road junction was discovered during excavations in 1958 (Musty and Rahtz, 1964, 136-139). Main road diversions are common in medieval planted towns: Beresford, 1967, 156; Butler, 1976, 39, 45; Aston and Bond, 1976, 89. Haslam, 1976, 93 places the Saxon town within the ramparts and on the slope outside the west gate, but offers no explanation. My reconstruction largely follows V.C.H.6, 1962, 53.

6. The council of London is described by Stenton, 1971, 666-667. Wilton's career as seat of a Saxon bishop is discussed by V.C.H.6, 1962, 7. Domesday book provides comparative material for Wiltshire boroughs in the eleventh century. Old Sarum in 1086 paid the third penny to the tune of £6, as did Malmesbury. Marlborough and Cricklade were less, but Wilton paid £50.

7. The most recent account of Old Sarum Cathedral is to be found in R.C.H.M., 1980, 15-24, with plan. An artist's reconstruction of the cathedral as it may have appeared in 1092 is reproduced in Shortt, 1957, 21. A new square-ended presbytery was added in the early twelfth century.

8. There is archaeological evidence for the Bishop's Palace: R.C.H.M., 1980, 21-22, and the Canons' houses are referred to after the site was abandoned: V.C.H.6, 1962, 61. Canons' houses outside the gates are mentioned in 1091: V.C.H.6, 60. The evidence for a planted town is a map of *ca.* 1700 showing burgage plots along a main road. The map is reproduced in V.C.H.6, 1962, 66, and the various possibilities of town plantation at Old Sarum are discussed by Beresford, 1967, 508-509 and Haslam, 1976, 48, who suggests that the burgage plots may have been laid out soon after the Norman conquest. The parliamentary tree, which was cut down in 1905 and is now commemorated by a plaque, is described in Anon. 1931 and V.C.H.6, 1962, 67. 'Nyweton Westyate' is first mentioned in 1353 (V.C.H.6, 1962, 64) and recent archaeological work seems to have located this outside the west gate: Musty and Rahtz, 1964, 141-142. Haslam's plan (Haslam, 1976, 93, see note 5 above) suggests that this western suburb is of Saxon date, but there seems to be no evidence for this. Its existence is noted also by Leland: Smith, 1964, 261.

9. Hatcher, 1843, 604, and plan facing, found evidence of a boundary wall running across the southern slope of Old Sarum, which he took to be the city wall. It is interesting to note that Hatcher, unlike later writers, did not fall into the trap of assuming that the city lay within the ramparts. A building excavated in 1958 (Musty and Rahtz, 1964, 138) appeared to have been built of timber and thatch or shingles at this period, although it was subsequently rebuilt in chalk and flint. The guild merchant is discussed

by Haskins, 1912, 13-16 and V.C.H.6, 1962, 62, the churches *ibid.* 65. The Church of Holy Cross is described as being 'over the east gate' in documents, and this is interpreted literally by Brown, 1963, 827. The grammar school is described by Robertson, 1937, 11-12 and Robertson, 1938, 28. Old Sarum is compared with Krakow and Zurich by Brooke, 1977, 461-463. Quotation, referring to Old Sarum, from Hatcher, 1843, 605.

10. The authorship of 'historia translationis veteris ecclesiae beatae Mariae Sarum ad novam' (Jones, 1884, vol. 2, 3ff') has been attributed to William de Wanda since the eighteenth century (Price, 1753, 2; Ledwich, 1771, 67) and his claim is discussed by Jones, 1884, vol. 2, x. Aubrey, 1847, 96 describes, 'the old records of the church that had been clung together and untouch for perhaps two hundred yeares.' The poem by Henry d'Avranches has been printed twice: Malden, 1899; Torrance, 1959 (with translation) and the penultimate couplet is quoted in Matthew Paris *Chronica majora*, A.D. 1229 (Rolls Series, vol. 3, 190) and *Historia Anglorum* (Rolls Series, vol. 2, 318). *Annales de Dunstaplia*, A.D. 1220 (Rolls Series *Annales monastici*, vol. 3, 62): '... Salesbiriensis ecclesia cathedralis infra castri sita procinctum, translata est ad veterem Salesbiriam, juxta cursum aquae fluentis constituta.'

11. The seventeenth-century copy of the legend is printed in Macray, 1891, 266-269. One fifteenth-century version is printed in Davies, 1908, vol. 1, 183-185; the other is preserved in a manuscript among the Bishop's records known as Miscellanea Decani MS., which is translated by Jones, 1884, vol. 2, cii-cvi. It is not clear whether they are all copies of a lost original or whether they are interdependent. A sentence found in the Davies version (184), 'Ostendit regi ... suo directas,' is missing in Macray, although it is necessary for the sense of the following words, 'Quibus inspectis ...,' which are common to both. Some of the discrepancies between these two versions, however, seem to be deliberate insertions by the copyist of the Davies manuscript (e.g. 184, 'et alias literas ... notatum est'), since they refer to additional material appended only to the Davies version. Bishop Beauchamp's account is printed in Hatcher, 1843, 164, and a similar version, preserved in the city muniments, is in Macray, 1891, 269, note 1.

12. Other medieval versions are to be found in Davies, 1908, vol. 1, 185-186 and 188, as well as Hatcher, 1843, 75, and the two examples cited above. For Leland's account, see Smith 1964, vol. 1, 260. Harrison's account prefixed Holinshed's *Chronicles*, and his description of Salisbury is printed in Ledwich, 1771, 54-55 and Duke, 1837, 385-386.

13. Ward's account is given by Aubrey, 1847, 96-97. Camden, 1695, 247. Celia Fiennes was a native of Newton Tony, and so perhaps her unusual explanation had some local currency: see Morris, 1949, 5.

14. Pope, 1713, reprinted in Ledwich, 1771, quotation from pp. 18-19. Perhaps his most memorable stanza occurs on p. 21: 'Then then the men of Old Sarum came down / From the hill where there was neither well nor spring, / That they might have a mill, and water at will, / And hear the sweet fishes sing.' Dugdale, 1819, 477. Child, 1844, 26-29. A recent summary by a folklorist is Whitlock, 1976, 106, 194. The ley-line theory is propounded by Garrard, 1980, 7-9. It is interesting to note that the motif of firing an arrow occurs in the very earliest account of the move, that of William de Wanda described above (Jones, 1884, vol. 2, 3-4). There Bishop Herbert Poore is compared to the sons of Ephraim, who 'intendunt arcum, id est bonum aliquid propositum concipiunt, et sagittas etiam emittunt ... sed in die belli ... retrorsum convertuntur.' There is no evidence, however, that Pope was aware of William's account, and it is probably coincidental. The final quotation is part of the title of Price, 1753.

15. Peter de Blois *Epistolae*, 104 is printed by Migne (*Patrologia Latina*, 207, 326-327) and quoted in V.C.H.6, 1962, 61. Parts are reproduced in Ledwich, 1771, 19 and Hatcher, 1843, 37.

16. The papal bull has often been printed, and is included in William de Wanda's account: Jones, 1884, vol. 2, 5-7, as is Richard Poore's charter of 1218, *ibid.* 7-9. Jones,

1884, vol. 2, 7 incorrectly dates the papal bull to 1219, and his mistake has been copied by most subsequent writers. In fact Honorius III became Pope on 18th July 1216 and so, 'quarta kalendas Aprilis pontificatus nostri anno secundo,' should be 29th March 1218. R.C.H.M., 1980 gives both the correct (16) and the erroneous (xxxii) dates.

17. The royal charter of 1227 is printed in Hatcher, 1843, 730 and Davies, 1908, vol. 1, 201-203, and translated in Haskins, 1927, 1-4, Richard Poore's charter of 1225 is in Hatcher, 1843, 728 and Davies, 1908, vol. 1. 187-188. William de Wanda's account is in Jones, 1884, vol. 2, 3ff, especially 9-13.

18. The chronology of decline at Old Sarum and Wilton, and references to 'Old Salisbury' meaning St. Martin's are taken from V.C.H.6, 1962, 62, 15, 51-52. On the development of towns in general see Postan, 1975, 235-245 and Reynolds, 1977, 46-65. Settlement before 1220 in the New Sarum area is discussed in R.C.H.M., 1980, xxix-xxxi. Beresford, 1967, 509 speaks of the possibility that the move was a penitent's return to an Old Salisbury. The actual site of New Sarum is discussed below.

19. The building history of Old Sarum Cathedral is fully described in R.C.H.M., 1980, 15-24. For Winchester see Pevsner and Lloyd, 1967, 668-671, and for Amesbury see Chandler and Goodhugh, 1979, 12-14 and Farmer, 1979.

20. For Devizes see V.C.H.10, 1975, 230-243. The chronology of town plantation and the profits which might accrue from new towns are described by Beresford, 1967, 55-97, 637-641. The Bishop of Winchester's plantations are discussed by Beresford, 1959. Quotation from the 1306 Bishop's charter, Hatcher, 1843, 75.

21. Most details are from Beresford, 1967. More recent general surveys are by Butler, 1976 and Aston and Bond, 1976. Devizes, Downton and Hindon are also described by Haslam, 1976.

22. Beresford, 1967, 142-163; Butler, 1976; Aston and Bond, 1976, 79-96.

23. These suggestions are derived largely from Rogers, 1969, 1-2; Haslam, 1976, 51; and R.C.H.M., 1980, xxxii-xxxiv. There is some evidence that the Cathedral in fact straddled the thoroughfare, which was regarded as running through it: Davies, 1968, 203. It will be apparent to anyone who has used the works of K. H. Rogers (Rogers, 1969) and D. J. Bonney (R.C.H.M., 1980, introduction) that this and the following paragraphs rely very heavily on archaeological and documentary references which they cite and on the arguments which they base upon them. I have deliberately adopted a less cautious approach to the evidence than its sketchiness perhaps merits. In the following notes from here to the end of the chapter I do not cite Rogers and Bonney, but their work has been used throughout.

24. The social organisation implicit in the houses of the Close is discussed by Edwards, 1939, 63-66. She notes that Peter de Blois refused an offer to live in the Close because he could not afford to do so. Leadenhall is described by Wordsworth, 1917.

25. The 'spontaneous' city is suggested by the Tropenell cartulary version of the legend: Davies, 1908, vol. 1, 185: 'Et anno Domini tunc sequente predictus episcopus Ricardus, perpendens populum ad predictum locum de Meryfeld confluentem, et ibidem ad capellam ligneam supradictam diversa munera devotissime offerent in honore beate Marie Virginis, ad regem Henricum accessit, eidem benignissime supplicando, ut de predicto loco de Merifeld, de gracia sua speciali, civitatem inde faceret, et ei libertates, fraunchesias, inde faceret et concederet.' The account in the corporation records (Macray, 1891, 269 note) gives a similar impression of the city as an afterthought, although it is more realistic about the Bishop's motives: 'But as it was thought by the wisedome of the sayd bishop and the chanons at that tyme, that forasmuch as the see was there where noe people was dwelling it would be convenient, and also for the church and them commodious and profitable, to have there a towne, the sayd bishop ... gave and

confirmed ... that there should be in that city of New Sarum a certain graunte, as they say, of free-hold ...'

26. The antiquity of Mitre House is discussed by Jones, 1884, vol. 2, cxi-cxii.

27. Aldermanries are first mentioned, though not by name, in two crown pleas in the Wiltshire eyre: Meekings, 1961, 254-255. The absence of any record of civic government in the thirteenth century outside the Bishop's jurisdiction is discussed by Street, 1916, 194-198, but this notwithstanding it would seem most likely that the ward divisions are part of the definition of the city's organisation which clearly took place in the 1225-1227 period. Meads Ward remained extremely small by comparison with the others throughout its history. There is some evidence that the Cathedral masons were originally settled to the east of the Cathedral Close, in the area which I suggest was the city's original focus: V.C.H.6, 1962, 75 and note 84.

28. The charter is printed in Hatcher, 1843, 730 and translated in Haskins, 1927, 1-4.

29. The point is forcefully made by Reynolds, 1977, 193. See also Beresford, 1967, 146-154.

30. The drainage system has been often described: see Rammell, 1851; Middleton, 1868; and Hammond, n.d. Haslam, 1976, 51 notes that streets in the eastern chequers follow the contours.

31. The size of tenements and annual rent are stipulated in the Bishop's charter of 1225, printed in Hatcher, 1843, 728 and Davies, 1908, vol. 1, 187-188. Crummy, 1979, has shown that the chequers east of the Endless Street-Exeter Street line are based on a 14×20 pole standard, which allows for streets of two poles wide and 6×2 tenements per chequer. The discrepancies of up to $1\frac{1}{2}$ poles which he (p. 150) attributes to inadequate surveying technique are more likely to have resulted from the need to follow contours.

32. Law suits were heard in the Wiltshire eyre of 1249: see Meekings, 1961, 254-258 and Clanchy, 1971, 136-141. The 1269 parish boundaries are described in a charter printed in Hatcher, 1843, 735 and translated ibid, 52-54.

33. Suburban growth is discussed by Keene, 1976, and Fisherton in V.C.H.6, 1962, 180-194. A series of deeds relating to Fisherton is printed in the Tropenell cartulary, Davies, 1908, vol. 1.

34. Market-infill is discussed by Aston and Bond, 1976, 96-97; and see below, chapter three.

35. V.C.H.6, 1962, 88-89; R.C.H.M. 1980, 50-51; Barley, 1976, 60; Turner, 1970, 198-199.

36. Hatcher, 1843, 75.

NOTES TO CHAPTER TWO: MATURITY

1. Total population figures from the 1801-1951 censuses are conveniently summarised in V.C.H.4, 1959, 356. Current figures are derived from estimates by Wiltshire County Council Planning Department.

2. The circumstances of the 1695 census are described by Glass, 1965, 169-183. Hatcher's figure (Hatcher, 1843, 822) may be traced back through Hatcher's earlier anonymous history (Hatcher, 1834, 162) to the annual issues of the Salisbury Guide from 1810 onwards (and perhaps a little earlier, though it is not included in the 1806 issue). In the 1830 issue the population section of the guide is attributed to Henry Wansey, and this author had first published the figures in 1801 (Wansey, 1801, 41). The common link between all these publications is Easton, the Salisbury printer. Wansey does not

indicate his source, but it is clear from his work (*op. cit.* 47) that he had examined St. Edmund's registers, where the figures ('2742 persons numbered in this parish, 2665 St. Thomas parish, 1569 St. Martin's parish') are to be found beneath entries for May 1695. Fortunately two other authors seem to have known the result of this census, or one taken a few years later, and these offer a check on its accuracy. A writer in the *Gentleman's Magazine* (vol. 23, 1753, 341) concerned with a smallpox epidemic, comments: 'The inhabitants of Salisbury in 1695 were 6,678, in the last year 6,586.' (This statement is reprinted in *Wiltshire Notes and Queries,* vol. 1, 1893-1895, 497.) Gregory King's journal also preserves population figures for Salisbury as follows (Laslett, 1973, fol. 92): 'Salisbury, St. Thomas parish 2364; St. Edmunds 2747; St. Martins, 1561; Total of Sarum 3 parishes 6672 ... Sarum by Mr. Hoskit [?] Oct. 1700.' Either, therefore, King's figure for St. Thomas's parish is 300 too low or the figure recorded in St. Edmund's register is 300 too high. The reference in the *Gentleman's Magazine* would suggest that the latter is at fault, and this is confirmed by comparing figures for the three parishes derived from the 1667 royal aid and supply (Nevill, 1910, 413-434), the 1675 religious census (Hatcher, 1843, 822, akin to the Compton census of 1676 for which no Salisbury figures survive), and the 1801 census (V.C.H.4, 1959, 356). These may be tabulated as follows (1667 wards have been translated into parishes, with possible error):

1667: St. Thomas's as % of St. Edmund's		80.0
1675: „	„	75.0
1695: „	„	97.2
1700: „	„	86.1
1801: „	„	70.2
1667: St. Martin's as % of St. Thomas's		65.4
1675: „	„	72.2
1695: „	„	58.9
1700: „	„	66.0
1801: „	„	78.9

Thus it is clear that the figures of King (1700) fit the pattern much better than those in the St. Edmund's register (1695). We conclude therefore that the St. Edmund's figure of 6,976 should be adjusted downwards by 300 to 6,676. The higher (erroneous) figure has been quoted, following Hatcher, by a number of authorities, including V.C.H.6, 1962, 72; Slack, 1972a, 198, n. 38; Clark and Slack, 1976, 83; Chalklin, 1974, 34. The 1775 census is recorded by Wansey, 1801, 41 and Hatcher, 1843, 822. The Italian estimate is to be found in Crino, 1968 and Hatcher, 1843, 470. The 1597 official estimate is reported by Slack, 1972a, 195 note 7.

3. The 1377 poll tax total is given in Hatcher, 1843, 822 and V.C.H.4, 1959, 306. I have applied the alternative multipliers of Russell and Postan as described by Stephens, 1981, 50-51. The 1523 subsidy is discussed, and an estimate made for Salisbury, by Hoskins, 1963, 68-73. The figures are transcribed by Sheail, 1968. The 1548 estimate is from the chantry certificates, and the figure is given by Carrington, 1887, 256. I have assumed that the figure given includes 60% of the population of the parish, as suggested by Stephens, 1981, 56-57. I omit another list of communicants, that of 1675 (mentioned in the preceding note), which is printed in Hatcher, 1843, 822. This would seem to have been made in conjunction with the Compton census of 1676, but it is missing from the surviving returns (Ruddle, 1901, 539) and so may have been compiled on a different basis. According to Hatcher it lists 'inhabitant householders,' but the total, 3,400 for the three Salisbury parishes, is too low compared with other seventeenth-century sources to represent the total number of communicants (it would yield a total population of 5,542 or 5,667 according to Ruddle's or Stephens's formulas) but far too high to represent the total number of families. Hatcher does not give his source for these figures and they remain enigmatic. I have also omitted from this discussion Slack's estimate of the total population in the 1630s (Slack, 1972a, 176 (table 12) and 198, n. 38). This

figure, 6,867, is arrived at by multiplying the average annual number of baptisms by 33, this multiplier being derived from Hatcher's 1695 total, which we have shown to be erroneous. The method of calculating total populations from baptisms has also been called into question: Rogers, 1977, 19 and 233–234, n. 33.

4. The only hearth tax return for Salisbury complete enough to be of any value is that of 1664, which contains a total figure and a little over half the returns. The total may have some use as a basis for comparison with other places, but cannot be used to calculate a population figure. The ward lists (WRO. G23/1/236), previously thought to date from the late fifteenth century (Rathbone, 1951, 81) have been shown on internal evidence to date from 1399 or 1400 (R.C.H.M. 1980, xxvi, n. 2). Laslett, 1969, 200 suggests a multiplier of 4.75 may be used to convert families to individuals throughout the post-medieval period. The 1455 list, from Bishop Beauchamp's *Liber niger*, is printed in Nevill, 1911, and the 1667 list, a royal aid, in Nevill, 1910. The 1626 estimate is in WRO. G23/1 uncatalogued box 4, doc 65A, and is quoted by V.C.H.6, 1962, 72 and Slack, 1972, 198, n. 38. The 1782 figure is printed by Wansey, 1801, 43. On a total of 1,424 houses he multiplies by five to give 7,120, but to his figure should be added, '50 more houses at least in courts and alleys,' to which he also refers. Law, 1972, gives a figure of 7,720 in 1782, but this seems merely to be a misreading of Wansey's 7,120.

5. The records of the three city parishes and Fisherton Anger are deposited in the Wiltshire Record Office (WRO. 1900, 1901, 1902, 1903). The graphs are based on a nine-year moving average derived from calendar year (1st Jan.–31st Dec.) totals.

6. A marginal note in St. Edmund's register 1604 reads: 'If you finde the book in eyther of theise sides Unperfect, impute it to the contagion of the time then.' The epidemics of 1563, 1627 and 1666 are each represented by only two of the three parishes, the other being lost. In 1579 and 1723 the register of St. Thomas's does not show any more burials than usual, but this is probably because the very limited size of its graveyard led to its parishioners being buried elsewhere (see below, chapter 6, note 75). The city's action to prevent overcrowding in 1580 is described by Hatcher, 1843, 289.

7. The signatories to the agreement of 1306 between the Bishop and the city (presumably, therefore, the most influential citizens) are listed in Hatcher, 1843, 742. The list of taxpayers of 1334 to the 15th and 10th assessment has not been printed, but is to be found in the Public Record Office, E179/196/8. I have considered all the topographical names from both sources, even though a few duplicate one another and some may have become true surnames. On this question see Reaney, 1958, xiii–xv. I have made the possibly dangerous assumption that most of the names I have not been able to identify (16%) are remote from Salisbury. The figures for vagrants are taken from the 1598 and 1599 entries in Slack, 1975, 17–26, and the apprentices serving Salisbury masters, 1710–1760, from Dale, 1961, *passim*. In addition to the 133 apprentices analysed a further 108 were stated to have come from Salisbury and 255 had no place of origin recorded.

8. Comparisons with planted towns are derived from data in Beresford, 1967, 251–289, and from towns in general the tables provided by Hoskins, 1972, appendix. The 1455 rental is from Nevill, 1911, and the impression of prosperity given by this survey seems to undermine the recent suggestion by Bridbury, 1981, that Salisbury appears more prosperous in the middle ages only because its position as an ecclesiastical manor led to fewer complaints of penury in order to evade national taxation.

9. Figures from Hoskins, 1972, appendix. In 1801 there were 43 English towns with populations in excess of 10,000, compared with Salisbury's 7,668. There is a good account of the problems faced by towns like Salisbury in the post-medieval period in Clark and Slack, 1976. For Coventry's problems see Phythian-Adams, 1979.

10. All figures derived from census reports. Boundary changes and the incorporation of suburbs – an integral part of town development since 1801 – make precise comparisons

impossible. I have tried to consider all English towns (other than a few northern industrial suburbs reckoned as separate towns) which had a recorded population in 1801 of between 6,700 and 8,000.

11. Hudson, 1978, 15.

12. The economic fortunes of Wiltshire generally are summarised by V.C.H.4, 1959, 1–6. Comparative figures for the population/wealth of Wiltshire towns may be derived from the following sources: 1334 (15th and 10th) - V.C.H.4, 1959, 294-303; 1377 (poll) - V.C.H.4, 1959, 304-311; 1545 (subsidy) - Ramsay, 1954; 1548 (chantry certificates) - Carrington, 1887, 256; 1576 (subsidy) - Ramsay, 1954; 1676 (ecclesiastical census) - Ruddle, 1901; 1801-1951 (census) - V.C.H.4, 1959, 339-361; 1971 (census) - county census report. Supplementary figures for Bradford, Devizes, Swindon, Trowbridge and Warminster may be taken from their respective V.C.H. entries. Since these various lists and censuses were compiled for different reasons they cannot be expected to provide a consistently accurate picture. The general picture, however, is remarkably consistent and may be accepted.

13. Hudson, 1978, 11.

14. See above, chapter 1, note 31. The total of about 500 standard tenements is based on the premise that standard chequers contained twelve tenements and that wherever possible the city was laid out in multiples of twelve. Thus Gores, Parsons, Vanners, Three Swans, Cross Keys, Black Horse, Swaynes, White Hart and Marsh chequers could all contain twelve; White Horse, Blue Boar and Three Cups could contain fifteen (12 plus 3) each; Antelope, Trinity and Rolfe's 24 each. Tenements lining one side of a street also seem to come in multiples of twelve; thus the west side of Castle Street, and St. Ann Street/St. Martin's Church Street from the Friary to the Church could each accommodate 24 tenements; Exeter Street as far as its medieval limit at Brickett's Almshouses, and the south side of New Street from High Street to St. John Street, would each take eighteen, as would Griffin chequer. If tenements are drawn out on this basis the total is approximately 500, although of course the exact boundaries of most tenements can no longer be recovered.

15. The problems presented by the division of tenements are discussed by Rogers, 1969, 4 and R.C.H.M., 1980, xlii–xlvi. No-one seems to have recognised a connection between the water channels and the layout of the tenements, although it was presumably the intention to supply water to as many tenements as possible. Note that certain east–west streets, where the tenements had to lie north–south, such as New Canal and New Street, were also supplied with water channels.

16. The 1455 list is printed by Nevill, 1911. 'Balle's Place' is described by Bonney, 1964.

17. Medieval building materials in Salisbury and the number of surviving buildings are described in R.C.H.M. 1980, lxi–lxii. One thirteenth-century house, which survived until the last century, is illustrated in Hall, 1834, following pl. xv.

18. The Hall of John Halle is the subject of a book: Duke, 1837, and the history of Church House is described in detail by Everett, 1941b. Merchants' houses in general are discussed in R.C.H.M. 1980, xliv–xlvi, and all the buildings used as examples in this and succeeding paragraphs are described there passim.

19. This building is the subject of an article by Drinkwater and Mercer, 1964, from which (241) the quotation is taken. The contract was first transcribed by Nightingale, 1875, although it was not then realised that it related to an existing building.

20. All details from R.C.H.M., 1980, passim. See also Reeves and Bonney, 1982.

21. Both maps are reproduced in R.C.H.M., 1980 (pls. 1 and 16), and elsewhere. The various editions of Naish's map are discussed by Rogers, 1963.

22. Leland: Smith, 1964, vol. 1, 260; Fiennes: Morris, 1947, 1 (she lived at Newton Tony); Evelyn: Hatcher, 1843, 467; Byng: Byng, 1934, vol. 1, 106; Pepys: Hatcher, 1843, 467; Cosmo de Medici: Hatcher, 1843, 470; Simond: Simond, 1817, vol. 1, 257; Kohl: Kohl, 1968, 159.

23. Statistics are derived from the descriptions given in R.C.H.M., 1980, *passim*, whence also comes the quotation (xlviii). The contemporary was Henry Wansey (Wansey, 1801, 44). In fact he was incorrect in believing that the population did not rise in the eighteenth century: as we have seen, his figure for 1695 – 6,976 – was 300 too high, and his figure derived from the 1801 census – 6,967 – is strangely at odds with that published in the 1801 census report – 7,126. Presumably Wansey, whose book was published in 1801, was working from provisional census figures which were subsequently amended.

24. The window tax assessments (arranged by ward in bundles in WRO. G23/1/188–191) were probably subject to widespread evasion, and so cannot be used for precise statistical calculations. I have chosen 1706, the earliest year for which returns to all four wards are available. I have used the inventory in R.C.H.M., 1980 for deductions about surviving buildings (including buildings demolished since *ca.* 1960). Wansey, 1801, 43 (note) gives the demolition of houses around the Guildhall as one of the reasons for a decrease in houses at the end of the eighteenth century.

25. Wansey, 1801, 43 calculated that 71 houses had been lost between 1782 and 1801, and records the number of poor in 1795 (*ibid.* 44).

26. Population and housing figures are taken from the decennial census reports, 1801–1971, and from the tables derived from them in V.C.H.4, 1959, 339-361. The acreage of the Salisbury parishes is taken from Ordnance Survey 1st ed. 1:10000 maps, and the successive boundary changes are described in V.C.H.6, 1962, 71-72 (with map).

27. A memorandum by Mr Squarey, printed in Rammell, 1851, 19-20, suggests that Salisbury, 'is surrounded on nearly all sides by property, the owners of which, from their rank and wealth, are indisposed to part with any portion of it, and in many instances, perhaps, are unable to do so without great expense, in consequence of the terms of the settlements under which they hold the land, whilst in other cases the owners are ecclesiastical corporations.' Fisherton, according to Mr Squarey, was the only exception.

28. Salisbury's expansion is summarised in V.C.H.6, 1962, 90-92, and individual buildings earlier than *ca.* 1850 are described in R.C.H.M., 1980, *passim*. Names are taken from Ordnance Survey 1st ed. 1:10000 and 1:2500 maps, *ca.* 1880.

29. See in general O'Dell and Richards, 1971, 191ff and Aston and Bond, 1976, 176ff. It is interesting to note that the western end of Windsor Road contains a row of cottages which appear to be built of Bath stone, in the fashion of New Swindon.

30. Tithe maps and awards for Fisherton Anger (1843), Milford (1845), Britford (*ca.* 1840) and Stratford-sub-Castle (*ca.* 1839), in the Wiltshire Record Office, depict the pre-expansion landscape.

31. The Coombe Road estate is described in detail in Mate, 1905, supplement (certain copies only, e.g. in Salisbury Museum Library and Wiltshire Record Office Library). Committee minutes of the Housing, Town Planning etc. Committee are contained in bound volumes of council minutes (WRO. G23/100/24-26). The committee's first meeting took place on 10th September 1917. Minutes 73, 95, 192, 332, 486, 514 are particularly relevant. A. C. Bothams was the principal architect of Macklin Road, and the winning layout was submitted by D. Edwards of Taunton (minutes 129, 132).

32. The dates of the principal housing estates are given in V.C.H.6, 1962, 91, from information supplied by the city council. They should, however, be regarded with some caution. Both the dates I have checked are incorrect – the first house in Wain-a-long

Road was opened in January 1922 (WRO. G23/100/29, Housing committee, minute 612), not 1924, as stated, and the houses in West Harnham were commenced in 1920 (WRO. G11/114/2, 5ff), not 1921. It is not clear from V.C.H.6, 1962, 91 that these houses were in fact built by Salisbury R.D.C. and not included within the city's jurisdiction until 1927. The survey and letter are both from WRO. G23/132/50 (1), and information on Finch's Court is from R.C.H.M., 1980, 91 (145).

33. Useful information about recent trends in housebuilding, and plans for future development, may be found in two planning documents: Wiltshire County Council, 1978, 28ff and Salisbury District Council, 1980, 44ff.

NOTES TO CHAPTER THREE: WORKING

1. Survey of 1306: Hatcher, 1843, 742. About one quarter of the 217 citizens listed have occupational surnames, and a few are given surnames and occupations. Ward lists of 1399/1400: WRO. G23/1/236. The date of the document is established by R.C.H.M., 1980, xxvi note 2. See appendix one below, where the lists are transcribed and discussed. Ledger entry, 1440: transcribed by Haskins, 1912, 60-62. According to Haskins (*ibid*) 'Then follow complete lists of the names of the members of the various guilds, each guild forming a separate entry,' but I can find no trace of such a list in WRO. G23/1/1 (Ledger A). Can it be that Haskins is referring to the list of 1474/1475 in WRO. G23/1/2 (Ledger B), which is cited in V.C.H.6, 1962, 133 and note 86? Register of city companies, 1612: WRO. G23/1/264. The register as originally compiled claims to list, 'first are mentioned the severall companyes, and then the names of every person of that empuye that hath geven any thinge and the severall summes by them geven, and then the name of such as are able to give and have lyved in the town and hath given nothing and lastlie the names of the poore persons of every companye that deserve well in respecte of their behaviour to be of the companyes and are not able to give anything.' To these lists have been added the names of those admitted into the various companies up to 1641, and in the index to the register names of those admitted during the period 1661-1710 have been included, although the name of the company is not always included. Names from this later period have been amalgamated, in our statistics, with the wills of a similar period. Although it is not possible to know how large would have been the contingents of weavers and tailors, had they been included in the register, some indication of the tailors' strength at this period may be gained from a reference in Haskins, 1912, 175 to a meeting in 1603 attended by 52 members of the tailors' guild. Occupations cited in the Sub-Dean's wills, 1611 to 1641, have been taken from the manuscript index in the Wiltshire Record Office, and I have added for statistical purposes the occupations of masters listed in a survey of the poor of the city in 1625, in Slack, 1975, 65-74.

2. Sub-Dean's wills: index in the Wiltshire Record Office. I have not extracted data from the index after 1710, neither have I included Salisbury wills from the consistory court of Sarum. Entries of the period 1660-1710 in WRO. G23/1/264 have been added to the figures derived from these wills - see above, note 1. Apprenticeship records: Dale, 1961, *passim*. Of the printed pollbooks which I have examined only that of 1819 includes occupations. I have chosen the dates 1851/1855 and 1911 for analysis, although other census years may equally well be used. 1976 data are from figures quoted in Salisbury District Council, 1980, 24 (table 3.7).

3. Pope, 1697, 67, quoted by Hatcher, 1843, 464; cf. 1718 estimate in Hatcher, 1843, 509; Haskins, 1912, 94.

4. See, in general, V.C.H.4, 1959, 7-42; Hony, 1926, 449-451; Poole, 1976, chapter 11. The antiquity of existing parish and manorial boundaries in the Salisbury area is discussed by Bonney, 1972 and Taylor, 1964. The customs of Winterbourne Stoke are

transcribed by Goddard, 1905; I quote from pp. 211-212. Yardland is often defined as an area of about 30 acres, but here it seems to mean each tenant's holding. Goddard suggests that 'a dead' means, 'a sheep fold, not shifted daily (?),' but it seems more likely that 'dead' simply refers to a fence or hurdles made of dead wood, as opposed to a quick-set hedge. If, as he suggests, this passage were to mean that the flock were turned loose into the whole field, there would be no need for hurdles to confine them. On wool as a by-product see V.C.H.4, 1959, 54-55 and Kerridge, 1972, 19; and on over-production Hony, 1926, 451 and Ponting, 1979, 22.

5. Ponting, 1979, 30; Hony, 1926, 451-452. The demesne and tenantry flocks of certain manors are tabulated in V.C.H.4, 1959, 21, 26, 28, and the flocks of the manors of Martin are discussed by Poole, 1976, 177. My estimate of the number of manors is derived from the 1377 poll tax returns in V.C.H.4, 1959, 306-311, which record approximately 180 manors in sixteen hundreds covering Salisbury Plain. Aubrey was perhaps the first to attempt this calculation: he estimated between 1,000-2,000 per tithing in the seventeenth century (Aubrey, 1847, 108).

6. The types of sheep are discussed by Ponting, 1979, 18-23. Examples of selective breeding are given in V.C.H.4, 1959, 20. On the suitability of Wiltshire wool for clothmaking see Kerridge, 1972, 19. The lists of wool-grades are described by Power, 1933, 49, and the later list, of ca. 1475, is given in full in Myers, 1969, 1028-1029.

7. Most details are from V.C.H.4, 1959, 21-29. It was said of one of the Hungerfords, Sir Thomas, in 1357, that he could ride on his own land all the way from Salisbury to Farleigh Hungerford Castle (on the Somerset border, near Trowbridge): Jackson, 1855, 86-87. Wiltshire demesne lessees have been studied by Hare, 1981.

8. The various forms in which wool might be sold are described by Power, 1933, 51. Hatcher, 1843, 60 describes illegal exporting of wool by Salisbury citizens in the thirteenth century. Tables showing comparative figures for the export of wool and cloths through Southampton between 1399 and 1482 are given by Gray, 1933, 356-358. According to Lloyd, 1977, 314: 'Unfortunately the passage of wool from sheep to the looms of the English weaver is the one almost totally obscure area of the medieval cloth trade.' The Southampton trade with Italy is described in Quinn and Ruddock, 1937-1938 and Ruddock, 1951, and summarised by Platt, 1973, 154-155 and Power, 1933, 44-47. In 1374 Salisbury merchants John Leghe and John Wiche had to under-take not to hinder, 'the Lumbards from gathering and buying wool in Wiltshire.' (Cal. Close, 1374-1377, 88, cited by Lloyd, 1977, 313.) According to Haskins, 1912, 34, Webb, Halle and Swayne were all merchants of the staple. The collection of wool for export is described by Power, 1933, 48-58, Hanham, 1975, xviii and Lloyd, 1977, 305-314. A table of 'th costs that run upon a sack of Cotswold wool before it is sold,' is printed by Myers, 1969, 1029. The role of wool-broggers is discussed by Ramsay, 1965, 9-11 (although he is dealing mainly with the period after 1500).

9. This account is based largely on Singer, 1956, 191-220, 364-369, but I have also used Mann, 1971, 280-307 (a detailed description of post-medieval processes); Ponting, 1957, 12-17 (based on Bristol); and Ponting, 1971, 7-12. As this book went to press a detailed account of clothmaking in Salisbury by an eminent medieval economic historian was published (Bridbury, 1982). Readers concerned to discover more about Salisbury's career in the national context are advised to refer to that work, which was not available to me when writing my account.

10. Eleven 'skevys' of teasels were imported to Salisbury in 1443-1444; Coleman, 1960-1961, 216, 271. A 'skevy' perhaps represents a basket of 600 teasels: Coleman, 1960-1961, 330. Twenty dozen and five pipes of cards were imported during the same year, but the precise quantity of a pipe in this context is not clear: Coleman, 1960-1961, 85, 106, 237, 330. A single cardmaker occurs in the poll tax fragment of 1379 (V.C.H.4, 1959, 127) and two appear in the ward lists of 1399/1400 (WRO. G23/1/236). The

guild of sadlers, cotelers, pewters, pynners and cardmakers is mentioned in the first city ledger (WRO. G23/1/1) and the entry is transcribed by Haskins, 1912, 61. The title 'spinster' in the 1379 poll tax fragment is discussed in V.C.H.4, 1959, 127, and in the sixteenth century by Ramsay, 1965, 13 - see also Hatcher, 1843, 288. William Coke, spyndeler, is mentioned in an indenture printed in Swayne, 1896, 377. Thomas Baker's crime is in *Cal. Inq. Misc.* 1399-1422, 377.

11. Spinning by wool producers is discussed by Ramsay, 1965, 13-14, and the yarn market in V.C.H.6, 1962, 86. The lists of masters and journeymen in 1421 are in WRO. G23/1/1 fol. 73-74, and the totals are given by V.C.H.4, 1959, 126-127; the 1474 totals, from WRO. G23/1/2 fol. 120-121, are in V.C.H.6, 1962, 133. The independence of the Salisbury weavers is noted by Ramsay, 1965, 20. V.C.H.6, 1962, 133-134 cites John Briggs (died 1491) as an example of a wealthy weaver. It is clear from his will that he possessed two broad looms and one narrow loom, and employed three journeymen, four apprentices and five female servants. Thomas Copter's will is in WRO. G/23/150/86; his property is also mentioned in the 1455 rental, Nevill, 1911, 85-86. Of 24 names included in the 1455 rental who are either referred to as weavers or may be identified as weavers from other sources, all appear to own or have owned at least one tenement (they are Walter Bride, Thomas Copter, John Chapman, Richard Cokle, John Durnford, Edward Fonteigne, Thomas Glover, John Hamersmyth, John Huysh, John Handsmyth, John Hayne, William Mede, Thomas Payn, Robert Playe, John Purdy, John Ruddok, William Soper, Nicholas Schote, Thomas Wageyn, Thomas Whityng, John Woton, John Wyoth and William Wheler). I have only discovered four names of journeymen weavers (according to the 1421 list) which appear in the 1455 rental (John Baudry, John Chitren, John Charelton and Thomas Pese), but it may be significant that they all appear as tenants, not owners. John Woton's tenement, rated $17\frac{1}{2}$d, is in Nevill, 1911, 87, and his import of oil in Coleman, 1960-1961, 179; cf. Thomas Whityng, a weaver (Nevill, 1911, 71) who imported wine (Coleman, 1960-1961, 127, 203). For Thomas Payn see Haskins, 1912, 36, 60. William Pridy is in V.C.H.4, 1959, 126. Nicholas Shete is in *Cal. Pat.* 9th May 1449. Edward Goodyer is described as a tailor in Haskins, 1912, 113 and is included on the tailors' bede roll (Haskins, 1912, 128). His occupation of 10 Queen Street is described in R.C.H.M. 1980, 84. However his name appears on the list of master weavers in 1421 (WRO. G23/1/1, fol. 73) and he is described as a weaver formerly occupying premises in Endless Street in the 1455 rental (Nevill, 1911, 73). Perhaps they are different people. John Durnford similarly appears as a master weaver in WRO. G23/1/1 fol. 73, but as a dyer in Nevill, 1911, 79. The ward lists (WRO. G23/1/236) figures are: Market Ward 7; Martins Ward, 24; Meads Ward, 7; New Street Ward, 7. V.C.H.6, 1962, 133 suggests that most weavers lived in the south-east part of the city. The weavers' guildhall was in Endless Street: Haskins, 1912, 95; V.C.H.6, 1962, 133, 137; R.C.H.M. 1980, xlvii.

12. See, in general, V.C.H.4, 1959, 126-127; V.C.H.6, 1962, 134. Thomas Copter's will in WRO. G/23/150/86. According to Ramsay, 1965, 20, Salisbury's fullers in the sixteenth century were independent and in competition with one another. The development of the fulling mill is described by Carus-Wilson, 1967, 183-210. On specific mills, Stratford-sub-Castle (Old Sarum): V.C.H.4, 1959, 119; Ford: V.C.H.4, 1959, 121; Milford: Rogers, 1976, 25; Harnham: Rogers, 1976, 254, R.C.H.M. 1980, 171-172, where it is thought more likely to have been primarily a paper mill; Mumworth; will of Thomas Mylbourne, *Cal. I.P.M. Hen VII*, vol. 1, 829; Town Mill: Rogers, 1976, 255. Kenneth Ponting (in Jenkins, 1972, 237, and Ponting, 1971, 12) seems to believe that the city's artificial water channels were used to power fulling mills, but I know of no documentary evidence to support this. No mills are mentioned in the 1455 rental, and one property built to straddle a watercourse in Trinity chequer (R.C.H.M. 1980, 113, no. 234), which might appear to be a good candidate, was in fact owned by a grocer, a merchant and a vintner and subsequently became an inn. Racks in Salisbury are

described in V.C.H.4, 1959, 121 and Haskins, 1912, 83; they are frequently encountered in medieval documents. William Hanleygh's will is in WRO. G23/1/212, fol. 26v; the interpretation of 'hanlyn' as teasel handles is suggested in V.C.H.4, 1959, 127. The will of William Purchase in 1418 (Davies, 1908, vol. 1, 248) includes a bequest of a 'parvam pelvem cum lotorio,' which may also refer to fulling equipment. George Joce's will is in WRO. G23/1/214, fol. 25. John Colyngborn, tucker, occurs in Davies, 1908, vol. 1, 240, and as a woad merchant in Bunyard, 1941, 115. However, another John Colyngborn also seems to have lived in Salisbury: Nevill, 1911, 79.

13. 1306 list: Hatcher, 1843, 742-743. 1399 lists: WRO. G23/1/236 (the figures are Market, 8; Martins, 3; New Street, 1). The location of dyers in the Castle Street and Cheesemarket area is discussed by R.C.H.M. 1980, xli. John Cupper in 1455 held a tenement 'juxta superiorem pontem de Fysherton' (Nevill, 1911, 71) and a dyer from Longbridge Deverill had premises on the site of the present public library (R.C.H.M. 1980, 54). 'The Diers Guylde' is quoted by Haskins, 1912, 380, and 61. 1455 rental: Nevill, 1911, 71, 79, 87. John Durneford is described as a weaver in WRO. G23/1/1, fol. 73. Woad imports are discussed by Coleman, 1960-1961, xxvii-xxviii. The lucrative nature of the trade was recognised by the Bristol merchants, who described it as the 'moost chieff, noblest and pounderoust merchaundys of good & able Wode, thencrece whereof in old tyme causyd, manteynyd and susteynyd the noble felicitee of this Worshipfull Town.' (Power and Postan, 1933, 207.) See also Bridbury, 1982, 78.

14. See Duke, 1837, *passim* and Collier, 1908. The quarrel is recorded by Hatcher, 1843, 136, 161-169, including the following 'flowers of civic eloquence' (as Hatcher describes them): 'I defy thee; what art thou? I am as rich as thou, churl, knave, harlot. I am as rich as thou, and greater beloved than thou ... I am better of birth than thou, and have borne the worship and estate of this city, and kept it as well as thou.' See also Haskins, 1912, 147-159. The importance of Halle was recognised as early as Aubrey in the seventeenth century: Aubrey, 1847, 113.

15. The 1396-1397 aulnage account and the 1399/1400 ward lists have been transcribed and are printed as appendix one, see above, pp. 257-272. All the evidence presented in this paragraph is described more fully there.

16. William Lightfoot: mayor: Hatcher, 1843, 696; member of Parliament: Hatcher, 1843, 707; merchant's mark: R.C.H.M. 1980, 26; properties: Nevill, 1911, 70; Church House: Everett, 1941b; R.C.H.M. 1980, 73-76; export trade (generally): Platt, 1973, 152-163, V.C.H.6, 1962, 125-126; 1445 confiscation: *Cal. Pat.* 20th December 1445; 1444 imports: Coleman, 1960-1961, 100, 114, 140, 191, 206. On this import trade generally see Coleman, 1960-1961, xxvi-xxix; Coleman, 1963, 10; V.C.H.6, 1962, 126.

17. Most details from V.C.H.6, 1962, 125-128. See also (for Thomas Freeman) *Cal. Pat.* 21st October 1434 and 2nd May 1440.

18. Conyers, 1973, 54-64.

19. Quotation from Carus-Wilson, 1967, xxiv-xxv, whose table of exports of raw wool and woollen cloth 1347-1544 (*ibid*) charts the progress of this transformation.

20. Little is known about Salisbury's early economic history: see summaries in V.C.H.6, 1962, 124; Rogers, 1969, 6. References to 'Stapulhall' are given in Haskins, 1912, 33-34.

21. Ponting, 1971, 12 suggests that it began as soon as the city was built but this is not borne out by the 1306 list of free citizens (Hatcher, 1843, 742-743) which includes very few occupational surnames connected with the woollen industry. The rise of woollen exports is traced by Carus-Wilson, 1967, 245ff, who shows that Bristol's export trade began earlier than that through Southampton, where record levels were achieved in 1391-1396 (*ibid*, 259). Southampton's Italian trade is described by Platt, 1973, 154.

22. The growth of the rural industry is discussed by Ponting, 1957, 22–36 and Ponting, 1971, 13–20. The accounts in V.C.H.4, 1959, 123–128 and V.C.H.6, 1962, 125 have been used *passim* throughout this section.

23. See appendix one.

24. The types of cloth are discussed in V.C.H.4, 1959, 124–126. Hatcher, 1843, 113–114 describes rays as medleys, but the word later came to mean cloth manufactured from wool dyed before spinning. Quotations from V.C.H.4, 1959, 124. Southampton's overseas trade is described by Platt, 1973, 154–157.

25. Haskins, 1912, 91–94 suggests that the weavers continued to prosper in the sixteenth century. By 1582 Salisbury seems to have captured from Southampton the distribution of French products such as canvas: Platt, 1973, 220. The town mill development is recorded in a lease cited by Rogers, 1976, 255.

26. The decline of the Southampton Italian trade is discussed by Platt, 1973, 218–220; Ramsay, 1965, 23. Imports of woad dwindled almost to nothing in the 1480s: Coleman, 1960–1961, 321, 324. The west Wiltshire trade in undyed broadcloth is described in V.C.H.4, 1959, 138–140.

27. See in general V.C.H.6, 1962, 128–129. In 1612 the guild of fullers was not represented in the list of trade companies, but seems to have been replaced by a company of clothworkers, probably the employees of clothiers: Haskins, 1912, 381–382. The development of the capitalist clothier in west Wiltshire is brilliantly described by Ramsay, 1965, 31–49; he is also responsible for the suggestion that the market was the reason for a similar development not occurring in Salisbury: *ibid*, 20–21.

28. V.C.H.6, 1962, 129. Quote from Aubrey, 1847, 112. The suitability of Salisbury cloth for mourning, and its imitation at Painswick, are cited by Mann, 1971, 9, 43.

29. Free citizens: WRO. G23/1/264 (the index at the end of the volume serves as a continuation after 1660). Loans: WRO. G23/1/4, G23/1/59. The system is discussed and extracts are given by Haskins, 1912, 390–396. Clothworkers' company: Haskins, 1912, 380–387. The composition of the various trade guilds is derived from WRO. G23/1/246, listed in Rathbone, 1951, 82–84. Inventories among wills of the Sub-Dean of Sarum in Wiltshire Record Office. The use of a crook to facilitate shearing is discussed by Mann, 1971, 302. Petitions: 1720 cited by Mann, 1971, 33; 1718 in Haskins, 1912, 94–95.

30. See in general V.C.H.4, 1959, 151–155; Ramsay, 1965, 71–84. Plague: see above, chapter 2. There was however a proposal in 1658 to employ a Dutchman to teach workhouse children the Spanish trade: Hatcher, 1843, 441; Mann, 1971, 11. This seems to have had no effect and in 1727 Salisbury was not among the medley-producing areas inspected by Quarter Sessions: V.C.H.4, 1959, 158.

31. Salisbury flannels, unlike Welsh flannels, used a worsted warp: Hatcher, 1843, 579. Salisbury's flannel industry is discussed in V.C.H.4, 1959, 159–160; Mann, 1971, 43. The woolcombers' company is described by Haskins, 1912, 397–400. Types of flannel and other cloth: Hatcher, 1843, 579. Wyndham anecdote: Hatcher, 1843, 649. Haskins, 1912, 386 recounts the story and assigns it to 1795, the year of Wyndham's election to Parliament. But the story loses its point if Ogden was already 'Draper to his Majesty' (V.C.H.4, 1959, 161) and so is perhaps earlier than 1786.

32. Sun fire insurance records: Ponting, 1974, 161–172. Thirty-one Salisbury clothiers insured £30,000; cf. Trowbridge: £34,000; Bradford: £24,750; Heytesbury, £18,000; Wilton: £10,750; Devizes: £8,500; Chippenham: £6,100; Warminster: £5,800. It should be borne in mind that these figures refer only to the business of one insurance company and may not be representative. 1770 undercutting: Mann, 1971, 86. Hussey: Ponting, 1974, 170. Hinxman: Ponting, 1974, 169 and Haskins, 1912, 396. Hutchings: Haskins, 1912, 386–387. Wansey: V.C.H.4, 1959, 168; Mann, 1971, 132. In general, see Rogers,

1976, especially pp. 17-23, 37, 253-254. I am most grateful to Mr Rogers for discussing these points with me and allowing me access to his unpublished notes on Salisbury clothiers. Factory sales: *Salisbury Journal*, 21st December, 1807; 6th June, 1808; 20th July, 1812.

33. V.C.H.4, 1959, 171-172; V.C.H.6, 1962, 129; Hatcher, 1843, 580. I am grateful to Mr Rogers for several of these suggestions.

34. Quote from Noyes, 1913, 121.

35. I have made extensive use of Watkins, 1915 and Everitt, 1967. The work of Watkins seems to be little known, although it is a most valuable discussion of the organisation of markets. The definition of a market is that of the Royal Commission on Market Rights and Tolls, 1888, discussed below, and is quoted by Watkins, 1915, 22.

36. A recent statement of the prehistoric origin of fairs is in Dyer, 1981, 23-26; see also Grinsell, 1957, 305 and Whitlock, 1976, 26-30. Lists of charters for markets and fairs are given in Richardson, 1974, 232-251. My figures are derived from adding all the Wiltshire entries before 1350 (except Cardestok, which is presumably Chardstock in Dorset, and Poulton, which is now in Gloucestershire) to those of Henry III where the county is not given, but which may reasonably be identified with Wiltshire places, 34 entries in all. On later markets in general see Everitt, 1967, 467-469, and in Wiltshire and neighbouring counties Dyer, 1979 (from which figures are taken, p. 129) and Chartres, 1973. Comparative figures for 1792 and 1888 (from the Royal Commission on Market Rights and Tolls) are reproduced in Richardson, 1974, 251-269. On Yarnbury, see the remarks of Jim Carpenter of Wylye in Curry, 1981: 'And I can remember going with my father to what was nearly the last Castle Fair, up top of the forest. The gypsies used to come, and there were animals, horses, colts, sheep and cattle. It stopped because the war was on.'

37. Most details are taken from V.C.H.6, 1962, 138-141. A nominal $6\frac{3}{4}$ mile distance between market towns was normally considered the minimum permissible (Watkins, 1915, 26) and is often quoted, but has no legal basis (Salzman, 1928). A horsefair in Salisbury cathedral is cited by Davies, 1968, 56.

38. This exercise has often been attempted and my account adds little to the information provided by Hatcher, 1843, 93-94; Haskins, 1912, 262-266; Gover, 1939, 19-22; V.C.H.6, 1962, 85-87; Rogers, 1969, 5-6; R.C.H.M. 1980, xl-xli. There are a number of inconsistencies and uncertainties.

39. See the sources listed in note 38 above. The use of the elm tree as a yarn market is suggested by Shortt, 1957, 43. Hog Lane and Cow Lane seem to be alternative names for that part of Salt Lane bordered by Gore's and Three Swans chequers: see Haskins, 1912, 228 and Donn's map of Salisbury 1797. Melemonger Street (and variants) is the former name of Greencroft Street, and occurs commonly: see Gover, 1939, 21. Hatcher, 1843, 94 suggests that Smiths' Row was in Winchester Street, but without stating his authority. Tanner Street is probably a corruption of St. Ann Street (and not the other way round), although it is likely that tanners lived in the area: R.C.H.M. 1980, xlii. Shipstrete (Sheep Street) – Gover, 1939, 21 sv. Market Place - is perhaps a variant of Chipper Street, referred to as Shiperestrete in 1415 – Gover, 1939, 20. Occupational street names are discussed further below, note 50.

40. 1455 figure: Rogers, 1969, 6. Meaning of shop: Watkins, 1915, 35, cf. the common occurrence of the word in seventeenth-century probate inventories. Shops in fysschamels: V.C.H.6, 1962, 86 quoting *Cal. Pat.* 1313-1317, 112; see also *Inq. ad quod damnum*, xcv. 12 (P.R.O. list xvii, 137). 1368 building regulation: Hatcher, 1843, 84. Fourteenth- and fifteenth-century survivals: R.C.H.M. 1980, 59-66 *passim* (nos. 35, 52, 55-57, 60, 63, 68, 71-72); see also Reeves and Bonney, 1982, 103. 'Pentyse': WRO. G23/1/44/1 translated in *Salisbury Journal*, 26th Jan. 1884, p. 3. Its location is not known,

and so it may not have been in the Market Place. One of the tenants was the proprietor of Pynnock's Inn, High Street. Pentices in general are discussed by Everitt, 1967, 484–485. The arrangement of houses around the Bishop's Guildhall is ambiguous. Naish's map, 1716 and 1751, suggests an open courtyard, but two well-known prints, R.C.H.M. 1980, pl. 2a, pl. 8, seem to depict the existence of houses adjoining the Guildhall on both north and south sides. The Speed map, 1611, reproduced as R.C.H.M. 1980, pl. 1b includes a curious circular mark in this area. The mark does not appear on an original map, nor on Lea's 1689 reprint (both in W.R.O.), nor on a commonly available modern reproduction. Is it simply a blemish? According to Wansey, 1801, 43 note, the Guildhall was formerly surrounded with houses.

41. Poultry cross: R.C.H.M. 1980, 15; the legend of the penitent, *ca.* 1375–1388, is recounted by Noyes, 1913, 125–126. First Council House: V.C.H.6, 1962, 87; R.C.H.M. 1980, 61 (no. 38). Elizabethan Council House: H.M.C. 1907, 225 (the decision to build); V.C.H.6, 1962, 87, quoting WRO. G23/1/3, f. 27 notes that it was built 'where the great elm late stood'. It is interesting that the vignette of the Council House on Speed's map 1611, has a large tree depicted immediately to its east. The building of similar council houses at this period is discussed by Everitt, 1967, 482. Several illustrations of the Council House exist; see R.C.H.M. 1980, pl. 2a; Shortt, 1957, pl. 43; Burnett, 1978, 54. It continued in use after the fire: Hatcher, 1843, 537. Negotiations about the new Council House are summarised in V.C.H.6, 1962, 87, and the building is described in R.C.H.M. 1980, 46–47. Bell: H.M.C. 1907, 213, quoting WRO. G23/1/2, f. 247. Weighbeam: V.C.H.6, 1962, 86 note 42. Seventeenth-century legislation about the use of the weighbeam is printed in H.M.C. 1907, 237, 242. The pillory is depicted on Speed's map, 1610, and, with the stocks and whipping post, is referred to on Naish's map, 1751 (not on the 1716 edition). The case of John Selloway is recorded by Shortt, 1957, 104.

42. 1306 regulations: Davies, 1908, vol. 1, 195–197 (nos. 19–23). Hatcher, 1843, 76 summarises these provisions, but his translations of items 19 and 23 contradict each other, and readers should refer to the original Latin; see also Street, 1916, 216, note 3. It should be noted that this reference to a striking clock (if indeed it is a clock and not simply a bell rung at the time of a service) in the Cathedral predates by 80 years the earliest reference usually offered in discussions of the surviving medieval clock, e.g. Backinsell, 1977a. 1416 regulations: H.M.C. 1907, 194. 1521 quotation: H.M.C. 1907, 213. John Ivie quotation (from his declaration, 1661): Slack, 1975, 111–112.

43. The Bishop's right to allocate market pitches: Davies, 1908, 194 (no. 16), cf. Hatcher, 1843, 76. Fifteenth-century rearrangement: H.M.C. 1907, 193–195. Horses: *ibid.* 193. Butchers: *ibid.* 195. Chandlers: *ibid.* 221–222 (the dispute was a long-standing one). Coal merchants: *ibid.* 212. Vintners: *ibid.* 228. 1607 tradesmen: Williams, 1960, 10 (no. 19). Weighbeam orders: H.M.C. 1907, 237, 242. Thomas Raye: Hatcher, 1843, 365. Thomas Raye was mayor in 1611 and Thomas Raye junior in 1652: Hatcher, 1843, 696–697. The question of medieval refuse disposal is discussed by Keene, 1982.

44. General: Watkins, 1915, *passim*; Everitt, 1967, *passim*. 1306 regulations: Davies, 1908, 195–196 (no. 19). 1416 orders: H.M.C. 1907, 193, 195. Faggots: *ibid.* 216, 236. Leathersellers: Williams, 1960, 90–92 (nos. 1151, 1159–1171). Engrossers: *ibid.* 64, 66, 68, 94 (nos. 788–790, 810–811, 834, 1200). John Warden: Haskins, 1912, 242. General decline of the open market: Chartres, 1973, 68, 70–71.

45. 1673 guidebook: Blome, 1673, 240–242 (Wiltshire) and *passim* (other counties); 1798 directory: U.B.D. 1798, sv. Salisbury; 1888 inquiry: R.C.M.R.T. 1889, 332 (12, 939); 1929 report: M.A.F. 1929, 134; city and Bishop: V.C.H.6, 1962, 87, 139 with notes; 1888 inquiry: R.C.M.R.T. 1889, 332 (12,949), 325 (12,630–12,631), 328 (12,750).

46. Day book: W.R.O. G. 23/1/29. That the Michaelmas fair was used as a hiring fair is suggested by the occurrence of 55 names listed without a trade, some of whom are described as men, and one as maiden. Corn dealers: WRO. G23/1/30.

47. See in general V.C.H.6, 1962, 139-140, although the Market House is wrongly dated to 1865 instead of 1859. A good summary of attempts to improve the market comes in a report submitted to the city council on 10th Feb. 1854 (WRO. G23/100/2, pp. 387-389). It includes a reference to competition from a new market at Bishopstoke (Eastleigh). On the Salisbury Railway and Market House Company see Lee, 1956 and Backinsell, 1977b, which both make use of company records not available to the V.C.H. Neither, however, seems aware that a memorial (petition) by tradesmen advocating a market house and tram road was presented to the city council on 31st May 1855 (WRO. G23/100/3 pp. 22-25) several months before the meeting on 17th October which they present as the first suggestion of such a scheme.

48. All details from R.C.M.R.T. 1889, 325-334 *passim*. The song is 'Wilton Fair,' variously known as 'Marlborough Fair' (these two versions in Cologne and Morrison, 1981, 28-29) and 'Bridgwater Fair' (Addison, 1953, 175-176). I see no reason why it should not be applied equally to Salisbury fair.

49. Quote from Devenish, 1948, 77-78. Most other details from M.A.F. 1929, 134 and from Leslie Brindley in Curry, 1981 (including quotation). Recent history from V.C.H.6, 1962, 140 and Backinsell, 1977b.

50. See Gover, 1939, 19-22 (which however omits a number of streets - e.g. Bellfounder Street, Cow Lane, Hog Lane, Smiths' Row - and omits many early references); V.C.H.6, 1962, 79-84 (which gives few definitions); Rogers, 1969, map showing medieval street names; R.C.H.M. 1980, xxxvi-xxxvii, xl-xli. Hart, 1976 is unreliable and should be used only for examples of modern folklore. In my text I have modernised the spelling of names, which may not occur in documents in these forms. The 1455 list is transcribed by Nevill, 1911. Mealmonger Street residents: Johanne Slegge (Nevill, 1911, 69, widow of Johannis, Haskins, 1912, 61); Thomas Croos (Nevill, *ibid.* 78); Johannis Colyngborn (*ibid.* 79); Johannis London (*ibid.*) 80); Ricardus Spershor (*ibid.* 86); Johannis Stone/Johannis Huyssh (*ibid.* 86; WRO. G23/1/214, sv. 1418). The owners of the eighteen properties (all from Nevill, 1911) are as follows (with source, if occupation not given by Nevill): Ricardus Stille, cook, formerly Henricus Chubbe, baker; Johannis Wily, merchant (Haskins, 1912, 36 etc.), formerly Robertus Warmwell, draper (Hatcher, 1843, 134 etc.); Johannis Chippenham, butcher, formerly Robertus Canne, leatherdresser (WRO. G23/1/2, 120); Johannis Wynchester, barber, formerly Johannis Glaser, chandler; Johannis Glaser, chandler, formerly Johannis Noble, fisher (Swayne, 1896, 361); Ricardus Hayns, tailor, formerly Johannis Dannell, goloshmaker (WRO. G23/150/97); Willelmus Swyngel, baker (Haskins, 1912, 60), formerly Robertus Stonard, baker (WRO. G23/1/214, sv. 1419); Walterus Hynde, smith? (Swayne, 1896, 358), formerly Georgius Joce, tucker (WRO. G23/1/214, sv. 1431); Johannis Chittern, weaver's journeyman (WRO. G23/1/1, 73b), formerly Willelmus Purchase, tucker (Davies, 1908, vol. 1, 248); Willelmus Schipton, cordwainer, formerly Johannis Swyft, ironmonger (Davies, 1908, vol. 1, 179); Johannis Symond, clerk, formerly Johannis Bodyngton, salmonmonger (Davies, 1908, vol. 1, 250); Johannis Wise, draper, formerly Willelmus Wilmote, draper; Simonis Pasford, cook, formerly Johannis Hayne, weaver (WRO. G23/1/2, 121); Johannis Dogood, brewer, formerly Johannis Forest, dubber (Swayne, 1896, 10); Johannis Ston, tailor, formerly Johannis Huyssh, weaver (WRO. G23/1/214, sv. 1418); Ricardus Spershor, saddler, formerly Willelmus Mede, weaver (WRO. G23/1/1, 73); Walterus Sharioth, sawyer, formerly Johannis Atkyn, dyer; Johannis Crickmor, dubber (Haskins, 1912, 61), formerly Robertus Gilbert, tanner (Davies, 1908, vol. 1, 230).

51. In using the 1399/1400 ward lists for this purpose I have calculated that they are arranged in approximately the following order: Market Ward – St. Thomas's Church, Minster Street, Cheesemarket, Castle Street, to bar and back, Chipper Street, Blue Boar Row, Market Place, Endless Street, Bedwin Street, return to Market Place, Pot Row, Wheeler Row, etc.; Martin's Ward – perhaps Three Cups, Black Horse, Swaynes, Griffin, Barnard Cross, Rolfes, Trinity chequers; New Street Ward – New Street, High Street, Silver Street, New Canal, Catherine Street. I have deduced this itinerary by identifying as many holdings as possible from other sources, but I have no great confidence that it is correct. The difficulty in using the 1455 list (Nevill, 1911) is twofold: very few occupations are given (and so they must be derived from other sources, such as the city ledgers and domesday books); and although street names are usually given, they generally refer to much longer stretches of road than now, and so the addresses given are not very precise. Archaeological evidence suggests that metalworking took place at this period in the Milford Street-Guilder Lane area, and so the names Guilder Lane and Bellfounder Street may have preserved their original meaning: R.C.H.M.1980, xlii, and see note 57 below.

52. This description is based on the evidence presented in appendix two.

53. Kelly, 1855, 99–103.

54. This account is based on Reynolds, 1977, 80–84 and Clark and Slack, 1976, *passim* (general considerations); and Haskins, 1912, *passim* and V.C.H.6, 1962, 132–138 (Salisbury).

55. Processions: Wordsworth, 1901, 207; Haskins, 1912, 67–69; Shortt, 1982. The 1496 procession to greet the king is in WRO. G23/1/2, fol. 194 and 194v, which outlines the preparations for the royal visit. It is clear that the guilds were involved: 'Also the maire causid the Stewardes of any crafts in the Cyte to bring to him in Wryting how many men of any crafte ghuld ryde with hym to reseve the kyng and the quene to the cyte.' There are also instructions about cleansing the streets, but I do not see any mention of the tailors' giant, as claimed by Stevens, 1914, 63. His claim is perhaps derived from a misreading of Haskins, 1912, 67–68, who mentions the 1496 visit and the existence of the giant in the same paragraph, but without actually claiming that the giant was present on this occasion (see Shortt, 1982). His existence a few years later is perhaps implied in the passage quoted, 'Tailours with the Pagent,' which is from WRO. G23/1/2, fol. 210, giving the order of the Watch on Seynt Osmundys nyght, ca. 1503. The tailors' procession is quoted from Haskins, 1912, 111. The couplet about St. Christopher is translated from a Latin inscription in Bibury church, Gloucestershire, quoted by Stevens, 1914, 62–63. The bede-rolls are in Haskins, 1912, 37 and 129.

56. Tailors' regulations: Haskins, 1912, 122, 170, 171; other companies: Haskins, 1912, 223, 367, 279, 257, 223, 277, 359.

57. Salisbury bellfounders: V.C.H.4, 1959, 252–253; Barbur's bells: Walters, 1927, 255–258; Chitterne bell: Walters, 1927, 57; Tyssen, 1907–1908, pl. opp. p. 366; his house: R.C.H.M. 1980, 95 (169); site reconstructed by Tyssen, 1907–1908, 363–364; 1972 excavations: notes by Algar, 1973, 137 (report forthcoming); bellcasting techniques: Price, 1980, 435; text and discussion of wills of John and Alice Barbur: Tyssen, 1907–1908. I am most grateful to Mr Algar for his comments on this passsage.

58. Details of Beckham's possessions and lifestyle from his will and inventory, 1671, among the Sub-Dean's wills in the Wiltshire Record Office, published by Chinnery, 1979, 556–557 I surmise from the 1667 royal aid (Nevill, 1910, 427) that he lived in White Bear chequer and, as this property is not left to anyone in his will, it was rented. Beckham's accounts as chamberlain in 1621 are in Haskins, 1912, 351–352. His monument is described and illustrated in R.C.H.M. 1980, 30, pl. 47, and Chinnery, 1981, 34 suggests that the carving was originally an overmantel.

59. Chinnery, 1981, 33-35. Beckham's early career is from Ledwich, 1771, 207-214, which was drawn on by Hatcher, 1843, 617 and Haskins, 1912, 357, and reprinted in Chinnery, 1979, 551-553. Note that, besides his memorial in St. Thomas's church, a carved chimneypiece by Humphrey Beckham may be seen in John a Porte's house in Queen Street: R.C.H.M. 1980, 82 (128). The Joiners' Hall is described by Hatcher, 1843, 599.

60. Seven members of the Beckham family are known: Chinnery, 1981, 34. I assume from the fact that Christopher Braithwaite was a constable in 1627 (see below) that he was born *ca.* 1600 or earlier. William and Thomas Braithwaite (the name is spelled in various ways) are mentioned in the Lenten recognisances of 1620: Williams, 1960, 41 (493), 45 (547), 47 (570); see Moore, 1972, 7, 11. William Braithwaite also served as an assistant overseer for the poor for Dolphin chequer in 1625: Slack, 1975, 71 Trade company: Haskins, 1912, 373, 375. Will of Edmund Paley: WRO. Sub-Dean's wills 1613. The premises formerly of Christopher Braithwaite in Dolphin chequer were assessed for the royal aid in 1667 (Nevill, 1910, 415); since, according to Christopher's will (WRO. Sub-Dean's wills, 1666) Elizabeth Braithwaite, John's widow, owed her father-in-law rent, I assume that John had been his father's tenant in Dolphin chequer, the only premises Christopher is recorded as having owned. Ivie's declaration is in Slack, 1975, 117. Ivie's note that Christopher was then (1661) still alive suggests that we are dealing with the same man, and not an ancestor of the same name. His gift of muskets is recorded in the Falstone day book: Waylen, 1892, 356.

61. John Braithwaite's inventory is in WRO. Sub-Dean's wills, 1666. John Bishop and John Banister are mentioned as tenants in 1667: Nevill, 1910, 415 – see appendix two. Stephen Gibbs, referred to as servant in Christopher's will, appears in 1667 as the owner of the premises (Nevill, *ibid.*) and is described as a swordcutler in his own will, in WRO. Sub-Dean's wills, 1690. Francis Braithwaite married in Marlborough in 1657 and Christopher Braithwaite in 1664 (both from Mormon index). A John Braithwaite of Marlborough, ironmonger, is mentioned in a deed of 1735: WRO. 212B/5218. The later history of the cutlery industry in Salisbury has been described by Fullford, 1914, 71-72; V.C.H.6, 1962, 130 and Moore, 1972.

62. On clay pipes in general I have used Oswald, 1975. His list of Wiltshire pipemakers (pp. 197-198) includes names, such as Solomon Sanger, not found in Atkinson's articles (see below). A good brief introduction to the subject is by Ayto, 1979. Salisbury pipes and pipemakers are described by Atkinson, 1970; Atkinson, 1972; and Atkinson, 1980, which supersede V.C.H.4, 1959, 242-244.

63. See the sources listed in note 62 above. Other details from Joel Sanger's will, in WRO. Sub-Dean's wills, 1750 and from Dale, 1961, items 526, 743, 2108, 2495, 2618. Joel Sanger (junior) is described as a common brewer in his will, WRO. Sub-Dean's wills, 1772.

NOTES TO CHAPTER FOUR: TRAVELLING

1. The best account of Wiltshire ridgeways is by Timperley and Brill, 1965. Ridgeways mentioned in Saxon charters are described by Grundy, 1918. See also a discussion on ridgeways in relation to settlements by Taylor, 1979, 31-39.

2. The Roman roads radiating from Old Sarum are described, with references, by Margary, 1973, 99-104. That there was no important Saxon settlement at Old Sarum before 972 is shown by a charter described by Bonney, 1969 and quoted in R.C.H.M., 1980, xxix. Evidence of Saxon and early medieval use of the roads from Old Sarum to Winchester and Old Sarum to Badbury is provided by Grundy, 1918, 98-99, 112, and by the place names Stretford (Stratford Toney), Stratford (-sub-Castle), and Winter-

burneford (Ford), which all refer to Roman river crossings. It has been suggested, however, that the Roman road to the Mendips fell into disuse and was not revived: see Musty, 1958, 31.

3. See, in general, Taylor, 1979, and Grundy, 1918. The Avon valley route is given in R.C.H.M., 1980, xxix, and its continuation south since Roman times is suggested by Stone and Algar, 1955, 110, although some doubt is cast by Musty, 1958, 182. A Wilton-Milford road is postulated in R.C.H.M., 1980, xxxiii. The name 'Wiltway' occurs in the fifteenth century and later in Amesbury and Durrington parishes, Pugh, 1947, 19, 34 and Ruddle, 1900, 7. 'Wiltenweye' is used of the Damerham-Wilton road, according to V.C.H.6, 1962, 2. Other roads converging on Wilton are described by Crawford, 1928, 178-179.

4. Names and derivations are taken from Gover, 1939. Charford ('Cerdicesford' in the Anglo-Saxon Chronicle) is discussed by Crawford, 1931. Domesday or pre-Domesday 'ford' names are as follows: Barford (in Downton); Barford St. Martin; Britford; Charford (in Breamore, Hants.); Deptford (in Wylye); Durnford; Great Wishford; Landford; Langford; Little Wishford (in South Newton); Longford (in Britford); Milford (in Laverstock); Pinding Ford (in South Newton - now preserved only in Pin Marsh); Stapleford; Stoford (in South Newton); Stratford-sub-Castle; Stratford Toney; Ugford (in Burcombe); Wilsford; Woodford.

5. Grant of privileges: Hatcher, 1843, 730: 'Concedimus etiam predicto episcopo et successoribus suis quod ad emendacionem eiusdem civitatis vias et pontes ad eam ducentes mutent et transferant et faciant sicut viderint expedire salvo iure cuiuslicet alterius.' Bull Bridge, Wilton (modern Bulbridge) had given its name to a parish by ca. 1200: Macray, 1891, 61. Ayleswade Bridge, see Hammond, n.d., 3-5; Moberly, 1891, 121-122; Fletcher, 1937b, 64; V.C.H.6, 1962, 88. Leland, see Smith, 1964, 260.

6. Gough Map (Bodleian) ca. 1360. The course of the roads is discussed by Rogers, 1969, 3; V.C.H.6, 1962, 79; R.C.H.M., 1980, xxiii-xxiv. St. Thomas's Bridge is recorded by Leland, ca. 1540 (Smith, 1964, 269), but the present structure dates from the late eighteenth century (Jervoise, 1930, 70). Clarendon is shown as a park on Saxton's map of Wiltshire, 1576. The transference of the name 'Winchester Street' seems to have occurred 1550-1600: see V.C.H.6, 1962, 79, 84. Southampton traffic: Coleman, 1960-1961, xxvii, referring to the year 1443-1444. This road, but not its continuation towards Bristol, is described by Ogilby, 1675, pl. 51.

7. Hinton, 1977, 182-184, discusses not only the navigability of rivers in southern England but also the economics of water transport in the context of Oxford and the Thames. See also Dyos and Aldcroft, 1974, 38. On the commission of sewers see Hatcher, 1843, 460 and Hammond, n.d., 6-9. On St. Martin's churchwarden see Baker, 1906, 45. The suggestion that there was a wharf in Crane Street (hence the name) - see Hammond, 1910, 371-372 - cannot be sustained. The road is named after an inn. It is interesting to note that a ship, the Catherine of Salisbury, is mentioned in a will of 1419 (Hatcher, 1843, 95; V.C.H.6, 127). Presumably it was so-called because it was owned by Salisbury merchants. In view of the surviving medieval bridge at Fordingbridge (mentioned in 1252: see Jervoise, 1930, 75) as well as the obstacles described in the foregoing paragraph, it is hard to see how the Catherine could ever have visited Salisbury.

8. John Aubrey describes Seth Ward and many of his circle as 'ingeniose' men: Aubrey, 1972, 474. John Taylor's pamphlet, 'A discovery, by sea, from London to Salisbury,' 1625, is quoted in Hatcher, 1843, 460 note and Haskins, 1912, 301-303; see also Willan, 1937, 592. Ivie's scheme is mentioned by Slack, 1975, 9. Mathew's scheme in 1655 is referred to by Hatcher, loc. cit. For the Act of Parliament see Hadfield, 1955, 23, 26.

9. From the evidence of Pope, 1697, 77, Pope, 1713, 11, and documents quoted by Hatcher, 1843, 460-461, 471-472 it is clear that Ward was the driving force behind the

scheme. The disillusionment of 1677 is seen in Hatcher, 1843, 472 and Brentnall, 1947, 11-12. The subsequent revivals up to 1729 are described by Willan, 1937, 593-594, and the 1771 survey by Priestley, 1831, 37 and Braun, 1962, 171.

10. Naish's map of Salisbury (1716 and 1751 editions) includes the river from Salisbury to Christchurch marking all the cuts that were made. Cross, 1970a and Cross, 1970b describes the remains of the navigation and cites WRO. 490/1683 as evidence of use. Hatcher, 1843, 497 prints the regulations.

11. See Hatcher, 1843, 529-530; Braun, 1962, 171; Welch, 1966, 3; WRO. 1553/4. The dates of the two surveys given by Hatcher should be noted and compared with the dates of the meetings given by Braun. It is clear that someone – presumably George Yalden Fort, who was an active trustee of the Salisbury and Eling turnpike trust and is described by Braun as the, 'principal protagonist for the project' – took the first survey (of waggons and cart passing through Petersfinger gate 10th January-10th July 1770) and only called the first meeting (for 21st August 1770) once he had analysed the results of his survey. The second survey (from 27th August 1770 to 28th [sic] August 1771) was clearly demanded by the meeting, which fixed it to start on the following Monday morning (27th August 1770 was a Monday). Not until the whole year had elapsed and the results of the new survey had been analysed would the committee reach its decision (on 18th September 1771). This chronology I take to be evidence of the committee's cautious response to the proposal. The proposal failed because the Andover Canal Bill (upon which the Salisbury Canal was dependent) was not enacted, and because of the death in 1772 of the engineer James Brindley. The second proposal, by Christopher Gullet, failed either because of opposition on the grounds of it being monopolistic (Hatcher) or because of lack of money and the American war (Welch).

12. Details from Waylen, 1859, 467-469, and Hadfield, 1955, 71-75. Braun, 1962, 173 suggests that a map of the proposed canal from Salisbury to Pewsey Wharf, published in 1792, sparked off the ride to Devizes.

13. V.C.H.4, 1959, 278-279; Welch, 1966, 5-9; Hatcher, 1843, 549 mentions a figure of £55,400 subscribed. The Act is 35 Geo III, c. 51.

14. Derived entirely from Welch, 1966 and Braun, 1962.

15. I have not questioned the accuracy of Ogilby, 1675, although clearly his choice of the 'principall roads' must have been subjective. It is interesting that he does not describe a road from Salisbury to Bristol via Wilton and Warminster or Edington and Trowbridge. The roads are also omitted from most seventeenth-century county maps. I am inclined to believe that the importance of such a road in the medieval and post-medieval period has been overrated, e.g. by V.C.H.6, 1962, 124. The vagrancy figures are from Slack, 1975, 56-58, who also notes (3) that of 666 vagrants recorded in Salisbury between 1598 and 1669 about 20% claimed places of settlement more than one hundred miles from Salisbury.

16. Details from Slatter, 1965, 62-65 and *passim*. Thirty-one journeys are recorded during 1708. It is interesting to note that only once in the whole diary (36) does he hint at any mishap while travelling; this – obstruction by 'abusive people' at the Dolphin inn in Southampton in 1696 – he describes as 'a rare accident'.

17. It is clear from entries in WRO. G23/1/84, which describes the remedies, that the basic problem was the clogging of the channels by road metalling thrown up by wheeled vehicles.

18. See WRO. G23/1/83-84. The principal offending streets (with number of presentments in WRO. G23/1/84) are as follows: Brown Street (16); Culver Street (15); Winchester Street (14); Castle Street, Gigant Street, Milford Street and the Town Ditch (New Canal) (all 12); Catherine Street and Dragon Street (Exeter Street) (both 9);

St. Ann Street (8). Most of these presentments date from the period 1710-1730, and show clearly that most of the problems occurred in Winchester Street and southwards and Catherine Street and eastwards, along the roads which would have been used by traffic on the Exeter road. The presentment quoted (WRO. G23/1/84) is by George Allen, dated 24th February 1734, and his view was shared by early travellers such as Defoe and Fiennes.

19. The petition to Parliament is described by Hatcher, 1843, 518, and resulted in an act, 10 Geo II, c. 6. Details of improvement carried out under this act are taken from the first of the Highways minute books, WRO. G23/1/85.

20. Details from V.C.H.4, 1959, 254-271.

21. Most details from WRO. 1316/4, the trust's earliest minute book. See especially entries for the following dates: June 1753; 3rd Dec. 1753; 14th Jan. 1754; 9th Feb. 1756; 13th Apr. 1756; 30th May 1757; 3rd Nov. 1757. All meetings in the latter half of 1768 were inquorate, as were most meetings between June 1777 and April 1782. Quotation, from Arthur Young, is given by V.C.H.4, 1959, 259 note 34.

22. Hatcher, 1843, 523. 1 Geo III, c. 37 and 2 Geo III, c. 51. The trust's archives appear not to have survived. In WRO.1316/4, meetings 19th Feb. 1777 and 21st Apr. 1786 the Sarum and Eling trust agreed to emulate road works at Stoford and Fisherton tollhouse.

23. Morgan Morse, the Salisbury carrier in 1625, is mentioned by Hatcher, 1843, 358. An account of the 1684 snowstorm is appended to Anon, 1841, 13-16. The 1770 survey is discussed above, note 11.

24. Slatter, 1965, 59. In general, see Chandler, 1980. Hatcher, 1843, 520-521. Quotation from an unnamed traveller in Hatcher, 1843, 580 note. The accident at St. Thomas's Bridge is recorded in the Sarum and Eling trust minutes, WRO. 1316/4, 15th July 1754. Statistics from Hatcher, 1843, 529-530 and Chandler, 1980.

25. Most details from Chandler, 1980. The 1839 survey is preserved by Hatcher, 1843, 571 note.

26. The London to Bristol railway line was opened throughout in 1841. Annual income statistics are taken from returns to Quarter Sessions, WRO. A3/7/2/12; A3/7/2/21; A3/7/2/24; A3/7/2/40. The success of the Kennett and Amesbury trust is described in Chandler, 1979.

27. Alderbury wooden railway: Welch, 1966, 17-19. The 1803 railway line was suggested in a *Salisbury Journal* editorial and is noted by Braun, 1962, 176. The 1834 proposal is described by Farrant, 1969, and the 1837 proposal by V.C.H.4, 1959, 285. The city council set up a committee to watch the proceedings of the railway companies in November 1844, and the council minute books (WRO. G23/100/2-3) contain frequent references to railways from then until 1859. Mr Walkingshaw appears in WRO. G23/100/2, 95-105.

28. *Salisbury Journal*, 30th Jan. 1847, 4; 6th Mar. 1847, 1-2.

29. The Milford terminus was described in the railway's act (7 & 8 Vic, c. 63) as, 'near Smith's Close, otherwise Fowler's Croft, at Milford, in Salisbury, by the turnpike road to Southampton.' The railway mania as it affected Salisbury is well described by Ruegg, 1878, 4-39, and the council's negotiations are recorded in the council minutes (WRO. G23/100/2-3), especially entries for 20th Feb. 1851; 13th May 1853; 2nd Feb. 1854; 30th Mar. 1855; 7th Feb. 1856; 18th Apr. 1856. Quotation from Ruegg, 1878, 1.

30. Warminster line: MacDermott, 1964, 142-151; Thomas, 1981, 164-176; *Salisbury Journal*, 5th Jul. 1856. Andover line: Matthewson-Dick, 1978, 20; *Salisbury Journal*, 2nd May 1857.

31. Most details from Ruegg, 1878, admittedly a partisan source. Particularly relevant are pages 41, 43, 50, 61.

32. Matthewson-Dick, 1978, 20; *Salisbury Journal*, 7th May 1859, 5; City council minutes, 9th Nov. 1859 (WRO. G23/100/3, 294); V.C.H.6, 1962, 181; V.C.H.4, 1959, 322–323; Hudson, 1968, 251; Nock, 1965, 86–97.

33. Backinsell, 1977b.

34. Details from Matthewson-Dick, 1978.

35. Olivier, 1941, 67. Her dates were 1873–1948. A good introduction to the Salisbury carriers may be found in Mullins, 1978, 29–35.

36. Anon, 1774, 68–77.

37. Anon, 1825, 91–94; Harrod, 1865, 462–465; Greening, 1971.

38. Quotation from Jefferies, 1889, 237. I am indebted for most of the information in this paragraph to Mullins, 1978. Coombe Express: see plate 29. According to Mr Frank Brooks, quoted in Harnham W.I., 1981, 18, 'she always made a stop at the old and picturesque inn called "The Swan", for a last refresher for herself and the donkeys, generally, I think, from the same jug.' The Salisbury carriers rarely appear in published material about Wiltshire villages, but see Wakelin, 1979, 11 for a description of the Pitton carrier.

39. I owe the suggestion of grouping of carriers at certain inns to Mullins, 1978, 33.

40. Pennells, 1963, *passim*; Kelly's directories, 1915–1939; *Motor transport yearbook*, 1923–1924. Much information about early bus services may be derived from local newspapers, e.g. advertisements for new Wilts and Dorset services, to Trowbridge, in *Salisbury Journal*, 5th Aug. 1921, 5; to Southampton, in *Salisbury Journal*, 30th Sep. 1921, 5.

41. *Motor transport yearbook*, 1923–1924, 328. Sparrow and Vincent is described by Pennells, 1963; see also *Salisbury Journal* reports between June and November 1930, especially an account of dangerous driving on 12th Sep. 1930, 10. Silver Star is described by Pennells, 1965.

42. Scout buses: Farrant, 1967, 13–14. Statistics from Kelly's directories of Wiltshire and of Salisbury, various years. Silver Star: Pennells, 1965, *passim*.

43. Most details from Pennells, 1963. In 1908 Salisbury City Council had set up a sub-committee to formulate a scheme for providing an omnibus service (WRO. G23/100/15 General Purposes Committee minutes 896 (18th June 1908)) and shortly afterwards the London Electrobus Co. Ltd. were approached with a view to running electric buses in the city (WRO. G23/100/16, Council minutes 2425 and 2462 (3rd Dec. 1908)). Nothing further is heard of this scheme. Wilts and Dorset's joint services are described by Biddiscombe, 1974, 1975. Until 1956 Kelly's directories of Salisbury included lists of bus services provided by Wilts and Dorset, including, for the period 1950–1956, city services. The opening of the bus station is amusingly described by Olivier, 1941, 67–68. The Wilts and Dorset fleet shortly after its takeover by Hants and Dorset is described by Kaye, 1966, 73–77.

44. Mere complaint: WRO. W.C.C. Roads and Bridges Committee minutes 110 (17th Oct. 1902); April 1904 statistics: *ibid.* 65 (15th Apr. 1904), and WRO. Register of motor cars, book 1; occupations of owners from Kelly's directories of Wiltshire, 1903 and 1907; complaint of damage to roads: WRO. W.C.C. Roads and Bridges Committee minutes 77 (14th July 1905); Mr Targett: *ibid.* 7 (20th Jan. 1905); St. Thomas's Bridge: *ibid.* 78 (14th July 1905) – the letter had been sent by the motorist to the secretary of the Motor Union, who had forwarded it to Wiltshire County Council.

45. Cyclists' guide: Inglis, 1905, routes 513, 661, 683-692, 703; the county surveyor's annual report, June 1903 is similarly complimentary about all the roads in Salisbury city and district, and Wilton urban and rural districts; metalling of county roads: WRO. W.C.C. Roads and Bridges Committee minutes 17 (22nd Jan. 1904). Details of city streets from WRO. G23/100/13-15, Road Committee minutes 12 (23rd May 1906), 342 (19th July 1906), 402 (25th Oct. 1906), 428, 434 and 436 (22nd Nov. 1906), 672 (24th Oct. 1907), 815 (19th Mar. 1908), 860 (21st May 1908); abstract of accounts, 1912-1913. The first streets to be treated with tar were Castle Street, Blue Boar Row, Queen Street, New Canal, Catherine Street, High Street, Bridge Street, and Fisherton Street. The tar-sprayer cost £370.

46. Statistics from Salisbury directories: Brown, 1912; Kelly, 1925; Kelly, 1939-1940. Four Salisbury firms applied for general identification marks (trade plates) in 1904, including Lowther and Sons and Rowland and Sons: WRO. Register of motor cars, book 1; Arthur Edwards registered three cars in 1904: AM290, AM369 and AM544 (*ibid.*) and so was presumably a motor trader at this date. Scout Motors are fully described by Farrant, 1967 – the advertisement is quoted on page 10.

47. All details from WRO. G23/100/38, 41, General Purposes Committee Minutes, 5330 (20th Nov. 1930); City lands 3585 (18th Sep. 1931); Watch 4118 (23rd June 1931) and 4471 (18th Sep. 1934).

48. All details from WRO.G23/100/39-42, committee minutes: City Lands 3657 (19th Feb. 1932), 3746 (8th July 1932) and 3811 (20th Jan. 1933); Council-in-Committee 164 (19th Jan. 1935); Watch 4360 (24th Oct. 1933), 4347 (19th Sep. 1933) and 4541 (19th Mar. 1935); General Purposes 5724 (22nd Sep. 1932) and 6243 (22nd Nov. 1934). See also Salisbury City Council annual abstracts of accounts for the years 1932 to 1936.

49. This paragraph relies heavily on the annual reports of the chief constable of Salisbury, as reported in the *Salisbury Journal* (usually the first issue in February of each year). The account in *Salisbury Journal* 8th Feb. 1935, 7 is particularly helpful. Statistics for 1968-1977 are taken from published summaries by Wiltshire Constabulary and from the Wiltshire chief constable's annual reports. For more general considerations and statistics see Plowden, 1973, 267-291 and 482-483. Quotation from Olivier, 1941, 74.

50. 1949 car parks: Sharp, 1949, 58, estimates the following capacities – New Canal, 65; Cheese Market, 35; Salt Lane, 200; Market Place, 200; New swimming baths, 300 approximately. The development of car parking may easily be traced through the city's official guides issued periodically between 1953 and 1974. A survey conducted in 1979 (Wiltshire County Council, 1980, table 2.3.1) shows the following off-street car-parking capacity: Central, 1,377; New Street, 643; Brown Street, 227; Market Place, 219; Salt Lane, 175; Culver Street, 136; College Street, 80; etc. The total was 3,172. It is interesting to note that multi-storey car parks in New Street and Brown Street were first proposed as long ago as 1949 – Sharp, *loc cit.*

51. The extent of road improvements may be assessed from the published annual abstracts of accounts of Salisbury City Council. Harnham Bridge: V.C.H.4, 1959, 266. 1949 plans: Sharp, 1949, 45-54. Modern main road developments are summarised in the annual reports of the Wiltshire County Council County Surveyor, especially 1972/3 and 1977/8. The one-way system's aims are described in Wiltshire County Council, 1965, para. 41.

NOTES TO CHAPTER FIVE: GOVERNING

1. 15th September 1981. In this chapter no attempt is made to offer a systematic account of city government, which more than any other topic covered in this book, has

been competently and comprehensively described in print elsewhere. Readers desiring such an account should consult Street, 1916 and V.C.H.6, 1962. The present discussion attempts only to convey something of the nature and flavour of city government, and so is selective in the events it describes.

2. This summary is derived largely from Reynolds, 1977, chapters 5 and 6.

3. Street, 1916, 212–214; V.C.H.6, 1962, 95, 105.

4. Records of the Bishop's courts survive among both the city muniments: WRO. G23/1/73–82; and the diocesan records: WRO. Bishop: Administration: City Courts, bundles 1–25 (brief list in Wiltshire Record Office). 1464 regulations: WRO. G23/1/2, f.71, translated in H.M.C., 1907, 204–205. Sinecure bailiffs: Street, 1916, 321–324. 1566 proceedings: WRO. G23/1/80, f.1. 1687 court baron: uncatalogued book of late seventeenth century court baron proceedings in a box with WRO. G23/1/68–71. 1718 court leet: WRO. diocesan records: Bishop: Administration: City Courts, bundle 1. Seth Ward's comments are quoted by Street, 1916, 355–356. 1835 winding-up: V.C.H.6, 1962, 105. A book of procedures has in fact survived and is among the diocesan records: WRO. Bishop: Administration: City Courts, bundle 25. It appears to be of eighteenth-century date and derived from a standard textbook of court procedure.

5. All details from Street, 1916, which is probably the most competent and detailed essay on any aspect of Salisbury's history to have been published. It is followed by V.C.H.6, 1962, 101–103.

6. Street, 1916, 356–361; Bridbury, 1981, 7–8; Reynolds, 1977, 115–116.

7. Street, 1916, *passim*. The issue of the monarch's power in granting or refusing requests for incorporation is discussed in political terms in Clark and Slack, 1976, 126–140.

8. Reynolds, 1977, 172–177; Clark and Slack, 1976, 127–134; Street, 1916, 200 note 2, 343–344, 227, 233.

9. Street, 1916, *passim*, especially p. 346, where is quoted a submission of 1603 asking, 'That the Cittie may be made a Countye and soe incorporated with the trades therein for the prevencion of the decaye thereof.' – this suggests that the method of government may have contributed to the city's decline. The quotation continues: 'Lastly, many offenders escape, by reason the power of reformacion resteth more in others than in the mayor and his brethren,' suggesting that the split responsibility impeded justice. In addition complaints of drunkenness and disorderly behaviour were made against two of the Bishop's officers during the 1593–1596 dispute: Rundle, 1979, [9].

10. Most details from V.C.H.6, 1962, 117–121. Quotations from Hatcher, 1843, 380 and Slatter, 1965, 47, 69.

11. V.C.H.6, 1962, 113, 117–118. Hatcher, 1843, 578 (the passage may in fact have been written by Benson, since it later describes the office of recorder, which office Benson held).

12. Byng, 1934, vol. 1, 106; Wheeler, 1889, 39 sv. 1796; Spire, 1935, 6; Spire, 1958, 28; Wiltshire County Council, 1978, 92, table 9.2.

13. Simond, 1817, vol. 1, 257; Hudson, 1978, 17; Spire, 1935, 7.

14. This account is based largely on Street, 1916, 220–224; Rathbone, 1951, 63–64; V.C.H.6, 1962, 96–100. An important collection of 'Divers Ordinances and Constitutions,' 1408–1428 has been translated from WRO. G23/1/1, ff. 147–148 in H.M.C., 1907, 193–195, and I have quoted from this. Agincourt: Hatcher, 1843, 113. St. George's guild: Haskins, 1912, 26–47.

15. Most sources are the same as note 14 above. Coroners are described in Hunnisett, 1981, xxix. Quotes from H.M.C., 1907, 193, 194.

16. Reynolds, 1977, 171-177 may be used to place Salisbury's procedures (described in V.C.H.6, 1962, 96-97) in a national perspective.

17. The 1612 charter describes the various offices and their holders. The full Latin text is in Hatcher, 1843, 773-783, and there is an English summary in Haskins, 1927, 8-9. V.C.H.6, 1962, 105-113 provides a detailed account of civic government during the period. On the link between oligarchy and incorporation see Clark and Slack, 1976, 128-135. Quote by John Ivie in Slack, 1975, 124.

18. The best discussion of John Ivie and his circle is by Slack, 1972a, passim, especially pp. 183-189. The appointment of Peter Thatcher is described in Swayne, 1896, 173-174. The connection between St. Thomas's Church and the Dean and Chapter is described by V.C.H.6, 1962, 147-148, and its sympathies are illustrated by its appointment of the Bishop to deliver a weekly lecture (Hatcher, 1843, 330). Maurice Greene, in 1610-1612, and Thomas Hancock, in 1633-1634, who were both prominent brewers and opponents of the puritans, served as churchwardens at St. Thomas's Church: Swayne, 1896, 306-307, 317. The arrangements for co-ordinating poor relief between the three city parishes and the Close are described by Slack, 1975, 8. Quotes from Slack, 1975, 116 and Hatcher, 1843, 356. The English Dialect Dictionary defines 'stepple' as a hoof-mark, or a short, neat flight of steps. This is the closest I can come to an intelligible meaning for 'stupples.'

19. Slack, 1972a, 181-183, 189-192; Slack, 1975, 9-15 and passim.

20. Charters of 1630, 1675 and 1707 printed in Hatcher, 1843, 786-798 and summarised in Haskins, 1927, 9-11. Charter of 1656 printed and discussed by Hall, 1907. A general account of city government during the period 1612-1835 is provided by V.C.H.6, 1962, 105-113.

21. Derived largely from council minute book WRO. G23/1/22, sv. 1800, which is duplicated in WRO. G23/1/6; also from a minute book of meetings of the mayor, aldermen and justices, WRO. G23/1/15, sv. 1800. These meetings seem to have acted also as the city lands committee, to which the highways committee referred the question of New Canal, WRO. G23/1/87, sv. 27th February and 17th April 1800. The dangerous state of this watercourse was confirmed in January 1805 when it claimed the life of a man from Wilton, who was swept as far as Dairyhouse Bridge before his body could be recovered: Wheeler, 1889, 41. Fines: Wheeler, 1889, 39 sv. 1796 and passim; V.C.H.6, 1962, 109. Bishop's clerk: Hatcher, 1843, 556.

22. WRO. Salisbury City Q.S. Q/126/1-2, sv. 1800.

23. WRO. G23/1/50, pp. 162-170. My figures are based on the financial year beginning 8th November 1799. V.C.H.6, 1962, 108-110.

24. V.C.H.6, 1962, 113-117. Statistics, which apply to the financial year beginning 1st April 1930, are taken from the abstract of accounts for that year (in Salisbury Local Studies Library).

25. All details from WRO. G23/100/37 passim. The Watch Committee meeting described took place on 22nd April, 1930. the General Purposes Committee on 26th June, 1930, and the Public Health Committee on the 24th March 1930.

26. WRO. G23/100/36-38, sv. Special Unemployment Grants Committee (later Unemployment Committee); also newspaper accounts, as follows: October 1929 council meeting: Salisbury Journal, 11th Oct. 1929, p. 9; Labour party: Salisbury Journal, 20th Dec. 1929, p. 5; letter: Salisbury Journal, 17th Jan. 1930, p. 7; Ratepayers Association: Salisbury Journal, 24th Jan. 1930, p. 5; Salisbury Times, 24th Jan. 1930, p. 10; editorial: Salisbury Journal, 20th Dec. 1929; letter: Salisbury Journal, 3rd Jan. 1930, p. 11.

27. WRO. G23/100/36-38; Salisbury Journal 1st Aug. 1930, p. 5; quotes from Salisbury Times 5th Dec. 1930, p. 9. In WRO. is a file (G23/132/41) pertaining to the official

opening of the bridge on 22nd July 1931. The corresponding newspaper account (*Salisbury Times*, 24th July, 1931, p. 5; *Salisbury Journal*, 24th July, 1931, p. 9) provide useful information about the history of the bridge, and there is a photograph of the tollgate in *Salisbury Times*, 10th July, 1931, p. 10.

NOTES TO CHAPTER SIX: LIVING

1. The best account of medieval education in Salisbury is by Orme, 1976, 65–78; see also his introduction, *ibid*, 1–34. For John of Salisbury (*ca.* 1120-1180) see Chibnall, 1956. xi–xl; Ponting, 1975, 15–21.

2. Robertson, 1938, *passim*, especially 39–45, 68–94; Orme, 1976, 69–72; V.C.H.3, 1956, 175–176, 179; Robertson, 1937; Wordsworth and Robertson, 1938.

3. Orme, 1976, 72–73, 76; Robertson, 1938, 37, 123.

4. Theological school: Orme, 1976, 73–74; Robertson, 1938, 38–39. De Vaux College: V.C.H.3, 1956, 369–385; Edwards, 1954; Orme, 1976, 68–69; R.C.H.M. 1980, 130-131.

5. De Vaux College: V.C.H.3, 1956, 384; Friaries: V.C.H.3, 1956, 330, 333; Revived grammar school: V.C.H.5, 1957, 357; Robertson, 1938, 124-127; Theological college: V.C.H.3, 1956, 68.

6. 1569 establishment: Endowed charities, 1907, 1-2; V.C.H.5, 1957, 349; V.C.H.6, 1962, 100; Orme, 1976, 75. Hatcher, 1843, 284-285 misprints the date 1559, and this is followed by R.C.H.M. 1980, 149 (423). George Inn, 1590-1624: V.C.H.6, 1962, 81; Hatcher, 1843, 314 (1608 complaint); Haskins, 1912, 295 (quote). The date for moving to the George Inn, 'about 1590,' is given by Haskins and followed by V.C.H., but Hatcher found an entry in a city ledger of 1616 proposing the move there (Hatcher, 1843, 327), and so it may be that the 1608 complaint preceded the move to the George Inn. School charges (1631): Hatcher, 1843, 380-381. Thomas Naish: Slatter, 1965, 41 and note. Nineteenth-century decline: Endowed charities, 1907, 1-2, 151-152.

7. St. Edmund's church school: Swayne, 1896, xxiv, 153, 187, 241; Old Council House: Hatcher, 1843, 366; V.C.H.6, 1962, 87; Jacobite school: Waylen, 1857b, 125; 1714 private schools: V.C.H.5, 1957, 350.

8. 1731 charity schools: Cox, 1731, 198-199. The work is quoted by V.C.H.5, 1957, 350 and note 27 as an undated 'Account of Wiltshire,' of *ca.* 1727 in Salisbury Museum Library. The publication date is in fact 1731. V.C.H. also gives Salisbury's total as 170, not 200. This is because the school in St. Edmund's parish is described as taking 50 pupils, and then 30 pupils taught spinning. I assume that the two figures are separate, but the V.C.H. presumably regards the larger figure as including the smaller. This problem cannot be resolved. Nowes's school, 1718: Endowed charities, 1907, 62-63, 180-182; Talman's school, 1755: Endowed charities, 1907, 58-59, 222; Godolphin school, 1725: Endowed charities, 1907, 99-114; V.C.H.5, 1957, 362-363; Douglas and Ash, 1928, *passim* (quotes from 11, 10, 26-27 - the memories are those of Miss Kate Leigh, at Godolphin from 1861 and recalled *ca.* 1926).

9. Mrs Voysey: Robertson, 1938, 252-253; Joseph Moon: Hatcher, 1843, 546-547, note; Henry Hatcher: Britton, 1847, 15-16.

10. Pigot's directories, 1822, 1830, 1842, sv. Salisbury. The 1833 figures are contained in a Commons Paper, H.C.1835, 62 *Education enquiry, vol. 3: abstract of education returns 1833*, p. 1046. The 1851 educational census is summarised in a Command Paper, C.1692, *Report of commissioners for taking a census of Great Britain on Education, 1852-1853*, p. 119.

11. Ransome, 1972, 4, 17–18, 96. Wesleyan Sunday school: WRO. 1150/181, 1150/184 (quote). 1819 survey: H.C.1819, 9. *Digest of parochial returns ... on education of the poor*, pp. 1035–1036; 1833 survey: H.C. 1835. 62 *Education enquiry, vol. 3: abstract of education returns 1833*, p. 1046; 1851 census: C.1692 (see previous note) p. 119.

12. St. Edmund's parish school: V.C.H.6, 1962, 164; St. Martin's National school: according to Hatcher, 1843, 558 (followed by V.C.H.6, 1962, 164), the school was established in 1811, but a broadside among the Radnor papers, WRO. 490/1406, clearly envisages an opening date of 1812, even though the meeting it describes may have been held in 1811. Quote from WRO. 490/1406. Statistics and quote by the rector of St. Martin's (Thomas Davis) are from V.C.H.6, 1962, 164 and the Parliamentary papers quoted in the previous two notes. Schools between 1825 and 1850: V.C.H.6, 1962, 162–165 *passim*. 1851 census, see above, note 10. According to the 1851 population census 905 children attended eight public day schools and 408 25 private schools. There were 1,086 children aged under five, 941 aged five to ten, and 855 aged ten to fifteen. No fewer than 1,766 children were described as scholars, with a further 65 'scholars at home'. At least 450 of these 'scholars' probably attended Sunday school only, although a few may have been receiving full-time education outside the city.

13. Hardy, 1895, part 3 *passim*. Mary Hardy, 1860, and Katherine Hardy, 1877, appear in the list of students printed in Steward, 1891, 37–47. Mary was still there in 1862 and there was a rumour that, 'she got out one night and went on the river, and it has been out of bounds to us ever since' – Deacon, 1975, 9. The reminiscences are in Steward, 1891, 22–28, and it would be interesting to know whether Hardy had read them. He describes, 'the species of nunnery known as the Training-School at Melchester,' and Steward, 1891, 26 has, 'Our College friends at Winchester dubbed us the Nuns of St. Margaret.' On the history of the college in general, see V.C.H.5, 1957, 363–364, and on its connection with King Alfred College, Winchester, see Rose, 1981.

14. Most details are from W.R.O. Education records: Salisbury School Board Minute Book, 1871–1879, pp. 10–12, which has a useful survey of education in Salisbury in April and May 1871. Plans of the two new National Schools are in W.R.O. 782/88 (St. Edmund's) and W.R.O. 782/89 (St. Thomas's). Additional details from V.C.H.6, 1962, 161–168.

15. V.C.H.6, 1962, 161 offers a résumé of this affair. More detail is supplied by a scrapbook, mostly of newscuttings compiled by a supporter of the nonconformist faction, in Salisbury Local Studies Library, and I have used this *passim*. The Bishop's letter to British school parents (from *Salisbury Journal*, 19th Jan. 1889) is on p. 5; a copy of the letter from Lord Fitzmaurice is on p. 62; accounts of the public meeting are on pp. 64–73. The Bishop's remark was quoted in the *Daily News* (see p. 64), but I have used the fuller (*Salisbury Journal?*) account, p. 69; *The Times* correspondence and an account of the Parliamentary debate (28th March 1890) are also in the scrapbook, on unnumbered pages towards the end.

16. Sources as previous note. Quotes from scrapbook pp. 69, 71. The Bishop's speech to the synod is reported in *Salisbury Journal*, 19th April 1890, supplement p. 1. The history of Bishop Wordsworth's School (Happold, 1950, 19–21) and Wordsworth's biographer (Watson, 1915, 201–203) tend to gloss over the background to the school's establishment.

17. V.C.H.6, 1962, 161–168. The analysis of schools in 1903 is derived from W.R.O. Salisbury Education Committee minute book 1, 1903–1905, pp. 98–100, 167. Comparative figures for 1945 are from W.R.O. Salisbury Education Committee minute book 16, 1943–1945, pp. 221–222. According to V.C.H. (*ibid.* 162) 'there was a steady rise in the number of children attending elementary schools', after 1927, as might be expected, but this does not seem to be borne out by our figures, which show an inexplicable small decline between 1903 and 1945.

18. All details from W.R.O. Wilts. C.C. Education Committee log books: Salisbury St. Martin's boys, 1911-1933, *passim*.

19. All details from W.R.O. Wilts. C.C. Education Committee log books: Salisbury George Herbert girls, 1927-1951, *passim*. After 1930 this school was known as St. Martin's junior girls' school, and, to avoid confusion, I refer to it by this name, even though my first reference is a slight anachronism.

20. Current attendance figures are taken from the 1982 edition of the *Education authorities directory*. Bishop Wordsworth's: Happold, 1950, 24-30; V.C.H.5, 1957, 366-367. Other details are from V.C.H.6, 1962, 161-168 and V.C.H.5, 1957, 352-355.

21. V.C.H.6, 1962, 143. College of Technology: Grant, 1968, 1-18. Libraries: Little, 1981 *passim*; Museum: Willoughby, 1960a, 1960b, *passim*.

22. General works for medieval religion: Bettey, 1979; Platt, 1981; Anderson, 1971; Davies, 1968; Cox, 1913. The best architectural description of Salisbury's churches is R.C.H.M. 1980, 24-39; see also V.C.H.6, 1962, 144-154. St. Edmund's churchwardens' accounts are transcribed and printed by Swayne, 1896; the introduction to this edition, by Amy Mary Straton (c.f. Straton, 1892-1896), is particularly useful. St. Thomas's doom painting is discussed by Hollaender, 1944.

23. St. Edmund's service books and vestments: Swayne, 1896, 3-7; St. Martin's lectern and pulpit: R.C.H.M. 1980, 34-35; St. Edmund's organ: Swayne, 1896, 19 (also introduction p. xxix) - the list of books includes 'i boke for the organes' (p. 4); St. Edmund's seats: Swayne, 1896, xxi, 359. Pew rents as a separate heading in the accounts first appear in 1477-1478: see Cox, 1913, 67. According to R.C.H.M. 1980, 39, fifteenth-century carved oak bench-ends survived at St. Edmund's incorporated into modern choir-stalls. The Life of St. Osmund: Swayne, 1896, xxxvi, 19.

24. Fonts: R.C.H.M. 1980, 29, 34, 38. Wedding door: Swayne, 1896, xxviii. Receipts from ringing the forthfare bell occur in most churchwardens' accounts: see Swayne, 1896, xix. Quotes from Swayne, 1896, 27: 'pro una laterna empta ad usum ecclesie ad portandum diebus et noctibus cum sacramento altaris viid,' *ibid*. p. 36: 'pro una libra cere empta pro lumina portando cum sacramento in visitacionibus infirmorum viiid;' Funeral expenses: Swayne, 1896, xix-xxi, 57.

25. Payments to banner-carriers: Swayne, 1896, xviii, 9, 11 etc.; Veils: *ibid*. xiv, 7 ("i veyle to be drawen in lenton tyme to fore the hye auter"); Christmas lights: *ibid*. xiv, xv; Saints' days: *ibid*. xv; Easter sepulchre: Bettey, 1979, 23-24; Swayne, 1896, xxv, 7 ('ii palles of cloth of goolde for the sepulcre with a shete of Raynes'), 363 ('to William Kerver for the makyng' of a newe Sepulture vis viiid,' - in 1476-1477); Daunse of Powles: Bettey, 1979, 52. It is so named from a famous example of the painting in old St. Paul's Cathedral. Earlier writers (Swayne, 1896, xvii; Cox, 1913, 66; Davies, 1968, 55) assumed it referred to maypole dancing. A Salisbury example of the *danse macabre* theme existed in the Hungerford chantry in Salisbury Cathedral until its destruction *ca*. 1790. It is illustrated in Hatcher, 1843, opp. p. 502 and Duke, 1837, opp. p. 105.

26. A full account of the painting is given by Hollaender, 1944; the 'permanently-exposed lantern slide' is his felicitous description (p. 352). See also R.C.H.M. 1980, 30-31, and plate 35.

27. Chantries in general: Wood-Legh, 1965; Platt, 1981, 106-120 (the notes, pp. 175-176, refer the reader to the extensive literature on the subject); William Kensyngton's will (in Latin) is printed in Swayne, 1896, 379-380; Swayne's chapel: Haskins, 1912, 136-139; V.C.H.6, 1962, 149; R.C.H.M. 1980, 24, 26-27; Hatcher, 1843, 701 (list of appointments of chantry priests). The inscriptions are in Latin. Altars and guild chapels are summarised in V.C.H.6, 1962, 145, 148-149, 152-153. The confraternity of Jesus Mass is discussed by Clutterbuck, 1897, 142; the accounts are printed in Swayne, 1896,

248-272. Tailors' bede-roll: Haskins, 1912, 128-129. Other names, 1505-1581, were added later. An earlier tailors' bede-roll is discussed and transcribed by Haskins, 1916.

28. 1380 clerical poll tax: Kirby, 1956, 164-165; St. Thomas's staff list, 1432: Hatcher, 1843, 190, who makes it clear that to this list of 57 should be added at least four more important church officials; Guild of St. George: Haskins, 1912, 26-47. V.C.H.6, 1962, 149 seems unconvinced by Haskins's argument that the guild had its chapel in St. Thomas's Church, but I find his references (p. 43) to the removal of the George (from Swayne, 1896, 275) and (p. 38) to the chaplain of St. George living in a tenement in St. Thomas's cemetery, are persuasive. Council meetings and mayor-making in church: Haskins, 1912, 41-42; Corporation seats in church: Swayne, 1896, xxi-xxii, 163, where in 1613 it is described as an 'Auncyent Custom'. Tailors' and weavers' guilds: V.C.H.6, 1962, 149, 152-153; Haskins, 1912, passim.

29. 1473-1474 gifts: Swayne, 1896, 14. I have deducted the sale of pardons from the total in the text, as this is considered in the next paragraph. The Easter offerings are described in Swayne, 1896, xiv and Cox, 1913, 53-55. Rebuilding St. Thomas's chancel: V.C.H.6, 1962, 150; Haskins, 1912, 135-136; R.C.H.M. 1980, 26.

30. Fair: Davies, 1968, 55-56; Swayne, 1896, xxxii, 37, 50; Pardons: Swayne, 1896, xv-xvi; Relics: listed in the 1472 inventory – Swayne, 1896, 6; Pew rents: Swayne, 1896, xxi-xxii, 359; Cox, 1913, 67-69; V.C.H.6, 1962, 153.

31. Swayne, 1896, xvi-xvii and passim; Cox, 1913, 62-65 (to whom I owe the 1510 anecdote); Bettey, 1979, 49-52, 58-59 (who observes the connection between church houses and the introduction of pews); Davies, 1968, 48-52 (who notes that Richard Poore, Bishop of Salisbury, condemned ales in 1223). The possibility that the scotale house was in, and gave its name to, Scots Lane (Swayne, 1896, xvi; Cox, 1913, 62) cannot be substantiated; Scots Lane is in all probability derived from John Scot, who lived there in 1269 - R.C.H.M. 1980, xxxvii.

32. Swayne, 1896, page references as follows: grouping of pews, 199; north aisle pews, 179; gallery, 205; removal of font, 217, 219; folding seats, frequent references, e.g. 224; portable seats, frequent references, e.g. 205, 219; pews nailed up, 225; treatment of strangers, xxiii; locks, frequent references, e.g. 206; meeting to change seats, 225; checking on absentees, xxiii.

33. Swayne, 1896, page references as follows: aldermen's seats, frequent references, e.g. 179; quote, 187; scholars, 205, 213; youth, 207; weavers' company, 193, 205; midwives, 204; mistresses, 199; poor seats, 190; children, 325, 338.

34. Swayne, 1896, page references as follows: ten commandments, etc. 202; communion tokens, etc. 184; communion wine, 190. John Strickland: see Fletcher, 1926, 14-16. The extract of a sermon is taken from a volume of his printed sermons in Salisbury Local Studies Library. Entitled 'Mercy rejoycing against judgement' it was preached before the House of Commons in 1645. We quote from p. 19. 'After-clap' (i.e. consequence) has continued in Wiltshire dialect in the form 'atterclaps.'

35. Swanton's pew: Swayne, 1896, 209. January 1630 meeting: Swayne, 1896, 190. Other details from Slack, 1972b. There is a brief biography of Sherfield by Bettey, 1980.

36. Most details from Slack, 1972b. Shortt, 1957, pl. 20 reproduces a window from St. Edmund's similar to that destroyed. Hatcher, 1843, 371-374 is useful.

37. The account of Richard Grafton and James Harwood for 1652-1653 is in Swayne, 1896, 226-228. Richard Grafton left a will (WRO. Sub-Dean's wills 1674) and his place of residence is known from Nevill, 1910, 430. The reorganisation of pews is in Swayne, 1896, 223-224. The average receipts in the five available previous accounts (for 1647-1648, 1648-1649, 1649-1650, 1651-1652, 1652-1653) are as follows: pews: £7.17.0d (20.2%); burials, £5.2.10d (13.1%); quarter-book, £15.18.3d (40.9%); gravestones,

£4.5.0d (10.9%); other, £5.14.7d (14.9%) total, £38.17.7d. 1650 supplementary rate: Swayne, 1896, 221–222.

38. The average expenditure in the same accounts (see note 37 above) is as follows: salaries, £13.6.5d (34.2%); bells, £1.19.3d (5.0%); church fabric, £13.1.5d (33.6%); wine, candles, etc. £3.19.0d (10.2%); other, £6.11.2d (17.0%). Thomas Fort: Swayne, 1896, 208, 214. 1648–1649 work: Swayne, 1896, 220.

39. Swayne, 1896, 227–228.

40. Statistics derived from P.R.O. HO 129/263-264. The churches provided accommodation for 3,558 (Anglican) and 4,491 (Nonconformist), total 8,049 worshippers. The population of the three city parishes and Fisherton Anger (excluding the Close) in 1851 was 11,422: V.C.H.4, 1959, 348, 356. No figures are available for attendance at the Cathedral. Church attendance on 30th March 1851 was as follows: morning – 1,897 plus 513 Sunday scholars (Anglican), 1,221 plus 393 Sunday scholars (Nonconformist), total 4,024; afternoon – 1,677 plus 521 Sunday scholars (Anglican), 595 plus 327 Sunday scholars (Nonconformist), total 3,120; evening – 1,100 (Anglican), 2,018 plus 30 Sunday scholars (Nonconformist), total 3,148.

41. P.R.O. HO 129/263; quotes from Glynne, 1923, 199 and Cossor, 1931, 23–24; other information from V.C.H.6, 1962, 191–192; R.C.H.M. 1980, 41–42; Wheeler, 1889, 66.

42. P.R.O. HO 129/264. Painting: see above and note 50. Other details from Lear, 1910, 121–122 and *Salisbury Journal*, 1st March 1851, p. 2, col. 5. The interior of St. Thomas's Church at this period is depicted in Hatcher, 1843, plate opp. p. 588.

43. Sarum S. Edmund, 1907, 14, 17–18; Lear, 1910, 122; R.C.H.M. 1980, 36–39; P.R.O. HO 129/264. The Roman numerals are M = 1,000, D = 500, C = 100, L = 50, III = 3.

44. Baker, 1906, 5–6. Tatum is described by Foster, 1888, 1390; Lear, 1910, 122; obituary notice in *Salisbury Journal*, 9th April 1870, p. 8, col. 2. See also Alexander, 1976 for a discussion of one of his antecedents. P.R.O. HO 129/264.

45. Abel, 1978, 1–3, 13, V.C.H.6, 1962, 156–159; V.C.H.3, 1956, 101–115 *passim*.

46. P.R.O. HO 129/264; Moore, 1955, 29; *Salisbury Journal*, 24th December, 1853.

47. V.C.H.6, 1962, 159, 192–193; W.R.O. 1150/158 (a statement about the chapel's financial position in 1852); W.R.O. 1150/50 (circuit plans 1844–1870); P.R.O. HO 129/264.

48. The Wesleyan Reform Movement in general is discussed by Wilkinson, 1978, 318–323; and William Griffith is included in Beckerlegge, 1968. The progress of the movement in Salisbury can be traced through documents and newspaper reports, as follows: W.R.O. 1150/487 (tract society minute book 1846–1871); W.R.O. 1150/488 (bazaar committee, 1857–1882); W.R.O. 1150/464 (Milford Street Church trustees meeting minutes, 1851–1857); W.R.O. 1150/475 (Milford Street chapel pew rent book, 1858–1877); *Salisbury Journal*, 1st February, 1851, p. 2. col. 6; 24th May, 1851, p. 2, col. 4; 31st May, 1851, p. 2, col. 4; 9th August, 1851, p. 2, col. 6; 4th October, 1851, p. 3, col. 1; 1st November, 1851, p. 2, col. 7; 20th December, 1851, p. 3, col. 1; 27th December, 1851, p. 2, col. 6. The effect of this secession on the existing Wesleyan congregation may be gauged from the circuit plans, W.R.O. 1150/50 (from which it is apparent that many local preachers rallied to the reform movement); P.R.O. HO 129/264; and W.R.O. 1150/158, a statement of 1852 about the chapel's financial position.

49. Primitive methodism: V.C.H. 1962, 160, 193; P.R.O. HO 129/263; W.R.O. 1150/273; W.R.O. 1150/286. Roman Catholicism: V.C.H.6, 1962, 155–156; V.C.H.3, 1956, 93–94; R.C.H.M. 1980, 44–45; personal communication, Mrs Alexandra Wedgwood,

June 1982; P.R.O. HO 129/264; *Catholic directory*, 1851, p. 67. New Jerusalem Church: V.C.H.6, 1962, 160; P.R.O. HO 129/264.

50. The quotation is from 'Our God, our help in ages past,' by Isaac Watts, 1674-1748.

51. This and the following two paragraphs are based on newspaper accounts of the inquest and trial: *Salisbury Journal*, 8th August 1842, p. 4; 15th August 1842, p. 4; 22nd August 1842, p. 3; *Devizes and Wiltshire Gazette*, 18th August 1842, p. 2; 25th August 1842, p. 3 (two letters about the case). The husband's name is derived from P.R.O. ASSI 25/29/24. Margaret Easter's age is from P.R.O. HO 27/68; it is also given, with other details, by Dowding, 1855, sv. 1842. The house is possibly 68 St. Ann Street, the kitchen of which adjoined Pelican Place (R.C.H.M. 1980, 123 (no. 289)) and what appears to be a drain leading away from a privy in the yard is marked on Kingdon and Shearm's map of 1854.

52. See above, note 51. The newspaper reports of the trial describe the tramp as Philip Happy, but the indictment, P.R.O. ASSI 25/29/24, is endorsed William Happy, and this is also the name given at the inquest.

53. Nineteenth-century statistics derived from tables in Dowding, 1855. 1249 crimes: Meekings, 1961, 254-258. 1293 fight: Pugh, 1978, 77 (no. 291). Ann Bodenham: Hatcher, 1843, 418-419.

54. Richard Stevenson: Haskins, 1912, 175. Thomas de Colne: Jones, 1884, vol. 2, 23-24.

55. Hatcher, 1843, 253, 577; V.C.H.6, 1962, 113.

56. W.R.O. G23/1/85 sv. 1737-1738; V.C.H.6, 1962, 110.

57. Graham, 1886, 1-12, 70-80, 222-223.

58. General accounts in V.C.H.5, 1957, 289; V.C.H. 6, 1962, 115. Details from WRO. G23/111/1, *passim*.

59. *Salisbury Journal*, 8th August 1842, p. 4; 15th August 1842, p. 4.

60. I know of no satisfactory brief account of the administration of justice in Wiltshire. I have used V.C.H.5, 1957, *passim*; also Rathbone, 1951, 66; Wiltshire County Council, 1959, ix-xii; Fowle, 1955, vii-lxv. On Devizes as an assize town see V.C.H.10, 1975, 252.

61. This and subsequent paragraphs are derived from P.R.O. ASSI 21/59; *Devizes and Wiltshire Gazette*, 18th August 1842, p. 2.

62. See previous note. The precise wording of the indictment is found in P.R.O. ASSI 25/29/24.

63. See above, note 61. Details also from correspondence printed in *Devizes and Wiltshire Gazette*, 25th August 1842, p. 3.

64. Quotations and most details from *Devizes and Wiltshire Gazette*, 18th August 1842, p. 2. According to the second letter, from 'A lover of justice,' in *Devizes and Wiltshire Gazette*, 25th August 1842, p. 3, the verdict of the jury excited considerable surprise in the court.

65. Margaret may not have been returned to Fisherton immediately, even though her return was decreed by the judge in the passage quoted above. Correspondence in P.R.O. HO 13/81, p. 63 implies that on the 22nd August she was still held in Devizes (or at least that the Secretary of State believed that she was still there). But a note in the *Salisbury Journal*, 5th September 1842, p. 4, makes it clear that she had returned to Fisherton by 3rd September. Old Sarum gaol: V.C.H.5, 1957, 21-22; V.C.H.6, 1962, 182. City gaol, 1246: V.C.H.6, 1962, 95-96, derived from Meekings, 1961, 257 (no. 564). Bishop's letter: Jackson, 1866, 83-84. Old Fisherton gaol: R.C.H.M. 1980, 157 (no. 476); Jackson, 1866, 84-87.

66. W.R.O. A4/2/1/1.

67. Hatcher, 1843, 603; Dowding, 1855, tables of rations (note that the prison regime was more indulgent between 1823 and 1835 than it became thereafter); V.C.H.5, 1957, 239-240; W.R.O. A4/2/7/1.

68. Fisherton gallows: V.C.H.6, 1962, 183. Executions on the Green Croft: Haskins, 1927, 61. Buckingham's execution: Wheeler, 1889, 12. Stourton's execution: Wheeler, 1889, 14 (Hatcher, 1843, 273, wrongly gives the date as 1556). Henry Wynn's execution: *Devizes and Wiltshire Gazette*, 17th March 1836, p. 3; Dowding, 1855, sv. 1836.

69. Dowding, 1855, sv. 1826.

70. *Devizes and Wiltshire Gazette*, 25th August 1842, p. 3 (editorial and letters). The instigator of the memorial seems to have been a Mr Starky (*Salisbury Journal*, 12th September 1842, p. 3) presumably John E. A. Starky, of Spye Park, Bromham, who died in 1843 (V.C.H.7, 1953, 181, 186), and who was a member of the grand jury at the assize in question (*Devizes and Wiltshire Gazette*, 18th August 1842, p. 2). The first memorial was forwarded to the Home Office by Messrs Fennell and Kelly, of Bedford Row, London (P.R.O. HO 13/81, p. 63), but letters were also sent in reply to petitions from T. H. S. Sotheron of Bowden Park, Lacock, and T. G. Thorpe, of Devizes (P.R.O. HO 13/81 pp. 86, 100, 114). Sotheron, 1801-1876, was M.P. for Devizes from 1835-1844: see his obituary in *Wiltshire Archaeological Magazine*, vol. 16, 1876, 340-343. The sequence of events may be reconstructed from the Home Office letters quoted above (also P.R.O. HO 13/81, pp. 81, 108) and from newspaper accounts quoted above (also *Salisbury Journal*, 29th August 1842, p. 4; 5th September 1842, p. 4; 19th September 1842, p. 4).

71. Dowding, 1855, sv. 1842.

72. Mr. Donald Dickinson, who died in January 1981. He came to work in Salisbury in 1929.

73. Trinity Hospital was entirely rebuilt in 1702: R.C.H.M., 1980, 56-57 (no. 27). St. Nicholas's Hospital: the account in V.C.H.3, 1956, 343-356 may be supplemented by Wordsworth, 1902, *passim* (the quotation is translated from p. 24); Endowed Charities, 1907, 64-68; and R.C.H.M., 1980, 54-56 (no. 26).

74. V.C.H.3, 1956, 357-361; Baker, 1910, *passim*, especially 378-379, 384, 392.

75. Leper hospitals: V.C.H.5, 1957, 318-319; V.C.H.3, 1956, 361-362; Hatcher, 1843, 92, 335. Plague: 1477: Hatcher, 1843, 198; 1579: *ibid.* 288-289; 1604: *ibid.* 309-311; 1627: *ibid.* 359-363; 1643: *ibid.* 393-394; 1665: *ibid.* 456; 1666: *ibid.* 458. The demographic effects of plague are discussed above, in chapter two. 1625 precautions: Hatcher, 1843, 357-358. Besides the 1579 change of venue, the Council House was used in 1604 and the Close in 1666. Tailors' guild: Haskins, 1912, 180; Slack, 1975, 123. George Inn: Haskins, 1912, 295. Fumigation: Swayne, 1896, xx. St. Thomas's Churchyard: *ibid.* 324. Plague burial grounds: Haskins, 1927, 61; Swayne, 1896, 324.

76. 1579: Hatcher, 1843, 288-289; 1627: Slack, 1975, 121-122, 125-126.

77. Barber surgeons and apothecaries were formed into trade companies: see Haskins, 1912, 50-54, 363-369. Thomas Naish: Slatter, 1965, 79. Seth Ward: Pope, 1697, 66; H.M.C.1907, 10; W.R.O. Diocesan Records: Bishop: Administration 24 (Seth Ward's *Liber notitiae*), f. 182 and 182 verso.

78. Pope, 1697, 98-108; Hatcher, 1843, 465-467; James, 1926; Snyder, 1965.

79. Smallpox and the inoculation controversy: V.C.H.6, 1962, 112; V.C.H.5, 1957, 322. Infirmary: Haskins, 1922, 2-7; Shemilt, 1967, 13-20. The identification of 'Mr. Wood of Bath' is made by R.C.H.M. 1980, 52.

80. Haskins, 1922, 4-8; Shemilt, 1967, *passim*. Quotation from Hudson, 1978, 16. The description of the building is based on a plan of 1819 reproduced in R.C.H.M. 1980, 53. John Tatum's cure: Gubbin and Longridge, 1967, 49; see also Alexander, 1976.

81. Haskins, 1922, 3-15 *passim* (quote from p. 3); Shemilt, 1967, 25-31. Quotation from Hudson, 1978, 16.

82. Smith, 1982, prologue has 'after 1754' as the date of founding of Laverstock House; V.C.H.5, 1957, 329 suggests the 1760s. On Laverstock House in general see Parry-Jones, 1972, 116-119, and on Fisherton House see Smith, 1982 *passim*. Statistics from Parry-Jones, 1972, 42-43.

83. Categories of lunatics: Parry-Jones, 1972, 50-70. Quote from Anon, 1860, 59. Laverstock House: V.C.H.5, 1957, 329; Parry-Jones, 1972, 116. County asylum: V.C.H.5, 1957, 331. Criminal lunatics at Fisherton: Parry-Jones, 1972, 65-66; Smith, 1982, *passim*.

84. Pamphlets: Anon, 1850 (quote from pp. 12-13); Anon, 1860, 57-64. Lunacy Commissioners' reports: Parry-Jones, 1972, 255, 118; Smith, 1982, 35-36. Rotatory chair: Parry-Jones, 1972, 198; Smith, 1982, 15. Treatment: Smith, 1982, 63, 15-17. Finch family: *ibid.* 1-9; Dr. Lush: *ibid.* 5-7; W. C. Finch's report: *ibid.* 44.

85. Cholera: V.C.H.5, 1957, 325-326; Rammell, 1851, 116-117. Isolation hospital (this is the smallpox hospital described above): Rammell, 1851, 93-94. Cholera-ridden cottages: Rammell, 1851, 98-99. This court, Smith's Cottages, Castle Street, belonged to Alderman W. Smith, one of the directors of highways and a leading opponent of drainage improvements: P.R.O. MH 13, 160, letter 2nd May 1852.

86. In general: Rammell, 1851, 68-87 *passim*; Middleton, 1864, 15-17. Mineral spring: Middleton, *loc. cit.* At times the water in the street channels was clean enough to support fish. Two weeks before the inquiry was held one of its opponents, R. Farrant, sent by rail to the Chairman of the Board of Health a trout caught in one of the channels: P.R.O. MH 13, 160, letter 29th May 1851. Similar catches were reported in the *Salisbury Journal*, 17th May 1851, p. 2, col. 3 and 15th January 1853, p. 2, col. 7.

87. 1850 meeting: W.R.O. G23/1/91; Middleton, 1852, 14-15; Rammell, 1851, 72-76. Catherine Street: W.R.O. G23/1/91, 21st February, 1851; 21st March, 1851; 4th April, 1851. Middleton's opposition: P.R.O. MH 13, 160, letters 20th March 1851; 3rd April 1851; 14th May, 1851 etc.; Middleton, 1864, 14. Barrel drains: W.R.O. G23/1/91, 9th May 1851; Rammell, 1851, 77-81 (including quotes).

88. Rammell, 1851, 81-84 (barrel drains and pumps); 8, 93-100 (tours of inspection - quote from p. 94).

89. V.C.H.6, 1962, 114; P.R.O. MH 13, 160, letters 2nd February, 1852.

90. Rammell, 1851, 110-114.

91. Middleton, 1864, 15; Middleton, 1852, *passim* (quote from pp. 10-11). Memorials: P.R.O. MH 13, 160, 31st January 1852, 5th August 1852. Drainage works: V.C.H.6, 1962, 114; Middleton, 1864, 17-20. Benefits: *ibid.* 20-26. Quote: Middleton, 1868, 16.

92. V.C.H.5, 1957, 333-342; V.C.H.6, 1962, 117, 183-184; Salisbury 200, 1967, *passim*; Smith, 1982, *passim*.

93. Every inventory attached to probate records proved in the court of the Sub-Dean of Sarum between 1696 and 1715 inclusive (Wiltshire Record Office) has been used in this analysis, a total of 39, viz: (in chronological order) 1696. 16: Tusker; 1696. 15: Staples; 1696. 12: Pasby; 1696. 10: Snooke; 1697. 6: Swayne; 1697. 2: Viner; 1697. 1: Ray; 1698. 9: Quaile; 1698. 8: Mills; 1699. 7: Mack; 1699. 1: Millett; 1700. 5: Greene; 1700. 2: Brune; 1700. 1: Norris; 1701. 9: Peirce; 1701. 3: Bell; 1702. 9: Seale; 1702. 5: Merritt; 1702. 13: Weste; 1703. 9: Eyers; 1704. 15: Strong; 1704. 14: Cole; 1706. 14:

Clements; 1706. 13: Godfrey; 1709. 3: Loversage; 1709. 12: Munday; 1709. 2: Brune; 1710. 5: Austin; 1710. 3: Jones; 1711. 11: Hellier; 1712. 5: Prince; 1713. 9: Frowde; 1714. 7: Keile; 1714. 6: Zelle; 1714. 10: Bishop; 1715. 10: Tinham; 1715. 6: Case; 1715. 8: Holmes; 1715. 9: Nutbeam. However 1702. 9: Seale has been ignored for some purposes because it describes the contents of an inn rather than a private house. Few probate inventories survive after 1715. Salisbury wills proved in the Consistory Court of Sarum during the period have not been included in this analysis.

94. All amounts have been rounded up or down to the nearest pound. For reasons which are obscure the inventory of John Weste (1702. 13) carries vastly inflated prices (the timber and firewood left in the gardens were valued at over £400) and so I have had to omit him from most of my calculations, although I include him among the elite ten as debts owing to him and ready money, which are presumably genuine, place him indisputably in this bracket. The reader should be warned that all calculations in this paragraph rely ultimately on the subjective valuations of the persons drawing up the inventories and so must remain approximate.

95. Eleven out of 39 inventories are not described room-by-room and I have omitted also 1702. 9 (Seale) which is an inn. In counting the number of rooms I have excluded cellars, washhouses, closets, outhouses, sheds, stables, passages and stairs.

96. Cook- 1709. 12. Munday; butcher- 1709. 2: Brune; currier- 1709. 3: Loversage; saddler- 1700. 1: Norris; milliner- 1706. 13: Godfrey, brazier- 1699. 7; Mack; plateworker- 1702. 13: Weste; weavers- 1713. 9: Frowde; 1714. 7: Keile; clothworker- 1715. 10: Tinham.

97. Statistics used in this paragraph are based on furniture in all rooms other than shops, workshops and outbuildings, in 35 inventories. Three inventories are too brief to describe furniture and the inn (1702. 9: Seale) is also omitted.

98. Godfrey: 1706. 13; Greene: 1700. 5.

99. Because a number of inventories give only very vague descriptions of beds this study is drawn from a sample of 27 out of the 39. For details of individual inventories see above, note 93.

100. See Lindsay, 1964 and Roberts, 1981 for discussions of the change from wood- to coal-burning fires. Coal-carriers in Salisbury have been discussed above in chapter 3. Mr Mintorne features in Simon Forman's autobiography, and is cited in an anonymous note in *Wiltshire Archaeological Magazine*, vol. 50, 1942-1944, 102. The word firepan has two meanings, a portable grate (*Shorter Oxford English dictionary*) and a fire shovel (*English dialect dictionary*). It is probably employed in both senses in the inventories; when it is coupled with tongs it is presumably intended to convey the second meaning.

101. The items described in this paragraph all occur in the sample of probate inventories. The following are the total numbers of each: gridiron, 11; frying-pan, 10; skillet, 51 plus; pot, 34 plus; hook, 32; hanger, 7; cottrells, 28 pairs; kettle, 65 plus; spit, 39; andirons, 39 pairs; jack, 13; chain, 4; weight, 5; dripping pan, 9; ladle, 14; skimmer, 17; chafing-dish, 11; saucepan, 5; mortar, 5; colander 3; coffee pot, 4. For their use see Lindsay, 1964 and Roberts, 1981.

102. This and the succeeding paragraphs are based largely on a reading of the 1871 census enumerators' returns, used in conjunction with the first edition Ordnance Survey 1:500 sheets of 1879 (Figure 27). So far as I can tell there has been no significant change in the house numbering (except in St. John Street and 5 St. Ann Street) between 1871 and the present. Architectural details are derived from R.C.H.M. 1980, 107-111, 116-119.

103. I have tried to follow Constable's guidelines (Constable, 1977, 11-25) wherever practicable so that my figures may be compared with his 10% sample of Salisbury as a whole. I have therefore omitted from my figure of 109 families three 'secondary house-

holds.' 210 male, 274 female, 484 total in 109 households = 4.4 (1.9 male, 2.5 female) per household. Size of household (with Constable's percentage for his 10% sample in brackets): 1: 7 = 6% (6%); 2: 21 = 19% (14%); 3: 15 = 14% (19%); 4: 15 = 14% (17%) 5: 21 = 19% (10%) 6: 14 = 13% (11%); 7: 4 = 4% (8%); 8 and over: 12 = 11% (12%). 187 children of householders (not necessarily infants) lived at home (38.6%). Number of householder's and/or wife's children (Constable's percentage in brackets): 0: 34 = 31% (32%); 1: 26 = 24% (22%); 2: 19 = 17% (13%); 3: 13 = 12% (10%); 4: 7 = 6% (7%); 5 and over: 10 = 9% (16%). Children of school age: Catherine Street: 12 = 18%; Brown Street: 31 = 47%; Ivy Street: 13 = 20%; elsewhere: 10 = 15%; total 66.

104. Handicaps were separately enumerated, and five are identified in our sample: a deaf male aged 61; a female blind from birth aged 40; a blind female aged 85; a blind male aged 83; a female deaf and dumb from birth aged 51. Six out of twelve single-parent families (with children under 20) lived in Brown Street. Twelve illegitimate children are recorded, mostly in Brown Street; none is admitted in Catherine Street.

105. Figures for various principal occupations are as follows (from a total of 184): building trades, 8; manufactures- woodworking, 8; carriages, 4; cloth, 27; food, 6; jewellery, cutlery, etc, 5; printing, 5; leather, 8; dealing- dress, 11; food and drink, 26; transport, 16; domestic service, 31; other service, 17.

106. It is not the case that the wealthier Catherine Street tradesmen were much more permanent than the Brown Street labourers. Fourteen premises changed hands and twelve remained in the same occupancy between 1861 and 1871. The best example of continuity in fact is in Brown Street where only one of seven properties between numbers 38 and 54 changed hands.

107. The history of Antelope Square is discussed in R.C.H.M. 1980, 108 (208).

108. The Barracks, and its successor, Cromwell Place, are described in R.C.H.M. 1980, 118 (258).

109. Most of the casualties in this area occurred ca. 1967: R.C.H.M. 1980, 111 (223, 224). W. A. Wheeler wrote *Sarum chronology* and *Supplemental Sarum chronology*, and contributed historical articles to the *Salisbury Journal*. The Journal offices are opposite the site of his house, and it is likely that his employment as an overseer printer was with that newspaper.

110. WRO. 1900: parish records 36 (1574) and 43 (1600); Register of electors, 1981–1982 Salisbury constituency, St. Martin nos. 1, 2 and 3. If 227, the 1600 total, is multiplied by 1.6 to allow for children, the resulting figure of 363 is 6% of 6050 and 5% of 7260. In calculating the 1871 totals I have included everyone over 16, but have excluded the three hotels – the Red Lion, the White Hart and the Waggon and Horses. The 1574 easter book has a heading, 'Brown Street' which must include only the parts of Brown Street which concern us (the remainder lying in other parishes), but Milford Street and Ivy Street are probably included with New Street and the Town Ditch and so cannot be separately identified. The 1600 Easter book describes the remainder of

TABLE: ADULTS IN ANTELOPE AND WHITE HART CHEQUERS 1574-1981

| | White Hart | | | | | Catherine Street | | | | | Antelope (rest) | | | | | Totals | | | | |
	M	F	S	T	H	M	F	S	T	H	M	F	S	T	H	M	F	S	T	H
1574	28	38	3	69	32	27	36	12	75	32	incomplete					incomplete				
1600	32	33	13	78	33	29	34	19	82	34	27	34	6	67	35	88	101	38	227	102
1871	36	64	1	101	43	45	53	25	123	35	35	40	1	76	31	116	157	27	300	109
1981	21	26	–	47	20	8	11	–	19	12	6	6	–	12	6	35	43	–	78	38

M (Male) F (Female) S (Servants) T (Total) H (Houses)

Antelope chequer as 'The Blewe lyon checker,' which must be derived from an earlier name for the Queen's Arms Inn: WRO. 1075/90 (259). NOTE: The WRO. numbers of the easter books are likely to be changed during 1983.

111. The main sources used to supplement the easter books have been WRO. 1900/5 (St. Thomas's parish registers), WRO. G23/1/264 (the catalogue of free citizens of 1612), and the index of Sub-Dean's wills in the Wiltshire Record Office. Despite an exhaustive search the evidence remains too fragmentary to draw any but the most tentative conclusions. Madalen Lewes is in Slack, 1975, 19. Information about the Talbot family is culled from the sources described above.

112. Deeds: WRO, 897/1. Architectural description, date, merchant's mark and illustration of the first-floor fireplace are all in R.C.H.M. 1980, 63–64 and plate 90. Earlier occupation along Minster Street may be deduced from the 1399 ward lists (see appendix one), read in conjunction with the city domesday books and other contemporary sources. See also Reeves and Bonney, 1982. Assuming that the ward lists were compiled systematically in house-by-house order we know that numbers 4 (John Spencer); 8 (John Harnham); and 18 (John Swyft), all lived in Minster Street (see Davies, 1908, 224; WRO. G23/1/213, f. 3v; and WRO. G23/1/213, f. 3, 3v respectively) and so we may assume that the street in 1399 contained at least fifteen properties. William Eaton is listed in Easter books (WRO. 1900) from 1574 (36) to 1596 (42). He is not in the book for 1600 (43). He served as a St. Thomas's churchwarden in 1597/1598 (Swayne, 1896, 302), and he appears in an undated Easter book (48) which may probably be dated to 1599 (it omits for the first time his next-door neighbour, Henry Hammond senior, who died in August 1598: WRO. 1900/5). He probably died, therefore, between Easter 1599 and Easter 1600, but this cannot be checked from St. Thomas's burial register as there is a lacuna at this point. Toby Halle and his wife appear in the Easter books for 1600 (43) and 1602 (45). The 1612 inventory is among the deeds. Robert Jole is described in Haskins, 1912, 319–323, whence the quotations are taken. Although during his mayoralty he was regarded as a brewer, his occupation in these deeds and in the register of free citizens, also of 1612 (WRO. G23/1/264) is given as tanner. But there are unlikely to have been two Robert Joles, and no brewer of that name is listed in WRO. G23/1/264.

113. This narrative is deduced from deeds in WRO. 897/1; WRO. Sub-Dean of Sarum's wills 1663. 9: Mason (the inventory is in fact dated September 1662); 1687. 11: Mason; and 1691. 8: Carter. I may be found to have made a few unwarranted assumptions but I am confident that the general drift is correct.

114. Sources as in the previous note; also WRO. Sub-Dean of Sarum's wills, 1742. 11: Tinham.

115. Deeds: WRO. 897/1; Fauconer pedigree: Maskelyne, 1896–1898. The names of tenants may be discovered from St. Thomas's parish rate books, used in conjunction with references in the deeds, but without their trades the names are not of particular interest. Solomon Sweetapple appears in the 1816 rate book, but is replaced by Joseph Sweetapple in the 1817 rate book. William Henry Coates is listed as a surgeon in directories, e.g. Pigot 1822; his will (among the deeds) was made in 1848, but he was still alive in 1852 or shortly before, as he appears in Hunt's directory of 1852, and the documents surrounding the 1853 sale give the impression that he had recently died.

116. Deeds: WRO. 897/1. Occupants: directories and electoral rolls, various dates; for details of events during the present century I am indebted to Mr Stanley Holmes, the present occupier.

Bibliography

Note: Apart from recognised abbreviations for state papers and other national sources, the only terms abbreviated in the notes which are not explained in the bibliography are P.R.O. for Public Record Office and W.R.O. for Wiltshire Record Office. In the bibliography *W.A.M.* is used to abbreviate *Wiltshire Archaeological and Natural History Magazine*.

Abel, George. 1978. *A history of the Presbyterian Congregational United Reformed Church in Salisbury, 1662–1978*. Salisbury: Salisbury United Reformed Church.

Addison, William. 1953. *English fairs and markets*. London: Batsford.

Akerman, John Y. 1857. 'On pilgrims signs found in Salisbury.' *W.A.M.* 3, 94–97.

Alcock, Leslie. 1972. *'By South Cadbury is that Camelot. . .' : the excavation of Cadbury Castle, 1966–1970*. London: Thames and Hudson.

Alexander, B. W. 1976. 'John Tatum, M.D. (1724–1783) and his near medical relations.' *Salisbury Medical Bulletin*. 28, 91–95.

Algar, David J. 1973. 'Wiltshire archaeological register for 1972: medieval: Salisbury.' *W.A.M.* 68, 137.

Anderson, Mary D. 1971. *History and imagery in British churches*. London: John Murray.

Anon, 1717. *The proceedings in the Star-Chamber, against Henry Sherfield, Esq . . . for breaking a glass window in the Church of St. Edmonds in the said city. . . 1632*. London: S. Noble.

Anon, 1774. *The Salisbury guide; giving an account of the antiquities of Old Sarum, and of the ancient and present state of the city of New Sarum. . .* 3rd ed. Salisbury: Easton.

Anon, 1825. *The Salisbury guide comprising the history and antiquities of Old Sarum, the origin and present state of New Sarum. . .* 30th ed. Salisbury: Easton.

Anon, 1841. *The late flood: an account of the disastrous inundation. . . Saturday, January 16, 1841 to which is added a true relation. . .* Salisbury: Brodie.

Anon, 1850. *A visit to the Fisherton House Asylum, near Salisbury, Wilts, under the superintendence of W. C. Finch, M.D. August 21, 1850, by a London reporter*. London: Harding (printer).

Anon, 1860. *Our holiday at Laverstock House Asylum; how we visited Stonehenge and what we learned there*. London: John Churchill.

Anon, 1931. 'Old Sarum Parliamentary tree.' *W.A.M.* 45, 504.

Aston, Michael and Bond, James. 1976. *The landscape of towns*. London: Dent.

Atkinson, Donald R. 1970. 'Clay tobacco pipes and pipemakers of Salisbury, Wiltshire.' *W.A.M.* 65, 177–189.

Atkinson, Donald R. 1972. 'Further notes on clay tobacco pipes and pipemakers from the Marlborough and Salisbury districts.' *W.A.M.* 67, 149–156.

Atkinson, Donald R. 1980. 'More Wiltshire clay tobacco pipe varieties.' *W.A.M.* 72/73, 67–74.

Aubrey, John, 1847. *The natural history of Wiltshire*; by John Aubrey, edited, and elucidated by notes, by John Britton. London: Wiltshire Topographical Society.

✓ Aubrey, John. 1972. *Aubrey's brief lives*; edited with the original manuscripts and with an introduction by Oliver Lawson Dick. Harmondsworth: Penguin.

Ayto, Eric G. 1979. *Clay tobacco pipes*. Princes Risborough: Shire.

Backinsell, William G. C. 1977 (a). *The medieval clock in Salisbury Cathedral.* Salisbury: South Wiltshire Industrial Archaeology Society.

Backinsell, William G. C. 1977 (b). *The Salisbury Railway and Market House Company.* Salisbury: South Wiltshire Industrial Archaeology Society.

Baker, Thomas H. 1906. *Notes on St. Martin's Church and parish.* Salisbury: Brown.

Baker, Thomas H. 1909. 'Notes on some Wiltshire merchants' marks.' *W.A.M.* 36, 324–328.

Baker, Thomas H. 1910. 'The Trinity Hospital, Salisbury.' *W.A.M.* 36, 376–412.

Barley, Maurice W. (ed.). 1976. *The plans and topography of medieval towns in England and Wales.* London: Council for British Archaeology.

Barton, Gwendolen. 1977. 'Salisbury Infirmary: an 18th century foundation.' *Hatcher Review.* 3, 16–24.

Bavin, John. 1976. *Heart of the city: the story of Salisbury Playhouse.* Salisbury: Salisbury Playhouse.

Beckerlegge, Oliver A. 1968. *United Methodist ministers and their circuits...* London: Epworth Press.

Beresford, Maurice W. 1959. 'The six new towns of the Bishops of Winchester, 1200–1255.' *Medieval Archaeology.* 3, 187–215.

Beresford, Maurice W. 1967. *New towns of the middle ages: town plantation in England, Wales and Gascony.* London: Lutterworth Press.

Bettey, Joseph H. 1979. *Church and community: the parish church in English life.* Bradford-on-Avon: Moonraker Press.

Bettey, Joseph H. 1980. 'Henry Sherfield of Salisbury: a seventeenth century puritan, lawyer and agricultural innovator.' *Hatcher Review.* 9, 20–25.

Biddiscombe, Brian. 1974, 1975. 'How the green buses got to Salisbury.' *Omnibus Magazine.* 293, 135–136; 294, 1–4.

Blome, Richard. 1673. *Britannia: or a geographical description of the kingdoms of England, Scotland and Ireland.* London: Roycroft.

Bonney, Desmond J. 1969. 'Two tenth-century Wiltshire charters concerning lands at Avon and at Collingbourne.' *W.A.M.* 64, 56–64.

Bonney, Desmond J. 1972. 'Early boundaries in Wessex.' *In:* Fowler, Peter J. *Archaeology and the landscape: essays for L. V. Grinsell.* London: John Baker. 168–186.

Bonney, Helen M. 1964. '"Balle's Place," Salisbury: a 14th-century merchant's house.' *W.A.M.* 59, 155–167.

Bradbeer, Firmin S. 1909. *The Haunch of Venison Salisbury: a short description.* Salisbury: Haunch of Venison.

Bradley, Richard. 1978. *The prehistoric settlement of Britain.* London: Routledge and Kegan Paul.

Braun, Hugh. 1960. 'The earthworks of Old Sarum.' *W.A.M.* 57, 406–407.

Braun, Hugh. 1962. 'The Salisbury Canal: a Georgian misadventure.' *W.A.M.* 58, 171–180.

Brentnall, Harold C. 1947. 'A Longford manuscript.' *W.A.M.* 52, 1–56.

Bridbury, Anthony R. 1975. *Economic growth: England in the later middle ages.* 2nd ed. Hassocks: Harvester Press.

Bridbury, Anthony R. 1981. 'English provincial towns in the later middle ages.' *Economic History Review,* 2nd series. 34, 1–24.

Bridbury, Anthony R. 1982. *Medieval English clothmaking: an economic survey.* London: Heinemann.

Britton, John. 1847. *Memoirs of the life, writings and character of Henry Hatcher...* London: Britton.

Brooke, Christopher N. L. 1977. 'The medieval town as an ecclesiastical centre: general survey.' *In:* Barley, Maurice W. (ed.) *European towns: their archaeology and early history.* London: Council for British Archaeology. 459–474.

Brooks, Nicholas. 1965. 'The unidentified forts of the Burghal Hidage.' *Medieval Archaeology.* 8, 74–90.

Brown, Reginald A. *et al.* 1963. *The history of the king's works.* vols. 1-2. London: H.M.S.O.

Bunyard, Barbara D. M. 1941. *The brokage book of Southampton, from 1439-40.* vol. 1. Southampton: Southampton Record Society.

Burnett, David. 1978. *Salisbury: the history of an English cathedral city.* Tisbury: Compton Press.

Butler, Lawrence. 1976. 'The evolution of towns: planted towns after 1066.' *In*: Barley, Maurice W. (ed.) *The plans and topography of medieval towns in England and Wales.* London: Council for British Archaeology.

Byng, John. 1934. *The Torrington diaries.* vol. 1. London: Eyre and Spottiswoode.

Camden, William. 1695. *Camden's Britannia newly translated into English: with large additions and improvements.* Published by Edmund Gibson. London: Swalle.

Carrington, Frederick A. 1887. 'Notes on the manor of Aldbourne.' *W.A.M.* 23, 254-267.

Carus-Wilson, Eleanora M. 1954. *Medieval merchant ventures.* London: Methuen.

Chalklin, Christopher W. 1974. *The provincial towns of Georgian England: a study of the building process, 1740-1820.* London: Arnold.

Chandler, John H. 1979. *The Amesbury Turnpike Trust.* Salisbury: South Wiltshire Industrial Archaeology Society.

Chandler, John H. 1980. *Stagecoach operation through Wiltshire.* Salisbury: South Wiltshire Industrial Archaeology Society.

Chandler, John H. and Goodhugh, Peter S. 1979. *Amesbury: history and description of a south Wiltshire town.* Amesbury: Amesbury Society.

Chartres, John A. 1973. 'The marketing of agricultural produce in metropolitan western England in the late seventeenth and eighteenth centuries.' *In*: Havinden, Michael (ed.) *Husbandry and marketing in the South-West, 1500-1800.* Exeter: University of Exeter.

Chevallier, Raymond. 1976. *Roman roads.* London: Batsford.

Chibnall, Marjorie. 1956. *John of Salisbury's memoirs of the papal court.* London: Nelson.

Child, Miss F. 1844. *The spinster at home in the Close of Salisbury: no fable, together with tales and ballads.* Salisbury: Brodie.

Chinnery, Victor. 1979. *Oak furniture: the British tradition: a history of early furniture in the British Isles and New England.* Woodbridge: Antique Collectors' Club.

Chinnery, Victor. 1981. 'Some notes on the members and products of the Salisbury Joiners' Company in the early seventeenth century.' *Hatcher Review.* 2 (11), 32-35.

Clanchy, M. T. 1971. *Civil pleas of the Wiltshire eyre, 1249.* Devizes: Wiltshire Record Society.

Clark, Peter and Slack, Paul A. 1976. *English towns in transition, 1500-1700.* London: Oxford University Press.

Clutterbuck, Robert H. 1897. 'The fraternities of Sarum.' *W.A.M.* 29, 137-146.

Cobbold, Debbie. 1980. A survey of Salisbury railways and market house. B.A. thesis, University of Southampton.

Coleman, Olive. 1960, 1961. *The brokage book of Southampton, 1443-1444.* 2 vols. Southampton: University of Southampton.

Coleman, Olive. 1963. 'Trade and prosperity in the fifteenth century: some aspects of the trade of Southampton.' *Economic History Review.* 2nd series. 16, 9-22.

Collier, B. F. 1908. 'John Halle, merchant and mayor of Salisbury.' *Journal of the British Archaeological Association.* 2nd series. 14, 221-242.

Cologne, Celia and Morrison, Jean. 1981. *Wiltshire folk songs.* Devizes: Wiltshire Folk Life Society.

Constable, Derek. 1977. *Household structure in three English market towns, 1851-1871.* Reading: University of Reading.

Conyers, Angela. 1973. *Wiltshire extents for debts: Edward I - Elizabeth I.* Devizes: Wiltshire Record Society.

Cossor, W. E. and Cossor, Robert H. 1931. Historical notes relating to St. Clement's and St. Paul's Churches [Fisherton Anger]. Unpublished manuscript in Salisbury Local Studies Library.

Cowan, Michael. 1981. 'A local battle in A.D. 552.' *Hatcher Review*. 2 (11), 3-11.

Cox, John C. 1913. *Churchwardens' accounts from the fourteenth century to the close of the seventeenth century*. London: Methuen.

Cox, Thomas. 1731. *Magna Britannia et Hibernia, antiqua et nova*. vol. 6. London: Matt.

Crawford, Osbert G. S. 1928. 'Our debt to Rome?' *Antiquity*. 2, 173-188.

Crawford, Osbert G. S. 1931. 'Cerdic and the Cloven Way.' *Antiquity*. 5, 441-458.

Crino, A. M. 1968. *Un principe di Toscana in Inghilterra e in Irlanda nel 1669*. Rome: Temi e Testi.

Cross, Donald A. E. 1970 (a). 'The Salisbury Avon Navigation.' *W.A.M.* 65, 172-176.

Cross, Donald A. E. 1970 (b). 'The Salisbury Avon Navigation.' *Industrial Archaeology*. 7, 121-130.

Crummy, Philip. 1979. 'The system of measurement used in town planning from the ninth to the thirteenth centuries.' *In*: Hawkes, Sonia C. *et al.* (ed.). *Anglo-Saxon studies in archaeology and history, I*. Oxford: British Archaeological Reports. 149-164.

Cunliffe, Barry W. 1978. *Iron age communities in Britain*. 2nd ed. London: Routledge and Kegan Paul.

Curry, Jennifer. *et al.* (ed.) 1981. *Wiltshire lives*. Salisbury: St. Edmund's Arts Centre.

Dale, Christabel. 1961. *Wiltshire apprentices and their masters, 1710-1760*. Devizes: Wiltshire Archaeological and Natural History Society, Records Branch.

Davies, J. S. 1908. *The Tropenell cartulary, being the contents of an old Wiltshire muniment chest*. 2 vols. Devizes: Wiltshire Archaeological and Natural History Society.

Davies, John G. 1968. *The secular use of church buildings*. London: S.C.M. Press.

Deacon, Lois. 1975. *Thomas Hardy and the Salisbury see*. Guernsey: Toucan Press.

Devenish, Dorothy. 1948. *A Wiltshire home: a study of Little Durnford*. London: Batsford.

Dolley, Reginald H. M. 1954. 'The sack of Wilton in 1003 and the chronology of the "long cross" and "helmet" types of Aethelraed II.' *Nordisk Numismatisk Unions Medlensblad*. May, 1954, 152-156.

Douglas, Mary A. and Ash, Cecily R. 1928. *The Godolphin School, 1726-1926*. London: Longmans, Green.

Dowding, William. 1855. *County of Wilts. Fisherton Gaol. Statistics of crime from 1801 to 1850 compiled by the Governor of the County Gaol*. Salisbury: Blake.

Drinkwater, Norman and Mercer, Eric. 1964. 'The Blue Boar Inn, Salisbury: an existing 15th-century building and the contract for its erection.' *Archaeological Journal*. 120, 236-241.

Dugdale, James. 1819. *The new British traveller, or, modern panorama of England and Wales...* 4 vols. London.

Duke, Edward. 1837. *Prolusiones historicae; or, essays illustrative of the Halle of John Halle, citizen and merchant, of Salisbury...* vol. 1 [all published]. Salisbury: Brodie.

Dyer, Alan D. 1979. 'The market towns of southern England, 1500-1700.' *Southern History*. 1, 123-134.

Dyer, James, 1981. *Hillforts of England and Wales*. Princes Risborough: Shire.

Dyos, Harold J. and Aldcroft, Derek H. 1974. *British transport: an economic survey from the seventeenth century to the twentieth*. Harmondsworth: Penguin.

Edwards, Kathleen. 1939. 'The houses of Salisbury Close in the fourteenth century.' *Journal of the British Archaeological Association*. 3rd series. 4, 55-115.

Edwards, Kathleen. 1954. 'The activities of some fellows of De Vaux College, Salisbury, at Oxford and elsewhere.' *Oxoniensia*. 19, 61-91.

Eltringham, G. J. 1951. 'Salisbury companies and their ordinances, with particular reference to the woodworking crafts.' *W.A.M.* 54, 185-191.

Endowed Charities. 1907. *Endowed charities (County of Wilts): Return... City and Parish of Salisbury or New Sarum*. London: H.M.S.O.

Everett, Cyril R. 1941. 'Notes on the history of the Diocesan Church House, Salisbury.' *W.A.M.* 49, 435-479.

Everett, Cyril R. 1944. 'Notes on the Decanal and other houses in the Close of Sarum.' *W.A.M.* 50, 425-445.

Everitt, Alan. 1967. 'The marketing of agricultural produce.' *In*: Thirsk, Joan (ed.). *The agrarian history of England and Wales, vol. 4: 1500–1640.* Cambridge: Cambridge University Press. 466–592.

Farmer, David H. 1979. 'The refoundation of Amesbury Abbey.' *In*: Chandler, John H. (ed.) *The Amesbury millennium lectures.* Amesbury: Amesbury Society. 47–57.

Farrant, Jeremy P. 1967. *The history of Scout Motors Limited of Salisbury.* Salisbury: Salisbury and South Wiltshire Group for Industrial Archaeology.

Farrant, John. 1969. 'A railroad to Salisbury: the proposal of 1834.' *Wiltshire Industrial Archaeology.* 1, 10–13.

Fletcher, James M. J. 1926. *Incumbents of the Salisbury churches during the period of the commonwealth.* Salisbury: Salisbury Times.

Fletcher, James M. J. 1937. 'Robert Bingham, Bishop of Salisbury, 1229–1246.' *W.A.M.* 48, 59–67.

Foster, Joseph. 1888. *Alumni Oxonienses: the members of the University of Oxford, 1715–1886*... 4 vols. Oxford: Parker.

Fowle, John P. M. 1955. *Wiltshire quarter sessions and assizes, 1736.* Devizes: Wiltshire Archaeological and Natural History Society, Records Branch.

Fullford, George. 1914. 'Old Salisbury industries and their remains.' *In*: Stevens, Frank. *The festival book of Salisbury.* Salisbury: Salisbury, South Wilts and Blackmore Museum.

Garrard, Bruce. 1980. *The arrow: the founding of the new cathedral at Salisbury.* Woodcutts: Garrard.

Glass, David V. 1965. 'Two papers on Gregory King.' *In*: Glass, David V. and Eversley, David E. C. (eds.) *Population in history.* London: Arnold.

Glynne, (Sir) Stephen. 1923. 'Notes on Wiltshire churches.' *W.A.M.* 42, 167–214.

Goddard, Cecil V. 1905. 'Customs of the manor of Winterbourne Stoke, 1574.' *W.A.M.* 34, 208–215.

Gover, John E. B. *et al.* 1939. *The place-names of Wiltshire.* Cambridge: Cambridge University Press.

Graham, Henry. 1886. *The annals of the yeomanry cavalry of Wiltshire.* Liverpool: Marples.

Grant, Eric. *et al.* 1968. *The Tech comes of age.* Salisbury: Salisbury and South Wilts College of Further Education.

Gray, Howard L. 1924. 'The production and exportation of English woollens in the fourteenth century.' *English Historical Review.* 39, 13–35.

Gray, Howard L. 1933. 'English foreign trade from 1446 to 1482.' *In*: Power, Eileen E. and Postan, Michael M. *Studies in English trade in the fifteenth century.* London: Routledge and Kegan Paul.

Greening, Alan. 1971. 'Nineteenth-century country carriers in north Wiltshire.' *W.A.M.* 66, 162–176.

Grinsell, Leslie V. 1957. *The archaeology of Wessex: an account of Wessex antiquities from the earliest times to the end of the pagan Saxon period*... London: Methuen.

Grundy, George B. 1918. 'The ancient highways and tracks of Wiltshire, Berkshire, and Hampshire, and the Saxon battlefields of Wiltshire.' *Archaeological Journal.* 75, 69–194.

Gubbin, J. H. and Longridge, Robert G. M. 1967. 'The development of medical care.' *In*: *Salisbury 200: the bi-centenary of Salisbury Infirmary, 1766–1966, by members of the hospital staff.* Salisbury: Salisbury General Hospital.

H.M.C. 1907. Historical Manuscripts Commission. *Report on manuscripts in various collections.* vol. 4. Dublin: H.M.S.O.

Hadfield, Charles. 1955. *The canals of southern England.* London: Phoenix House.

Hall, Hubert. 1907. 'The commonwealth charter of the city of Salisbury, September 1656.' *In*: *Camden miscellany.* vol. 11. London: Royal Historical Society.

Hall, Peter. 1834. *Picturesque memorials of Salisbury: a series of original etchings and vignettes*... *to which is prefixed, a brief history of Old and New Sarum.* Salisbury: Brodie.

Hammond, John J. n.d. *Missing chapter of Salisbury history.* Salisbury: Bennett.

Hammond, John J. 1910. 'Notes on Audley House, Salisbury.' *W.A.M.* 36, 364-372.

Hanham, Alison. 1975. *The Cely letters, 1472-1488.* London: Oxford University Press (Early English Text Society).

Happold, Frederick C. 1950. *Bishop Wordsworth's School, 1890-1950.* Salisbury: Bishop Wordsworth's School.

Hardy, Thomas. 1895. *Jude the obscure.* London: Osgood, McIlvaine.

Hare, John N. 1981. 'The demesne lessees of fifteenth-century Wiltshire.' *Agricultural History Review.* 29, 1-15.

Harnham W.I. 1981. Harnham Women's Institute. *The history of Harnham.* rev. ed. Harnham: Harnham Women's Institute.

Harrod, J. G. and Co. 1865. *Postal and commercial directory of Wiltshire, containing a brief descriptive account of each town, parish, village, and hamlet, followed by a directory.* London: Harrod.

Hart, Evelyn. 1976. 'Salisbury and its street names.' *Hatcher Review.* 2, 24-34.

Haskins, Charles. 1909. 'The Church of St. Thomas of Canterbury, Salisbury.' *W.A.M.* 36, 1-12.

Haskins, Charles. 1912. *The ancient trade guilds and companies of Salisbury.* Salisbury: Bennett.

Haskins, Charles. 1916. 'The original bederoll of the Salisbury tailors' guild.' *W.A.M.* 39, 375-379.

Haskins, Charles. 1922. *The history of Salisbury Infirmary.* Salisbury: Salisbury and District Infirmary and Hospital League.

Haskins, Charles. 1927. *The charter of Henry III (1227), with a translation... A summary of the translation of the nine other royal charters in the corporation muniments. New Sarum in the middle ages and the history of St. Edmund's College, Salisbury.* Salisbury: Salisbury Times.

Haslam, Jeremy. 1976. *Wiltshire towns: the archaeological potential.* Devizes: Wiltshire Archaeological and Natural History Society.

Hatcher, Henry. 1834. *An historical and descriptive account of Old and New Sarum, or Salisbury.* Salisbury: Clapperton.

Hatcher, Henry. 1843. *Old and New Sarum, or Salisbury,* by Robert Benson and Henry Hatcher. London: Nichols (*The history of modern Wiltshire,* by Sir Richard Colt Hoare, vol. 6).

Hill, David. 1971. 'The Burghal Hidage: the establishment of a text.' *Medieval Archaeology.* 13, 84-92.

Hinton, David A. 1977. *Alfred's kingdom: Wessex and the south 800-1500.* London: Dent.

Hollaender, Albert E. J. 1944. 'The Doom-painting of St. Thomas of Canterbury, Salisbury.' *W.A.M.* 50, 351-370.

Hony, G. B. 1926. 'Sheep farming in Wiltshire, with a short history of the Hampshire Down breed.' *W.A.M.* 43, 449-464.

Hoskins, William G. 1963. *Provincial England: essays in social and economic history.* London: Macmillan.

Hoskins, William G. 1972. *Local history in England.* 2nd ed. Harlow: Longmans.

Hough, Alfred J. n.d. *The adventures of Plouman Jahn, at Zalisbury Vair: a poem in the Wiltshire dialect.* Salisbury: Salisbury Times.

Hudson, Kenneth. 1968. *The industrial archaeology of southern England.* 2nd ed. Newton Abbot: David and Charles.

Hudson, William H. 1978. *A shepherd's life.* new ed. Tisbury: Compton Press.

Hunnisett, Roy F. 1981. *Wiltshire coroners' bills, 1752-1796.* Devizes: Wiltshire Record Society.

Hunt and Co. 1852. *Directory of Hampshire and Dorset... Weymouth:* Hunt.

Inglis, Harry R. G. 1905. *The contour road book of England.* London: Gall and Inglis.

Jackson, John E. 1855. 'On the Hungerford Chapels in Salisbury Cathedral.' *W.A.M.* 2, 83-99.

Jackson, John E. 1866. 'Wiltshire county gaols.' *W.A.M.* 9, 82-87.

James, R. R. 1926. 'Turberville of Salisbury.' *British Journal of Ophthalmology*. 465-474.

Jefferies, Richard. 1889. *Field and hedgerow, being the last essays of Richard Jefferies, collected by his widow*. London: Longmans.

Jenkins, John G. 1972. *The wool textile industry in Great Britain*. London: Routledge and Kegan Paul.

Jervoise, Edwyn. 1930. *The ancient bridges of the south of England*. London: Architectural Press.

Jones, William H. R. 1884. *Vetus registrum Sarisberiense alias dictum registrum S. Osmundi episcopi: the register of S. Osmund*. vol. 2. London: Longman.

Kaye, David. 1966. *British bus fleets; 3: South central*. London: Ian Allan.

Keene, D. J. 1976. 'Suburban growth.' *In*: Barley, Maurice W. (ed.) *The plans and topography of medieval towns in England and Wales*. London: Council for British Archaeology. 71-82.

Keene, D. J. 1982. 'Rubbish in medieval towns.' *In*: Hall, A. R. and Kenward, H. K. (eds.) *Environmental archaeology in the urban context*. London: Council for British Archaeology. 26-30.

Kelly and Co. 1855. *Post Office directory of Wiltshire...* London: Kelly and Co.

Kerridge, Eric. 1972. 'Wool growing and wool textiles in medieval and early modern times.' *In*: Jenkins, John G. *The wool textile industry in Great Britain*. London: Routledge and Kegan Paul.

Kirby, John L. 1956. 'Clerical poll-taxes in the diocese of Salisbury, 1377-81.' *In*: Williams, Neville J. *Collectanea*. Devizes: Wiltshire Archaeological and Natural History Society, Records Branch.

Kohl, Johann G. 1968. *England and Wales*. London: Cass.

Laslett, Peter. 1969. 'Size and structure of the household in England over three centuries.' *Population Studies*. 23, 199-223.

Laslett, Peter. 1973. *The earliest classics*. New York: Gregg.

Law, C. M. 1972. 'Sources for urban history, 4: Some notes on the urban population of England and Wales in the eighteenth century.' *Local Historian*. 10 (1), 13-26.

Lear, Francis. 1910. 'Reminiscences of eighty years.' *Salisbury Diocesan Gazette*. 23, 121-123, 140-143, 158-161.

Ledwich, Edward. 1771. *Antiquitates Sarisburienses...* Salisbury: Easton.

Lee, Charles J. 1956. *The first 100 years: a short survey of the work of the Salisbury Railway and Market House Company*. [Unpublished typescript in Salisbury Local Studies Library.]

Lindsay, John S. 1964. *Iron and brass implements of the English house*. 2nd ed. London: Tiranti.

Little, Andrew G. 1935. 'Grey Friars of Salisbury.' *W.A.M.* 47, 36-54.

Little, Bernard M. 1981. *A history of libraries in Salisbury, 1850-1922*. M.Phil. thesis, Polytechnic of North London.

Lloyd, Terence H. 1977. *The English wool trade in the middle ages*. Cambridge: Cambridge University Press.

M.A.F. 1929. Ministry of Agriculture and Fisheries. *Report on markets and fairs in England and Wales, part 4: Eastern and southern markets*. London: H.M.S.O.

Macdermot, Edward T. 1964. *History of the Great Western Railway*, revised by C. R. Clinker. 2 vols. London: Ian Allan.

Macray, William D. 1891. *Charters and documents illustrating the history of the Cathedral, city, and diocese of Salisbury, in the twelfth and thirteenth centuries...* London: H.M.S.O.

Maggs, Colin. 1982. *The Bath to Weymouth line including Westbury to Salisbury*. Tisbury: Oakwood Press.

Malden, Arthur R. 1899. 'A contemporary poem on the translation of the Cathedral from Old to New Sarum.' *W.A.M.* 30, 210-217.

Mann, Julia de L. 1971. *The cloth industry in the west of England from 1640 to 1880*. Oxford: Clarendon Press.

Margary, Ivan D. 1973. *Roman roads in Britain*. 3rd ed. London: John Baker.

Maskelyne, Anthony S. 1896. 'Fawconer of Salisbury.' *Wiltshire Notes and Queries*. 2, 29–33, 75–79.

Mate and Co. 1905. *Mate's illustrated Salisbury: a literary and pictorial souvenir*. Bournemouth: Mate.

Mathewson-Dick, Thomas D. 1978. 'Railways.' *In*: Corfield, Michael C. (ed.) *A guide to the industrial archaeology of Wiltshire*. Trowbridge: Wiltshire Library and Museum Service.

Meekings, Cecil A. F. 1961. *Crown pleas of the Wiltshire eyre, 1249*. Devizes: Wiltshire Archaeological and Natural History Society, Records Branch.

Middleton, Andrew B. 1852. *An address to the inhabitants of Salisbury on sanitary reform, shewing the benefit of the Public Health Act, and the small cost thereof, with some remarks on the proceedings of the directors of the highways*. Salisbury: George Brown.

Middleton, Andrew B. 1864. *The benefits of sanitary reform, as shown at Salisbury, in nine years' experience thereof*. London: Simpkin.

Middleton, Andrew B. 1868. *Salisbury: the English Venice. The Town Ditch the last canal thereof. Three letters... to which is added a postscript...* Salisbury: Brown.

Moberly, Robert C. 1891. 'St. Nicholas' Hospital, Salisbury.' *W.A.M.* 25, 119–164.

Moore, Charles N. 1972. 'The Salisbury cutler industry.' *Wiltshire Industrial Archaeology*. 4, 7–13.

Moore, G. A. 1955. *The story of Brown Street Baptist Church, 1655–1955*. Salisbury: Brown Street Baptist Church.

Morgan, Faith de M. 1958. 'An excavation at St. Martin's Church, Salisbury: St. Martin's Church construction.' *W.A.M.* 57, 40–49.

Morris, Christopher. 1949. *The journeys of Celia Fiennes*. rev. ed. London: Cresset Press.

Mullins, Sam. 1978. '"And old Mrs. Ridout and all:" a study of Salisbury's county [*sic*] carriers.' *Wiltshire Folklife*. 2 (1), 29–35.

Musty, John W. G. *et al*. 1958. 'The Roman road from Old Sarum to the Mendips: the Grovely Wood-Old Sarum section.' *W.A.M.* 57, 30–33.

Musty, John W. G. 1959. 'A pipe-line near Old Sarum: prehistoric, Roman and medieval finds including two twelfth century lime kilns.' *W.A.M.* 57, 179–191.

Musty, John W. G. 1968. 'Water-mills on the River Bourne, south Wiltshire: the excavation of the site of Gomeldon Mill with a note on local post-medieval pottery.' *W.A.M.* 63, 46–53.

Musty, John W. G. and Rahtz, Philip A. 1964. 'The suburbs of Old Sarum.' *W.A.M.* 59, 130–154.

Myers, Alec R. 1969. *English historical documents 1327–1485*. London: Eyre and Spottiswoode.

Nevill, Edmund R. 1910. 'Salisbury: a royal aid and supply for 1667.' *W.A.M.* 36, 413–434.

Nevill, Edmund R. 1911. 'Salisbury in 1455. (Liber Niger.)' *W.A.M.* 37, 66–91.

Nightingale, James E. 1875. 'An indenture for building a house at Salisbury, 23rd Henry VI.' *W.A.M.* 15, 329–336.

Nock, Oswald S. 1965. *The London and South Western Railway*. London: Ian Allan.

Noyes, Ella. 1913. *Salisbury Plain: its stones, cathedral, city, villages and folk*. London: Dent.

O'Dell, Andrew C. and Richards, Peter S. 1971. *Railways and geography*. 2nd ed. London: Hutchinson.

Ogilby, John. 1675. *Britannia, volume the first; or, an illustration of the kingdom of England and dominion of Wales, by a geographical and historical description of the principal roads thereof*. London: Ogilby.

Olivier, Edith, 1941. *Country moods and tenses: a non-grammarian's chapbook*. London: Batsford.

Orme, Nicholas. 1976. *Education in the west of England, 1066–1548*. Exeter: University of Exeter.

Oswald, Adrian. 1975. *Clay pipes for the archaeologist.* Oxford: British Archaeological Reports.

Palmer, Charles F. R. 1879. 'The black friars of Wiltshire.' *W.A.M.* 18, 162–176.

Parry-Jones, William Ll. 1972. *The trade in lunacy: a study of private madhouses in England in the eighteenth and nineteenth centuries.* London: Routledge and Kegan Paul.

Pennels, David J. N. 1963. *The fleet history of Wilts and Dorset Motor Services Ltd., and Venture Ltd.* London: P.S.V. Circle.

Pennels, David J. N. 1965. 'The Silver Star story: a tribute to Silver Star Motor Services Ltd.' *Buses Illustrated.* 118-120, 2-89 *passim.*

Pevsner, Nikolaus and Lloyd, David, 1967. *Hampshire and the Isle of Wight.* Harmondsworth: England.

Phythian-Adams, Charles. 1979. *Desolation of a city: Coventry and the urban crisis of the late middle ages.* Cambridge: Cambridge University Press.

Pigot and Co. 1822. *London and provincial new commercial directory for 1822-3...* Manchester: Pigot.

Pigot and Co. 1830. *... Directory of ... Wilts.* Manchester: Pigot.

Pigot and Co. 1842. *... Directory of... Wilts.* Manchester: Pigot.

Platt, Colin. 1973. *Medieval Southampton: the port and trading community, A.D. 1000-1600.* London: Routledge and Kegan Paul.

Platt, Colin. 1981. *The parish churches of medieval England.* London: Secker and Warburg.

Plowden, William. 1973. *The motor car and politics in Britain.* Harmondsworth: Penguin.

Ponting, Kenneth G. 1957. *A history of the west of England cloth industry.* London: Macdonald.

Ponting, Kenneth G. 1971. *The woollen industry of south-west England.* Bath: Adams and Dart.

Ponting, Kenneth G. 1974. 'Wiltshire woollen mills: insurance returns, 1753-1771.' *W.A.M.* 69, 161-172.

Ponting, Kenneth G. 1975. *Wiltshire portraits.* Bradford-on-Avon: Moonraker Press.

Ponting, Kenneth G. 1979. 'Sheep in Wiltshire.' *Wiltshire Folklife.* 2 (3), 18-30.

Poole, Edward H. L. 1976. *Damerham and Martin: a study in local history.* Tisbury: Compton Russell.

Pope, Walter. 1697. *The life of the Right Reverend Father in God Seth, Lord Bishop of Salisbury ...* London: Keblewhite.

Pope, Walter. 1713. *The Salisbury ballad: with curious, learned and critical notes.* London [reprinted Salisbury: Easton, 1770 and included in Ledwich, 1771].

Postan, Michael M. 1975. *The medieval economy and society: an economic history of Britain in the middle ages.* Harmondsworth: Penguin.

Power, Eileen E. 1933. 'The wool trade in the fifteenth century.' *In*: Power, Eileen E. and Postan, Michael M. *Studies in English trade in the fifteenth century.* London: Routledge and Kegan Paul.

Power, Eileen E. 1941. *The wool trade in English medieval history, being the Ford lectures.* London: Oxford University Press.

Power, Eileen E. and Postan, Michael M. 1933. *Studies in English trade in the fifteenth century.* London: Routledge and Kegan Paul.

Price, Francis. 1753. *A series of particular and useful observations... upon that admirable structure, the Cathedral-Church of Salisbury...* London: Baldwin.

Price, Percival. 1980. 'Bell.' *In*: Sadie, Stanley. (ed.) *The new Grove dictionary of music and musicians.* vol. 2. London: Macmillan. 424-437.

Priestley, Joseph. 1831. *Historical account of the navigable rivers, canals, and railways, of Great Britain.* London: Longman, Rees, Orme, Brown and Green.

Pugh, Clarence W. 1933. 'Some domestic and other bills of the Wyndham family (Salisbury).' *W.A.M.* 46, 185-197.

Pugh, Ralph B. 1947. *Calendar of Antrobus deeds before 1625.* Devizes: Wiltshire Archaeological and Natural History Society, Records Branch.

Pugh, Ralph B. 1978. *Wiltshire gaol delivery and trailbaston trials, 1275-1306.* Devizes: Wiltshire Record Society.

Quinn, D. B. and Ruddock, Alwyn A. 1937, 1938. *The port books or local customs accounts of Southampton for the reign of Edward IV.* 2 vols. Southampton: Southampton Record Society.

R.C.H.M. 1980. Royal Commission on Historical Monuments (England). *Ancient and historical monuments in the city of Salisbury.* vol. 1. London: H.M.S.O.

R.C.M.R.T. 1889. Royal Commission on Market Rights and Tolls. *Minutes of evidence taken before Arthur J. Ashton Esquire, Assistant Commissioner, at inquiries held by him in England, together with his reports on the markets.* vol. 3. London: H.M.S.O. (Commons Papers, 1888, liv).

Rahtz, Philip A and Musty, John W. G. 1960. 'Excavations at Old Sarum, 1957.' *W.A.M.* 57, 353-370.

Rammell, Thomas W. 1851. *Report of the General Board of Health on a preliminary inquiry into the sewerage, drainage, and supply of water, and the sanitary condition of the inhabitants of the city and borough of Salisbury, in the county of Wilts.* London: H.M.S.O.

Ramsay, George D. 1954. *Two sixteenth century taxation lists, 1545 and 1576.* Devizes: Wiltshire Archaeological and Natural History Society, Records Branch.

Ramsay, George D. 1965. *The Wiltshire woollen industry in the sixteenth and seventeenth centuries.* 2nd ed. London: Frank Cass.

Ransome, Mary. 1972. *Wiltshire returns to the Bishop's visitation queries, 1783.* Devizes: Wiltshire Record Society.

Rathbone, Maurice G. 1951. *List of Wiltshire borough records earlier in date than 1836.* Devizes: Wiltshire Archaeological and Natural History Society, Records Branch.

Reaney, Percy H. 1958. *A dictionary of British surnames.* London: Routledge and Kegan Paul.

Reeves, John A. and Bonney, Helen M. 1982. 'No. 15 Minster Street, Salisbury, a fourteenth century timber-framed house.' *W.A.M.* 76, 99-104.

Reynolds, Susan. 1977. *An introduction to the history of English medieval towns.* Oxford: Clarendon Press.

Richardson, John. 1974. *The local historian's encyclopaedia.* New Barnet: Historical Publications.

Roberts, Hugh D. 1981. *Down hearth to bar grate: an illustrated account of the evolution in cooking due to the use of coal instead of wood.* Devizes: Wiltshire Folk Life Society.

Robertson, Dora H. 1937. 'Notes on some buildings in the city and Close of Salisbury connected with the education and maintenance of the Cathedral choristers.' *W.A.M.* 48, 1-30.

Robertson, Dora H. 1938. *Sarum Close: a history of the life and education of the Cathedral choristers for 700 years.* London: Jonathan Cape.

Rogers, Alan. 1977. *Approaches to local history.* 2nd ed. London: Longmans.

Rogers, Kenneth H. 1963. 'Naish's map of Salisbury.' *W.A.M.* 58, 453-454.

Rogers, Kenneth H. 1969. 'Salisbury.' *In:* Lobel, Mary D. (ed.) *Historic towns: maps and plans of towns and cities in the British Isles, with historical commentaries, from earliest times to 1800.* vol. 1. London: Lovell Johns.

Rogers, Kenneth H. 1976. *Wiltshire and Somerset woollen mills.* Edington: Pasold Research Fund.

Rose, Martial. 1981. *A history of King Alfred's College, Winchester, 1840-1980.* Chichester: Phillimore.

Rowe, Cyril M. 1966. *Salisbury's local coinage (seventeenth century trade tokens).* Salisbury: Tisbury Printing Works.

Rowlandson, Thomas. 1963. *Rowlandson's drawings for a tour in a post-chaise,* with an introduction and notes by Robert R. Wark. San Marino: Huntington Library.

Ruddle, Charles S. 1900. 'Notes on common lands in and around Durrington.' *W.A.M.* 31, 1-7.

Ruddle, Charles S. 1901. 'A census of Wilts in 1676.' *Wiltshire Notes and Queries.* 3, 533-539.

Ruddock, Alwyn A. 1951. *Italian merchants. and shipping in Southampton, 1270-1600*. Southampton: University College.

Ruegg, Louis H. 1878. *The history of a railway*. Sherborne: Sherborne Journal.

Rundle, Penelope. 1979. *Salisbury: the city and its charters*. Salisbury: Salisbury Charter Trustees.

Salisbury District Council. 1980. *Salisbury, Wilton and Alderbury district plan: report of survey and issues, July 1980*. Salisbury: Salisbury District Council.

Salisbury 200. 1967. *Salisbury 200: the bi-centenary of Salisbury Infirmary, 1766-1966, by members of the hospital staff*. Salisbury: Salisbury General Hospital.

Salzman, L. F. 1928. 'The legal status of markets.' *Cambridge Historical Journal*. 2, 205-212.

Sarum S. Edmund, 1907. *Quingentenary festival*. Salisbury: St. Edmund's Church.

Sharp, Thomas. 1949. *Newer Sarum: a plan for Salisbury*. London: Architectural Press.

Sheail, John. 1968. The regional distribution of wealth in England and Wales as indicated in the 1524/5 lay subsidy returns. Ph.D. thesis. University of London.

Shemilt, Philip. 1967. 'Beginnings.' *In: Salisbury 200: the bi-centenary of Salisbury Infirmary 1766-1966 by members of the hospital staff*. Salisbury: Salisbury General Hospital.

Shortt, Hugh de S. 1957. *City of Salisbury*. London: Phoenix House.

Shortt, Hugh de S. 1982. *The Giant and Hob Nob*. 2nd ed. Salisbury: Salisbury and South Wiltshire Museum.

Simond, Louis. 1817. *Journal of a tour and residence in Great Britain during the years 1810 and 1811*. vol. 1. Edinburgh: Constable.

Singer, Charles. *et al.* 1956. *A history of technology, vol. 2: The Mediterranean civilizations and the middle ages, c. 700 B.C. to c. A.D. 1500*. Oxford: Clarendon Press.

Slack, Paul A. 1972 (a). 'Poverty and politics in Salisbury 1597-1666.' *In*: Clark, Peter and Slack, Paul A. *Crisis and order in English towns 1500-1700*. London: Routledge and Kegan Paul. 164-203.

Slack, Paul A. 1972 (b). 'Religious protest and urban authority: the case of Henry Sherfield, iconoclast, 1633.' *In*: Baker, Derek. *Schism, heresy and religious protest*. Cambridge: Cambridge University Press.

Slack, Paul A. 1975. *Poverty in early-Stuart Salisbury*. Devizes: Wiltshire Record Society.

Slatter, Doreen. 1965. *The diary of Thomas Naish*. Devizes: Wiltshire Archaeological and Natural History Society, Records Branch.

Slow, Edward. 1910. *Reckerlections an yarns of a woold Zalsbury carrier var auver vifty years rote in the Wiltshire dialect*. Salisbury: Edwards.

Smith, Gertrude. 1982. *The Old Manor Hospital, Salisbury, Wiltshire: private madhouse, licensed house, psychiatric hospital*. Salisbury: Smith.

Smith, Lucy T. 1964. *The intinerary of John Leland in or about the years 1535-1543, parts I to III*. vol. 1. London: Centaur Press.

Snyder, Charles. 1965. 'Turberville of Salisbury, physician for the eyes.' *Archives of Ophthalmology*. 73, 897-900.

Spire. 1935. *Annual report: Friends of Salisbury Cathedral, year 1935*. Salisbury: Friends of Salisbury Cathedral.

Spire. 1958. *Twenty-eighth annual report: Friends of Salisbury Cathedral*. Salisbury: Friends of Salisbury Cathedral.

Stenton, Frank M. 1971. *Anglo-Saxon England*. 3rd ed. Oxford: Clarendon Press.

Stephens, William B. 1981. *Sources for English local history*. 2nd ed. Cambridge: Cambridge University Press.

Stevens, Frank. 1914. *The festival book of Salisbury*. Salisbury: Salisbury, South Wilts and Blackmore Museum.

Steward, Edward. 1891. *Salisbury Diocesan Training School, its annals and register for fifty years together with divers reminiscences and some facts about the King's House*. Salisbury: Bennett.

Stone, John F. S. and Algar, David J. 1955. 'Sorviodunum.' *W.A.M.* 56, 102-119.

Straton, Amy M. 1892-1896. 'An introduction to the churchwardens' accounts of the parishes of St. Edmund and St. Thomas, Sarum.' *Transactions of the Salisbury Field Club*. 2, 21-65.

Street, Fanny. 1916. 'The relations of the bishops and citizens of Salisbury (New Sarum) between 1225 and 1612.' *W.A.M.* 39, 185–257, 319–367.

Swayne, Henry J. F. 1896. *Churchwardens' accounts of S. Edmund and S. Thomas, Sarum, 1443–1702, with other documents.* Salisbury: Bennett.

Taylor, Christopher C. 1964. 'The Saxon boundaries of Frustfield.' *W.A.M.* 59, 110–115.

Taylor, Christopher C. 1979. *Roads and tracks of Britain.* London: Dent.

Thomas, David St. J. 1981. *The West Country.* 5th ed. Newton Abbot: David and Charles.

Timperley, Harold and Brill, Edith. 1965. *Ancient trackways of Wessex.* London: Phoenix House.

Torrance, W. J. 1959. 'A contemporary poem on the removal of Salisbury Cathedral from Old in [*sic*] Sarum.' *W.A.M.* 57, 242–246.

Turner, Hilary L. 1970. *Town defences in England and Wales: an architectural and documentary study, A.D. 900–1500.* London: John Baker.

Tyssen, Amherst D. 1908. 'John Barbur, of Salisbury, brazier.' *W.A.M.* 35, 351–369.

U.B.D. 1798. *The Universal British directory of trade and commerce.* vol. 4. London: Barfoot and Wilkes.

V.C.H.3. 1956. Pugh, Ralph B. and Crittall, Elizabeth (eds.). *A history of Wiltshire.* vol. 3. London: Oxford University Press. (The Victoria History of the Counties of England.)

V.C.H.4. 1959. Crittall, Elizabeth (ed.) *A history of Wiltshire.* vol. 4. London: Oxford University Press. (The Victoria History of the Counties of England.)

V.C.H.5. 1957. Pugh, Ralph B. and Crittall, Elizabeth (eds.). *A history of Wiltshire.* vol. 5. London: Oxford University Press. (Victoria History of the Counties of England.)

V.C.H.6. 1962. Crittall, Elizabeth (ed.) *A history of Wiltshire.* vol. 6. London: Oxford University Press. (The Victoria History of the Counties of England.)

V.C.H.10. 1975. Crittall, Elizabeth (ed.) *A history of Wiltshire.* vol. 10. London: Oxford University Press. (The Victoria History of the Counties of England.)

Wacher, John. 1975. *The towns of Roman Britain.* London: Batsford.

Wakelin, Arthur. 1979. 'The Pitton of Arthur Whitlock, part I: village life.' *Wiltshire Folklife.* 3 (1), 3–13.

Walters, Henry B. 1927. *The church bells of Wiltshire: their inscriptions and history.* Bath: Kingsmead Reprints [facsimile reprint, 1969].

Wansey, Henry. 1801. *Thoughts on poor houses with a view to their general reform, particularly that of Salisbury... to which is added, an account of the population of Salisbury with observations thereon.* London: Cadell.

Watkins, O. S. 1915. 'The medieval market and fair in England and Wales.' *Y Cymmrodor.* 25, 21–74.

Watson, Edward W. 1915. *Life of Bishop John Wordsworth.* London: Longmans, Green.

Waylen, James. 1855. 'County gaol at Fisherton.' *W.A.M.* 2, 259–260.

Waylen, James. 1857. 'Wiltshire notes and queries.' *W.A.M.* 3, 125–127.

Waylen, James. 1859. *A history, military and municipal of the ancient borough of the Devizes...* London: Longman, Brown.

Waylen, James. 1892. 'The Falstone day-book.' *W.A.M.* 26, 343–391.

Welch, Edwin, 1966. *The bankrupt canal: Southampton and Salisbury, 1795–1808.* Southampton: Southampton City Council.

Wheeler, William A. 1889. *Sarum chronology: a brief record of the most salient events in the history of Salisbury.* Salisbury: Brown.

Whitlock, Ralph. 1976. *The folklore of Wiltshire.* London: Batsford.

Wilkinson, J. T. 1978. 'The rise of other Methodist traditions.' *In*: *A history of the Methodist Church in Great Britain.* London: Epworth Press.

Willan, Thomas S. 1937. 'Salisbury and the navigation of the Avon.' *W.A.M.* 47, 592–594.

Williams, Neville J. 1960. *Tradesmen in early-Stuart Wiltshire: a miscellany.* Devizes: Wiltshire Archaeological and Natural History Society, Records Branch.

Willoughby, R. W. H. 1960 (a). 'The Salisbury and South Wilts Museum: founded 1860.' *W.A.M.* 57, 307–315.

Willoughby, R. W. H. 1960 (b). 'The Blackmore Museum.' *W.A.M.* 57, 316–321.

Wiltshire County Council. 1959. *Guide to the Record Office, part I: Guide to the records in the custody of the Clerk of the Peace for Wiltshire.* Trowbridge: Wiltshire County Council.

Wiltshire County Council. 1965. *Salisbury: the town centre plan.* Trowbridge: Wiltshire County Council Planning Department.

Wiltshire County Council. 1978. *South Wiltshire structure plan: report of survey.* Trowbridge: Wiltshire County Council Planning Department.

Wiltshire County Council. 1980. *Salisbury urban area transportation study: report of survey.* Trowbridge: Wiltshire County Council Planning Department.

Wood-Legh, Kathleen L. 1965. *Perpetual chantries in Britain.* Cambridge: Cambridge University Press.

Wordsworth, Christopher. 1901. *Ceremonies and processions of the Cathedral Church of Salisbury.* Cambridge: Cambridge University Press.

Wordsworth, Christopher. 1902. *The fifteenth century cartulary of St. Nicholas' Hospital, Salisbury, with other records.* Salisbury: Brown.

Wordsworth, Christopher. 1917. 'Elias de Derham's Leadenhall in Salsibury Close, 1226–1915.' *W.A.M.* 39, 433–444.

Wordsworth, Christopher and Robertson, Dora H. 1938. 'Salisbury choristers: their endowments, boy-bishops, music teachers, and headmasters, with the history of the organ.' *W.A.M.* 48, 201–231.

Index

This is an index of names and subjects mentioned in the text of the book. The appendixes and notes have not been indexed. Additional information about many subjects mentioned in the text may be found by referring to the appropriate note.

Wylye Valley, 105, 141, 144,
146, 150
Wyndham family, 59, 206
Wyndham, Henry, 91
Wyndham estate, 61, 63, 174
Wyndham Road, 175, pl.10
Wynn, Henry, 218

Yarmouth, 43
yarn, 97, 103
Yarnbury, 94, 95
Yarnmarket, 78, 98–99
yeomanry, 213
Yeovil, 132, 141, 142
York, 42, 43, 193

Yorkshire, 39, 132
Dales, 73
Young, Bertrand, 191

Zelle, Richard, 236
Zillwood, Mr and Mrs, 188
Zurich, 11

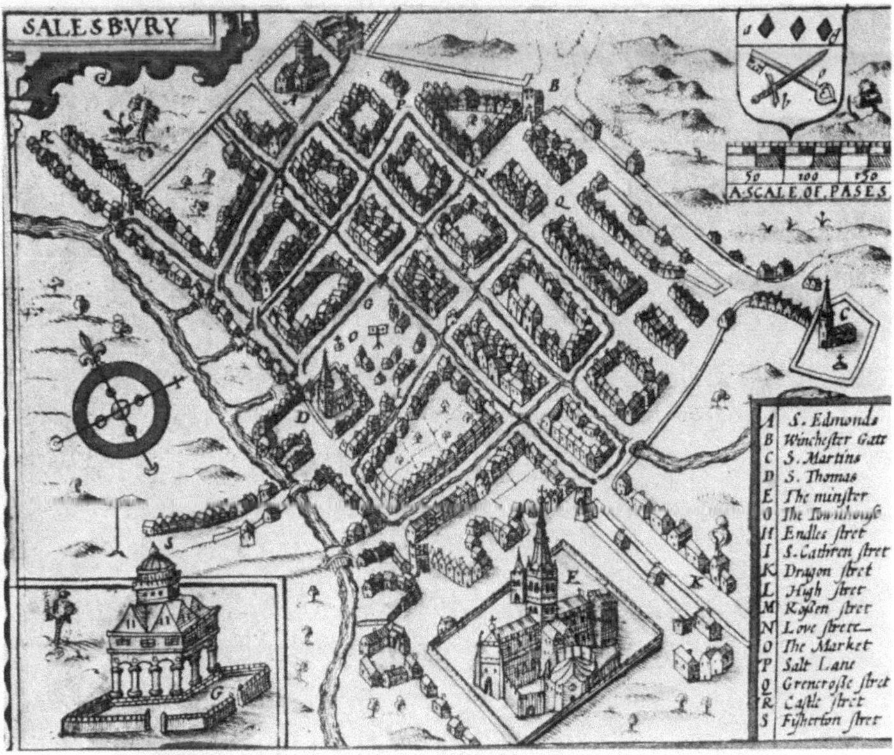
SALESBVRY
50 100 150
A SCALE OF PASES
A S. Edmonds
B Winchester Gatt
C S. Martins
D S. Thomas
E The minster
G The Townhouse
H Endles stret
I S. Cathren stret
K Dragon stret
L High stret
M Rosten stret
N Love strete
O The Market
P Salt Lane
Q Grenecrosse stret
R Castle stret
S Fysherton stret

'The first street map of the city was published by John Speed in 1611, in a corner of his map of Wiltshire.' (p. 53)

2. 'Can it really be that there was once a city on this windswept hill?' (p. 3) Old Sarum from the east, 1982.

3. 'It is a mysterious, bewitching building, which has rarely failed to provoke the visitor's curiosity. Every generation that has lived in its shadow has had to come to terms with it, and to work out its own explanation of this marvel.' (p. 11) Salisbury Cathedral from Harnham Hill, 1982.

4. 'He had to devise a street plan which would allow for the best and most convenient division of land.' (p. 22) The original extent of the Market Place and part of the grid street pattern may be clearly seen on this aerial photograph, taken in the 1930s.

5. 'It has been noticed that one of the north–south alignments ... is not entirely straight but wanders slightly to one side and the other in order to take account of the contours.' (p. 27) Looking towards St Edmund's Church, along Gigant Street, Pennyfarthing Street and St Edmund's Church Street, 1982.

6. 'Clearly to have premises fronting the road that connected two of the most important towns in southern England was a worthwhile proposition.' (p. 29) The Waggon and Horses Inn, Fisherton Street, a pencil and wash drawing by W. Bothams, believed to have been taken from a photograph before 1870. The bridge in the foreground is Summerlock Bridge, and the view shows the north side of Fisherton Street looking towards the city.

7. 'In Guilder Lane, however, a row of seven cottages survives, which ... offers the best remaining example in the city of the kind of housing in which its poorer medieval citizens were accommodated.' (p. 53) 1982.

8. 'The attractions of spaciousness and vista which drew the Victorians here, but led them to build their homes on a scale which few can now afford to maintain.' (p. 58) House at the top of Fowlers Hill, 1982.

9. 'And largely because of the presence of the railway stations Fisherton's population increased by over 2,000 in the twenty years from 1861 to 1881. Such rapid growth is reflected in the many terraces of small town cottages which are concentrated to the north-east of Devizes Road.' (p. 59) Meadow Road, Fisherton, 1982

10. 'All the segment of land between Castle Street and London Road was built over, with terraces of small villas marching up the hill . . .' (p. 59) Wyndham Road, 1982.

11. 'Macklin Road is reminiscent of the textbook "garden-city" concept of town planning, with its carefully irregular siting of thoughtfully-designed houses, and still, 60 years on, the estate proclaims the pride and idealism with which it was planned.' (p. 62) 1982

12. 'A survey of the city in 1919 found 153 houses unfit for habitation and 400 occupied by two or more families.' (p. 63) Fulford Place lay behind buildings in Castle Street a few metres north of Scot's Lane.

13. 'Most of the condemned houses lay in courts; ... one example, Finch's Court in Winchester Street, is still standing, though no longer inhabited.' (p. 63) 1982.

14. 'The workers in leather, ... were concerned with a by-product of the pastoral rural economy, which had to be treated in various ways before it could be converted into items of clothing and other useful products.' (p. 70) A saddler at work in the city, *ca.* 1945.

15. 'The present Harnham Mill dates from about 1500 and may have originated as a fulling mill.' (p. 80) 1982.

16. 'It was the Salisbury merchant, with his forceful cosmopolitan ways, who ensured that the wealth thus created returned to the city, and it was he, rather than the craftsman, who grew fat on the city's success.' (p. 81) The Hall of John Halle survives as an ostentatious reminder of a brash and influential merchant. This engraving, by J. Fisher, was published by Hall, 1834, to show a proposed restoration by Pugin.

17. '"The Faucon" survives as part of the present Church House in Crane Street.' (p. 82) A nineteenth-century drawing of Church House from Crane Bridge.

18. 'The trades in this part of the market were enabling the city to survive by feeding and providing for its citizens, as well as offering specialist products and services to citizen and stranger alike.' (p. 97) An engraving by W. H. Bartlett, looking down Minster Street towards Silver Street, published in 1829.

19. 'The present Poultry Cross ... probably dates from the late fifteenth century, although it was remodelled in 1852–1854.' (p. 101) An oil painting depicting tradesmen around the Poultry Cross shortly before its reconstruction.

20. 'When this Council House was damaged by fire in 1780 the opportunity was taken to convince the Bishop that it was time to demolish his Guildhall.' (p. 101) An original drawing by E. Valter showing that for a few years in the 1790s the Elizabethan Council House, and its replacement, the present Guildhall, stood side-by-side.

21. 'The Market Place was devoted primarily to cattle ...' (p. 106) This very early photograph, possibly of the 1850s, suffers from the limitations of the camera, but vividly depicts, nevertheless, the disorganised state of the Victorian market.

22. '"For miles all round both far and near. They come to see the rigs of fair"' (p. 107) Salisbury Michaelmas Fair, 1930s?

23. 'Special occasions ... might also bring out the scarlet and crimson robes, the mace and insignia, and all the paraphernalia of civic pageantry.' (p. 113) Salisbury celebrates the coronation of Edward VII in 1902 with a public dinner (for men only) in the Market Place.

24. 'Six grotesque carved mannikins, possibly the product of a Beckham imagination, may still be seen from the street holding the first-floor windows in position.' (p. 117) The Joiners' Hall, St Ann Street, 1982.

25. 'In 1244 Bishop Bingham replaced "Aegel's ford" across the Avon with a fine stone bridge – Ayleswade or Harnham Bridge – which is still in use.' (p. 126) An anonymous oil painting in Salisbury Museum.

26. 'The rivers provided drinking water for man and beast, a plentiful supply of fish, water for cleaning, sanitation and irrigation, water to drive mills and to use in the various processes of an industrial city; rivers could be used too in place of walls, to act as barriers or boundaries, and as highways, the most ancient highways of all.' (p. 127) The River Avon behind Castle Street.

27. 'Gradually after about 1860 . . . the trusts sold off their tollhouses, their boards, gates and posts, and were absorbed into local authority highway boards.' (p. 139) Fisherton tollgate and house stood near the present Wilton Road roundabout. It was sold by auction in 1858 and demolished during the 1860s.

28. ' "We have had so much cold water thrown upon us before that a bucket or two extra can make no difference now." ' (p. 141) The commencement of the Salisbury and Yeovil Railway in 1856 as depicted by the *Illustrated London News.*

29. 'Salisbury folklore has not quite forgotten the Coombe Bissett carrier, Mrs Ridout and her donkeys who, trading under the rather optimistic title, the "Coombe Express," were to be seen every week enjoying the sustenance provided by a Harnham inn on their way home.' (p. 146) Oil painting, *ca.* 1870, by Frank Brooks, in Salisbury Museum.

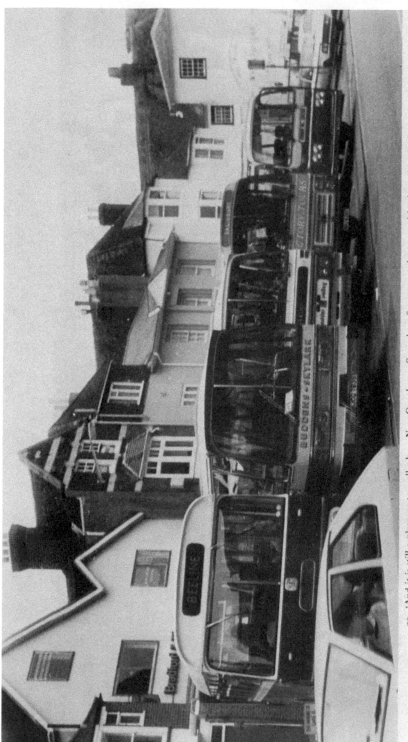

30. 'And it is still a pleasure to walk along New Canal on a Saturday afternoon and see a multi-coloured rank of private buses ... the last remnants of the carriers' centuries-old web of service.' (p. 148) 1982.

31. 'Wartime, which brought a huge influx of servicemen into the area, was Wilts and Dorset's finest hour . . . For a few years everyone travelled by bus . . .' (p. 148) Salisbury bus station, opened in 1939, and seen here *ca*. 1945.

32. '. . . protesting about the difficulty he had recently experienced in driving 70 head of cattle through the streets to market on account of the congestion from motor traffic.' (p. 151) Cattle at the junction of Crane Street and High Street in 1936.

33. 'The accommodation of 3,000 large metal boxes, although it has been essential for Salisbury's survival as a real city, seems to have upset some indefinable equilibrium, which lay at the heart of Salisbury's character.' (p. 152) Even on a winter Sunday afternoon Salt Lane car park is well used. 1982.

34. 'The Bishop's court continued, on paper at least, until 1835, and for most of its long history was held in the Bishop's Guildhall, on the site of the present Guildhall, although its power and influence were gradually eroded by the growing municipal administration.' (p. 158) In this eighteenth-century view the Bishop's Guildhall is over-shadowed by the Elizabethan Council House.

35. 'The line of inns fronting the medieval High Street ... bears witness to the stream of messengers and pilgrims trekking into the city by reason of business or penance.' (p. 164) An engraving of the High Street, by W. H. Bartlett, published in 1829.

36. 'Included in this scheme was a proposal to buy a privately-owned road and tollbridge ... which had been built across the river north of the city by Thomas Scamell in 1899 ...' (p. 174) Scamell's Bridge and the railway bridge, from the ring road, 1982.

37. 'The Grammar School, which seems to have lain dormant for seventy years, was revived in 1540 and moved into the Close.' (p. 181) Choristers playing on Choristers' Green, in front of their school, which was rebuilt in 1714. The photograph was taken in about 1945, two years before the school moved into the Bishop's Palace.

38. 'The establishment of a free grammar school, controlled by the city council, in 1569 was probably not the enlightened act that it may at first appear.' (p. 182) This engraving, by J. C. Buckler, dated 1822, shows the Grammar School building behind railings on the right of the picture. It lay in Castle Street, opposite Chipper Lane.

39. 'The stamp of vigorous Victorian discipline began to be impressed on generations of young ladies... Most looked back on their college days with a wistful mixture of respect, affection and discomfort.' (p. 188) Salisbury Training College, group portrait, 1888.

40. 'The largest, St Edmund's National School, with nearly 500 pupils, occupied purpose-built premises near the church.' (p. 188) 1982.

41. 'St Martin's, older and wiser than Salisbury, tucked in its comfortable backwater at the city's limits . . .' (p. 193) The building directly below the church spire is St Martin's School, Salisbury's first National School, dating from 1812, but extensively rebuilt in 1930. 1982.

42. 'Here is a medieval guidebook to heaven and hell, more vivid and direct than any theological treatise.' (p. 195) Part of the doom painting in St Thomas's Church, depicting heaven (above) and hell (below) 1982.

43. '... as long as ther shall bee one stone upon another in Edmundes Church ...' (p. 204) The tower was completed in 1655, after its predecessor had collapsed. The nave, which occupied the grassed area in the foreground, was demolished at the same time. An inscription over the tower door commemorated the event. 1982.

44. 'John Wesley himself preached in the predecessor of the present chapel in St Edmund's Church Street, and described it as, "the most complete in England."' (p. 208) 1982.

45. 'The real value of the Infirmary was that it offered the sick poor a chance to tackle their illnesses in a warm, reasonably comfortable environment, where they would be given better food and cleaner bed-linen than they could expect at home, and so would stand a far greater chance of recovery.' (p. 224) Salisbury Infirmary in the nineteenth century, by Frank Highman.

46. 'Looking down Catherine Street today the impression is of a nearly continuous line of small shopfronts on either side beneath assorted eighteenth- and nineteenth-century upper storeys . . .' (p. 244) 1982.

47. A Salisbury middle-class home, *ca.* 1945.

48. A Salisbury working-class home, *ca.* 1945.